The Attractions of Fascism

Contents

Introduction

'Conference volumes are a publisher's nightmare', says a colleague of mine who took refuge in Australian academe after twenty years with a leading West German *Verlag*. I hope this book is an exception; it grew out of an unusual conference and an unusual project, to which the conference itself was essential. The attempt to understand the attractions of Fascism, the appeal of a 'quick fix' which was potent not only in Hitler's Germany and Mussolini's Italy but in other countries as well, demands a broad and multi-disciplinary perspective. Fascism has been 'explained' over and over again, pressed into system after system. However, the essential question of those who regard 'die Gnade der späten Geburt' ('the blessing of having been born later': FRG Chancellor Helmut Kohl) not as an alibi but as a responsibility remains largely unanswered, and no amount of purely political or economic analysis can answer it. How was it that the vast majority of apparently 'civilized' communities could tolerate, accept, even welcome regimes whose ideology and its brutal realization stood in such absolute contrast to accepted standards of political, social and individual morality?

To have asked the question is to have demonstrated its continuing importance. Brecht's biologist image is of little use, for all its menace ('The womb is fertile still from whence this crawled'); it too is an alibi, which sees Fascism as the product of others. We must rather assume a Fascist foetus which we all carry within us, and which can all too easily be brought to unappetizing life. Brecht's *Questions of a Working-Class Reader* need to be asked of Fascism as well, and the answers are desolate; its monuments were not built without the hands – the willing hands – of many. The sentimental prognosis of Fritz Lang and Thea von Harbou's film *Metropolis* – that the hands and minds which constructed the new and enduring Tower of Babel, the edifice of modernity, would need a 'mediator' – was realized, as Siegfried Kracauer saw, in the ideology of Fascism, which replaced idealized remnants of bourgeois ethics with a far deeper appeal to the repressed 'by-products' of bourgeois socialization, the phantasies of national, social and sexual domination which formed its 'other' from the beginning. The double heritage of the European Enlightenment was at the forefront of our consciousness during 1989, the bicentenary of the French Revolution – reason and rationalization, democracy and nationalism, freedom and domination, and enough other 'polar pairs' to delight any structuralist. Fascism is its 'black sheep', the hypertrophy of its other into gross and horrific reality.

To ask this question, and to arrive at some partial answers to it – the contributors to this volume are united, if in anything, in their rejection of 'global theories' – it was necessary to bring together colleagues from a wide variety of backgrounds and disciplines, to range from personal experience to explorations of the murkier products of high and very low culture, from theory to social history and social psychology. Fascism was no natural catastrophe. It was made by people, and it is to the people, in their often disarming or pathetic ordinariness, that we must look for an explanation. There is a clear sympathy in many of the chapters for a 'revisionist agenda' of a different kind to that currently being advocated by some historians in the Federal Republic: to strip Fascism of its 'aura', so that we may understand the continuities that link it to what went before and came after. All historical events are, in a sense, unique; to understand the uniqueness of Nazism or the Holocaust, however, we need to relate them not to the killing fields of Cambodia, but to the 'normalities' of the societies from which they emerged.

Most of the chapters, again, betray their debt to the attempts of the Frankfurt School and other 'outsiders' of the Weimar Republic like Wilhelm Reich and Ernst Bloch to penetrate to the grounds of Fascism; they add to this theoretical concern, however, an awareness of the achievements of social history as a necessary base and corrective. It is perhaps no accident that those with a feminist perspective come closest to extending the questions of the conference into contemporary reality; feminist history must embrace, by definition, the comparative and international perspective our project assumes as a precondition for any real advance in understanding.

I send the book on its way in the hope that it will be more than an addition to the academic discussion, that it will contribute to an approach to one of the darkest chapters in European history which resists the temptations of demonology and abstraction, and enables the kind of productive identifications which aid self-recognition. To understand may or may not be to forgive, but guilt and forgiveness may in the long run be far less important than an understanding which results in change to our selves and our uneasy societies.

John Milfull
Sydney

PART I

Reconstructing the Past

–1–

The Child and the She-Wolf

Memories of a Fascist Childhood

SILVIO TRAMBAIOLO

Preface

In this chapter I shall attempt to offer a sample of micro-history based on personal experience of Fascist rule. The focus will be on the life of a small village community (approximately 3,000 people) in the Bassa Padana, in the north-eastern region of the Po valley, as witnessed by myself as a child from 1937, when I was only two, to the end of the Second World War.

The major instrument for this maieutic operation will be my own memory, which I believe to be lucid enough but which must inevitably be affected by unconscious barriers and distortions over which I cannot claim much control. However, given that my journey into the past is likely to prove far richer in sentiment than in analytical depth, it should none the less shed some light on the topic under general discussion.

From my particular perspective, the period from 1937 to 1945 appears to be divided into three distinct phases:

(1) Village life under Fascist rule before the war (1937 to 1940).
(2) The effects of the first years of war on village life (1941 to 1943).
(3) The new Fascist rule after the Armistice (September 1943 to April 1945).

I shall deal with these in chronological order, but it should be apparent that many of my considerations will apply to the period as a whole.

In order to evoke what it was like to grow up in those years, I shall look at the following: the physical environment, the living conditions of villagers and their expectations, the family, the church, the state, schooling, social life and so on. Naturally, my emphasis will be on those aspects of village life on which the impact of Fascism was more clearly discernible.

A Village without History

To the outsider, Piacenza d'Adige, where I was born in 1935, might have appeared totally indistinguishable from the numerous country villages strewn across the Bassa Padana, the lower region of the Po valley. Like most country villages, it consisted of a small group of houses huddled together next to the church to form a piazza and a few more running along in opposite directions on both sides of the provincial road connecting Padua to Rovigo.

To me, for the first ten years or so of my life, Piacenza d'Adige was the whole world, and it is about this village and those years that I would like to write.

In 1937 Piacenza d'Adige was a village of about 3,000 people. These people were mostly farm labourers or small share-croppers, with a dozen or so tradesmen and shopkeepers. There was only a handful of large landowners and none of them lived in the village. The people with some degree of authority were: the parish priest, the village doctor, the marshal in charge of the *carabinieri* station, the *podestà* (the Fascist-appointed mayor) and the chemist, who, together with the doctor, could boast a university degree.

Just before my generation, literacy had been the privilege of individuals whose families were able to spare child labour for the two or three years of primary schooling that were then available. Numeracy was much more widespread and of a higher, if intuitive, level. This is understandable. In a world of scarce commodities, low wages and a long tradition of bartering and price bargaining, nobody worth his salt could afford not to master his arithmetic. Naturally, in a place so remote from towns and big cities, the common medium of communication was a local strand of the Venetian dialect. Even the priest, whilst using Latin for the liturgical parts of church services, would address his congregation in dialect for the sermon.

The road along which the village had been built was a primitive, pebbly affair, dusty in summer and full of pot-holes in winter. On the other hand, since it was used mostly by people on bicycles or horse-drawn carts, the road could happily be used by children for endless soccer or other games without a single car passing to disturb their leisure. Children would usually scamper around barefooted for most of the year. In winter they wore laced boots with a thick wooden sole reinforced by steel tacks to prolong wear. There was only one car in the whole village. Occasionally it was used in emergencies such as when people needed to be taken urgently to hospital in the nearest township. Usually women gave birth in their own homes and people died in their own beds.

It was a village almost without history. People's memory did not go back further than a couple of generations. No one seemed to take much notice of or question the few relics of time past which still survived here and there in the form of place-names with a definite Venetian ring to them: Mocenigo, Contarini, Morosini. As I was to learn much later, these were names of the patrician families of the *Serenissima* Republic of Venice who had owned the land before Austrian rule and the eventual unification of Italy.

Possibly the only event which still loomed large in the people's minds was the natural disaster of 1881, when the Adige burst its raised banks and flooded the village with a wall of water, causing death and devastation. It was recalled with awe that the rush of waters had reached the 'doors' of Padua some thirty miles away. This event had been handed down to later generations through an irreverent mock-heroic folk-song that was, ostensibly, a good example of popular exorcism.

More recent calamities like the Great War and the Spanish flu had affected my parents' generation, and many families had lost relatives because of one or the other. Every year, on 4 November, the village's invalids and veterans from the Great War would dress up in their medals and uniforms and march to the dead soldiers' memorial to celebrate the anniversary of a victory that had been sorely paid for. War, plagues and suffering were accepted meekly as part of the human lot. Only religion seemed to allow for some hope.

I remember being struck at a very early age by the cogency of the pleading chant intoned by the priest during the early spring processions, the Rogationes, 'A peste, fame et bello', immediately followed by the congregation's response, 'Libera nos, Domine' ('From plague, famine and war, deliver us, O Lord').

Given the general condition of illiteracy or semi-literacy of the people in the village just before my generation (my mother, for example, had had just two years of primary schooling, my father three), the only repositories of any form of culture or tradition were the old people. In their lives and generally through incredible hardships they had acquired experience and insight that they were willing to pass on to the new generations.

One such person was a sprightly old lady who was almost a

hundred years old. She loved reminiscing about the times when the whole of the Venetian region was still under Austrian rule, before its annexation to the kingdom of Italy in 1866. Being totally illiterate, she had obviously not been affected by nationalistic rhetoric and, drawing from her personal experience, she had no qualms in saying that the change had not been for the better. She would actually call the new masters 'that bunch of thieves'. However, she seemed to have an even greater and very personal aversion to Mussolini, and this was extremely puzzling to the little boy who on the one hand was very fond of the old lady, but on the other fervently yearned to be a true *Balilla.*[1] It took the little boy quite a few years to realize that she was quite right on both accounts.

The Years before the War

My introduction to Fascism could not have been a smoother one. As a baby I was literally lulled into it by my older sisters who, having been exposed to Fascist indoctrination in their five years of primary schooling that had by now become compulsory, would send me to sleep to the majestic tune of Horace's 'Carmen Saeculare' (in the new Italian version commissioned by the regime) and more popular songs like 'Giovinezza', 'Roma rivendica l'Impero', 'Faccetta Nera' and many more that were part of the school curriculum.

I have still got a record of my early beginnings as a Fascist. In the scanty photo album of my family there is a picture of myself at the age of two, dressed up as a *Figlio della lupa*, my right hand duly raised in the Fascist salute (though the fingers of my hand are outrageously spread out like a fan). Being a *Figlio della lupa* was the very first step in the Fascist *cursus honorum* and was part of the Fascist revival of the myth of Rome, meant to instil a sense of pride in our nationhood. My family's finances could not possibly have stretched to outfitting me in this fancy dress, and it was later explained to me that it had been a gift thought up by some relatives who were far better off than ourselves. It had also been done more for fun than out of any deep conviction.

However, what still puzzles me to some extent is not the photo in itself, but rather the message that it carries on the back. Scribbled in the handwriting of one of my older sisters there is a message

1. *Balilla*: member of the nation-wide Fascist organization of primary school children.

addressed to my father: 'Dear Dad, I hope you will like this picture of our own "child of the she-wolf". Yours. . . .' The said irony was that my father received this photo with the accompanying message while he was in Ethiopia, where he had been more or less forced to go and work as a civilian in order to gain the right to a Fascist Party card. Because of his socialist leanings my father had refused it for years. Now a family of seven and the difficulty of finding a job without a party card had made him forgo ideological principles and settle for the hard realities of the times. What is more, his efforts were all in vain, for he died in Africa not much later.

As I grew older I slowly came to realize that the two main and inescapable forces affecting the lives of everybody in the village were religion and Fascism. The former, deeply rooted in the people's consciences, promised life after death and threatened eternal damnation for sinners. The latter promised better and better living conditions, a destiny of grandeur for the whole country, and was supported by an all-pervasive organization which left no room for anything that was not in line with the regime's directives.

After the 1929 Concordat, these two forces actively cooperated with each other. I grew up in a period when consensus with the regime could not have been greater. People now dared only speak in whispers of earlier times when socialists had been beaten up by Fascists, and the priest had been forced out of the parish and sent into a long period of confinement for publicly denouncing from the pulpit a group of Fascist youths who had disrupted a procession on the day of the village's patron saint and torn to pieces the flags of the local Catholic youth organization.

Before the war I was not aware of any opposition or even mild resistance to the regime. Even my mother decided to join the local branch of the Massaie Rurali, a nation-wide women's association of country workers. Maybe Mussolini, with his campaign for population growth, had made her feel that she too had contributed to a greater *patria* with her five children. She received a monthly magazine and went along to meetings where a city lady would talk on improved methods of child raising, house management or vegetable growing. Everybody seemed to be benefiting in one way or another from the regime and, contrary to the general habit, people were saying for once how things had been much worse in the past. The regime was much appreciated not only for its enforcement of law and order, but also for the definite overall improvement in living standards in the village. Many people still lived just above the poverty line, but labourers and peasants did not have to work as many hours as before, poor people were assured a hot meal in winter, five years of primary schooling had become compulsory, and children were duly vaccinated. When necessary, school children were sent free of charge to a mountain or seaside resort during the summer vacation. The rest of the children were looked after for the same period in the village's own *colonia elioterapica* (solar therapy camp). In spite of its pompous name, this special Fascist institution worked very effectively. As one of its beneficiaries, I can recall that it was with sheer joy that about two hundred children went to it after the school year had come to an end. In previous times, the majority of them would have been left all day to their own devices with very little food, while the parents worked in the fields. In this *colonia* the children were very nicely fed and spent time lying in the sun to absorb its supposed benefits. This sunbathing took place on a bed of knee-deep river sand which had been transported to a field in the village in order to simulate a sandy shore. Games were organized for the children's entertainment by specially appointed supervisors. Hot showers were provided at the end of the day; this was certainly a novelty, as none of the children would have had a shower in their own home.

Acceptance of Fascism in our village, and probably in the whole country, might well have been the product of wishful thinking, but it was genuine and passionate. Fascist indoctrination, based as it was on the dictator's fiery slogans and relentless propaganda, might have been more superficial than a religion, but the beliefs engendered by it were just as strong.

All the men would respectfully remove their hats whenever they gathered in the public square to listen to Mussolini addressing the nation. On these occasions the atmosphere was one of great reverence. The speeches were broadcast from a window in the Casa del Fascio on the only radio receiver existing in the village.[2] Naturally enough, local Fascist authorities did not command anywhere near this respect. In spite of all his military posturing in uniform at every opportunity, the Segretario del Fascio (secretary of the local branch of the Fascist Party) was still considered first as very much a *paesano* and second as a Fascist authority of doubtful importance. I remember an old man cutting him down to size in public one day: 'Hey you, Leonida! You think you're the Duce himself, don't you! Well, don't forget that when you were a snotty boy not so long ago I caught you many times crapping all over my cabbage patch.'

2. Casa del Fascio: the village building that housed Fascist activities and offices.

The War

With the outbreak of war everything changed. Mussolini's mass rallies in support of his decision to declare war did not have much impact on the village people. Instead, everybody seemed to be fretting and fearing the worst. At school I was asked to write letters of encouragement to soldiers at the front line. Food rationing, stockpiling and black market practices started almost immediately. The *colonia elioterapica* functioned for the last time in the summer of 1942, but the supervisors now spent more time in teaching children pathetic war songs than in organizing games. I still remember with some embarrassment one of these songs. It went more or less like this: 'They've said that ten Italians cannot cope with one English soldier; we say instead that a single Italian soldier can teach a lesson to fifty English soldiers. This much we've always shown in the past, and if another lesson is required, the Brits had better go and learn it from our troops.'

Then the first news arrived from the front line of servicemen from the village who were missing, wounded or killed. The gloom became general. Some still wanted to believe the bombastic war bulletins broadcast over the radio but, as time went on, these bulletins lost all credibility. War had become the only topic of conversation for adults and children alike. There were many theories about how the war was going and when and how it would end.

On 8 September 1943 the bells of the village church started ringing at an unusual hour, as if for a festive day, and were immediately followed by those of nearby villages. The festive chorus was to announce the Armistice, and everyone rejoiced at the thought that the war was over. Unfortunately, the worst was yet to come.

For a few months afterwards no one seemed to have a clear idea of what was happening. Apparently the war had not ceased, yet servicemen from the village, dressed in civilian clothes, were returning in throngs. Effigies of Mussolini and Fascist slogans on walls were openly defaced. The word *Fascista*, which had appeared in relief on the kindergarten facade, had been gouged out, leaving it not only still legible but even more conspicuous than before.

The period of general euphoria did not last long. Two things happened almost simultaneously to quash any optimism. First, the local *carabinieri* disappeared overnight and were replaced by a bunch of youths in Fascist uniform who would strut about the village constantly armed to the teeth. They were called either *Repubblichini* or *Perugini*. The first denomination qualified them as faithful followers of Mussolini and supporters of the Repubblica Sociale founded by the Duce after he had been ousted from power in Rome. The second name simply labelled them as originally coming from Perugia, in central Italy. Neither of the two names had positive connotations for the village people, with the exception of a handful who, in order to cling to positions of privilege, had chosen to side with armed strength. For this they were even more hated by the rest of the villagers than were the *Repubblichini* themselves.

Secondly, German troops, who had so far been seen only passing through the village in small numbers, began more and more to make their powerful presence felt. They took over first the town hall and then the school building, and eventually they even requisitioned rooms in private dwellings.

The German *Kommandantur* stationed in the village claimed one of the two bedrooms in our house. Groups of three or four passing troops would stay for a couple of days or a few weeks to sleep and rest. The German soldiers had far more food than we did, and on the whole were willing to share part of their rations with us, especially if they required any cooking or washing of my mother.

To my younger brother and myself (respectively eight and nine years old), these guests were objects of intense interest and wonder. Their foreign language, a few words of which we mastered quickly with their help; their unusual manners; the strange loaves of black bread which were transported piled up like bricks on trucks; their own characteristic army smell (so very different from the smell of English soldiers, as we couldn't help noticing when, much later on, a group of 'liberators' stayed for a few nights in the same room); these soon made us forget the discomfort of overcrowding at night.

From the time the room was requisitioned to the end of the war I must have come into contact with at least a hundred German soldiers, but I can recall only one unpleasant experience during the enforced presence of these strangers in our house. Nothing dramatic happened in this particular case; there was simply a clear show of contempt towards us, against which we were powerless to react in any way. This came unexpectedly after many examples of goodwill and cameraderie shown by the Germans, especially to us children but also towards our whole family. Maybe it had something to do with the fact that the two Germans who caused trouble were officers, while all the others who stayed at our place were common soldiers. Anyway, for no apparent reason, these two officers started shouting abuse at everyone in the house. They did so in perfect Italian, which to us dialect speakers was not much more comprehensible than German. One of their words has stayed with me to this day: *tegame*, Italian for frying-pan, which we in Venetian dialect called *tecia*. Our inability to understand our own language enraged them, and eventually they ignored us and started looking themselves for what they needed to cook their meal, throwing pots and pans about and breaking some plates in the process.

Whilst most people in the village lived in terror of the *Repubblichini*, especially families with youths who had refused to enlist in Mussolini's army, the Germans treated the *Repubblichini* with the disdain of the regular soldier for the mercenary. I recall one particular summer evening when for some reason the *Repubblichini* had put the whole village under curfew. At the time we had an oldish German soldier staying at our place and we were sharing our supper with him. Four *Repubblichini* came pacing along the street. They stopped in front of our house shouting abuse and threats because the shutters on our windows had not been closed as prescribed. It had seemed ludicrous to us to take our supper by electric light when outside it was hot and there was still plenty of light. As the shouting continued, we looked silently at Max, waiting for his reaction. He winked at us and smiled. Then he stood up, went to the window and shouted back in German. To our surprise, he pulled out his gun and fired a round of shots into the air. The *Repubblichini* fled without saying another word, and after supper my brother and I were only too happy to be allowed to go out into the courtyard and play soccer till dark.

Soccer was actually the one element that had, at least on one occasion, brought the village people and the *Repubblichini* together. This occasion took place not long after the *Repubblichini* had taken over from the *carabinieri* and well before their many odious deeds.

I do not know how the idea came about, but somehow it had seemed proper at the time that the newcomers from Perugia should show their prowess in a soccer match against the local youths. Most of the village servicemen had just returned, fleeing from wherever they had happened to be at the time of the Armistice. By this time they should have enlisted with the military forces of Mussolini's Repubblica Sociale, but hardly anyone had complied. On the other hand, the resistance movement hadn't yet started to pose a threat to the *Repubblichini*. So it happened that many a future partisan from the village came out of cellars and hay barns where they had been hiding to avoid conscription, to make up a team of eleven and defend the sporting honour of Piacenza d'Adige against that of Perugia. For one day the combination of the common passion for soccer with *campanilismo* proved stronger than ideological differences.[3]

The match was played on an impromptu field because, owing to wartime penury and the fact that most of those who usually played had been called up, the village's soccer field had been ploughed and sown with corn. So it was a real battle in more ways than one, but pride was maintained on both sides as the match ended in a 1–1 draw.

The fair play of the *Repubblichini* was, unfortunately, destined to be confined to that one occasion. In the following months the 'partisans' looked for safer hiding places (there never was a real armed resistance to speak of in the village), and the *Repubblichini*, feeling more and more hated and trapped, retaliated with vengeance. I eventually saw the end of a *rastrellamento*, the thorough military search for 'partisans' and their supporters.

One morning over fifty people, both young and old, were paraded in the village square after being captured during one such operation carried out by what looked to me like an army of *Repubblichini* and German soldiers in full combat gear. The prisoners had their hands tied to a long rope and their eyes looked terrified in their pale, unshaven faces. They were dragged by force and frequently jabbed with rifle butts; one crying old man was brutally beaten up. It was the *Repubblichini* who distinguished themselves for brutality against their fellow countrymen. The Germans looked on in total silence, showing no sign of emotion.

In the afternoon I saw these prisoners, together with others from the village (including my own brother-in-law) arrested on that day, being hauled into buses and taken away to the district jail. Five of them were to be executed two months later. I knew all of them pretty well; one, who was only fifteen, worked in the village's bicycle repair shop and used to exchange a joke or two while he fixed my bike.

Danger was now coming from all directions, even from the sky. The road passing through the village was by no means an important artery of communication, but probably for this very reason the Germans used it for their never-ending convoys of trucks and tanks heading for the front and for Red Cross buses packed with bandaged soldiers coming back from it. The village school building had been transformed into a military hospital. For a while I went to school in a very unattractive building. Then things precipitated and

3. *Campanilismo*: the instinctive and passionate attachment to one's own birthplace, symbolized by the bell tower (campanile) of the parish church.

I spent most of my fourth year of primary school as a private pupil, together with four or five boys and girls of the same age. The teaching was excellent, but the fee must have been minimal, otherwise my mother could not have afforded it.

As the front line of war slowly advanced towards us, our village became more and more often the target of strafing planes while nearby towns were heavily bombed. Fear grew in everybody to the point of panic. I remember a friend of mine who, though usually a very tough boy, would tremble and whimper as soon as he heard the awesome noise of bomber planes approaching, becoming quite hysterical when bombs were dropped, even if it was miles away.

People seemed to have become more devout than usual and their participation in church services seemed more fervent than before. We were taught a new hymn to the Virgin Mary in which we implored her from 'our vale of tears' for the cessation of hatred and the advent of peace.

I must confess that at the age of nine or ten war had a strange fascination for me and I was often plainly excited by the horrific things that happened around me.

One morning I watched with the keenest interest and a sense of amazement a dog-fight between American fighter planes, which were escorting a squadron of bombers, and Italian or German ones. Right above my head the planes looked like beautiful silver birds cavorting in the clear blue sky, and the crackling of the machine-guns reminded me of the merry sound of chestnuts bursting open on the fire, amplified to a deafening level. Then, in an attempt to escape the attack, the bombers started to drop their deadly load. Although fortunately the bombs fell several miles away, the shock waves caused by the explosions left me breathless. Some of the planes were hit and started falling with a trail of flames and smoke, and soon afterwards the sky was dotted with white parachutes undulating in the breeze.

A few days later, as an altar boy, I attended the funeral service for one of the airmen killed in this lethal duel – an American officer. I still remember his ashen face and light-brown uniform as he lay in an open coffin of unpolished pine, waiting for the priest's blessing before burial in the village cemetery. The poverty of the coffin was in stark contrast to the embroidered silk cushion on which the head of the dead officer rested. A mother from Piacenza, whose son had been killed in the war whilst serving in the air force, was responsible for this act of piety. Not even the *Repubblichini*, for all their brutality, had the heart to stop this old lady from paying the dead enemy a tribute that went well beyond military rules. This was surely one of the most humane things that I witnessed in those troubled times.

When the war was slowly and painfully drawing to an end, the German soldiers staying at our place looked much more worried than those who had stayed previously. I vividly remember one of them. It was New Year's Day 1945. In our house the kitchen was the only room that had any heating in that cold winter. The German soldier had stayed overnight, and in the early morning he had gone out to the village *osteria*; he came back looking totally distraught and thoroughly drunk. He sat next to the wood stove, drinking from a wine flask. With tears streaming from his eyes, he repeated over and over again in broken Italian, as if talking to himself: 'Moglie . . . kaputt! . . . figli . . . kaputt! . . . casa . . . kaputt! . . . alles kaputt!'[4]

I also remember the last two soldiers who spent some time together at our place immediately before the end of the war. One of them, Helmut, was young and outgoing; the other, Heinrich, was a thoughtful, greying man who looked to me too old to be in the army, and he probably thought so too. While Helmut spoke to us of Germany's secret weapons which would soon be used to give Germany the final victory, Heinrich would comfort us with news we desperately wanted to believe – that Germany had already been defeated, that the war was definitely coming to an end and that all would soon be well again. To a child, Helmut was much more appealing than Heinrich. He couldn't have been more than sixteen and was optimism personified. He drove a powerful motor bike which took up half a room in our house. In all sincerity he promised my brother and myself that he would give it to us if he was called up to the front, which, by now, was coming closer every day. He actually did leave the motor bike with us the day that he had to make a hurried departure, and he helped us hide it under a haystack. For a few weeks my brother and I couldn't believe our luck; our dreams were shattered when, as soon as the war was over, the village 'partisans' came out of hiding and took immediate possession of the splendid vehicle.

My own realization that the war was really drawing to an end came to me one day in mid April 1945. In the fields and gardens everything was green and budding. One afternoon I was playing on the road alone with my brother because most people had fled from the village centre to the inner countryside. As I raised my eyes

4. 'Wife . . . dead! . . . children . . . dead! . . . house . . . destroyed! . . . everything . . . finished!'

in the direction of an unusual noise, I saw something unusual and sad, even for those sad times. A German army truck was slowly coming towards us, pulled by two tired-looking cows. The German soldier at the wheel beckoned to us and opened the door of the truck to let us in. We thought that he wanted to give us a joy-ride and climbed into the truck without hesitation. In hindsight, it is likely that he was just looking for a little human warmth while enduring the loneliness of a journey that seemed to have neither purpose nor destination. We exchanged only a few words, and after a couple of miles on this queer means of transport we got off, as the truck had veered from the main road on to a muddy side track which seemed to be leading absolutely nowhere. That incident, much more than the sight a few days later of German soldiers' bodies floating down the Adige, signalled to me the end of the war, or at least the death throes of the mighty Wehrmacht.

After the war, village people took some pride in believing that the war had actually finished in Piacenza d'Adige itself, with the very last bullets of lone German riflemen being shot at the advancing tanks of the allied troops. The name of the village was apparently mentioned in a war bulletin, but I doubt that this would be recorded in any history book.

Certainly the liberators entered triumphantly and they were treated to a heartfelt welcome by the local population. Not only did they carry in themselves all the signs of victory, but also, at another not unimportant level, they brought a huge array of material things that almost everyone had had to go without for a long time: chocolate, perfumed soap (Palmolive), butter, canned meat, sultanas and so on.

Death and horror did not stop with the arrival in the village of the liberators' army. Not long after the arrival of the allied troops, village people who had lost relatives at the hands of the *Repubblichini* couldn't wait to take their revenge on the *paesani* who had supported the *Repubblichini* all along. The latter, naturally, had fled the village at the first signs of the German army's imminent collapse.

Early one evening I was with my mother in the vegetable garden, where she was planting the new season's tomato seedlings, when we suddenly froze at the sound of repeated bursts of a machine-gun firing, breaking the evening stillness. The ominous sound was coming from the banks of the Adige, less than three hundred yards away. Neither of us said a word. We both realized immediately that so-called justice was being done. We knew all five of the people (amongst them a woman and her old father) who at that very moment were being shot in anger by other people whom we also knew very well, and whom at that time we wished we didn't know. For, whatever the rights and wrongs, both executioners and victims were still very much part of the *paese*.

–2–

The Oppressors and the Oppressed in Interaction

A Shared Dimension of Everyday Life

MIRA CROUCH

This chapter examines the attractions of Fascism contained in the possibilities under Nazi rule for arbitrary and autonomous oppressive actions. I should first clarify the sense in which 'Fascism' is used. Firstly, the term is employed to denote the authoritarian political movement of Nazism (following common usage which has broadened the original Italian definition of the term) – and, as a kind of shorthand, for the general political and social conditions under Nazi rule. Secondly, 'Fascism' is used to refer to the ideology which inspired the Nazi movement, supported, nurtured and legitimized the structures and functions of the Nazi organizations, and justified the actions of individual members of those organizations. Thirdly, again following popular usage, the attribute 'fascist' is understood to denote oppressive, dictatorial and authoritarian actions to which a particular kind of ideological relevance can in some way be imputed. In this last sense, 'Fascism' can refer to a dimension of social conduct, intermittent or continuous, which can also be present in (otherwise) 'democratic' societies.

In authoritarian societies, the holders and executors of authority are usually highly visible, either in the flesh (normally distinguished through some kind of insignia) or as icons, and are clearly separate from those they govern and in whose interests they usually claim to act. Generally, these individuals constitute some kind of party which *internally* is hierarchically structured and *externally* is impervious to political influence. Its doings are secretive, both within and without the hierarchy – in direct contrast to the openness of the ways in which its members exercise their authority and influence the general conditions of life under their rule. The flaunting and promulgation of a specific ideology constitutes an important aspect of these activities; thus the ideology is a significant *property* of the party, in both senses of the word.

The attractions for the masses of the ideology of Fascism/Nazism (especially during the early phases of the movement and the Nazi state) have been widely discussed in publications too numerous to mention, and the parameters of these discussions now have the status of received wisdom; the same applies to analyses of social and economic conditions of the period. In this chapter the received wisdom will be taken for granted. The discussion will focus on some aspects of lived experience under Fascism associated with the manner in which authoritarian and repressive conditions appear to have been imposed by Nazi rule – especially in relation to social groups excluded, by ideological definition and by fiat, from the rights and privileges of ordinary citizenship (here Jews in particular, but also gypsies, political suspects, and many other inhabitants of militarily occupied countries). This exclusion, as is generally known, was underscored by various degrees of oppression and persecution.

Much of the lived experience of Fascism resided in the fabric of the actual social interactions between the oppressors and the oppressed – interactions which were a necessary part of the process of persecution. I will seek to examine, partly in the manner advocated by Simmel,[1] some formal features of these interactions, and to explore possible implications of their content. Recollections of life in an occupied country suggest that oppression was in many respects individualistic and arbitrary, albeit contained within an impersonal and explicitly rationalized system.[2] Thus it was possible to distinguish between, on the one hand, the general policy of the oppressors in relation to their ideologically defined aims, and, on the other, the specific and relatively autonomous acts of the individual oppressors as they went about the work of oppressing. The oppressors seemed to have considerable discretionary powers in their dealings – that is in social interaction – with the oppressed. For instance, the breaking of the curfew sometimes resulted in shooting on sight and sometimes merely in a reprimand – at the whim, one felt, of those who happened to be on patrol on a given evening. Civilian passengers on trains were sometimes searched, seemingly at random, or singled out for manhandling. Reprisals for subver-

1. With particular attention to specific circumstances of definite types of interactions – especially concerning relationships of supra- and sub-orientation. See G. Simmel, 'The Problem of Sociology', in *The Sociology of Georg Simmel*, tr./ed. K. Wolff, New York, 1950.
2. My childhood was spent in occupied Yugoslavia; my father was Jewish.

sive guerrilla activities varied enormously from place to place, from time to time, and in degrees of brutality: in one town, adult hostages were hanged in a public place; in another, all boys from the local high school were rounded up and shot. And so on.

This 'caprice' was most obvious in the treatment of the Jews, where the business of oppression and persecution constituted an intensely active scene for the oppressors. In the lives of Jewish people under Fascism it is possible to distinguish two broad phases: the 'rounding-up' phase and the 'internment' phase. (The 'final solution' appeared as a subcategory of the second phase; it was characterized by greater efficiency in the execution of general objectives which had already been formulated.) In the 'rounding-up' phase, many rules and regulations were operative: the wearing of the yellow star, restrictions of freedom of movement, prohibitions on the use of public transport, regular reporting, confiscation of property, and forced changes of residence. Finally came the 'transports', and with these the classification of persons into categories in terms of priorities for transportation and of types and destinations of transports. These are all well-known 'standard' procedures, though differing somewhat from country to country. There was, however, a considerable degree of variation in the way in which they were carried out. Excessive acts of brutality (that is, over and above what appeared to be the norm for particular circumstances) took place randomly and without apparent reason. Conversely, relative lenience was manifested from time to time in a similarly random fashion; for example, 'exemption' from a transport was approved, a stay of execution was suddenly granted during a raid, an extension of time at home – or in the ghetto – was given prior to departure with a transport, and so on. Neither the excessive brutalities nor the lenient acts – nor, indeed, the 'norm' itself – were generally explicable or intelligible in terms of what could be assumed to be the objectives of the oppressors.

These impressionistic generalizations from my own experience seem to be supported by written accounts of the period, which all contain evidence of the apparently arbitrary manner in which the oppressors interacted with the oppressed.[3] The same can be said about accounts of life in concentration camps. Indeed, Bettelheim places special emphasis on the general unpredictability of events in

3. One of the most moving – and telling – of those accounts is by Etty Hillesum, *Etty: A Diary 1941–1943*, London, 1985. This discussion was also informed by Nechama Tech, *Dry Tears: The Story of a Lost Childhood*, New York, 1984; and Halina Birenbaum, *Hope is the Last to Die: A Personal Documentation of Nazi Terror*, New York, 1971; many others are of course available.

the camps, suggesting that this was one of the main reasons for the total loss of the feeling of autonomy among inmates.[4] This was due, he maintains, to severe attrition of cognitive control, as such control is normally only possible in a context of ordinary routines and familiar structures. I will suggest that the need for cognitive control was also responsible for the capricious behaviour on the part of the oppressors, and for the arbitrary and unpredictable nature of their actions. Spontaneity and individual variation – within given limits – are characteristic of ordinary, habitual human action by autonomous human beings in ordinary, everyday situations. To render 'personal', even by means of imaginative atrocity, an extraordinary situation requiring completely bureaucratic treatment of human subjects as objects, was to gain control over that situation, to incorporate into it some typifications and constructions of a life-world that was still partially valid 'after hours' and was reminiscent of the structures of shared meanings and values that had encompassed, prior to 1933, the lives of both the oppressors and their victims.

We can now view this situation with the wisdom of hindsight and the benefit of time elapsed, which afford us the possibility of attempting to consider events relatively dispassionately. It may well be that some of this arbitrariness of behaviour was facilitated at the structural level by insufficient planning and bad organization, in the accepted sense of those terms (that is, taking as given what was being organized). This can be accepted as a serious possibility, despite the stereotype of Teutonic thoroughness, if we consider that, from the Nazi standpoint, there was in fact no need to take great care about detailed procedures, since those most affected by them did not have to be given any intrinsic consideration in the plans made for their disposition and disposal. The discretionary powers of those engaged in the actual work of oppressing and persecuting could then be seen to arise within the acceptably wide margins of error for the mode of the task at hand.

In lived experience, however, actions in such a context of meaning could become instrumental not only in terms of the task, but also for the selves carrying out that task. These actions could become a means of affirming and reaffirming one's autonomy and superiority, of effective and legitimate self-assertion, of exercise of power drawn from both the social structure and its ideology. Impressionalistically, one can observe that such opportunities may be attractive to many persons, not just members of the Gestapo and

4. B. Bettelheim, *The Informed Heart*, Glencoe, 1960.

the SS. Thus, for example, bus conductors and drivers, school teachers (and university lecturers), nurses and doctors and social workers, amongst others, can show signs of arbitrary use and display of socially structured authority: 'bureaucracies, democratic or totalitarian, are as rich in such situations as Belsen was in spectacle frames'.[5] It can be postulated that justification claims for such actions are made or implied on the basis of ideological propositions which define some groups and/or individuals primarily in terms of their category membership, such as 'passengers', 'pupils', 'patients' or, in this context, 'Jews'. The operations which constitute the treatment of people in such categories are determined by the defining properties of the categories themselves, and the ideological principles (including scientific knowledge, where appropriate) which underlie them. This process parenthesizes the actual persons involved – or, more precisely, their personhood, both individual and collective – and shifts the emphasis on to the task itself. This, in turn, separates the operators (to whom the task belongs) from their human objects (towards whom the task is directed). For the operators, a concern with the human objects as such is thus beside the point – as Milgram's experiments, for example, have amply demonstrated.[6]

This task orientation is further supported by 'moral righteousness', since the execution of the task is normally associated, according to its ideology, with benefits for the 'community'. In such a setting, individualistic, oppressive, arbitrary (that is 'fascist') acts can thus take place whenever the required action is not completely prescribed. This seems, in fact, to be normally the case: firstly, because it is difficult and impractical to anticipate every possible set of circumstances; and secondly, and more importantly, because in all probability organizations and systems survive and continue to function partly on the basis of the considerable psychological

5. O. Webster, 'The Age of Treason', in O. Webster (ed.), *Disenchantment*, Melbourne, 1972, p. 227. It is of interest here to list some of Webster's examples of 'authoritarian psychopathology': . . . 'the silly little Premier denouncing "the permissive society" . . . the headmaster whose school is his empire and who proves it with his loudspeaker system a score of times daily . . . the magistrate who offers a police cell to a father in which to thrash his delinquent son . . . policemen who will enjoy hunting a boy to his death because he is startled while joy-riding in a stolen car . . . the Chief Commissioner of Police who can write that the prerogative of the professional policeman is the right to take instant action by way of arrest, a weapon "to be used with all the physical force he can muster, all the determination at his command to neutralize the hostile, obstructive acts of louts, whether allegedly educated or otherwise"' (p. 228).
6. S. Milgram, *Obedience to Authority: An Experimental View*, London, 1974.

benefits that accrue to their operators from the possibility of discretionary action within their defined roles. In particular circumstances, some arbitrary actions can be given positive labels – 'initiative', 'involvement', 'efficiency', for instance. These, in turn, can reinforce other spontaneous actions generated by the particular situational and personal factors. The limits of tolerance within which, in such a context, 'fascist' action can occur and be perceived as acceptable, will be set by a complicated dynamic in which the structural position of the functionaries and the ideological definition of their task play the most important part.

Some accounts of Nazism suggest that its intrinsic character may have been particularly conducive to arbitrary and random oppressive activity. Stern states:

> Both party propaganda and party practice alike were concerned to establish a system of government and administration that should not be a 'system' at all, but should remain 'fluid' and 'dynamic'. 'Es ist immer was los' – 'there was always something going on' – is the phrase on the lips of people who . . . try to convey the atmosphere of the Third Reich.[7]

Hitler's own capricious and emotive style of dictatorship may have set the tone for the actions of other, lesser bearers of authority, and his rhetoric of the will and the authenticity of experience may have become legitimizing slogans for the controlled and institutionalized chaos which was the characteristic form of National Socialist government. 'The state of permanent institutionalised chaos, the fluidity of social status, the mobility of power and the controlled arbitrariness of its exercise – all of these were not part of an abstract ideology, but the conditions which best suited Hitler's personal rule and "artistic" temperament.'[8] The historian Raul Hilberg echoes these themes in Lanzmann's film *Shoah* (1985):

> Everything is left to inference from general words. General words – the very wording 'final solution' or 'total solution' or 'territorial solution' leaves something to the bureaucrat that he must infer . . . One cannot even read Göring's famous letter to Heydrich at the end of July 1941, charging him in two paragraphs to proceed with the 'final solution', and examining that document, consider that everything is clarified. Far from it. It was an authorization to invent . . . In every aspect of this operation, invention was necessary. Certainly at this point, because every

7. J. P. Stern, *Hitler: The Führer and the People*, London, 1986, p. 115.
8. Ibid., p. 175.

> problem was unprecedented. Not only how to kill the Jews, but what to do with their property thereafter. And not only that.[9]

It would seem then that this inventiveness was both necessitated and enabled ('constrained' in the sense in which Durkheim used the term); enabled by Hitler's chaotic administration, and necessitated by the racist and proscriptive *political* creed – a rigid constant in an otherwise fluid situation – which, as Wajda points out, rendered specifically directed brutality socially acceptable.[10]

Hitler was the progenitor of the racist creed (though not, of course, the originator of all of its facets), of this action-orienting centre of the Nazi ideology – and in that sense, at least, he was the Father of the Nazi movement. It was his creation, and built into it, into the actions of all those individuals who made it work, was Hitler's own mode of personification of tyranny, where private vision – inspired by the Father – and personal arbitrariness represented political, legal and moral rules. A displacement, an irrational (childish?) externalization of conscience was achieved by 'the miniature "supermen" [who] went on with the work of destruction'.[11] Intoxicated by emotive notions of superiority and identified by Hitler's righteousness, the Nazis ruled, collectively and individually, in the archetypal fashion of the Father, the One we all know in fear and shame from our nightmares (and in appreciative recall of the writings of Freud). We recognize this fear- and guilt-provoking image instantly in Kafka's words:

> Your opinion was right, every other opinion was crazy, unbalanced, *meschugge*, not normal. And with all this your self-confidence was so immense that you had no need to be consistent at all and yet never ceased to be in the right . . . You assumed for me that mysteriousness that belongs to all tyrants, whose right is founded, not in thought but in their persons.[12]

It is chilling to consider how well the Nazi collectives and the Nazi individuals projected these images. The racist ideology legitimized not only the actions but also the persons of the Nazis as troops in defence of moral principles of purity and guardians of its 'natural' state. 'The sin against blood and race' that so concerns Hitler in

9. *Shoah: An Oral History of the Holocaust*, the complete text of the film by Claude Lanzmann, New York, 1985, p. 70.
10. M. Wajda, *Fascism as a Mass Movement*, London, 1976.
11. Agnes Heller, *The Power of Shame*, London, 1985, p. 48.
12. From Kafka's 'Letter to his Father', quoted in Stern, *Hitler*, p. 60.

Mein Kampf (1924) must be repressed by them,[13] and Goethe's *verdammte Unnatur* kept at bay; those who do the job are naturally entitled to it and can therefore act at will. Indeed, the normative concept of *nature* has aided many authoritarian tactics, of which Fascism is possibly only the most telling example. The idea of 'the natural' seems to have very deeply entrenched 'good' connotations (at least in Judaeo-Christian cultures): 'It is one of the most useful means ever devised for establishing moral points, and can be used . . . in almost any context to establish anything at all.'[14] The moral power of fathers is 'natural' in just this sense, and the moralistic, masculine and 'manly' men of the Gestapo and the Schutzstaffel (SS: Nazi elite corps) clearly appeared to consider themselves entitled to such power in relation to the rest of humanity. In the case of Nazism, the 'good' connotations of the 'natural' were also used to justify a system which erupted under circumstances in which, to borrow J. S. Mill's remark, 'the native promptings of the mind [had] nothing to oppose them but reason'.[15]

The Nazis seem to have understood this well. Like fathers in general, they had superior strength, and demonstrated it constantly to ensure that submission was understood to be inevitable. One recalls, for example, the ceremonial procession of the Wehrmacht through newly occupied territory, especially towns, always headed by tanks. The sights and sounds of crude force were combined with the visual absence of men – all the more horrible and cruel to imagine as they crouched, steely-eyed and grim-faced, inside their death machines. We knew them immediately as the aliens who would live amongst us, but not with us, like the lethal ghosts one fathoms in one's own conscience. A similar principle governed the very first round-ups of the Jews at reporting centres – defined immediately by brutality, arbitrarily and randomly administered by the officiating Gestapo. It ranged from abuse, kicking, pushing and so on, to removal from the queue for immediate execution in full sight of everyone present. Such tactics made it clear, from the very beginning of the Nazi rule, that the oppressors could do anything at all, both systematically as an organization, and personally as autonomous operators under the licence of absolute power.

The arbitrariness of the acts of oppression constitutes the most convincing evidence of the superior strength of the oppressing

13. A. Hitler, *Mein Kampf* (1924), London, 1940.
14. Janet Radcliffe, *The Sceptical Feminist*, Harmondsworth, 1980, p. 80.
15. J. S. Mill, 'On Nature', quoted by Radcliffe, ibid., p. 80.

forces; its absolute nature is confirmed, rather than invalidated, by the randomness and inconsistency of its manifestations. In this context, the strategy of submission on the part of the oppressed was not only due to a realistic assessment of the futility of resistance. The arbitrary use of power made it seem feasible, in principle at least, to plead for mercy, to bargain, to offer evidence of good behaviour and special circumstances as reasons for various 'exemptions'; it made it seem possible to hope for arbitrary and wilful acts of lenience, as capriciously within reach of the oppressors as the brutality one sought to escape; it seemed one could actually be spared, however temporarily. For this one would plead as a child might, from a position of being (forcibly) regressed to a not-fully-human status, powerless and excluded from ordinary social life, reduced to physical dependence and at the mercy of one's body and of those who had power over it – like an infant, in fact. The humiliation, the guilt and the shame of this situation are private, personal and submerged for oppressor and victim alike, but for each have different consequences. Should the oppressors feel any kind of shame, the brutalization and the degradation of their victims must be intensified so that finally this shameful treatment is justified by the spectacle of the attrition of humanity which it has caused. As their authority over the victims is completely external, in stark reality a matter of sheer force, the oppressors' shame does not regulate their behaviour towards the out-group constituted by the victims; it can only affect their motivations for such behaviour. For the same reason, the out-group can only react in real terms by negotiation, as Heller has pointed out – since the shame its members feel is not intersubjectively constructed with the oppressors in a shared life-world.[16] As a result, the actual reality may assume the significance of a sign for the victims, and the shame and guilt may resonate with themes other than those plainly evident in the immediate situation. To be pardoned, then, in however insignificant a manner, may be much more than practically desirable. It may also be redeeming, a sign that one has gained the Father's favour in the face of annihilation; perhaps also a sign, more generally speaking, that one is exempt from the universal human wretchedness so abundantly obvious within the prevailing circumstances of the times.

The point was not lost, it seems, on 'the man in the street' – the many ordinary citizens in Germany, Italy, Hungary and other occupied European countries, who suspected, but might not

16. Heller, *The Power of Shame.*

always have known, what exactly took place to effect the 'final solution'. They also were constantly confronted with the spectacle of the oppressor's power as he marched down their streets, ate their food, restricted their freedom and menaced their lives – doing them harm but not, by and large, killing them.[17] Under these circumstances, what happened to the Jews (and others similarly operationally defined) was a comfort as well as a lesson (speaking generally, and leaving aside the reactions of those with strong anti-Semitic tendencies). Quite apart from feeling relief through contrast – which must have been reinforcing enough in itself – some might even have been secretly uplifted. Because they *did* know, in fact, that other people were being rounded up and penned like animals, beaten, tortured, suffocated and slaughtered, their nameless and filthy bodies heaped up to rot and burn. All of this, the sum of it and whatever was in evidence of it, was degrading; ultimately, those so treated were perceived as degraded in rèlation to oneself, however much one might have pitied them and abhorred their persecutors. If, in this process, one experienced the guilt of the survivor, there was all the more reason to seek evidence of deliverance and redemption, of which one needed assurance when confronted by destruction administered with such largesse as under the Nazi rule. Thus arises the fascination with Fascism, the spellbound, supplicating attitude of the general population in most authoritarian societies – the silent disquietude of those who do not have the motivating force of strong conviction, the revolutionary zeal or excess of pride to combat their acceptance of conditions which, on balance, are understood to deflect the wrath of vengeance on to others.

These observations suggest that some of the attractions of Fascism reside in the fabric of life within which Fascism is realized. This fabric is patterned with the forms in which absolute power manifests itself, and thus supports the experience, for the powerful, of being on the right side – and, for the powerless, of being *on the right side of those in power.* Absolute power corrupts – those who do not have it perhaps even more than those who do. Some of our current established constructions of morality, authority and legitimacy may well provide *in principle* the conditions for social acceptance of 'fascist' actions based *on principle.* Such circumstances are facilitated by cognate sociopsychological structures; much more could, of course, have been said on this subject. My aim has been to

17. This is an inversion of the well-known words of Socrates: 'Anytos and Meletos can kill me but they cannot do me harm', quoted in Heller, ibid., p. 42.

reach an explanatory level of *Verstehen* (understanding) in relation to the social meaning of arbitrary oppressive action. This has been arrived at by an eclectic – and to some perhaps inadmissible – mix of phenomenological and psychoanalytic concepts and propositions. There seems, however, little point in engaging in a methodological discussion at this stage; the reader is asked to suspend judgement on the prior existence of a problematic in this regard, and to treat the case presented on its own merits. Some of these may reside in questions implied here rather than addressed. Perhaps the most pressing of them should be asked with both urgency and humility: was indiscriminate annihilation – of Self and Other alike – Hitler's ultimate if unconscious aim, the *last* 'final solution'? Stern suggests that this was 'the secret that bound his followers to him; *and not his followers only*. On this dark understanding his whole career is based.'[18] That career is no more; but can the same be said of 'the dark understanding' shared by the rest of us?

18. Stern, *Hitler*, p. 224; my emphasis.

–3–

Giorgio Bassani
Historian of the Heart

SUZANNE KIERNAN

When *The Garden of the Finzi-Continis* came out in 1962, Giorgio Bassani became part of a new phenomenon in the history of Italian publishing: the boom in best-selling 'quality' novels. It was something he was responsible for before he became part of it, since it was he who had recommended for publication by Feltrinelli the 'quality best-seller' of a few seasons before, Giuseppe Tomasi di Lampedusa's historical novel *The Leopard* (1958),[1] when it had been rejected elsewhere by the 'dean' of the post-war culture of the Left, Elio Vittorini. The criticism of the Left quickly mobilized itself against the emergent neo-conservatism it perceived in Italian writing, seeing *The Leopard*'s success as its confirmation, and this mood or strain in Italian culture was soon neatly dubbed *Gattopardismo* ('Leopardism'). There had been an alarming resurgence of reactionary politics in Italy since the beginning of the decade – to the extent that the neo-Fascist movement had been able to constitute itself legally as the Movimento Sociale Italiano (MSI) and hold a national rally with impunity in 1952. In these years there are numerous instances of works of literature being judged first in the political arena, and found wanting there as works of literature. The question of whether they were 'good literature' or not left entirely aside, books like Beppe Fenoglio's *I ventitré giorni della città di Alba* of 1952,[2] and the 'book of the year' for 1955, Pratolini's *Metello*,[3] received perfunctory attention on their first appearance as to what it is that actually makes them literature and not something else.

The prevailing climate of the 1950s in Italy has been described in more recent times by the magisterial Moravia as one in which

1. Giuseppe Tomasi di Lampedusa, *The Leopard* [1958], *with A Memory and Two Stories*, tr. Archibald Colquhoun, London, 1986.
2. Beppe Fenoglio, *I ventitré giorni della città di Alba*, Turin, 1952.
3. Vasco Pratolini, *Metello*, Florence, 1955.

memories of Nazism-Fascism were so terrible that anyone declaring an anti-Stalinist attitude ran the risk of being pilloried as pro-Fascist.[4] It was in such a climate of opinion – characterized by ideological 'smogginess' or 'infestation' (to borrow suggestions from Calvino's fables of the 1950s),[5] and at the same time politically polarized – that Bassani was judged in the early 1960s. Privately, though from within the influential Einaudi citadel, Pavese had dismissed him – and by extension the conservative 'high-cultural' set who had taken him up – with the damning epithet *arcadico* in 1950.[6] Marxist criticism found him a bourgeois individualist. Gian Carlo Ferretti attributed to him a view of history as an arid chronicle of an undifferentiated reality:[7] the view, that is, of Geo Josz, the sole Jewish deportee from Ferrara to the Nazi camps to return in Bassani's story 'La passeggiata prima di cena'. Pasolini descried in his writing a kind of 'revulsion' in the face of reality that prevented him from taking up any 'clearly defined positions' in relation to it.[8] The 'neo-avant-garde' movement (Gruppo 63) found him entirely wanting, although Umberto Eco has since said that he was too hasty in the rush to judgement on Bassani as belonging to the 'enemy' alongside Cassola and Lampedusa, and that 'if we were back in 1963, I would greet him as a fellow traveler.'[9] Turning against him some words of quite admirably clear-sighted self-criticism made in 1964 (which I shall quote in conclusion), Carlo Salinari judged Bassani to be a fundamentally 'decadent' writer.[10] And in the early 1970s, a 'militant' critic from the Gruppo 63 referred scathingly to the regression by Bassani (along with several other 'oldies' of about fifty years) to subject-matter he found essentially 'stupid' and petty bourgeois, to life seen as 'the vicissitudes of the poor suffering heart':

4. Alberto Moravia, *Impegno controvoglia. Saggi, articoli, interviste: 35 anni di scritti politici*, ed. Renzo Paris, Milan, 1980, p. viii.
5. Italo Calvino, *La nuvola di smog e La formica argentina* (1959, 1952), Turin, 1972; the latter appears in an English translation in *Difficult Loves*, tr. William Weaver, London, 1983. It seems that Calvino contributed a new tag to the common pool with *La formica argentina*; references to the neo-Fascist 1950s as *gli anni delle formiche* abound, as testified by journalist Giovanni Cavallotti who, in *Gli anni cinquanta*, Milan, 1979, refers to the decade as 'la giornata delle formiche' (p. 7).
6. Cesare Pavese, *Lettere 1945–1959*, ed. Italo Calvino, Turin, 1966, p. 458.
7. Gian Carlo Ferretti, *Letteratura e ideologia: Bassani, Cassola, Pasolini*, Rome, 1965, p. 39.
8. Quoted in ibid., p. 39.
9. Umberto Eco, postscript to *The Name of the Rose*, tr. William Weaver, New York, 1984, p. 61.
10. Carlo Salinari, *Preludio e fine del realismo in Italia*, Naples, 1967, p. 336.

> They had gone back to churning out their stupid stories, all tentativeness and glancing suggestion, protesting how they were right in keeping faith with an inspiration closely allied to a particular life experience which for them – pathetic fools that they are – consists wholly in the vicissitudes of the poor suffering heart! Thus – they proclaim – have they saved poetry from the destructive onslaught of the Young Turks of the neo-avant-garde. The truth is they never were right and nor are they now. Their petty bourgeois muse is well dead and gone (if it ever existed in the first place).[11]

Bassani's narrative is motivated by the backward look, and in obeying the dictates of memory it fails to 'historicize' the past; this, I think, is the basis of the negative critical responses to his work, and is, I think, as true as any judgement in literature can be said to be 'true', which is to say appropriate to the case. But I am unaware of any discussion of Bassani that pays serious attention to one function in particular of memory in his writing. Generally missing is an acknowledgement of the author's intentions – regardless of whether or not he fulfils them.

In 1960 – that is to say, two years before the appearance of his most sustained novel, *The Garden of the Finzi-Continis* – Bassani drew attention to the 'dissimulated yet ever-present' narrator of all his writing to date as simultaneously 'story-teller, poet, judge and historian'. His main aim, he continues, is to approximate 'documentary' and poetry so that each somehow 'colours' the other.[12] An extraordinarily large claim in itself, it seems greatly at odds with the Bassani so often presented as an elegist, a nostalgist, the 'memorialist' lost in motionless contemplation of a past that has been made irretrievably private and 'immortalized' in poetry. And the dimensions of this ambitious 'writer's mandate' have been expanded in later years. Bassani has since closed off his 'Ferrara cycle' (consisting of short stories, novellas, and his single long novel) and collected it under the over-arching title *Il Romanzo di Ferrara* (The Romance of Ferrara).[13] No one could fail to register

11. Angelo Guglielmi, *La letteratura del risparmio*, Milan, 1973, p. 103; my translation, as are others where no English edition is given.
12. *Il Punto*, 8 October 1960; quoted by Ferretti, *Letteratura*, p. 64.
13. Giorgio Bassani, *Il Romanzo di Ferrara*, Milan, 1974; subsequently reissued with some slight changes, Milan, 1980. There is no English translation of the complete cycle. The 1980 edition is divided into six books, whose titles follow, accompanied by those of the English versions used for this essay: *Dentro le mura* (Within the Walls; first published as *Storie ferraresi*, 1956); *Gli occhiali d'oro*, 1958 (The Gold-Rimmed Eyeglasses; tr. William Weaver in *The Smell of Hay*, London, 1975 (see note 31 to this chapter); *Il giardino dei Finzi-Contini*, 1962

the weight of the claim implicit in the choice of title, given the illustrious history of the Romance tradition in Renaissance Ferrara from Boiardo to Tasso, with Ariosto as the great exemplar of a combination of poet and story-teller, historian and judge.[14]

In the years following the publication of *The Garden* in 1962 there were several more 'extra-literary' statements of literary intention from Giorgio Bassani. Far from considering himself a 'memorialist', he said in an interview in 1964, he thought himself on the contrary to be a 'thoroughly historical' writer, and asserted that 'there is no sentimental yearning after time past in my books. I do not write in order to recall it. I am attempting . . . objectively to construct the stages of a young writer's growing to maturity.'[15] And although he was one of Bassani's severest critics, Pasolini had observed as early as 1952 that the experience of nostalgia has no subjective grounding for this writer. For all its inadequacy, in Pasolini's view, its reference is ultimately historical: 'It is simply a hypothesis embedded in the past, regret for an error committed, or a destiny unfulfilled.'[16] In Bassani's 'extra-literary' statements, then, it seems that autobiographical writing is being placed firmly in the realm of historical writing, and it is arguably the historical and not the 'lyrical' subject he is putting forward when he concludes this same interview with a statement abolishing any distinction between 'life' and 'art': writing is 'merely the direct projection of my own life'.

Assuming that Bassani was not wilfully talking nonsense on this occasion (while bearing in mind that no author has a claim to be his own best critic, but merely his own best author), it is worth returning to the avowedly 'dissimulated' subject of the novels and stories to attempt to see how it is that, while their author claims for himself an historical dimension, so many readers can see only a decadent sensibility or a 'hermetic' quality. It is this very identity that is conferred on the narrator in *The Garden of the Finzi-Continis*

(The Garden of the Finzi-Continis; tr. Isabel Quigley, New York, 1965); *Dietro la porta* (Behind the Door), 1964; *L'airone*, 1968 (The Heron; tr. William Weaver, New York, 1970); *L'odore del fieno*, 1972 (The Smell of Hay; tr. William Weaver, London, 1975) (see note 31 to this chapter).

14. The *Orlando furioso* is *inter alia* an encomiastic legendary history of the d'Este dynasty, while in several of the exordiums to the forty-six cantos of the poem Ariosto is extremely critical of its contemporary strategies of power. See Ludovico Ariosto, *Orlando furioso* (1516), tr. Guido Waldman, New York, 1974.
15. Interview with Giulio Nascimbeni, *Corriere d'informazione*, 26–7 February 1964, p. 3.
16. Pier Paolo Pasolini, *Passione e ideologia (1948–1958)*, Milan, 1960, p. 422.

by the character Malnate; there, while he is plainly not comfortable with the definition, his only response is a vague ironic smile and a forbearing silence. 'Subivo, e tacevo' ('I bore it, and said nothing') he relates (although that is not the version in the English translation to which I refer elsewhere). Rhetorically, this is an exemplary sentence for Bassani, although it is by no means stylistically typical of his expansive and parenthetical way of proceeding; it is laconic, and speaks of silence. And in its paratactic structure it is an 'earnest', a token of an habitual thematic parallelism which I shall have occasion to speak about.

In the interview quoted above, Bassani makes an unambiguous assertion: 'Sono lo storico di quel passato.' Yet while he lays claim to the historian's role, his historically minded critics attribute to him a view of history that is entirely incompatible with such a role. It may be, however, that his is a different 'history'. For to the secular Jew – so terribly 'assimilated' as to be virtually *goy*, as Bassani's narrator defines himself in *The Garden*[17] – it may well seem that the Jewish historical experience is nothing but the experience of an interminable series of broken promises to the Chosen People. There is no secular 'Jewish history' common to all Jews of the Diaspora, and historians of the Jews in recent times (such as Léon Poliakov, by way of his account of the Italian dimensions of anti-Semitism, or Arnaldo Momigliano, most recently in his Brandeis University address)[18] always present Italian Jews as the product of specifically Italian historical conditions. All the same, one generalization is possible. Regardless of the differing regional experiences of Jewish communities in Italy, it seems that Italian Jews had long been able to live without the consolatory myth of the Promised Land. They had no need of it, because they had Italy, as Primo Levi wrote in *The Periodic Table* (1975): 'Piedmont was our true country, the one in which we recognized ourselves; the mountains around Turin, visible on clear days, and within reach of a bicycle, were ours, irreplaceable, and had taught us fatigue, endurance, and a certain wisdom. In short, our roots were in Piedmont and in Turin, not enormous but deep, extensive, and fantastically intertwined.'[19]

17. Bassani, *The Garden*, p. 259.
18. Léon Poliakov, *The History of Anti-Semitism*, London, 1975; Arnaldo Momigliano, *Essays in Ancient and Modern Historiography*, Oxford, 1977, and 'The Jews of Italy' (Brandeis University Address, 1984), *New York Review of Books*, 24 October 1985, 22–6.
19. Primo Levi, *The Periodic Table* (1975), tr. Raymond Rosenthal, London, 1985, p. 51.

The shocking and sickening realization on the part of its narrator that he had been declared an 'outsider' in the place that was so intimately 'home' to him is what Bassani's novella *The Gold-Rimmed Eyeglasses* (1958) is about. Ferrara was uniquely that place in which he 'recognized himself' without the need to make any distinction between a Jewish and an Italian self, but the impending promulgation of the Race Laws (the year is 1938) changes all that:

> And while Nino, filled with embarrassment, remained silent, I felt born within me, with unspeakable revulsion, the ancient atavistic hatred of the Jew toward everything that was Christian, Catholic: *goyish*, in other words. I thought also of Via Mazzini, of Via Vignatagliata, of the blind Vicolo Torcicoda: that labyrinth of narrow alleys, damp in winter and sweltering in summer, which had made up, once, the Ferrara ghetto. *Goy, goyim*: how shameful, what humiliation, what repugnance at expressing myself this way! And yet I could already do it – I said to myself – like any Jew from Eastern Europe who had never left the ghetto. In a more or less distant future, they, the *goyim*, would force us again to live there, in the medieval quarter from which, after all, we had emerged only seventy or eighty years ago. Huddled one against the other, behind the gates, like so many frightened animals, we would never escape it again.[20]

The historical trauma is before all else a private, 'visceral' experience (the term is one that Bassani used in reference to *Dietro la porta* (Behind the Door, 1964), a novella set further back in his narrator's life). That it can be felt no other way at first is the point of an earlier episode of *The Gold-Rimmed Eyeglasses* set on the town walls overlooking the Jewish section of the cemetery at Ferrara:

> I looked at the field below, where our dead were buried. Among the sparse tombstones, small in the distance, I saw a man and a woman moving . . . They moved among the graves with the caution and detachment of guests, outsiders. But then, looking at them, and at the vast urban landscape that was displayed to me, from up there, in all its extension, I felt suddenly filled with a great sweetness, a tender peace and gratitude. The setting sun, piercing a dark blanket of clouds, low on the horizon, illuminated everything vividly: the Jewish cemetery at my feet, the apse and spire of the church of San Cristoforo a bit farther on, and, in the background, high above the dark expanse of houses, the distant hulks of the Castello Estense and the cathedral. It had been enough for me to find again my city's maternal countenance, to have it,

20. Bassani, *The Smell of Hay*, p. 168.

> once more, all mine, and the atrocious feeling of exclusion that had tormented me during the past days abruptly fell away. The future of persecutions and massacres that, perhaps, lay in store for us (I had constantly heard it spoken of, since my childhood, as an eventuality always possible for us Jews) no longer frightened me.[21]

The protagonist is in the habit of viewing the city through the memorials to the Jewish dead, and just as the two are in the one continuous field of his vision, so Ferrara is assimilated to Jewish history, and there is no question of a distinction between 'civic' and 'racial' identity. With the promulgation of the Race Laws, the distinction originates. In this novella, and in *The Garden of the Finzi-Continis*, Bassani shows how a Jew may *lose* the promised land.

Writing on Jewish historiography, Arnaldo Momigliano has observed that the Jew has the religious duty to remember the past, and that to contemplate temporal history at any point is to be reminded of sacred history. He further draws attention to a parallelism between historical writing and literature in the Jewish tradition. Bassani, of course, is as thoroughly secular as the late historian; and yet, that same parallelism as a habit of thought is echoed in the author's own claim (alluded to above) to make 'documentary' value and 'poetic intuition' coincide as far as possible in his writing, and in an earlier assertion that 'every work of art should say at least two things: one apparent, the other concealed.'[22] Nothing is better concealed than a thing unspoken. What remains unsaid in Bassani remains so because the suffering heart, ultimately, is speechless and unknowing (and such is the burden of his epigraph from Manzoni's *The Betrothed* for *The Garden*, and of much of his late poetry). Yet, in the light of Renato Bertacchini's very reasoned and suggestive argument for seeing the key to Bassani's entire project in a *Bassani semita*,[23] it is equally possible that much remains unsaid in obedience to the strictures of the ancient prophets on the wisdom of keeping good counsel in the presence of the profane.

Clearly a 'poetics of memory' operates in Bassani's work, poetry and prose alike, though here I am concerned only with the prose narrative, which I have no hesitation in declaring infinitely better than the verse. Things present themselves to his narrator already suffused with the pathos of their deaths, bringing with them the foreknowledge that their only lasting place will be in memory, as

21. Ibid., pp. 161–2.
22. Quoted by Ferretti, *Letteratura*, p. 64.
23. Renato Bertacchini, 'Appunti sul semitismo di Bassani', in *Figure e problemi di narrativa contemporanea*, Rocca San Casciano, 1960, pp. 301–88.

the powerfully emblematic Jewish cemetery, with its conspicuous memorials to the dead, stands at the centre of *The Gold-Rimmed Eyeglasses* and as the induction into *The Garden of the Finzi-Continis*. Yet less attention has been paid to another aspect and another function of memory in Bassani. It has something approaching a forensic value for the narrator of the novel cycle, since it is the means by which he establishes a true record of events in his place and time. It is common knowledge that you might find your way about the city of Ferrara quite well simply from reading Bassani's *Romanzo di Ferrara*. Bassani even draws attention to the apparently redundant precision of the 'documentary' memory when he refers, for instance, to the 'odd exactness' with which his narrator in *The Garden* recalls every detail of the first supper he ate with the Finzi-Contini family at their villa.[24] This, of course, along with the great park that surrounds it (which tourists are said to come looking for year after year) is the one thing in Bassani's Ferrara which does not exist. Emblematic as the (real) Jewish cemetery, this imaginary demesne houses a modern Italian library equal to the public collection from which the narrator has been shut out by the Race Laws. Bassani's narrator is specific: this is a fully representative *national* library, with all the major authors of post-unification Italy, in *Jewish* keeping.[25] A similar point is made in the novel's opening pages, even as the 'decadent' theme of death-in-life is being laid down. A prologue recalling a visit to an Etruscan necropolis, where in life everyone had a second house awaiting him, gives rise to a meditation – ironic and elegiac in equal measure – on the most conspicuous tomb in the Jewish cemetery of Ferrara. The hideous funerary monument of great-grandfather Finzi-Contini dates from the years of the definitive abolition of the Ferrara ghetto, in the aftermath of the annexation of the Papal Romagna to the kingdom of Italy in 1860. Not only is it a memorial to the dead, however; in its festive operatic suggestiveness, it is a fitting expression of 'a mood of euphoria' brought on by a newly acquired civil equality in the new nation-state.[26]

It is this Promised Land that is taken away from Italian Jews with the enactment of the Race Laws in 1938. My argument is that the 'Ferrara cycle' is a project in secular Jewish historiography inseparable from its being an intimate lyrical and confessional 'novel of the interior'. No detail of experience at a time like the one in which it is

24. Bassani, *The Garden*, p. 172.
25. Ibid., pp. 174–5.
26. Ibid., p. 18.

set – 1929 to 1948 – is trivial: 'No, no: only we, born and brought up *intra muros* . . . could know and really understand these things, which were terribly subtle, of course, and maybe quite beside the point in everyday life, but none the less real for that.'[27] A young man's sense of affront at being excluded from a tennis club, his pain at seeing childhood friends grappling with the need to redefine him as a Jew, are not trivial; writ large, they are the millennial Jewish experience. Fadigati, in *The Gold-Rimmed Eyeglasses*, observes that destiny operates on the small scale as well as the large: 'Why, there are times, in a person's life, when it takes only a few months. A few months, sometimes, count for more than whole years.'[28] Bassani's insistence on returning to small-scale events and precise locations in memory differs in degree but not in kind, and in function not at all, from the repeated, incantatory and ritual 'I remember' of the agent of the Polish underground who undertook to travel Eastern Europe to 'witness' Nazi atrocities against Jews, and to inscribe them in memory. I am referring here to Jan Karsky, who in an interview for radio broadcast in recent years began almost every sentence with a formulaic and incantatory recital of the phrase 'I remember'.[29] (Interestingly, there is no sign and no mention of this apparent technique of memory in his book *The Story of a Secret State* (1944),[30] or in the interview with film-maker Claude Lanzmann for his historical documentary *Shoah*, completed in 1986.) Karsky was taken into the Warsaw ghetto and the Belzen death camp with the task of documenting them. In the absence of any other safe means of making and keeping a record under those conditions, his unassisted memories had the awesome responsibility of standing as the sole record – historically unfalsifiable and forensically sound – of that part of the Holocaust.

In one of the stories that stand as the foundation of Bassani's 'Ferrara cycle', 'Una lapide in via Mazzini' (A Plaque in Via Mazzini), a barely recognizable figure returns in 1945 from Buchenwald to Ferrara, the only one of 183 Jews deported from there in 1943 to do so. His return is a grave embarrassment to the citizenry: Geo Josz is a living memory, when they thought he had been taken care of in the commemorative plaque piously mounted in the synagogue wall. After three years, he disappears. The year is 1948, effectively the *terminus ad quem* of the *Romanzo di Ferrara*. Its

27. Ibid., p. 37.
28. Bassani, *The Smell of Hay*, p. 175.
29. Jan Karsky, radio interview broadcast on 'Background Briefing', Australian Broadcasting Corporation, 7 April 1986.
30. Jan Karsky, *The Story of a Secret State*, New York, 1944.

final structure has striking formal aspects: the first stories contain in germ all the later, longer narratives, and these in turn refer to each other. (In *The Garden*, a passing reference to the former location of a certain Dr Fadigati's consulting rooms has the effect of 'placing', in a kind of *mise-en-abîme* effect in the present text, the entire earlier novella in which he figures. Again, the scene of first childhood acquaintance with Micól is set against a sketch that – expanded – was to be the subsequent novella *Dietro la porta*.) The cycle begins in fragments, expands into a sequence of three novellas and a single novel, *The Garden*; it then peters out, so to speak, in another broken sequence of tales and first-person 'pieces' under the title *L'odore del fieno* (The Smell of Hay, 1972).[31] Thus the underlying form is the exact obverse of that of the poetry, which on the page most often assumes the unmistakable shape of the hour-glass (through which, it hardly needs to be said, the verse is measured and strained). The final prose fragment, 'Laggiù, in fondo al corridoio' (There at the End of the Passageway), whose title is the nucleus of the poetry to which Bassani has since devoted himself, is an account of the gestation of the single composite novel, now in six books. Its very last word is the one that bears its entire weight, the result of the accretion of the multiple roles the author has taken on: *io*.

Bassani has evidently completed the *Romanzo di Ferrara*. And since *The Heron* (1968) is set in 1941, the cycle therefore falls just short of formal closure by failing to touch 1948, the year of Geo Josz's second disappearance. Occurring in *Dentro le mura* (Within the Walls, 1956) the first set of stories – or equally properly *histories*, as proposed by an earlier title, *Storie ferraresi* – this stands at the beginning of a series of metaphoric suicides in Bassani's narrative. The withdrawal into solitude, the embracing of a destiny of 'isolation' which is the mark of his narrator, is a kind of unsought suicide: the parallelism of the conclusion of *The Gold-Rimmed Eyeglasses* makes this clear enough, when only in absolute solitude can its narrator speak aloud about the real suicide of Fadigati, another *escluso*. Micól Finzi-Contini – with the biblically suggestive name already settled upon her – knows there is no 'futurity' in her case; Bassani provides another allusion to the 'death-in-life' that is the lot of this generation of Jews in this place, even before the death camps, when he refers to the protagonist's little sister Fanny as

31. *The Smell of Hay* does not reproduce Bassani's *L'odore del fieno*. It includes the novella *The Gold-Rimmed Eyeglasses* and omits the concluding piece 'Laggiù, in fondo al corridoio' and the two stories that precede it. Thus my remarks on the 'ideal' structure of the 'Ferrara cycle' are based on the complete 1980 Italian edition of the *Romanzo*.

seemingly having decided not to grow out of childhood into adolescence. With *The Heron*, Bassani detached himself from his 'ever-present' narrator by moving for the first time in the longer works into third-person narration, and the novella concludes with the protagonist's firm decision to suicide. The year is 1947, the setting Ferrara and environs, and everything about the present reminds the 45-year-old Edgardo Limentani – who is not a literary man, this time – of the worst years he lived through under Fascism. He thinks the Communism that is now in the ascendancy is as bad. Bassani might just as easily have had Edgardo Limentani wait out his despair, had him hold out for 1948 and 'normalization' on the historical plane. But he did not, and 1948 in the *Romanzo* as a whole is represented only by Geo Josz's mysterious dematerialization in the group of stories giving rise to the cycle as a whole. The result is that the gap left in the circle is a manifestation of that same *vizio di forma* – some flaw at the very centre of things, ineradicable, irreparable and inseparable from their very identity with themselves – which Primo Levi made his guiding principle.

In an interview given well before *The Heron's* appearance, Bassani had the following words of clear-sighted self-criticism to which I alluded earlier (and raised against him by Salinari in a review article of the same year, 1964):

> I have always been taken up with decadent themes: with the sense of death, with the sense of dissolution that lies at the heart of things. But it has always been in a spirit that I have sought to keep clearly historicist. It is futile for us to deny 'decadentism': we are its children, and our parents were brought up on d'Annunzio. It's futile to pretend not to know the Italian language . . . Our real contribution ought to be an attempt at a thorough understanding: taking on 'decadent' themes without being taken over by them.[32]

Bassani's last novella is the one to which the adverse criticism provoked by the early works most aptly applies. The fruitful tension between the historical and the autobiographical projects has lapsed. Limentani seems impelled to suicide more by snobbery and spite than anything else (the Communists are an opportunistic rabble; he can no longer abide his vulgar wife). The analogy of the wounded heron and the suffering protagonist resembles nothing so much as an involuntary parody of the 'decadent' poetic sensibility that had managed to live to date – with intelligence and stoicism – alongside the *narratore, giudice e storico*.

32. Interview with Nascimbeni, *Corriere d'informazione*.

PART II

Constructing Fascism

–4–

The Birth of Fascist Man from the Spirit of the Front

From Langemarck to Verdun

BERND HÜPPAUF

The extraordinary impact of the First World War on the social-psychological and cultural development of European societies, in particular those which had to cope with the effects of defeat, has attracted considerable attention. In this essay I shall discuss two distinct interpretations of 'modern' warfare and the resulting concepts of history, both of which had considerable significance for the Weimar Republic and the emergence of Fascism.[1] I will argue that two mutually exclusive myths coexisted for some years: a traditional myth of heroism and personal sacrifice revolving around the strategically insignificant battles near Langemarck in 1914, and an aggressive myth with futuristic and nihilistic qualities primarily associated with the enduring battles at Verdun in 1916. While the former was popular with traditional conservative and nationalist

This chapter is a shortened and revised version of 'Langemarck, Verdun and the Myth of a New Man in Germany', *War and Society*, vol. 6, no. 2, September 1988, pp. 70–103.

1. The intention of this chapter is not a critique of myths as examples of a 'false consciousness', but their reconstruction and analysis in terms of their significance for the formation of mentalities and attitudes. For a recent overview see P. H. Hutton, 'The History of Mentalities: The New Map of Cultural History', *History and Theory*, vol. XX, no. 3, 1981. The chapter is also indebted to the approach adopted by authors of the Frankfurt School and Ernst Bloch, *Erbschaft dieser Zeit*, Frankfurt/M, 1934, which seems more appropriate to the issue of (bourgeois and Fascist) ideology than attempts to dismiss ideological matters as deception or delusion. An underlying assumption of the essay is that the success of National Socialism was partly due to the acceptability of its programme as it was perceived by different target groups, in particular as a result of an odd mixture of reactionary and modernist features. Modernist elements of the Verdun myth that gave the kiss of death to the ideals of Langemarck can well be seen in the context of a debate about the revolutionary modernist qualities of the Hitler movement, to which, in my view, the construction of a new man was central.

circles and, despite its strong emphasis on youth,[2] was representative of a mentality shared by the bourgeoisie of all ages, the latter was connected with a fascination with the age of modern technology, contained radical and in a sense revolutionary elements and had strong artistic potential. Its influence can be found in a whole range of works of literature and the arts from the 1920s and 1930s, but it never gained broad popularity. National Socialism, in so far as it defined itself as a radical movement, shared basic aspects of it. Whereas the Langemarck myth focused on a glorious past with ideals of chivalry and heroic warriors, the myth surrounding the battle of Verdun presented man as raw material in need of being shaped by the highly organized, amoral and merciless warfare of the age of modern technology.

Both myths were forced constructions based on a number of selected and even misrepresented events from military history, and each in a different way benefited the cause of National Socialism. The elemental imagery and the elaborate, often dark code associated with the name of 'Langemarck' occupied a central position in the mentality of the educated and patriotic middle classes and contributed to shaping their perception of and attitudes towards reality, which – as a result of the lost war which had left their basic beliefs and position in the social-historical world shattered – they were deeply afraid of losing. Since the dreams and attitudes for which 'Langemarck' was the suggestive name appeared to be realized by the NS movement, they can be interpreted as a driving force behind the inclination to Fascism. It was the Verdun myth, however, which was closest to Fascist ideology, in so far as its aim was a radical reconstitution of modern society. It contributed to the militancy of this ideology by creating the aggressive image of a fighting machine which served as a model for breeding the new man in the envisaged 'age of Fascism'. The combination of an interpretation of war as a modern technological system with the plan of creating a new man of superior qualities to function within that system makes the Verdun myth a central element in the revolutionary and modern appearance of the Fascist movement, thereby contributing to its attractions.

2. For a detailed analysis see Uwe-K. Ketelsen, 'Die Jugend von Langemarck', in Thomas Koebner, R. P. Janz and F. Trommler (eds), *'Mit uns zieht die neue Zeit.' Der Mythos der Jugend*, Frankfurt, 1985, pp. 68–96. See also other contributions to this volume, in particular those by F. Trommler, H. Mommsen, W. Mogge, J. Reulecke and K. Vondung.

Langemarck: The Myth of a Heroic Youth

The military events were complex, and some details remain in the dark.[3] After the southern part of the Western Front had frozen, the Entente and German armies turned to the northern sector of the front in an attempt to outflank each other. The British set their sights on Cologne and the Ruhr area, while the German high command (OHL) expected to regain the momentum lost at the Marne but central to the Schlieffen plan offensive: they looked to Calais and the French Channel coast. In a hasty action, a new army was recruited and named the Fourth Army. It consisted of six army corps, of which four were sent to Flanders. They were made up of a wide variety of groups of soldiers, including a considerable number of volunteers. In the controversy over various aspects of the battle in Flanders in October and November 1914, strong evidence has been put forward in support of the view that the proportion of such young volunteers and, in particular, of high school and university students, has been enormously exaggerated. It was less than 10 per cent in most of the battalions and no more than 20 per cent in others.[4]

It was common knowledge that this new army, after less than seven weeks of training, was ill-equipped and ill-prepared but full of enthusiasm when it was sent to the battlefield in northern France and Belgium. This view has now been substantiated in a detailed study, and it has become evident that in the battles near Langemarck, Dixmuiden and Bixschote, which formed the basis of the Langemarck myth, soldiers were sacrificed by a military leadership with no overview of the strategic situation, and no clear knowledge of the terrain, of the strength and positions of the enemy, or of appropriate fighting tactics.[5]

It is no surprise that Langemarck was never taken in 1914. After days of bloody fighting, the OHL issued a communiqué on 11 November 'informing' the German public about the ongoing

3. Karl Unruh, *Langemarck. Legende und Wirklichkeit*, Koblenz, 1986, gives the latest and most detailed account of the events. See also *Der Weltkrieg 1914–1918*, bearbeitet vom Reichsarchiv, Berlin, 1929, vols 5 and 6; Werner Beumelburg, *Ypern 1914, Schlachten des Weltkrieg*, vol. 10, Oldenburg/Berlin, 1926; H. W. C. Davis, *The Battle of Ypres-Amentière*, Oxford, 1915.
4. Unruh, *Langemarck*, pp. 61–9.
5. At the end of October the front line was closed from Belfort to the sea, and there were a few days with fighting on its entire length of 950 km. Between the coast and Arras, some 700,000 French, British and Belgian troops faced approximately 520,000 German troops. *Der Weltkrieg 1914–1918*; see also F. M. Kircheisen, *Die Schlachten bei Ypern und Dixmude*, Aarau, 1916.

battle in Flanders. Most papers printed this news on the front page, and it was this statement, or rather a few lines from it, which created one of the most powerful myths in modern German history. These few lines read: 'West of Langemarck, young regiments singing 'Deutschland, Deutschland über alles' broke forward against the front line of the enemy's positions and took them. Approximately 2,000 men of the French regular infantry were taken prisoner and six machine-guns captured.'[6]

The gist of the report was in full accordance with previous official reports from the front, in particular those covering the Marne battle. The intention on the part of the authors was clearly directed at the mood of the German population. Here, as in many other respects, the military command was convinced that high fighting spirits would be needed to compensate for the Entente's superiority in terms of numbers and equipment. Bad news from the military front was believed to lower the morale both of the fighting troops and of those at home. Lost battles were consequently carefully disguised in optimistic phrases.[7] Frequent jubilation about military victories and the continuous thrill experienced by the public quickly replaced a realistic evaluation of the military, political and economic position of the Reich and its army. The press release of 11 November is a splendid early example of the high command's belief that a lack of resources could partially be compensated by enthusiasm.[8]

To begin with, there is the name 'Langemarck', which appears to have been preferred over a number of names of other villages in the region for no reason other than its German sound (military histories of the time refer to the battles as 'near Ypres', often without even mentioning the name of Langemarck). 'West of' was not only a vague but also an incorrect geographical specification, and may have been used in order to connote the spirit of the offensive drive westwards. Then there is the keyword 'young', soon associated with students and schoolboys; and the combination 'young regiments' carries a much more romantic flavour than other more precise signifying terms, such as the 27th Reserve Corps. There is mention of movement and the long-awaited breakthrough is

6. *Kriegs-Kalender und Kriegsdepeschen. Nach den amtlichen Berichten*, Berlin, 1918, p. 74.
7. Karl Lange, *Marneschlacht und deutsche Öffentlichkeit 1914–1939. Eine verdrängte Niederlage und ihre Folgen*, Düsseldorf, 1974.
8. Bernd Hüppauf, 'Über den Kampfgeist. Ein Kapitel aus der Vor- und Nachbereitung des Ersten Weltkriegs', in A. A. Guha and S. Papke (eds), *Der Feind, den wir brauchen*, Königstein, 1985, pp. 71–98.

vaguely suggested. There is the song – the third stanza of Hoffmann von Fallersleben's poem 'Song of the Germans' – which, in this context, is obviously aimed at a deliberate misinterpretation in terms of an outbreak of nationalism combined with high-spirited youthfulness. There is success, and it apparently was of little importance for the enthusiastic reader that only the first lines had been taken, and that six machine-guns was an entirely insignificant number in a war where success was measured in hundreds and thousands of captured guns. But there is also an implicit message: contempt of death. Death is not mentioned in this statement. This silence, however, was more significant than a precise figure of casualties could have been. Every reader knew that such a brave action had to be paid for in blood, and the void in the press release was soon filled by colourful imagery. It is still difficult to find exact figures for the casualties. During the post-war years, astronomical figures were often mentioned in various publications, and sometimes it was simply stated that at Langemarck the 'prime of German youth' was sacrificed, leaving it to the imagination of the reader to interpret the flowery metaphor.[9]

On the first anniversary of the publication of the communiqué, most German papers published comments, reflections and editorials about the 'Day of Langemarck'. Some of the lines of the original statement, in particular those referring to the young regiments and the song, were repeated, and the most striking gap in the report, death, was finally filled. I quote only one example: 'The Day of Langemarck will forever remain a day of honour for the German youth . . . this day saw sheaves of the bloom of our youth slain. . . . But our grief for the bold dead is so splendidly surpassed by the pride in how well they knew how to fight and die.'[10]

This type of sermon was usually followed by the suggestion that a Day of Langemarck be introduced as a national day of remembrance. In all schools and in public ceremonies the memory of the heroes of 10 November 1914 would be kept alive and the bold warriors of Langemarck be commemorated 'as a shining example for the young generation to follow'. Keeping the memory of this day alive after the war was seen not only as a debt owed to the dead but also as a guarantee that the highest national values would be maintained and handed down to future generations. Such comments in 1915 set the tone for years to come. During the Weimar

9. Werner Beumelburg, *Sperrfeuer um Deutschland*, Oldenburg/Berlin, 1929, p. 79; *Flandern*, Oldenburg, 1933.
10. *Deutsche Tageszeitung*, 11 November 1915.

Republic, Langemarck was celebrated on many occasions, with important national events in 1919, 1924, 1928 and 1932.[11]

Throughout this period, Langemarck was associated with German honour and pride, national strength and unity, and above all with German youth, who were held up as the promise of a great national future. Indeed, Langemarck became a symbol of national unity; the sacrifice of their lives offered to the whole of the nation by her youth was interpreted as a spiritual bond stronger than social, political or military powers.

'Langemarck' and Post-War Society

It is the reality of the battle of Flanders in 1914 – the strategic failure and tactical incompetence of the military leaders, a disproportionately high number of casualties, and the feeling of despair and horror on the part of the soldiers – which gives the communiqué of the OHL its historical significance. Several of the military details in this statement have been challenged: it is particularly unlikely, for example, that charging soldiers running over wet and heavy clay or crawling through the muddy turnip fields of Flanders in late autumn would have sung a patriotic song. From the days immediately after the end of the war, this alleged incident has created much controversy and disbelief.[12] Yet it was this alleged singing of the 'Schoolboy Corps', as some British sources call them, which gave the Langemarck myth its core and special aura. The gulf between the military reality and its image created through a language appealing to the emotions forms the core of the ideological trans-

11. From 1919 onwards the national student organization at most German universities celebrated a Langemarck Day annually, around 10 November. Although high-ranking officers and representatives of conservative parties often participated, these celebrations received only unofficial support from governments. It was only in the late 1920s that the Berlin government was officially represented at ministerial level at celebrations and visits to the Langemarck cemetery.
12. Various explanations of the singing have been offered, as a result of the fighting conditions: an attempt to distinguish Germans from the enemy in the autumn mist, to keep in touch with one's neighbouring troops, and so on. Others tell of a piano in the back yard of a farmhouse where a few officers played and sang. Those who doubt that under the circumstances storming troops would sing a patriotic song have gathered the strongest evidence. It seems indicative of the importance attributed to this detail that even near the end of the Second World War the paper of the National Committee Free Germany published a contribution by General O. Korfes, entitled 'Langemarck – Truth and Legend', in which the legend of the song is rejected: *Freies Deutschland*, vol. 2, no. 45, 5 November 1944.

formation of insignificant military events into a national myth capable of mobilizing large masses, because it corresponded to social-psychological needs in such a way that its implausibility never got in the way of its success.

In order to achieve its tragic pathos, this pattern of interpreting reality constantly oscillated between two poles: the ineffable knowledge of catastrophe and the ritualized self-portrayal of omnipotence. The knowledge of defeat and the deaths of thousands, unacknowledged in the public statement, was nevertheless an integral part of the creation of the myth of enthusiastic young German soldiers who, like the martyrs of tradition, rejoiced and sang while they sacrificed their lives for the Fatherland.[13] It is the implicit dark background of death, fate and ruin which complemented the radiant image created by explicit words. This affinity to an ambivalent and tragic image of chivalry, characteristic of nineteenth-century bourgeois ideology, contributed to the great popularity of the Langemarck myth among the middle classes and, in particular, the educated youth. A few years after the end of the war, the *Vermächtnis* (legacy) of Langemarck formed a strong focal point for all but the politically left-oriented youth organizations, including the important Wandervögel and all other organizations that defined themselves as apolitical. In 1924 approximately 2,000 members of the Bündische Jugend (Youth Organizations) gathered in the Rhön, where a memorial commemorating the fallen soldiers of Langemarck was to be unveiled. R. G. Binding's report of the event, entitled 'German Youth and the War Dead', became one of the most influential writings for the youth movement. He said of Langemarck:

> These events, however, no longer form part of history, where some day they would be paralysed and buried, but belong to the continuously creative, continuously rejuvenating, continuously living, power of myth. The death of the brave has already established itself as such, since German youth has taken possession of it as the symbol and foremost image of youthful revolt, to which among all peoples on earth only this youth has a true entitlement.[14]

13. The most popular analogy was that of the fighters at Thermopylae, 480 BC. See B. Hüppauf, 'Der Tod ist verschlungen in den Sieg. Todesbilder aus dem Ersten Weltkrieg und der Nachkriegszeit', in B. Hüppauf (ed.), *Ansichten vom Krieg*, Königstein, 1984, pp. 55–91.
14. R. G. Binding, 'Deutsche Jugend vor den Toten des Krieges', in Werner Kindt (ed.), *Grundschriften der deutschen Jugendbewegung*, Düsseldorf/Cologne, 1963, pp. 431–5 (see p. 431). See also R. G. Binding, *Gesammeltes Werk*, Hamburg, n.d., vol. 2.

Here we find a key to the understanding of the unique success of the Langemarck myth in post-war German society. Its success was due not only, not even primarily, to the clever wording and promotion of the statement of 1914. These words fell on fertile ground. They met with a hunger for mythologies which had developed in the pre-war generation. Hölderlin and Nietzsche had become its heroes in its search for an identity beyond the framework of the modern technological society. Ernst Bertram's interpretation of Nietzsche as a secular prophet and originator of the new myth of an 'eleusinically rejuvenated millennium',[15] and Paul de Lagarde's, A. Bonus's and J. Langbehn's attempts to create the myth of a new man and a new time, gave expression to widespread dissatisfaction with the superficiality and purposelessness of life around the turn of the century.[16] The quest for heroes and grand historical situations and, above all, the renewal of life through the creation of a mythological horizon was common among the middle classes and particularly its younger members.[17] The war of 1914 created the long-awaited historical situation, and the press release of 11 November found many people well prepared to employ a few keywords and images in the text to create the myth they had been longing for. The specific arrangement of elements of the military events according to social-psychological requirements formed a bridge which linked pre-war anti-modern sentiments, and non-political opposition to the world of the fathers, with the anti-capitalist and anti-republican orientations of the post-war youth movement and various neo-romantic and nationalist organizations. The chivalry of the young warrior appeared as the strongest possible contradiction to modernity, technology and rationality, and hence the fighting in Flanders in 1914 was prepared for continuous

15. Ernst Bertram, *Nietzsche. Versuch einer Mythologie* (1918), Bonn, 1929, pp. 317–94; Julius Langbehn, *Rembrandt als Erzieher*, Leipzig, 1892; Paul de Lagarde, *Deutsche Schriften. Über das Verhältnis des deutschen Staates zu Theologie, Kirche und Religion* (1878), Munich, 1937. For a critical discussion of these authors see Fritz Stern, *Kulturpessimus als politische Gefahr. Eine Analyse nationaler Ideologie in Deutschland*, Berlin/Stuttgart, 1963.
16. Arthur Bonus, *Vom neuen Mythos. Eine Prognose*, Jena, 1911. For a critique see G. L. Mosse, *The Crisis of the German Ideology. Intellectual Origins of the Third Reich*, New York, 1964. Of overwhelming importance for this complex was the poetry and prose of W. Flex, *Gesammelte Werke*, 2 vols, Munich, 1925, and in particular W. Flex, *Der Wanderer zwischen beiden Welten*, Munich, 1917, of which 130,000 copies were sold by 1919.
17. Corona Hepp, *Avantgarde. Moderne Kunst, Kulturkritik und Reformbewegungen nach der Jahrhundertwende*, Munich, 1987. For the continuation of these trends see Ulrich Linse, *Barfüßige Propheten. Erlöser der zwanziger Jahre*, Berlin, 1983, p. 18. See Ketelsen, 'Die Jugend von Langemarck', pp. 72–5.

representation of these ideas by stripping it of its last concrete military and historical substance.[18] Through constant repetition in literature, the media, the school curriculum and public celebrations, it had become synonymous with the programme of rejuvenation of the German nation developed by political romanticism during the Weimar Republic.

National Socialism found it both easy and rewarding to exploit and actively participate in the shaping of this myth. It was easy because this bourgeois tradition overlapped so much, and its origins shared so many aspects, with NS ideology; and it was rewarding because 'Langemarck' could serve as an avenue into the NSDAP (Nazi Party) for the educated youth longing for metaphysical shelter and meaning in history.

A striking example of this closeness can be found in the widely distributed and highly acclaimed reflections by Hans Schwarz on *The Rebirth of Heroic Man*, published in 1930 and based on a Langemarck address given at the University of Greifswald where at that time the NS Student Organization had its highest representation.[19] In his attempt to define Germany's universal mission in opposition to the universal ideals shared by Britain, France and the United States, the Langemarck myth plays a central role. His reflections revolve around a dualistic view of the world, in which western democracies, and of course the new German Republic, are characterized by a whole range of qualities and features, every one of which is the antithesis of those attributed to the true Germany. The victorious western democracies celebrate Armistice Day (11 November), the 'official' Germany the Day of the Republic (9 November), but the true Germany, represented by her youth and those who did not abandon their deeper values and ideals, celebrates Langemarck Day (11 November).[20] Centred around

18. See Ketelsen, 'Die Jugend von Langemarck', pp. 72–5.
19. Hans Schwarz, *Die Wiedergeburt des heroischen Menschen. Eine Langemarck-Rede vor der Greifswalder Studentenschaft am 11. November 1928*, Berlin, 1930. The National Socialist Student Organization was founded in 1926, and two years later it had a representation of 53 per cent in Greifswald and 51 per cent in Erlangen; by 1930 the percentage in Erlangen had risen to 76, the highest ever during the Republic. One has to keep in mind, however, that only about 20 per cent of students participated in elections.
20. Political parties and various organizations were engaged in a bitter and ongoing fight over the day of national celebrations. Some wanted to replace the colourful celebrations of the Kaiser's birthday and the Day of Sedan with similarly pompous celebrations of the foundation of the Reich in 1871; others wanted to commemorate the foundation of the Republic in 1919. Entwined with this debate was another relating to military history: a Day of Mourning was introduced but not accepted by all states of the Republic. It had to compete with

these antagonistic days of celebration is a range of oppositions, such as: peace in the present, achieved through force, versus true peace of the future; the faceless unknown soldier, product of an abstract and international concept, versus the living image of the young hero protecting his nation; the coldness of the concept versus the love of the spirit; songs of revolution versus songs of the earth; men of technology and materialism versus men of enthusiasm, cult and nature; history and age versus the eternal youth of myth.

He associates Langemarck with a collective dream and state of ecstasy, which created the possibility of seeing through the surface of reality and coming closer to the truth. This emphatic 'truth' is not easily conceptualized, but is experienced outside verbal communication – an experience which leaves abstract rationalism behind and is linked to the body, the senses and intuition, and is expressed through body language, dancing and other forms of non-verbal communication. The collective experience of Langemarck, seen as the climax in a series of similar moments of collective ecstasy from the Wars of Liberation to the early days of August 1914, made it possible for the Germans to determine their own particular and true 'inner form'. Elements of a civil religion, fusing Christianity and Greek rites, are used in the attempt to explain that 'an ecstatic *Volk* changes life more deeply than the agitated masses of 9 November could [ever] have wished for.'[21] The new German Republic and democracy appear as a result of historical chance and mere political quarrels, a contingency with no relationship to the true tradition and core of the nation. The celebration of 9 November, that is, of revolution and new Republic, is seen as part of an externalized and meaningless history, whereas the experience of Langemarck fills the void in modern German history by creating a living myth. This myth is explicitly credited with the power of banishing horror in the face of a lost war and the threat of losing touch with history, whose culminating point, it was believed, was the 'Great War'. After the war was lost, the myth of Langemarck

---

an older Memorial Sunday for the dead and the Christian Reminiscere Sunday (the sixth Sunday before Easter), and students' and a few veterans' organizations pushed for a national celebration of the Day of Langemarck (various unpublished documents in Bundesarchiv Koblenz, R 32/22; 43 II/1265). L. Kettenacker correctly points at the lack of colourful and representative self-presentations of the state as one factor leading to a lack of popularity of the Republic, which appeared cold, rationalistic and dull: L. Kettenacker, 'Sozialpsychologische Aspekte der Führer-Herrschaft', in K. D. Bracher et al. (eds), *Nationalsozialistische Diktatur 1933–1945. Eine Bilanz*, Düsseldorf, 1983, pp. 97–131 (see p. 114).

21. Schwarz, *Die Wiedergeburt des heroischen Menschen*, p. 9.

provided an imaginary sphere for the shaping of a cultural identity, which fused pre-war traditions with the experience of battle and the years after the revolution. The quest for historical accuracy lay outside the realm of such an approach to the past. Langemarck became the name of a collective dream of a mythological age to come. It would overcome the cold and destructive age of technology and barren civilization and re-create transcendency. 'As soon as an untrodden land surfaces, we shall prepare the rebirth of myth by putting our lives at stake, bourgeois Europe will see its end, and a new age of all peoples will begin.'[22]

The new life in the name of Langemarck was envisaged outside the world of political realities. Despite its conservative or reactionary appeal and aggression against the Republic, this vision had no political power and no future. Its strange combination of negating historical facts and political realities and at the same time emphasizing change, action and a confidence in the history-making powers of mythology had no social-political foundations or agents. The Langemarck myth, powerful as it may appear, was in fact a continuation of the apolitical tradition of the middle classes in pre-war Germany.[23] 'Langemarck' was credited with turning the popular image of young men as filled with dreams and ideas removed from reality into an image of men of action and heroic deeds.[24] But a closer examination reveals that these actions achieved nothing, led nowhere and unfolded their potential in a sphere far from political decision-making. The frequent conjuration of the future as the period of the heroic generation of Langemarck and its heirs could hardly conceal the political emptiness of this claim.

The appropriation of this anti-republican and elitist myth by the Nazi movement, however, provided such a political basis and gave it a political function in the attempt to bring about a new state and society. The cult of youth, central to the Langemarck myth, was

22. Ibid., p. 10.
23. 'One does not die so joyfully and lavishly only to be used for politics', H. Schwarz wrote in a paper called 'Wir weihen Langemarck', which the board of the German Student Union sent to all universities in June 1932 as part of its preparation of the consecration of the newly completed cemetery at Langemarck (Bundesarchiv Koblenz, R 129/62). A strong contempt for politics was characteristic of the youth movement; N. Körber, 'Das Bild vom Menschen in der Jugendbewegung und unsere Zeit', in Kindt, *Grundschriften*, p. 472.
24. Quotations from Hölderlin were abundant; Kleist and Nietzsche were also frequently referred to. Hans Castorp in Thomas Mann's *The Magic Mountain* (1924) staggers across the turnip fields in Flanders with a romantic song of love and loneliness on his lips, in search of reality.

vitally important to National Socialism, since it served as a smokescreen behind which its close connection with traditional bourgeois and capitalist social powers could be hidden. The mythical heroes of Langemarck were not subject to ageing and could be conjured up year after year as the symbolic bond uniting every new age cohort with those who publicly, and with ever-increasing loudness, laid claim to the heritage of Langemarck. This integrating power of the myth was a brilliant means of blurring the contradictions between the image of a revolutionary workers' party and its real dependence on traditional power elites.[25] Reference to national enthusiasm and the fighting spirit of the young men of Langemarck worked like a social putty, filling cracks in the militant and National Socialist movements, since social contradictions were alien to the received image of the young, united, singing and dying fighters. The *Volksgemeinschaft* (unity of the people) envisaged by the NS found a historical point of reference in the shared sacrifice of Langemarck. Before 1933 the NS movement used the Langemarck myth as an example of a transformation of the quest for unity and national strength into reality, through action led by national enthusiasm and sacrifice.

Towards the end of the Republic such concrete political aims and the traditional Langemarck myth became entwined ever more closely. In 1928 the Deutsche Studentenschaft (German Student Union) acquired responsibility for building a war cemetery outside Langemarck.[26] Soon a Langemarck Foundation was established, considerable funds were raised, and architectural designs (by Tischler, a landscape architect, and Professor Hacker) were completed, and after three years of exhumations and construction works the new cemetery was consecrated in July 1932. The ceremonial opening of the 'place of pilgrimage and commemoration'

25. Hans-Peter Bleuel and Ernst Klinnert, *Der deutsche Student auf dem Weg ins Dritte Reich. Ideologien, Programme, Aktionen*, Gütersloh, 1967; Michael H. Kater, *Studentenschaft und Rechtsradikalismus in Deutschland 1918–1933*, Hamburg, 1975; Anselm Faust, *Studenten und Nationalsozialismus in der Weimarer Republik – Der Nationalsozialistische Deutsche Studentenbund*, 2 vols, Düsseldorf, 1973; Peter D. Stachura, 'Das Dritte Reich und die Jugenderziehung', in Bracher et al., *Nationalsozialistische Diktatur*, pp. 224–44; J. Radkau, 'Die singende und die tote Jugend. Der Umgang mit Jugendmythen im italienischen und deutschen Faschismus', in Koebner et al., *'Mit uns zieht die neue Zeit'*, pp. 97–127.
26. Various papers in *Langemarck-Spende* and *Deutsche Studentenschaft* in Bundesarchiv Koblenz, R 129/68, 216, 962. See also Hansgeorg Moka, 'Die Langemarck-Arbeit der deutschen Studentenschaft', in Karl A. Walther (ed.), *Das Langemarckbuch der deutschen Studentenschaft*, Leipzig, 1933, pp. 210–14. Josef Magnus Wehner's address appeared as a preface to a selection of war letters: *Langemarck. Ein Vermächtnis*, Munich, 1934.

was a delicate political event. The Student Union planned a 'quiet, unpretentious ceremony' and defended its decision – obviously against strong criticism, for failing to use the splendid opportunity for a great political demonstration – by emphasizing piety and reverence as particular attitudes of students towards the dead. This was a veiled attempt to defuse political tensions and rivalries. The Stahlhelm-Studentenring-Langemarck (Stahlhelm Student Group Langemarck) had clashed with the NS Student Organization on several occasions, and had protested against the NSDAP's heavy involvement in previous *Reichgründungstage* (national celebrations). There was clearly some danger of an outbreak of open hostilities and even the collapse of the Student Union as a result of conflicting views on the desirability of instrumentalizing 'Langemarck' for party politics. The opportunity of presenting themselves at a great public ceremony as the true heirs of the heroes of Langemarck was lost for the Nazis, but their influence on the Student Union was strong enough to ensure that their involvement was widely recognized. Josef M. Wehner, a prominent Nazi author at the time, gave the key address, and the speaker of the Student Union made his political affiliations clear by expressing views which largely coincided with those of the NS Student Organization. In simultaneous celebrations at all German universities, the unifying quality of the symbol was emphasized. In the name of the moral superiority of the sacrificed youth, the whole nation would be resurrected from its current ruins. Contributions to *The Students' Book of Langemarck*, which was produced in connection with the opening of the cemetery, came almost exclusively from Nazi authors or officers. Langemarck clearly played a significant role in NS strategies for conquering the minds of the young educated generation.

After 1933, this changed rapidly. There had been a few critical voices before 1933, emphasizing the lack of responsibility on the part of army commanders who appeared to have acted with no insight into the tactical and strategic situation at Ypres, where they sacrificed a large number of potential officers for no military gain.[27] This criticism was now expanded, and led directly to a glorification of the role of the leader who had been absent in 1914, but had

27. Examples of the critique of an irresponsible sacrifice of lives are Friedrich Kreppel, 'Nie wieder Langemarck!', in Kindt, *Grundschriften*, pp. 436–7, and Paul Plaut, *Geistige Wiedergeburt. Als Grundlage zum Wiederaufbau der Welt*, Berlin, 1922. For others, the lesson was to demand an increased military budget and intensified military education of youth: 'Oberland, Ziele und Wege', Bundesarchiv Koblenz NS 26/699; Gustav Sondermann, 'Jugendbünde und Wehrerziehung', 1925, Bundesarchiv Koblenz NS 26/700.

emerged in 1933. Another change was that the role of students in the regiments was no longer stressed. Now the heroes of Langemarck were referred to as young workers, craftsmen and teachers; it was often emphasized that only 'a few' or 'every tenth soldier had been a student'.[28] This more realistic view did not result from a wish for greater historical accuracy, but was politically motivated. The need for Langemarck to serve as the imaginary place for the preservation of German dignity and glory and the formation of a national identity disappeared soon after January 1933. Now the 'new realities' – Hitler, the party, and newfound military strength – were taking care of such problems in the real world of power politics and international affairs. National Socialists no longer felt the need to court bourgeois youth. 'Langemarck' could therefore be exploited for much more concrete purposes in the process of reshaping German society.

Langemarck and the War 'As It Really Was'

The NS movement considered itself fortunate in that a private of Austrian nationality by the name of Adolf Hitler had enlisted in the Bavarian Infantry Regiment no. 16 under Colonel List. As a result of mismanagement and a near collapse of the front, this Bavarian regiment was moved north from its position and served as reinforcements near Langemarck. In a chapter of *Mein Kampf* (1924) Hitler can thus introduce himself as one of the Langemarck fighters. He repeats a few of the clichés of the myth, in particular that of the song which, he claims, vaguely reached their ears from the far distance and then came closer and closer until, at the moment when death was about to decimate their ranks, it reached their group and was passed on to the neighbouring unit. His brief account is revealing in a number of respects.[29]

He does not remember himself acting as an individual, but appears only as a member of his unit. It is a 'we' that sings, combining the whole front line as a closed unit in the act of singing. It is apparent from the very first lines onwards that this is not meant to be an episode in Hitler's biography, and that the 'we' is a later

28. In 1934 W. Matthiessen wrote of the Langemarck regiments: 'They were the youth of the working class and from the farms. Craftsmen. Merchants. High school pupils. And about every tenth was a student.' Wilhelm Dreysse, *Langemarck 1914. Der heldische Opfergang der deutschen Jugend*, Minden/Berlin/Leipzig, 1934, p. 9.
29. Adolf Hitler, *Mein Kampf*, Munich, 1939, pp. 180–2.

construction. The singing is put in such abstract terms that it cannot be read as the reflection of a personal experience. It is clearly intended to represent the infamous community of the front, a major topic of NS propaganda.

The reader is also struck by the shortness of this passage. Wordy as *Mein Kampf* often is, this half page seems oddly insignificant, considering the importance which the Langemarck myth had for the world of nationalistic thought and emotions. Indeed, Hitler's little story is not only short but also critical of the events, or more precisely of the myth surrounding them. Apart from the song, Hitler makes no mention of other basic elements of the Langemarck myth: youth, affection and idealism. Even the death of the soldiers is not associated with sacrifice but is part of a 'lesson' the soldiers learnt. In his view, the positive result of the battle was the transformation of 'young volunteers' into 'old soldiers', who were now entirely led and governed by their will and had no room for emotions.[30] Neither the Hitler of *Mein Kampf* nor the later dictator can be seen as a convinced supporter of the Langemarck myth. He paid tribute to it, as this was politically opportune. The messages and telegrams he sent to Langemarck meetings and his opening words in Langemarck books were always short and never failed to play down the importance of students and of enthusiasm.[31] As the party was always anxious to capitalize on its success in arousing traditional national affections and individual and collective emotions and exploiting them for its own cause, the emotions associated with Langemarck became the field of responsibility of Baldur von Schirach, who staged numerous Langemarck activities, many of which were broadcast live.[32]

Within a few years, all independent Langemarck organizations came under the complete control of the party and its organs. In

30. 'Finally the will had become complete master. If I had stormed forward with jubilation and laughter during the first days, then I had now become calm and determined. This was what would last. It was only now that fate could proceed to the final test, without nerves cracking or one being driven to insanity. The young soldier had become an old soldier.' Ibid., p. 181.
31. In a letter dated 23 August 1932 the Student Union asked von Schirach and Hitler to contribute to a planned 'representative' book. The literary *crème* of the NS movement then contributed to the publication, which was a milestone in its public approbation of 'Langemarck'. Hitler sent a short and dry address. See Walther, *Das Langemarckbuch*. On a few similar occasions, Hitler appeared equally restrained.
32. In 1936 all radio stations broadcast the celebration 'Langemarck – heritage of the Hitler Youth', jointly organized by the 'old army' and the Hitler Youth in the Volksbühne Berlin: *Völkischer Beobachter*, 7 November 1936. In 1935, 1937 and 1938 similar events were staged.

1934 the Langemarck Foundation of the German Student Union was changed into a foundation of German youth and placed under the umbrella of the Hitler Youth. Less than three years later, the Langemarck Committee was incorporated in the responsibilities of the Berlin Ministry for the Youth of the Reich. In 1938 a compulsory monthly Langemarck pfennig, to be paid by every member of the Hitler Youth, was introduced.[33] From 1934 onwards, the annual celebrations of the Day of Langemarck, initiated by the German Student Union in 1928, came under the control of the Hitler Youth. Pompous ceremonies were held in the Deutschlandhalle (Hall of Germany) in Berlin. Representatives of the party, the government and the old and new officers' corps participated, and the hall was filled with Hitler Youth in uniform. Just as the Republic's Volkstrauertag (Day of Mourning) had been changed to Heldengedenktag (Day of Commemoration of Heroes), the emphasis in the celebration of Langemarck was now put on triumph and strength, symbolized by large numbers of flags, banners and endless rows of marching boys and girls in uniform. Langemarck plays were recited. In 1936 a Langemarck cantata by E. W. Möller was performed, and every year telegrams were sent to Hitler, who kindly responded, acknowledging that 'the ideals of the fallen soldiers of Langemarck are being put into reality in the new Reich'.[34] The Day of Langemarck also became the day on which students were admitted as new members of the party. The myth that had been dear to a disquieted and restless youth, uncertain of Germany's future, had ceased to exist, and 'Langemarck' had been incorporated into a uniformed society; Dr Moka could go as far as to claim that 'National Socialism and "Langemarck" are one and the same.'[35] A slogan from 1935, 'Banners high, and forward across the graves', illustrates the degree to which the interpretation and public presentation of memories of the First World War, and of 'Langemarck' in particular, had become part of Fascist language and iconography.[36] In 1938 a Langemarck educational programme was introduced to produce the 'new man' who would act in accordance with the slogan.[37]

33. Bundesarchiv Koblenz, R 129/68, 962 (*Langemarck-Spende*). See also 'Jungarbeiter und Studenten starben in Langemarck', *Berliner Tageblatt*, 7 November 1938.
34. *Völkischer Beobachter*, 18 November 1936.
35. Moka, 'Die Langemarck-Arbeit'.
36. 'Die Fahnen hoch und über die Gräber vorwärts!', *NS Partei-Korrespondenz*, no. 63, 15 March 1935.
37. Reichsstudentenwerk, Kurzberichte, 7. Folge, 1939 (Archive of the Institute for

This programme was offered at nine universities and jointly financed by German industry, the NS Student Organization and the party. Comments in party papers praised the Langemarck programme as a great achievement of the new state, as old privileges and ruthless intellectualism had been overcome in favour of the creation of a new Nazi elite: 'With Langemarck studies we have, for the first time and with consistency, practised the idea of a National Socialist selection for university.'[38] The apolitical enthusiasm of the Langemarck myth turned out to be a dead end. Instead of romantic warriors who would again link history with transcendency, the primitive idea of breeding a genetically clean and ideologically streamlined elite was now realized in the name of Langemarck. Of all the ways in which the Langemarck myth had come to overlap with the myth of Verdun, this one subordinated it most strikingly to the ideology and political programme of National Socialism.

Behind the pompous public show, the course of action adopted by the Third Reich in relation to the tradition of the First World War was aimed at a transformation of young boys who storm forward 'with jubilation and laughter' into 'calm and zealous' experienced fighters. As the battle in Flanders, in Hitler's view, replaced the 'romanticism of battle' with the 'horror' of modern war, the inherited Langemarck myth was not only put to rest but increasingly replaced by the Verdun myth of the emotionless and hardened modern warrior who functioned like a machine.

From 'Langemarck' to 'Verdun'

It has been argued that the youth myth, so significant for Italian Fascism, could not be accommodated in German National Socialism primarily because the latter lacked originality and openness.[39] It seems to me, however, that the relatively lesser importance attributed to youth by National Socialism (and Langemarck is representative in this respect) stems from a different concept of the party and its ideal membership. The image of the enthusiastic young fighter does not match the concept of the new man of the

Contemporary History, Munich, LB 48.08). The aim of the selection was the creation of a 'specific unified type' (ibid., p. 48).

38. Dr Scheel, 'Der vierte Lehrgang des Langemarck-Studiums eröffnet', *Völkischer Beobachter*, 10 December 1938; Dr U. Gmelin, 'Gedanken zum Langemarck-Studium', ibid.
39. See Radkau, 'Die singende und die tote Jugend', passim.

age of Fascism favoured by Hitler and the radical groups in the Schutzstaffel (SS: Nazi elite corps) and party. The Langemarck myth was dysfunctional in the image of a new thousand-year Reich based on new human material: amoral, cool, functional, experienced, hardened men who no longer needed ideals to identify with, or emotions as a basis for their fighting spirit. This new man would be able to pass the 'final test' without 'his nerves cracking' or being 'driven to insanity'.[40] He would no longer behave like the traditional warrior, but would be turned into a modern fighting machine. References to Langemarck by NS ideologists and politicians can thus more often than not be read as lip-service paid to youth – a youth considered important as a pool of boys and young men who were to be transformed into the new race of fighters, and girls who were to breed and raise them.

Langemarck, although a warrior myth, never really adopted specific militaristic qualities. Contrary to militaristic tradition, Langemarck emphasized spontaneity, individualism, education, ideals and individual responsibility, all of which are not easily reconciled with military hierarchy, drill or subordination. The ideals of the youth movement of the turn of the century were clearly embodied in this myth, and W. Flex's romanticism could easily be associated with the heroic young men of Flanders.[41] It was the rebellion of a generation which opposed the values and lifestyle of their parents, but without the intention of a radical revolt against a society of which they shared some of the initial aims and its revolutionary heritage: brotherhood and liberty, a Rousseauesque view of nature, an unspoilt humanity and an idealistic quest for the independence of the individual. This intergenerational conflict emphasized the readiness on the part of the young generation to sacrifice luxury, social security and even their lives in support of those ideals betrayed by the materialistic generation of their parents. Langemarck can be seen as the apotheosis of this cultural revolt and its ideals. During the celebration of its tenth anniversary there were recitals of nineteenth-century verses full of pathos, idealism and melancholy.[42] Hölderlin's 'Ode for the Fatherland' and verses from Nietzsche's *Zarathustra* about the rejoicing hero's death captured the mood and spirit of this anti-bourgeois assembly of a bourgeois youth which, despite its partiality for uniforms and

40. Hitler, *Mein Kampf*, p. 181.
41. W. Flex (see note 16). The events in Flex's short novel are based on his war experience in the east and at the Baltic Sea.
42. Binding, 'Deutsche Jugend vor den Toten des Krieges', passim; also Wolfgang Paul, *Das Feldlager. Jugend zwischen Langemarck und Stalingrad*, Esslingen, 1978.

banners, had little in common with the menacing militarism of NS organizations. The fact that National Socialism never really severed its links with the Langemarck myth was partly due to the internal contradictions so characteristic of the movement. The coexistence of the Langemarck and Verdun myths is another example of the surprising symbiosis between extreme anti-bourgeois and traditional bourgeois elements in the NS state and ideology.

While the memories of Langemarck were celebrated *ad nauseam*, the spirit of the front, central to the propaganda and social policies of the party, was increasingly associated with images of Verdun. The 'hell of Verdun' left no scope for bourgeois sentimentalities and ambivalences in relation to death. Their place was taken by the open menace of violence. The killing of enemies was an explicit element of this myth, and death and killing no longer had any connection with the quest for individuality or experience of reality from one's own sacrifice.

Verdun and the Somme in 1916: Background of a New Myth

The Verdun myth placed death in the context of well-organized and omnipresent violence, seen as an integral element of a military and political structure. The cold-blooded execution of deadly missions and fatal duties by the Verdun fighters appealed to a latent masochism and was highly functional in the reality of the Third Reich. The omnipresent menace of violence in this myth served as an element in the total command over society aimed at by National Socialism. The extermination of others under conditions experienced by everyone as 'hell' formed the core of the Verdun myth. It was this menace which made the events of Verdun so appropriate for NS ideology. The enemy, and those of one's own comrades who were too weak to survive this hell, were considered unworthy of living and consequently destroyed. This was the part of the war in which Hitler saw the real heroism of the German army emerge: 'the iron front of the grey steel helmet'. In contrast to the patriotic front of the singing youths, this new army, as Hitler put it, 'emerged old and hard from the continuous fighting, and he who was unable to stand up to the storm was naturally broken by it.' Hardness against enthusiasm, experience against affection, and old against young are basic differences between the two myths.

The military events of the fighting near Verdun in 1916 are well known, and I will only refer to them briefly. In 1916 both sides on the Western Front planned major military operations regarded as decisive in resolving the stalemate that had developed in 1914. Neither the combined British/French offensive at the Somme, nor the German operation near Verdun, achieved their aims. They were, however, battles of an unprecedented magnitude in terms of both casualties and quantities of equipment and ammunition. After the unprecedented barrage carried out by the French and British artillery in preparing their infantry attack, the Germans coined the word *Materialschlacht* (material battle), which rapidly became prominent in theories of modern warfare.

Falkenhayn, the architect of this battle, appears to have abandoned the aim of a breakthrough and tried instead to push the principles of the war of attrition to the extreme. He chose the strongest point in the French defence system because he planned to exhaust the human resources of the French army through repeated offensives against a fortress which France, for reasons of morale and national dignity, was unable to give up. The constant battles over a period of eight months were thus meant not primarily to lead to territorial gains, but to bleed the French nation to death. Falkenhayn did not confront the possibility that the attackers might have to pay as heavy a toll as the attacked. At the end of the brutal campaign, casualties were approximately 800,000. The French soon called Verdun the 'man-grinding mill' and the Germans 'hell', and the strategic plan was christened 'blood-pump'.[43]

From 1916 onwards, Verdun remained a magic word in France and Germany; it was from Verdun that the French unknown soldier was exhumed before being brought to Paris for his ceremonial burial at the Arc de Triomphe.[44] The massive system of fortifications, joined with the spirit of the soldiers who defended every square foot of this enormous defence structure, became the symbol of the final liberation of French soil from the enemy and the

43. A recent attempt to place the events into strategic and historical context and discuss issues of their ideological aftermath is German Werth, *Verdun. Die Schlacht und der Mythos*, Bergisch Gladbach, 1979. The series on 'Battles of the World War', edited by the Reichsarchiv, began with the volume *Douaumont*, Oldenburg/Berlin, 1926, by W. Beumelburg; vols 6, 13, 14, 15 and 18 (1926–9) were also devoted to the battle at Verdun. See also Michael Salewski, 'Verdun und die Folgen. Eine militär- und geistesgeschichtliche Betrachtung', *Wehrwissenschaftliche Rundschau*, vol. 25, 1976, pp. 89–96. Reflections on Verdun in German literature are discussed in Karl Prümm, 'Das Erbe der Front. Der antidemokratische Kriegsroman der Weimarer Republik und seine nationalsozialistische Fortsetzung', in H. Denkler and K. Prümm (eds), *Die deutsche Literatur im Dritten Reich*, Stuttgart, 1976, pp. 138–64.

44. *L'Illustration*, Paris, 15 November 1919; 6 and 20 November 1920; 10 and 17 November 1923; 22 July 1927.

saving of the nation. The statue of General Pétain, the originator and hero of this successful defence operation, now overlooks the battlefield. His words, engraved in the base of the monument, contain the core of the French legend of Verdun: 'Ils n'ont pas passé' ('They did not pass'). The French myth of Verdun resembles that of a massive wall with such a protective power that even the trumpets of Jericho would fail before it. This legend of the defence of the nation can be seen as the opposite of the dynamic myth that later emerged in Germany.

Verdun: Modernity at War

'La plus grande bataille' ('The greatest battle'), as it was called even as late as 1960,[45] played an equally significant role in post-war Germany, but here it contributed to the creation of an entirely different view of the First World War and, indeed, modern warfare as such. The names of the hills, forts and villages in the area, such as Douaumont, Pepper Ridge, the Dead Man and Fleury, were known to everyone and conjured up bloody images. The wave of war literature that emerged after 1928 was substantially based on the events of 1916, with the majority of books dealing with Verdun.[46]

For all these authors the war had become depersonalized and industrialized. There was no enthusiasm left and there were no general aims to fight for, only the close military targets of the day. Hopelessness and loneliness were combined with merely functional membership of a group of fighters organized on the principles of divided labour and responsibility, the monotony of the daily routine, grey mud everywhere, on faces, clothes, armour, food. Many

45. J.-H. Lefèbvre, *Verdun. La plus grande bataille de l'histoire*, Paris, 1960.

46. The first literary reflection of the battle in Germany was Fritz von Unruh's *Opfergang*. Commissioned and written immediately after the events in 1916, this small book did not appear until 1919 as it did not pass censorship as a result of its pacifist attitude. Written with a similar attitude but less emotional was Arnold Zweig, *Erziehung vor Verdun*, Amsterdam, 1935. From 1929 onwards a wave of nationalist novels by warmongers appeared, of which I mention only a few: Werner Beumelburg, *Gruppe Bosemüller*, Oldenburg/Berlin, 1930; P. C. Ettighofer, *Verdun. Das große Gericht*, Gütersloh, 1936; Alfred Hein, *Eine Kompanie Soldaten. In der Hölle vor Verdun*, Minden, 1929; Franz Schauwecker, *Aufbruch der Nation*, Berlin, 1930; Josef M. Wehner, *Sieben vor Verdun*, Munich, 1930; Hans Zöberlein, *Der Glaube an Deutschland*, Munich, 1931. The most recent publication, Ludwig Harig's *Ordnung ist das ganze Leben. Roman meines Vaters*, Munich, 1986, reconstructs the biography of his father, the decisive event in whose life was the battle of Verdun.

French novels about Verdun share this view, but they differ in one specific respect: there was success at the end. The German contributions to this topic have to deal with the fact that all was in vain. The small gains made during these eight months were all recaptured by the French after, and some already before, Hindenburg ordered the end of Operation Verdun in November 1916.

While in France victory was associated with the successful defence of strong fortifications at Verdun, the German experience was again one of interpreting defeat. Unlike Langemarck, Verdun was not presented as a glorious victory of superb ideals but as the experience of the climax of modern technological warfare, which made 'victory' and 'defeat' obsolete in the traditional sense of the words. *Vis-à-vis* the power of the material, victory seemed to have lost its meaning. The means seemed to have liberated themselves from the strategic and political ends to such a degree that, essentially, their destructive powers had become disproportionate to any conceivable aim. The possession of a few square metres of land had to be paid for by thousands of casualties and the complete destruction of the landscape. There are numerous documents and literary works which try to capture the experience of a war machine turning a once beautiful land into uninhabitable grey masses of mud, with no structured contours:

> 'This was once a trench,' said Süssmann, while they . . . walked towards that place which used to be called the village of Douaumont, with imposing houses and a church. Now there is nothing left, as everywhere else: ragged earth. And this earth begins to stink; sweet and putrid from rot . . . sunshine and wind make the stink even more awful . . . this whole decaying and pulverized region which stretches from here . . . to the inner belt of forts at Verdun.[47]

It was this view of the events at Verdun which stripped the war of any purpose and meaning. War had become self-contained, it entered a phase of independence, without need for supervision or planning. The war machine had become overwhelming, and it forced decisions on those partaking in its inexplicable movements. Human subjectivity had abdicated. The soldier no longer made his environment but was made by it. He appeared as a micro-system, whose actions maintained the momentum of a macro-system beyond his, or indeed anyone's, control.

47. Zweig, *Erziehung vor Verdun*, p. 190.

For a number of authors, this industrialized destruction of both man and the environment marked a shocking decline in western civilization. In his critical novel about an *Education at Verdun* (1935), Arnold Zweig described the scenario of a complete 'unmaking' of the world, both physical and mental, and portrayed the victims of this degeneration with a great deal of sympathy, the 'proletarians of destruction'.[48] But he, too, introduces a lieutenant who loses the enthusiasm of the early days of the war and turns into an emotionless fighting machine. His philosophy of action is taken from a murderous Islamic sect, the Assassins: 'There is no truth, and everything is permitted.' In Zweig's novel this attitude, generated by the battle of Verdun, signifies the threat to the future existence of European civilization, as its perfection of modern technology has also unleashed forces of primitive destruction and barbarism.

For other authors, it was precisely the industrialization of the battlefield which represented a radical new beginning, the advent of a modern period in which the forced exposure to the laws of technology would transform man into the new creature of modernity. The concept of *Materialschlacht*, central to Ernst Jünger's books, gives expression to the view that the material, that is technology, the sciences and abstract planning, has now become the dominant force on the battlefield, dwarfing the soldiers and reducing them to a dependent variable. Although the modern battlefield may look chaotic to the untrained eye, Jünger writes, it is in fact highly structured, imitating the scientific and mathematical principles underlying modern technology.[49] Under the menace of death, the soldier has no alternative but to adapt to the laws of this structure. His perception must become as objective and his eye as hard as the lens of a camera, his reactions as powerful and steady as a precision weapon. Contrary to tradition, which saw arms as an extension of the human arm, it is now the soldier who has been turned into an appendix of the technological structure of the battlefield.

Towards the end of the war, an iconography of this new type of soldier emerged. He had undergone the transformation process at Verdun or similar battles. The image was soon widely distributed in literature and the media, and normally shows a portrait of the side of a soldier's face reduced to basic lines: a sharp and marked nose, an eye directed to an imagined object in the distance, a

48. Ibid., p. 173. The term was first used by Henri Barbusse, *Le Feu* (1917), London, 1918: 'We factory workers of destruction . . .', p. 340.
49. Ernst Jünger, 'Über den Schmerz', *Werke*, Stuttgart, 1962, vol. 4, pp. 175–8 (1st edn in *Blätter und Steine*, 1934).

striking and robust chin, narrow lips. An 'iron will' seems to be concentrated in the eye. The whole face is centred around a penetrating glance, which often casts a conquering look at an imagined object. In these portraits the eye itself is active and aiming at a target like a weapon.

The posture is always one of strict control over the body and results from an unnaturally stylized carriage of the head, with every muscle in the face exerted. Reduced to a bare minimum of lines, the expression on the face and the atmosphere created by the whole appearance is one of stern, adamant and cold austerity. It gives expression to an extreme opposite of the ideal of the leisurely middle class of the nineteenth century as it appears in pictures and photographs, enjoying comfort and a posture of relaxation. Giedion describes how many skills and technical inventions were used in the nineteenth century in the attempt to create rooms and furniture which 'serve our physiological requirements' and make possible 'a complete bodily relaxation'.[50] He illustrates the interplay between the body and various technical mechanisms in chairs, sofas and so on, which were used to achieve a totally unconstrained posture.

The image of the soldier with a steel helmet also differs starkly from that of Langemarck fighters, or indeed of any soldier from earlier campaigns. Illustrations in Langemarck books present young faces with a softness of contour, natural movements and often romantic flair.[51] Their hair is visible, and there is often a decorative flower or oak leaf, or the traditional back pack with fur trimming, as carried by the youth groups.

The most striking aspect of the image of the Verdun fighter is the steel helmet, which often takes up three-fifths of the space. Its outer contours are sharply marked against the background, but the rest is a large empty plane, often fusing face and helmet. This depersonalized face largely covered by steel shows vigour, resoluteness and determination, but the proportions make it appear an extension of the large empty plane representing the steel helmet, which was introduced in 1916 and – more than any other part of the soldier's equipment – became the symbol of the changed face of the war and the men fighting it. The steel helmet replaced the cap or decorative leather helmets worn during the early phases of the war, and represented the modern functional and technical side of the war, at the same time resurrecting powerful archaic or medieval images of

50. Siegfried Giedion, *Mechanization Takes Command: A Contribution to Anonymous History*, New York, 1948, p. 398.
51. See e.g. Wilhelm Schreiner, *Der Tod von Ypern. Die Herbstschlacht in Flandern*, Herborn, 1917.

metal helmets, which had earlier gone out of fashion with the increasing power of firearms. The fusion of steel with flesh, and modern functional technology with memories of archaic protection and magic, made this stylized portrait of the Verdun fighter deeply significant for the image of the new man. Other less significant pieces of equipment could be added to this most exposed symbol of the fighting machine: the grey bag filled with hand-grenades, the flame-throwers, gas-containers and gas-masks. The body of the soldier appeared as the centre of coordination and movement in this collection of equipment. But it was a single icon, the steel helmet, which came to represent the essence of this war to an unprecedented degree. Many individuals and organizations soon did everything they could to make it omnipresent in the public sphere. It soon carried sufficient symbolic meaning to speak for itself, and once it was set up for conditioning people's minds, it appeared in the title of journals and papers, on book covers and as a mark between chapters. In the public perception, it came to represent that particular image of the war which blended associations of technology, determination, fighting spirit, destruction and heroism surrounded by an aura of mixed admiration and fear. The steel helmet developed into the logogram for 'fighting' as the essence of the period. Advertisements for postcards, colour prints, etchings and lithographs showing a soldier's profile with steel helmet appeared in the periodicals of veterans' organizations. The artists (such as Erich Mattschass or Ernst Vollbehr) were always introduced as active *Frontkämpfer* (fighters of the front), attesting to the authenticity of their work. Prices were moderate and rebates for orders of large quantities were offered.[52] One of the most powerful veterans' organizations called itself Stahlhelm (Steel Helmet) and used a stylized steel helmet as its crest. The constitution of its youth branch, the Jungstahlhelm, from May 1924 stated as one of its aims to make body and mind as 'hard as steel'.

The image of the man of steel was also promoted through film, and from the first years of the Republic, particularly from 1923 onwards, there were numerous occasions for shooting documentary films and newsreels.[53] At annual celebrations of soldiers of the front (Reichsfrontsoldatentag of the Stahlhelm; Reichskriegertag of the Kyffhäuser), thousands of ex-soldiers marched in columns and

52. The price of a four-colour postcard in 1926 was 8 Pf: various advertisements, e.g. in *Führer*, the news bulletin of the Stahlhelm, 20 September 1926.
53. There are eleven documentaries of Stahlhelm parades in the Bundesarchiv Koblenz (no. 696 passim) and various similar films from Oberland (no. 579), Kyffhäuser (no. 661), and so on.

lined up in geometrical formations. The Stahlhelm produced a whole series of films about such military parades with, they claimed, as many as 100,000 soldiers with 5,000 banners marching and falling in.[54] The continuous attempt to militarize the public consciousness was evident in the omnipresence of war through its symbols: uniforms, marches through the streets by military formations, celebrations of battles, the presence of soldiers in uniform at celebrations in the Reichstag, films, newsreels and special matinées for war films, and the steel helmet which could be seen almost everywhere. It was important for the success of this image of a new man in the age of technological warfare that it did not appear in isolation. Its acceptability was increased through a network of related conceptions of the period and visions of man in the age of technology, even if a glorification of war was not a part of them.

The aim of reconstructing man in the age of modernity did not emerge only in the First World War. The dissatisfaction with man as a product of nature, and attempts to reassemble mind and body in such a way that they did not appear outmoded *vis-à-vis* an artificially created world of technology, was older than the war and outlived the battlefields. Around the turn of the century, debates about reshaping and even re-creating man had not only become common in such disciplines as biology and economics, but formed a public discourse. The desirability of an 'economy of the human being' was widely accepted and was reflected in art and literature.[55] In a widely distributed book by an author who tried to blend a socialist and humanitarian commitment with an insight into the needs of the age of technology, the economy of the human being was defined as a breeding method aimed at improving man by eliminating the economically much too primitive procedure of natural selection. This, it was claimed, was particularly necessary at a time when no longer a minority but a large majority of the new-born survived childhood and would be capable of procreation.[56] Backed by scientific studies, sociological speculation and genetic ideologies, ideas and views of a new man more ideally adapted to modern living conditions were widespread.

Such ideas gained surprising momentum as a result of the war, which had certainly changed the appearance of man to a degree unimaginable before 1916. Art and literature now created images of

54. Der Stahlhelm am Rhein, 1930, Bundesarchiv Koblenz, 700/1–2.
55. Rudolf Goldscheid, *Höherentwicklung und Menschenökonomie*, Leipzig, 1911.
56. Ibid., p. 508, passim.

man as a product of the modern period, with his subjectivity shattered and no qualities of his own left.[57] In the 1920s this line was continued with stylized portraits of pilots or car and motorcycle drivers in black leather gear and helmets, which made their bodies look like artificial creations and their skulls appear as streamlined as eggs.[58] Shortly after the end of the war, George Grosz drew a picture of the new man as a stylized and technicized figure with an egg-shaped head, in front of a punching ball and surrounded by technical tools. Other Futurist or Dada artists presented an even more radical view of the new man as a depersonalized function in a technological environment. Such portraits or images of the human body as an artificial product share a common basis with those whose view of the new man was exclusively shaped by Verdun and the Somme, the main and decisive difference lying in the relationship to violence.

Verdun and Fascism

The mythical elevation of the Verdun soldiers to the ideal warrior of the modern age hinged on an extreme critique of Falkenhayn. He was portrayed as a man out of touch with modern times, and although his plan was considered worthy, its realization was declared incongruous with the fighting qualities of the new generation of soldiers.

In a pseudo-historical study, the conclusion was drawn that Falkenhayn sabotaged his own plan by holding reinforcements and supplies below the minimum necessary level.[59] Although there was no evidence to support this extravagant view, it became popular among nationalistic authors and was quoted or implicitly referred to. It is surprising to note that the Verdun myth which was so central to NS ideology was also based on an abortive military operation with an enormous number of casualties. The conclusion drawn from its outcome was a very simple one: of the two elements needed for military success, an army to fight and a commander to plan, it was the leader who had failed. The glory surrounding the army was even strengthened by the fact that it had

57. The title of Robert Musil's novel *The Man without Qualities* (1930–2) is representative of this modernist view of humanity.
58. *Die zwanziger Jahre im Porträt. Porträts in Deutschland 1918–1933*, Rheinisches Landesmuseum Bonn, 1976, pp. 10–12.
59. Hermann Wendt, *Verdun 1916. Die Angriffe Falkenhayns im Maasgebiet mit Richtung auf Verdun als strategisches Problem*, Berlin, 1931.

succeeded in realizing some of the most unlikely aims, and had taken Fort Douaumont despite incompetent leadership.

The Verdun myth, like Langemarck but unlike Tannenberg, was built exclusively around the image of the fighting soldier, with no importance attached to military leadership. The failure of the offensive was not interpreted in terms of its real cause, lack of resources, but in terms of the moral victory of the German soldier. The myth of Verdun symbolized the birth of a new man who developed a second nature, enabling him to move in a free and uninhibited way in an environment where death was a constant threat.

Not only were these warriors presented as well adapted to the special conditions of the front; the front itself was seen as a paradigm for life, and patterns of behaviour developed under its extreme conditions were presented as a model for humanity in the future. There was no 'generation of Verdun', for the Verdun myth presented itself as transcending the narrow chronological conditions of a generation. It was a myth of universal experience, revolving around the discovery of the intrinsic values of modern battle. If the word 'victory' can be applied at all in this context, then it is only as victory over the historical limitations of previous generations of soldiers. A trivialized shadow of Nietzsche's concept of the *Übermensch* (superman) was cast on this new man. His morality and psychological structure had finally caught up with scientific and technological progress. This leap into modern reality resulted from an exposure to the extreme consequences of the destructive powers of technology. In their battle against an extraordinarily powerful *Material*, the modern soldiers experienced for the first time the threat of mass extermination.

Out of this contradictory experience two types of image of a new man emerged. One was that of a functional being, artificially created and reflecting a technical world beyond emotion and meaning. This image, developed by Futurists and Dadaists, must be seen as both contradicting and overlapping with the Fascist view of a new man. It contradicted the Fascist view in that it was not presented as a legitimation for violence and destruction; however, it also overlapped with and, in a sense, supported the myth of the new man of a Fascist era in that it excluded even the faintest glimmer of human self-determination. No concept of transcendency, no soul or essence was left, and the empty plane which signifies the helmet can be interpreted as representing this void. Fascist authors partly succeeded in associating their views of modern man with those elaborated by critical and sensitive observers and analysts of the age of technology and mechanization. The extreme consequence drawn by these authors and materialized in the NS movement was an uncompromising propagation of man as an executioner of violence in an environment whose constitutive principles were presented as those of continuous war. It was partly due to this particular moulding of the experience of modernity as a fusion of technological progress and destruction, functionalism and archaic myths, rational organization and amoral aims, that National Socialism succeeded in associating itself with modern and modernizing forces in the turbulent society of the post-war years. Its dynamic drive incorporated a combination of rigid modernity and pre-civilized amorality. 'The force which sacrificed from 1914 to 1918 is now willing to construct. It fought all powers which were not prepared to accept it as the most eminent and noble value.'[60]

When Gottfried Benn wrote in 1933 of the new state in the process of being created and the new man so badly needed in the current collapse of western civilization, his *Typus* was largely a reflection of debates revolving around this particular experience of modern times.[61] Benn's combination of archaic and super-modern qualities, the absence of a historical *telos* and the lack of morality, the emphasis placed on struggle and domination, the stressing of a German experience different from that of the rest of the world, the forced coldness of his attitude, are as much indebted to myths of modernity based on the experience of the front as to Nietzsche's philosophy. And although Benn's flirtation with the NS was a short and unhappy episode, his essays gave expression to an attitude popular among radical and nationalistic groups in the late phase of the Republic. Their determination to change society in a fundamental way distinguished them from political conservatism and placed them in close proximity to European Fascist movements.[62]

Ernst Jünger is the best-known exponent of an 'unpolitical' literature who was drawn deep into radical right-wing politics through the particular mode in which the First World War was experienced in Germany, an experience to which his own books and articles made a considerable contribution.[63] Jünger who, like

60. Alfred Rosenberg, *Der Mythus des 20. Jahrhunderts* (1930), Munich, 1934, p. 620.
61. Gottfried Benn, *Gesammelte Werke*, ed. D. Wellershoff, Wiesbaden, 1968, vols 3 and 4.
62. These complex relationships are often splendidly visualized in Lina Wertmuller's films, such as *Love and Anarchy*.
63. Works by Ernst Jünger referred to in this chapter are: *In Stahlgewittern*, Berlin,

Carl Schmitt, mocked political romanticism, described the war as an experience of the overwhelming powers of modern technology, which had destroyed not only landscapes and lives, but also the humanity of the past, through operations of an almost mathematical precision. Jünger, whose experience stems from the battle at the Somme, produced the clearest and most radical contribution to the shaping of the myth of a new man. His worker-soldier, a futuristic construction with the qualities of a precision instrument, fascinated many a reader. He attempted to relocate the concept of the worker beyond the nineteenth-century left–right spectrum of politics and to base it on the experience of modernity realized in the *Materialschlachten* of the First World War. The new *Typus* of man, he wrote in 1932 in *Der Arbeiter*, had emerged from the war only in small numbers, as an elite or order, but would finally have consequences for 'den menschlichen Gesamtbestand' (the whole of humanity). After the definitive end of the romantic age of Langemarck, a new age with an entirely new attitude towards freedom, power, the elemental forces of life and *Sein* (being) was in the making. As a result of the experience of the constant threat of death at the front, this new man was in the process of emerging. 'Here, in the hidden power centres from whence the domination over the zone of death is carried out, we meet a new humanity, which grew out of new and particular demands.'[64] When this new humanity was turned into political reality after 1933, Jünger was barely able to recognize his vision.

The new man attained a high profile in the public sphere. As if they came from a source that never dried up, a critic observed after the war, soldiers often marched past the Führer for hours, like pistons of a huge machine, before filling an assembly ground where they formed huge uniform squares. Hundreds of thousands of uniformed men froze in a second to motionlessness, then made one short precise movement or raised their arm, as if these masses of men were one body directed by one will.[65] This militarist mechanical ballet formed the visual embodiment both of powerful dynamics and of the complete subordination of the men of steel to an external iron will. These were the formations of fighting machines with no emotions or traditional morality, capable of revol-

1922; *Der Krieg als inneres Erlebnis*, Berlin, 1922; *Der Arbeiter*, Hamburg, 1932; (ed.), *Das Antlitz des Weltkriegs. Fronterlebnisse deutscher Soldaten*, Berlin, n.d.; and 'Über den Schmerz' (see note 49).

64. Jünger, *Der Arbeiter*, p. 134.
65. Karlheinz Schmeer, *Die Regie des öffentlichen Lebens im Dritten Reich*, Munich, 1956, p. 124.

utionizing the world or, in the popular metaphor of the time, '[sie] aus den Angeln heben' ('turning it upside down').

It has been argued that the Langemarck myth formed an ideological bridge between the First and Second World Wars. The broad complex of emotions, ideas and attitudes towards the social and political reality associated with Langemarck certainly played an important part in the surprisingly quick and smooth incorporation of large sections of youth and its organizations into the NS state. Langemarck operated like a hinge on which enthusiasm and affection, often frustrated by the sober and unappealing Republic, swung many young people into the new state which, they believed, would be built on the idealistic foundations of the glorious moral victory of the generation of Langemarck. As Thomas Mann wrote in his diary in 1944, it should not be forgotten that at the beginning of the Third Reich enthusiasm and joy about the new beginning, the awakening of the nation, were predominant.[66]

While the Republic, with its origins in western rationality, the rejection of myth and the belief in progress, could be blamed for a devaluation of the symbols of the state and the glorious past of the Reich, numerous social organizations and groups worked towards a resurrection of symbols as elements in an encompassing project to restructure the public mind. Flags and uniforms, the swastika, a uniform body language or the steel helmet stylized as expressive symbols were used to lead the way to the coming age of irrationality. Nazi ideologues emphasized the elemental power of symbols springing from their unmediated connection with the subconscious. Their 'instinct' made them replace rational concepts with the visual symbol, Krieck wrote in 1932, and this connection with the irrational and elemental dynamics of life, he argued, gave them the power to create history afresh: 'This is called revolution.'[67]

It is doubtful whether there was a direct connection between the radical restructuring of German society under Fascism, the coming war and the romantic images of youth and sacrifice surrounding Langemarck. It was rather the modern warrior of Verdun, with no emotions and no ideal to identify with, who offered a model for the new elite formations of the state, the SS and the NS 'orders', and eventually for the soldiers of the Second World War, who were not characterized by enthusiasm and an identification with the just cause of their nation. The experience of August 1914 was not to be

66. Thomas Mann, *Die Tagebücher 1944–45*, ed. Peter de Mendelssohn, Frankfurt, 1986.
67. Ernst Krieck, *Nationalpolitische Erziehung* (1932), Leipzig, 1933, p. 38.

repeated in this century, and the divisive menace of violence took the place of feelings of enthusiasm and unity, even in 1933, when the joy Thomas Mann refers to formed only a thin layer over the horror of the victims of the events. For the soldiers in Hitler's war, Langemarck had become an empty word. And those who participated in the undeclared war against the Jews resembled the soldiers of Langemarck in no respect. The man who smoked a cigarette while sitting on the edge of a mass grave, dangling his feet over the corpses he had just shot,[68] was the man who, in Hitler's words, had killed the last remains of his conscience and replaced this romantic relic with a sense of duty. This, in Hitler's view, was the lasting lesson of the war: 'Only now could fate proceed to the last test without my nerves cracking or my mind failing.' Hannah Arendt was intrigued by the discovery of the banality of this mentality during the Eichmann trial in Jerusalem. Without a uniform and helmet, stripped of its military aura and placed in a civilian courtroom, the emotionless functionalism of this new man indeed seems banal. More than any other, the mentality expressed in the icon of the steel helmet needed a corresponding environment for its menace to unfold.

This disastrous environment, created by Fascism, remained an exception and lasted only a short while. But the technological vision of man as raw material with no core, who must therefore be moulded according to the perceived needs of the modern age, did not cease with the end of the Second World War. It is rooted more deeply in the present than its primitive and violent Fascist version would suggest, and while the First World War gave rise to it, its threatening consequences are still virulent.

68. Walther Hofer (ed.), *Der Nationalsozialismus. Dokumente 1933–1945*, Frankfurt, 1957, p. 302 (excerpts from H. F. Gräbe's eye-witness report of a massacre in Poland, 1942).

–5–

Georges Bataille's Diagnosis of Fascism and Some Second Opinions

ANTHONY STEPHENS

> Nietzsche is to Hegel what a bird breaking its shell is to a bird contentedly absorbing the substance within.
>
> Georges Bataille, 'The Obelisk' (1938)

The Doctor's Dilemmas

Georges Bataille's essay 'The Psychological Structure of Fascism' dates from the year 1933. It is a densely written and perspicacious attempt to render commensurable the phenomenon that had emerged and triumphed in Italy and Germany by proposing in little more than twenty pages a comprehensive explanatory model. My discussion sets out to place it in its philosophical rather than its political context, stressing its dependence on the vulgarized Nietzscheanism of the 1920s and 1930s, whilst not losing sight of the tensions within Bataille's thought which this creates.

Bataille's essay embodies the fascination which political power at its crudest and most charismatic can exert over sophisticated thinkers, and also something of the helplessness of philosophical abstraction before such realities as the rise of Mussolini and Hitler. A problem inherent in my analysis is that it is much easier to demonstrate the philosophical lineage of Bataille's essay than to specify what derives directly from the political situation in France particularly, and Europe generally, at the end of the 1920s and the beginning of the 1930s. The fact remains, however, that Bataille chose to translate his dilemmas into an idiom that combines concepts from Freudian psychology with others taken from both the Hegelian and Nietzschean traditions of philosophy. While Bataille's method can reveal much of the phenomenon of Fascism, it also tends to mask or simplify certain political realities, for the text itself is essentially a series of daring extrapolations from a set of abstract premises rather than any attempt at a *compte rendu* of the political scene which Bataille expected his readers to know so well.

While Bataille's diagnosis gets only the briefest of mentions from Klaus Theweleit, Wolfgang Fritz Haug and Manfred Behrens, I think its lasting interest lies in its recognizing and confronting the central dilemma still facing aetiologies of Fascism: does the emphasis belong more on socioeconomic causes or on psychogenetic dispositions?[1] This, in turn, makes the essay into a fascinating gloss on the struggle between the rearguard of Enlightenment individualism and the shock troops of collective identity, regardless of what political colour such collectives assume. Bataille begins his discussion by announcing that Marxism is in need of further development on this question 'because it did not undertake any general elucidation of the modalities peculiar to the formation of religious and political society' (B, 137). While the early part of the essay considers the conditions of production in industrial society, the main focus is on the nature of religious and military power and the relation of Fascism to 'royal sovereignty' (B, 149). Bataille's conclusion seems quite unequivocal: 'It thus appears that the unity of fascism is located in its actual psychological structure and not in the economic conditions that serve as its base' (B, 157).

What he means by 'psychological structure' is – by implication – a set of behavioural constants that supersedes the specifics of history on the one hand, while still needing to account for unique contemporary events on the other: 'The possibility of fascism nonetheless depended upon the fact that a reversion to vanished sovereign forms was out of the question in Italy, where the monarchy subsisted in a reduced state' (B, 158). This is indicative of the

1. Georges Bataille is quoted from Allan Stoeckl (ed.), *Georges Bataille. Visions of Excess. Selected Writings, 1927–1939*, Manchester, 1985, using the abbreviation (B, 143) etc. The Bataille works used in the chapter and contained in Stoeckl are: 'The Critique of the Foundations of the Hegelian Dialectic', 1937; 'The Notion of Expenditure', 1933; 'Nietzsche and the Fascists', 1937; 'Nietzschean Chronicle', 1937; 'The Obelisk', 1938; 'The Practice of Joy before Death', 1939. Other translations are the author's and from the editions named, unless otherwise indicated. The neglect of the essay is evidenced by the very brief mentions of it in literature on Fascism in general, e.g. Klaus Theweleit, *Männerphantasien*, Reinbek, 1980, vol. I, p. 224; Wolfgang Fritz Haug, 'Annäherung an die faschistische Modalität des Ideologischer', in Manfred Behrens (ed.), *Faschismus und Ideologie*, Berlin, 1980, vol. 1, p. 79; Manfred Behrens, 'Ideologische Anordnung und Präsentation der Volksgemeinschaft am 1. Mai 1933', ibid., p. 101; John Brenkmann, in *New German Critique*, winter 1979, pp. 59–63. There is a good introduction to Bataille in English in the volume of translations by Allan Stoeckl cited here, and an excellent overview of his work by the same author in his article 'The Death of Acéphale and the Will to Chance: Nietzsche in the Text of Bataille', in *Glyph*, vol. 6, Baltimore, 1979, pp. 42–67.

main tension within Bataille's construction of Fascism. For, on the one side, he sets out to be sober, concrete and empirical. Not only does he see his theory of the 'superstructure' as presupposing 'a Marxist analysis of the infrastructure' (B, 137), but he also offers a textual scrutiny of Mussolini's 'divinization of the State' (B, 155) in terms that show his theory is willing to be tested by its applicability to what the Fascists have actually said and done.

Against this, on the other side, is the whole force of his sweeping categorizations of human experience as such. With enormous aplomb he imports into a model of social behaviour that is already limited to the modulations of two concepts only, the homogeneous and the heterogeneous, a stripped-down version of Freudian terms, and then blandly pronounces the two systems to be in harmony:

> The exclusion of *heterogeneous* elements from the *homogeneous* realm of consciousness formally recalls the exclusion of the elements, described (by psychoanalysis) as *unconscious*, which censorship excludes from the conscious ego. The difficulties opposing the revelation of *unconscious* forms of existence are of the same order as those opposing the knowledge of *heterogeneous*. As will subsequently be made clear, these two kinds of forms have certain properties in common and . . . it would seem that the *unconscious* must be considered as one of the aspects of the heterogeneous. (B, 141)

The shifts in Bataille's position within the essay are as follows. Nothing in his opening stance would seem at odds with the commandment Max Horkheimer was later to enunciate in 'The Jews and Europe' of 1939: 'Whosoever refuses to speak of capitalism should equally be silent on the subject of fascism.'[2] In the second phase of the essay, the field of history is abandoned in favour of an exploration of anthropological concepts of the sacred which acknowledges Emile Durkheim's *The Elementary Forms of the Religious Life* of 1912. This in turn shifts the focus to Bataille's own preoccupation with the experience of the violent release of psychic energies, as outlined in 'The Notion of Expenditure', published in early 1933. At the same time the model expands to include the Freudian concepts of repression and the unconscious. Not only does this open a perspective on Fascism as a disposition of the individual psyche, but it enables the subsequent diagnosis of contemporary Fascist societies on the analogy of mentally disturbed individuals. These analogies remain active during the subsequent

2. Max Horkheimer, 'Die Juden und Europa', *Zeitschrift für Sozialforschung*, vol. 8, 1939, p. 115.

discussion of structures of dominance in society as such, culminating in the definition of 'royal sovereignty' as a composite of the 'other two powers, the religious and the military' and Fascism as something which 'once again unites military and religious authority to effect a total oppression' (B, 149). The conclusion of the essay addresses aspects of the contemporary realities of Italy and Germany, but, more significantly, admits that its own tendency has also been to effect a blurring of the political identities of the Left and the Right. For the present is 'this moment when a vast convulsion opposes, not so much fascism to communism, but radical imperative forms to the deep subversion that continues to pursue the emancipation of human lives' (B, 159).

Bataille begins by subscribing to the view that Fascism is the 'continuation of capitalist economic practice by political means', but immediately insists that there is much more that needs to be included in any adequate explanation.[3] His search leads him away from homogeneous society, which is 'productive society, namely useful society' (B, 138), towards the construction of its other: what he calls – generally in italics – 'the heterogeneous world' which 'includes everything resulting from unproductive expenditure (sacred things themselves form part of this whole)' (B, 142). The initial distinction has already established the paradigmatic antithesis which determines the whole later argument:

homogeneous	versus	heterogeneous
historical	versus	timeless
profane	versus	sacred

For Bataille neatly relegates historical capitalism to the negative side before setting out to define his own positive values:

> Thus in the present order of things, the *homogeneous* part of society is made up of those men who own the means of production or the money *destined for their upkeep or purchase*. It is exactly in the middle segment of the so-called capitalist or bourgeois class that the tendential reduction of human character takes place, making it an abstract and interchangeable entity. (B, 138)

The negativity of this social dimension is not least 'the inability . . . to find in itself a reason for being and acting' (B, 146ff.).

In opposition to this stands 'the general positive character of

3. Cf. Haug, 'Annäherung', p. 44.

heterogeneity' (B, 140), which derives essentially from Durkheim's definition of the sacred, formulated in turn from ethnographical data and seeking to fix social phenomena immune to historical change. Durkheim, in fact, serves as the bridge to a Nietzschean position. The positive quality of 'heterogeneity' is, in one sense, not far removed from the Dionysian liberation of energy in the extinction of rational consciousness: '*Violence, excess, delirium, madness* characterize heterogeneous elements to varying degrees . . . *Heterogeneous* reality is that of a force or shock' (B, 142ff.) In the years immediately before the outbreak of the Second World War, Bataille was to go as far as to preach the foundation of a Nietzschean religion.[4] In 1933, when he is ostensibly still writing from a Marxist point of view, the positive value of 'excess, delirium, madness' is closely allied with what Bataille at the end of the essay calls the 'deep subversion that continues to pursue the emancipation of human lives' and which is a cipher for revolution from the Left.

The essay seems to reach a point where Bataille needs Freud to keep Nietzsche under control. It is all very well to class as heterogeneous those such as 'cadavers and menstruating women . . . persons, words or acts having a suggestive erotic value . . . the warrior, aristocratic and impoverished classes' (B, 142), but the worship of Otherness which underlies such a concept of the sacred inevitably leads to an acknowledgement of the attraction historical Fascism exerts through the *mana* (B, 41) of its leaders:

> If these suggestions are now brought to bear upon actual elements, the fascist leaders are incontestably part of *heterogeneous* existence. Opposed to democratic politicians, who represent in different countries the platitude inherent to *homogeneous* society, Mussolini and Hitler immediately stand out as something other. Whatever emotions their actual existence . . . provokes, it is impossible to ignore the *force* that situates them above men, parties and even laws: a force that disrupts the regular course of things, the peaceful but fastidious *homogeneity* powerless to maintain itself. (B, 143)

It is fascinating to observe how Bataille's excursion into 'psychological structures' steered by a thoroughly uncritical Nietzscheanism brings him back to present reality, proclaiming with a certain awe that 'the *force* of a leader is analogous to that exerted in hypnosis' (B, 143).

Fascism indeed has the charms of the heterogeneous, but Bataille

4. Cf. the note on Bataille's essay 'Nietzschean Chronicle' (B, 263) and the first pages of Stoeckl, 'The Death of Acéphale'.

has run into the contradiction that this category not only 'tends to constitute authority as an unconditional principle' (B, 145) but also has to include the liberating energies he classes as 'subversive' (B, 158). This contradiction is paralleled by his inexact use of Freudian concepts, since on the one hand the very process by which the heterogeneous is constituted is analogous to repression, while on the other hand 'the knowledge of a *heterogeneous* reality as such is to be found in the mystical thinking of primitives and in dreams: it is identical to the structure of the *unconscious*' (B, 143). Heterogeneity thus has to be both the mechanism of repression and absolute social dominance *and* at the same time the 'unconscious' as such, the reservoir of primal energies which can burst forth as the 'effervescent masses in revolt' (B, 158).

There is a way around this problem in Freudian terms, but Bataille's first explicit strategy is to argue a line that is taken up again forty years later by André Glucksmann in his essay of 1972, 'Fascisms: The Old and the New'.[5] Glucksmann observes succinctly: 'Fascism tries to take over revolutionary movements that pre-exist it . . . Fascism does not just manipulate anything at all, but precisely those popular ferments left unexploited by the non-intervention of the proletariat.'[6] Bataille formulates his view of the conversion of revolutionary energy into unconditional authority as a function of the structures of dominance: 'The imperative presence of the leader amounts to a negation of the fundamental revolutionary effervescence that he taps; the revolution which is affirmed as a foundation is, at the same time, fundamentally negated from the moment that internal domination is militarily exerted on the militia' (B, 153). Illustrating what he calls Hitler's 'work of transformation on the material of political discourse', Wolfgang Fritz Haug interprets passages of *Mein Kampf* (1924) to demonstrate the recognition of the success of Marxism and the determination to take advantage of political ferment to 'forge granite principles from the wavering conceptual world of the masses'. The text seems to express quite clearly a naked opportunism clothed in but hardly disguised by the metaphors of ideology.[7] I think that one of the blind spots of Bataille's analysis is to discount the cynical pragmatism of Fascist politics in favour of much more tortuous explanations of the way in which social unrest could be usurped, exploited and channelled into authoritarian paths.

5. André Glucksmann, 'Fascisms: The Old and the New', *Les temps modernes*, vol. 310, 1972, pp. 266–334.
6. Ibid., 302ff.
7. Haug, 'Annäherung', pp. 54–9.

I do not think much is gained by criticizing Bataille for involving himself in a number of contradictions. These result largely from his determination to blend a social with a psychological perspective, so as to present the Fascism of 1933 as a unified phenomenon, and also from his consequent and inadvertent discovery of the intractable problems of reconciling Marxist and Nietzschean viewpoints. These are hardly more amenable to synthesis today, although the common understanding of Nietzsche is much more sophisticated than it was in the early 1930s.[8] They are also explicable in terms of his closeness to the object of investigation. This is not merely closeness in time. Bataille shows great courage in his willingness to confront and elucidate what made Fascism attractive; this means venturing into emotional proximity as well, as his depiction of the Otherness of Mussolini and Hitler reveals, but his account of the phenomenon is the richer for it. I do think, however, that Bataille's contempt for middle-class homogeneity leads him to romanticize Fascist modes of dominance. This takes the form of a needlessly complex dramatizing of the interaction of his own prime categories, as in the following: 'The mode of *heterogeneity explicitly undergoes a thorough alteration, completing the realization of intense homogeneity* without a decrease of the fundamental *heterogeneity*' (B, 151). What this means, basically, is that armies can be characterized by uniformity of behaviour without thereby becoming identical with the middle class.

What I find most lacking in Bataille's description of Fascist power is the balancing effect of the sort of awareness that permeates Brecht's *Arturo Ui* (1941). Brecht is perfectly aware of the Nazi leadership's bid for 'Otherness' in something of the sense that Bataille willingly concedes it, but his counterpointing of attempts at image-making with unadorned gangsterism achieves much the same effect as a semantic deconstruction of the text of *Mein Kampf* in our own day. It is not that Bataille is unaware of the criminal dimension of Fascism. Rather he is fascinated by the symmetry he perceives between the highest and lowest strata of society: 'If the heterogeneous nature of the slave is akin to that of the filth in which his material situation condemns him to live, that of the master is formed by an act excluding all filth: an act pure in direction but sadistic in form' (B, 146). Unpleasant as its human reality might be, the Fascism that has endowed Mussolini and Hitler with quasi-

8. See the interesting and incisive discussion by Jeff Minson of the conflict between Marxist and Nietzschean elements in the thought of Michel Foucault: 'Strategies for Socialists: Foucault's Conception of Power', in Mike Gane (ed.), *Towards a Critique of Foucault*, London, 1986, especially pp. 111–23.

royal status establishes a patterning of heterogeneity that Bataille seems to find aesthetically appealing:

> This process, which blends the different social formations from the bottom up, must be understood as a fundamental process whose scheme is necessarily given in the very formation of the chief, who derives his profound meaning from the fact of having shared the dejected and impoverished life of the proletariat. But, as in the case of military organization, the affective value characteristic of impoverished existence is only displaced and transformed into its opposite; and it is its inordinate scope that gives the chief and the whole of the formation the accent of violence without which no army or fascism could be possible. (B, 154)

Soldiers may be individually the 'scum of the earth', but the army may collectively dominate society; Hitler may have been a down-and-out, but 'fascist authority . . . is only one of the numerous forms of royal authority, the description of which constitutes the foundation of any coherent description of fascism' (B, 146). When the 'composite character of royal power' gets defined it is as a synthesis of 'the other two powers, the religious and the military' (B, 149). Thus the definition of Fascist power feeds back into that of the sacred: 'On the whole the king is considered in one form or another to be an emanation of a divine nature, along with everything that the principle of emanation entails in the way of identity when dealing with *heterogeneous* elements' (B, 152).

But the heterogeneous in turn not only manifests itself in the 'mystical thinking of primitives and in dreams' (B, 143), but is also the social 'unconscious', the only source of the 'deep subversion that continues to pursue the emancipation of human lives' (B, 159). If Bataille had been content with a simpler and more pragmatic explanation of the affinity between Fascism and crime, then I doubt he would have been led into such circularity. But his initial paradigm demands an explanation of any authoritarian structure in terms of *mana* (B, 141), and Hitler appears, on this reading, as additionally qualified for his role as a sacred king by his previous experience as a social pariah.

The analogy to Freudian psychology that Bataille introduced at the same early stage of his essay as the concept of *mana* could provide a counter-argument to this, but Bataille seems unwilling to develop its full implications. For if repression in Freud's sense can be likened to 'the exclusion of *heterogeneous* elements from the *homogeneous* realm of consciousness', and if this resembles in turn the social process whereby 'diverse elements . . . have been banished to heterogeneity as a result of social decomposition', then what has been repressed does not re-emerge as itself, let alone in the apotheosis of the sacred, but produces instead, in Freudian terms, the symptom, the disorder, the malfunction requiring treatment.[9] The way to such an argument is quite open, but Bataille declines to take it.

Despite this reluctance, Bataille does not let go of the analogy of the rise of Fascism as the remanifestation of forces that have once been repressed. Rather, he restates it vigorously towards the end of his discussion: 'Stirring up such apparently anachronistic phantoms would surely be senseless if fascism had not, before our very eyes, reappropriated and reconstituted from the bottom up – starting, as it were, with nothing – the very process described above for the establishment of power' (B, 153). The very words 'anachronistic phantoms' seem to imply that the political realities of 1933 are not the primal social and psychic energies that may once have been banished to the depths. But Bataille does not pursue the diagnosis in terms that state plainly what is the disease.

This is *not*, as Rita Bischof suggests, because contemporary Fascism lacks the 'revolutionaries' free renunciation of individual sovereignty' that she thinks Bataille attributes to socialist societies.[10] For he expresses a conviction, albeit rather tortuously, that the political Left had lost its grip on the proletariat and that the decision for Fascism – 'the imperative solution' – was a free choice on the part of the bulk of the societies concerned:

> Under these new conditions . . . the lower classes no longer exclusively experience the attraction represented by socialist subversion, and a military type of organization has in part begun to draw them into the orbit of sovereignty. Likewise, the dissociated elements (belonging to the middle or dominating classes) have found a new outlet for their effervescence, and it is not surprising that, given the choice between subversive or imperative solutions, the majority opted for the imperative. (B, 158)

For all his difficulties with the concept of the heterogeneous, I think there is none the less a certain intellectual toughness and realism in Bataille that prevents him from synthesizing a combined Marxist/Freudian perspective with the same facility as Wilhelm Reich.[11]

9. Cf. Jacques Lacan, *Écrits*, Paris, 1966, pp. 280ff. and in the index to this volume under 'symptôme'.
10. Ruth Bischof, 'Über den Gesichtspunkt, von dem aus gedacht wird', in her translation of Georges Bataille, 'Die psychologische Struktur des Faschismus', Munich, 1978, p. 98.
11. Cf. Mark Poster, *Foucault, Marxism and History*, Cambridge, 1984, pp. 122ff.

While Betaille allows the Freudian analogy to stand, he seems unwilling to force it. Part of the reason may be his recognition that neither Italian nor German Fascism had to disenfranchise the populace to assume power. Emphasizing this point in 1972, André Glucksmann says: 'Fascism is not born of a *coup d'état* . . . Fascism is already within the State.'[12]

It is certainly within the state as Bataille has defined it, and he leaves the implication open that it may be in the individual as well, without venturing to specify a particular pathogenesis that may dispose people towards Fascism, as does Klaus Theweleit in adopting part of the theory of Deleuze and Guattari.[13] I suspect that one reason he does not proceed in this direction is that the main thrust of his description of Fascism is somewhat at odds with his use of the Freudian unconscious in a social analogy. While he may well propose 'that the *unconscious* must be considered as one of the aspects of the *heterogeneous*' (B, 141), it is not really consistent with the rest of what he says to maintain: 'The difficulties opposing the revelation of *unconscious* forms of existence are of the same order as those opposing the knowledge of *heterogeneous* forms.' For the inaccessibility of the Freudian unconscious to knowledge on the part of the conscious mind is of a quite different order from the 'Otherness' of the bulk of the social phenomena that are labelled heterogeneous: 'mobs, the warrior, aristocratic and impoverished classes, different types of violent individuals or at least those who refuse the rule (madmen, leaders, poets, etc.)' (B, 142). In summary, Bataille seems to confuse thresholds of perception with thresholds of social demarcation.

The problem may lie, more specifically, in the Nietzschean values that are implicit in the bulk of Bataille's text. For certain manifestations of the heterogeneous seem to have the status for Bataille of epiphanies of the Dionysian – in the sense of the popular reception of Nietzsche in the 1930s. The strong, the violent, the atavistic can represent an intrinsic value, and Bataille hesitates in this essay to brand unequivocally the Fascist leaders as in any way sham or spurious versions of archaic expressions of power. When he differentiates the Fascist order in Italy and Germany from 'classical royal society', then it is in relatively obscure terms. There is no suggestion that these regimes are not as monolithic as they represent themselves to be: 'Fascist power is characterized by a foundation that is both religious and military, in which these two

12. Glucksmann, 'Fascisms', pp. 276ff.
13. Theweleit, *Männerphantasien*, pp. 216–34.

habitually distinct elements cannot be separated: it thus presents itself from the outset as an accomplished concentration' (B, 153). Had Bataille at this point been willing to cast a cold eye on the genesis and rise of Nazism in Germany, then he would have had to acknowledge that its foundation was neither 'religious' nor 'military' in the absolute sense he intends the terms. Rather, he shows a willingness to accept the Nazis as much nobler than all the facts suggested – the same willingness that determined, for varying lengths of time, the attitudes of Ernst Jünger, Gottfried Benn and Martin Heidegger.

By 1937, in a polemic entitled 'Nietzsche and the Fascists', he does finally pour scorn on the Fascist leadership, but then it is in terms which betray just how emotional and simplistic his own Nietzscheanism can be. I have pointed out elsewhere that Nietzsche's devastating critique of language somehow stopped short of the adjective generally, its comparative form in particular, and most especially the comparative of *vornehm*, which means basically the opposite of 'vulgar'.[14] When Bataille finally lambastes the Fascist leaders, it is from a position of Nietzschean *Vornehmheit*. Taking issue with Lukács's views to the contrary, he proclaims:

> Fascism and Nietzscheanism are mutually exclusive, and are even violently mutually exclusive, as soon as each of them is considered in its totality: on one side life is tied down and stabilized in an endless servitude, on the other there is not only a circulation of free air, but the wind of a tempest; on one side the charm of human culture is broken in order to make room for vulgar force, on the other force and violence are tragically dedicated to this charm. How can one not see the abyss that separates a Cesare Borgia, a Malatesta, from a Mussolini? The former were insolent scorners of tradition and of all morality, making use of bloody and complex events to benefit a greed for life that exceeded them; the latter has been slowly enslaved by everything he was able to set in motion only by paralysing, little by little, his earliest impulses. Already, in Nietzsche's eyes, Napoleon appeared 'corrupted by the means he *had* to employ'; Napoleon 'lost *noblesse* of character'. An infinitely more burdensome constraint no doubt weighs on modern dictators, reduced to finding their force by identifying themselves with the impulses that Nietzsche scorned in the masses. (B, 186)

This is quite mild as far as Bataille's Nietzschean proclamations of the late 1930s are concerned.[15] But Cesare Borgia as a true Nietzschean

14. Anthony Stephens, 'Nietzsche: The Resurrection of Parts', in *Thesis 11*, no. 13, pp. 104ff.
15. Cf. Bataille's *Nietzschean Chronicle* (B, 202–12).

hero – 'making use of bloody and complex events to benefit a greed for life that exceeded [him]' – is surely also a manifestation of '*heterogeneous* force' in the sense of the essay on Fascism of 1933.

I suggest that the underlying Nietzschean values of 'The Psychological Structure of Fascism', rather than his simple preference for abstractions over historical realities, account for what is least satisfying about Bataille's diagnosis in this otherwise challenging and complex text. He begins it in the vocabulary of Marxism and with an attack on the 'so-called capitalist or bourgeois class' (B, 138) and ends it with 'socialist subversion' still on the positive side of the paradigm (B, 158). But in 'The Notion of Expenditure', published earlier in 1933, the class struggle is seen to culminate in an apotheosis of blood sacrifice. The 'masters and exploiters' will get theirs on that '*great night* when their beautiful phrases will be drowned out by death screams in riots. That is the bloody hope which, each day, is one with the existence of the people, and which sums up the insubordinate content of the class struggle' (B, 128).[16] Germany's *Kristallnacht* endows this vision, in retrospect, with a terrible irony.

It is therefore not surprising that the Fascist leaders and their dominance structures usurp in 'The Psychological Structure of Fascism' something of the glamour of the Dionysian in crudest Nietzschean terms, for they clearly seem to be more potent manifestations of 'force' (B, 143) than anything 'socialist subversion' can muster. I think this may account for Bataille's strange blindness towards two aspects of Fascism most obviously open to his line of criticism: the falsity of its self-representations and the imperative inherent in its drive for dominance to find its ultimate legitimation in war.

On the first point, he seems to take the pernicious absurdities of Nazi racism entirely at face value:

> National Socialist Germany . . . has not been afflicted with the theoretical difficulties resulting from the necessity of officially articulating a principle of authority: the mystical idea of race immediately affirmed itself as the imperative aim of the new fascist society; at the same time it appeared to be incarnated in the person of the Führer and his followers. Even though the conception of race lacks an objective base, it is none the less subjectively grounded, and the necessity of maintaining the racial value above all others obviated the need for a theory that made the State the principle of all value. The example of Germany thus demonstrates that the identity established by Mussolini between the State and the sovereign form of value is not necessary to a theory of fascism. (B, 155)

16. For the relationship of blood sacrifice to the sacred, cf. B, 119.

On the second, his discussion of the relation of the Fascist leader to military power takes the following surprising turn: 'But this internal domination is not directly subordinated to real or possible acts of war: it essentially poses itself as the middle term of an external domination of society and of the State, as the middle term of a total imperative value' (B, 153ff.). Bataille's view seems quite implausible if it is contrasted with the following passage from Walter Benjamin's short text of 1930, 'Theories of German Fascism'. It is quite apparent to Benjamin, well before Hitler's accession to power, that the fatal entelechy of German Fascism is war:

> One should indeed direct all the light that language and reason still give towards showing up that 'primal experience' from out of whose silent gloom this mysticism of world-death crawls forth on its thousand derisory conceptual feet. The war that is exposed in this light is no more the 'eternal' war to which these new Germans pray than it is the 'last' one of the pacifists' delusion.[17]

When, in his essay of 1933, Bataille's focus on the realities of Fascism blurs or when he fails to pursue the implications of his own arguments, then I think it is possible to detect interference by those Nietzschean values that he articulates much more clearly in texts that precede and follow this one. The interference takes the form of a willingness to accept the self-mythifications of Fascism uncritically because it has for him the charisma of naked power, and, still worse, to mythicize further certain aspects of the very phenomenon he is subjecting to analysis.

The Nietzschean Legacy

If Flaubert were writing his *Dictionnaire des idées reçues* (Dictionary of Received Ideas) today, then the entry for Nietzsche would have to begin 'misrepresented by the Fascists', and in the West German edition continue 'and by Lukács as well'. Nietzsche presently enjoys the prestige of having been so thoroughly misrepresented from opposite ideological points of view that critics vie with one another in being charitable to him, lest they too inadvertently slip into the heresy of suggesting that there is anything at all in Nietzsche that

17. 'Theorien des deutschen Faschismus', in Walter Benjamin, *Gesammelte Schriften*, eds R. Tiedemann and H. Schweppenhäuser, Frankfurt/M, 1972, vol. III, p. 249.

Hitler could have read without gagging – if, of course, he had *really read* him.

Bataille's Nietzscheanism is an interesting case in point, and I think it is relevant for an understanding of later thinkers such as Gilles Deleuze and Michel Foucault. I have tried to show how it colours his diagnosis of Fascist psychology and, indeed, produces certain blind spots in the analysis. The fact that the Fascists crudely and cynically misrepresented some parts of Nietzsche and could have no use at all for other parts is quite indisputable. But this in no way affects the problem that a lot of Nietzsche's most cherished conclusions are both irrational and contrary to humane values. While Hegel and Marx are scarcely less irrational, they do not muddle the values of the European Enlightenment with anything like Nietzsche's insensate vigour. I suggest that an adherence to such Nietzschean values as he knew could indeed sway a thinker of Bataille's perspicacity towards a voluntary mythicization of the very phenomenon he had set out to dissect.

We must be aware that Bataille's attachment to Nietzsche becomes more fervid and declamatory as the 1930s progress, seems to cool down after the beginning of the Second World War, but remains a dominant influence in his later thought. His 'Nietzschean Chronicle' of July 1937 seems to represent its apogee and contains the following:

> In the image of the one he wanted to be to the point of madness, Nietzsche is born of the Earth torn open by the fire of the Heavens, he is born blasted by lightning and in that way he is imbued with this fire of domination that becomes the FIRE OF THE EARTH . . . WHEN THE SACRED – NIETZSCHEAN – FIGURE OF TRAGIC DIONYSOS RELEASES LIFE FROM SERVITUDE, IN OTHER WORDS, FROM THE PUNISHMENT OF THE PAST, HE RELEASES IT AS WELL FROM RELIGIOUS HUMILITY, FROM THE CONFUSIONS AND TORPOR OF ROMANTICISM. HE DEMANDS THAT A BRILLIANT WILL RETURN THE EARTH TO THE DIVINE ACCURACY OF THE DREAM. (B, 207)

The salient point is that a more muted Nietzscheanism, glorifying 'sacrifice', 'loss', 'expenditure', the 'tragic', the 'bloody hope' of the class struggle and so on, was already well established in Bataille's thinking before he undertook his delineation of the psychology of Fascism, avowedly as the necessary complement to a Marxist explanation.

It surely says something about Bataille's Nietzscheanism that it is only when in 1937 he feels roused to defend Nietzsche against Fascist misrepresentations that he finds Mussolini 'vulgar' by contrast to Cesare Borgia and Nazi racism a 'crudely and consciously fabricated falsehood' (B, 183ff.). Both verdicts are conspicuously not brought down in the relevant passages of 'The Psychological Structure of Fascism', as I have already shown. In 1933, the visible presence of power in abundance seems in both instances sufficient for Bataille to acquiesce to the ideological import of Fascist self-representation. In other words, I suggest that Bataille in 1933 has succumbed to a mythicization of presence that genuinely derives from Nietzsche's thought because myths of presence have little significance in either a Hegelian or a Marxist dialectic. Bataille only turns his critical talents loose on such myths once it becomes obvious that the Fascists have in some sense made Nietzsche their victim, notably by ignoring totally that dimension of his thought that is destructive of ideological positions as such.

To illustrate what I mean by a myth of presence, I must briefly turn to Bataille's critique of Hegel, which also predates the essay on Fascism and is pursued later. Bataille's assimilation of Hegelian and Marxist perspectives on history was rendered difficult by what he saw as an exclusive concentration on objective manifestations of power.[18] The fundamental antagonism between individual experience in Bataille's sense and the processes of history limited for him the applicability of dialectical thought to physical and subjective reality. In the 'Critique of the Foundations of the Hegelian Dialectic', published in 1932, he objects strongly to a global application of dialectic thought – rather, one must pick and choose:

> The precise point where introduced dialectical thought starts to express real relations must be determined in particular cases. For example, no opposition of terms can account for the biological development of a man who successively is an infant, an adolescent, an adult, and an old man. On the other hand, if one envisages the psychological development of the same man from a psychoanalytic point of view, one can say that the human being is first limited by the prohibitions that the father sets in opposition to his urges. (B, 112)

The criterion which makes a dialectical description of the relationship of child and parent acceptable to Bataille is that the structure is, in the first instance, 'lived' and not a categorically imposed abstraction: 'The importance of this theme comes from the fact that it

18. Bischof, 'Über den Gesichtspunkt', p. 96, makes this point well.

constitutes an *experience lived* by each human being. Through this the terms of dialectical development become elements of real existence' (B, 113). It is evident why Bataille was later to prefer an explanation of Fascism that gave more weight to psychology than to economics and why he added a Freudian dimension to his own categories, even if it did not quite fit. The development of his Nietzscheanism certainly did nothing to displace intense subjective experience from the top of his hierarchy of values; on the contrary. The whole movement of his thought shows a preference for states of consciousness that need not be legitimized by any historical pattern but simply derive their value from their own intensity. A myth of presence is not only one in which time appears as simultaneity, but also a configuration whose elements present themselves as an ideal cohesion. Dialectical constructs may, by contrast, exploit various modes of temporal and emotional discordance.

When in his essay of 1938, 'The Obelisk', he counterpoints the Hegelian and Nietzschean concepts of time, it seems that pathos has become the criterion of philosophical validity:

> Even Hegel describing the movement of Spirit as if it excluded all possible rest made it end, however, at HIMSELF as if he were its necessary conclusion. Thus he gave the movement of time the centripetal structure that characterizes sovereignty, Being, or God. Time, on the other hand, dissolving each centre that has formed, is fatally known as *centrifugal* – since it is known in a being whose centre is already there. The dialectical idea, then, is only a hybrid of time and its opposite, of the death of God and the position of the immutable. (B, 219)

The Hegelian concept of time loses out because it is emblematic of a consciousness divided against itself with no hope of knowing the ecstasy of union. On the other hand:

> Nietzsche's thought, which resulted in the sudden ecstatic vision of the eternal return, cannot be compared to the feelings habitually linked to what passes for profound reflection. For the object of the intellect here exceeds the categories in which it can be represented, to the point where as soon as it is represented it becomes an object of ecstasy – object of tears, object of laughter . . . In order to represent the decisive break that took place – freeing life from the humilities of fear – it is necessary to tie the sundering vision of the 'return' to what Nietzsche experienced when he reflected upon the explosive vision of Heraclitus, and to what he experienced later in his own vision of the 'death of God': this is necessary in order to perceive the full extent of the bolt of lightning that never

> stopped shattering his life while at the same time projecting it into a burst of violent light. (B, 220)

'Doch alle Lust will Ewigkeit/Will tiefe, tiefe Ewigkeit!'[19] I think it is now clear how the disposition towards creating myths of presence, certainly enhanced by and very likely derived straight from Bataille's reading of Nietzsche, influences the diagnosis of Fascism in the essay of 1933.

Michel Foucault, in his epitaph for Bataille, 'A Preface to Transgression', published in 1963, speaks of a central experience of *l'être sans delai* (instantaneous selfhood) in Bataille's whole work, and continues:

> Transgression opens onto a world that is scintillating and always affirmed, a world without shadow, without twilight, without that creeping negation which eats into the fruit and embeds in them the contradiction of themselves. It is the sunlit obverse of satanic denial; it has a bond with the divine, or rather: it opens, beyond that limit which designates the sacred, the space in which the divine is manifest. . . . No dialectical movement, no analysis of constitutions and their transcendental bases can be of any assistance in conceiving such an experience or even giving access to it. May not this instantaneous play of limit and transgression be for our age the essential proof of that concept of 'origin' to which Nietzsche dedicated us from the inception of his work – a concept that would be, absolutely and in the one motion, at once Critique and Ontology, a mode of thought that would simultaneously encompass finitude and being?[20]

Foucault seems in no doubt about the Nietzschean origin of Bataille's myths of presence and about their incompatibility with dialectical concepts of time and history. Thus his text echoes, whether consciously or not, Bataille's counterpointing of the Hegelian experience of time and the Nietzschean epiphany of 1938. Sharing Bataille's Nietzschean enthusiasms, as he does here, involves Foucault in certain difficulties with his own thinking about Nazism in other contexts. His line on Nazi racism is consistently that, with all its 'quasi-medieval mythology' and resuscitated apocalyptics, it represents a disastrous reversion to outworn modes of discourse.[21]

19. Friedrich Nietzsche, *Sämtliche Werke*, Kritische Studienausgabe, Munich, 1980, vol. 4, p. 404: 'Yet all pleasure craves eternity/Craves deep, deep eternity.'
20. Michel Foucault, 'Préface à la transgression', *Critique*, 1963, p. 757.
21. Michel Foucault, *Vom Licht des Krieges zur Geburt der Geschichte*, Berlin, 1986, pp. 52ff.

However, he cannot ignore the affinities between some of Bataille's enthusiasm for sacrifice and bloodshed, as release mechanisms for the experience of 'instantaneous selfhood' and the Nazi 'Myth of the Blood'. Thus, at the end of the first volume of his *History of Sexuality* of 1976, Foucault is obliged to consign Bataille's central enthusiasms to the realm of the anachronistic, the regressive: 'And nothing can prevent thinking of the sexual order in terms of the law, death, the blood and sovereignty – no matter how much one may call on de Sade and Bataille as witnesses for 'subversion' – from being ultimately nothing more than a nostalgic regression into past history.'[22]

Foucault's shift in attitude towards Bataille between 1963 and 1976 poses the central dilemma in evaluating Bataille's myths of presence. When Foucault saw them as timely and promising, he also traced them directly to Nietzsche and to a positive evaluation of the experience of 'origin', something that cannot be very far from the Dionysian release from the observing consciousness. When he sees Bataille, for all his championship of 'subversion', as imprisoned in the 'nostalgia' of regressive mythicizations, he omits Nietzsche and substitutes the less complex case of de Sade. Not surprisingly, Foucault himself has been criticized, in a trenchant analysis by Jeff Minson of his conception of power, precisely for having 'some untenable "Nietzschean" ingredients' in his thinking.[23]

Certainly Foucault has not been averse to mythicizing Nietzsche in terms which reject any perspective of historical relativism towards his thought. Just as his tribute to Bataille of 1963 unreservedly affirms the contemporary relevance of Bataille's 'concept of "origin"' in its full implications, so he lauds Nietzsche in *The Order of Things* of 1966 in terms which seem to create their own myth of presence:

> He has once more taken up the theme of the End of Time so as to make of it the Death of God and the wanderings [errors] of the last of humankind. He has taken up once more the finitude of anthropology so as to launch from it the mighty leap of the Superman. He has taken up once more the great, continuous chain of history, but so as to bend it in the infinity of the Return . . . In any event: before we were even born, Nietzsche had burnt to ashes, for our sakes, the garbled promises of the Dialectic and of anthropology.[24]

22. Michel Foucault, *Sexualität und Wahrheit. Der Wille zum Wissen*, Frankfurt/M, 1977, p. 179.
23. Minson, 'Strategies'.
24. Michel Foucault, *Die Ordnung der Dinge* (1966), Frankfurt/M, 1974, p. 322.

Of course, there are a large number of different 'Nietzschean' positions that one may develop from the whole corpus of Nietzsche's work. To be fair to Foucault, he has not gone on endlessly repeating this anti-historical apocalyptic, but has concentrated instead on the lines of Nietzschean thought that are destructive of ideology as such. But to distance himself from Bataille, as he does in 1976, he must also implicitly distance himself from that brand of Nietzscheanism that abounds in Bataille's works and that Foucault seems to share in the rhetoric of 1966. That he groups Bataille with de Sade instead ten years later may be no more than a tacit recognition of the complexity of the whole Nietzschean phenomenon. Or else it could simply be that Nietzsche has 'gone underground' in Foucault's later thought because he still offers the most potent antidotes to Marxism and because these are genuinely anti-historical.

Against Seduction

I should like, finally, to return to the problem of mythicization in Bataille's study of Fascism of 1933. I have tried to show how his Nietzschean perspective affects his analysis of Fascist self-representation, rendering him, it seems, insensitive to the hollowness of much Fascist ideology and susceptible to overlooking pragmatic aspects of how Fascist power was generated and worked in practice. Because Fascist displays of 'force' have affinities with the preferred scenarios of his own myths of presence, his delineation of a 'psychological structure' from an initially and ultimately still oppositional viewpoint drifts into a positive mythicization of what he is trying to expose to the cold light of reason – so that he fails to demolish Fascist ideology at precisely those points where it was most vulnerable. His one sentence on the Nazi's 'mystical idea of race' (B, 155) is the most flagrant example of this.

In tracing this to Bataille's Nietzscheanism, I am not saying that Bataille thought Hitler was the Nietzschean 'superman' or anything like it. Rather, I am arguing that what Bataille seems to have absorbed from Nietzsche was the structure of values that emerges in his own myths of presence and the proclivity to create such myths around manifestations of 'force'. I would further suggest that his earlier allegiance to Hegel and Marx also did little to help him avoid such traps. This has two major consequences for his analysis: firstly, it means that the 'psychological' dimension is not pursued rigorously; secondly, it intensifies the aura around aspects of Fascism instead of dissipating it.

On the first point, I have shown above how the Freudian analogy is postulated but left implicit or inchoate. Surprisingly, Bataille totally excludes the sexual dimension from his 'psychological structure'. Klaus Theweleit's insistence on it makes for a certain deadening prolixity, but his perspective is indubitably a valid corrective to Bataille's in this regard. Surely, if Bataille had been willing to carry the Freudian analogy further, he would have reached a point where the sexual implications of Fascist self-representation were inescapable.

On the second point, Bataille's depiction of force as a manifestation of the heterogeneous seems an excellent example of what Roland Barthes in his *Mythologies* of 1957 was to call 'myth as depoliticised speech'.[25] By this he means speech which disguises the political character of the realities it describes or evokes. He cites the example of the cover photograph on a copy of *Paris-Match* in which 'a young Negro in a French uniform is saluting, with his eyes uplifted, probably fixed on a fold of the tricolour' and generalizes from this example:

> In the case of the soldier-Negro, for instance, what is got rid of is certainly not French imperiality (on the contrary, since what must be actualised is its presence); it is the contingent, historical, in one word fabricated, quality of colonialism. Myth does not deny things, on the contrary, its function is to talk about them; simply, it purifies them, it makes them innocent, it gives them a natural and eternal justification, it gives them a clarity which is not that of an explanation but that of a statement of fact. . . . In passing from history to nature, myth acts economically: it abolishes the complexity of human acts, it gives them the simplicity of essences, it does away with all dialectics. . . . it organises a world which is without contradictions because it is without depth.[26]

Clearly, a great deal of Bataille's analysis does not fit this description. His argument is, in the main, tortuously complex and the interplay of his principal categories involves any amount of contradiction. Moreover, many parts of his discussion open critical perspectives and leave them open, whereas mythical discourse will close them off. But equally clearly, some of it does apply to his treatment of Fascist ideology and dominance structures. Where he could have shown in detail how these have been 'fabricated', he

25. Roland Barthes, *Mythologies* (1957), tr. Annette Lavers, London, 1972, p. 143.
26. Ibid.

leaves their self-representation untouched; by associating them with such atemporal categories as the sacred, he at times does come close to giving them 'the simplicity of essences'; he tends to let Fascist manifestations of force drift free from their historical contingencies and acquire the aura of 'Otherness'. The category of the heterogeneous, as Bataille defines it from the outset, contains so much that is 'nature' rather than 'history' that its repeated application to manisfestations of Fascist power quite clearly produce a mythification in Barthes's sense.

But how should we understand the stricture 'it does away with all dialectics' in relation to Bataille's text? For his starting point is precisely in Marxist dialectics, and at the end of the text he is still advocating 'socialist subversion'. Moreover, the relationship of the homogeneous to the heterogeneous presents itself at times as a complex dialectic, even if not consistently so. But yet the assessments of Fascist self-representation all too clearly represent suspensions of dialectical reasoning. The fundamental problem with Bataille's analysis is that the dialectical and Nietzschean modes of thought remain quite unmediated. The opposition exemplified by Bataille's own contrasting of the Hegelian and Nietzschean experiences of time is an absolute one and permits no productive interaction. What gives the text its shifting quality is that the one mode of thought simply displaces the other and vice versa, whilst the terminology remains the same. The attractions of Fascism for Bataille may be seen as luring him out of a dialectical and historical perspective into a Nietzschean cult of simultaneity. Once there, his description of Fascist power forms itself into myths of presence in which the ideologies of Fascist self-representation stand unchallenged.

I suspect this is a problem which Foucault may have inherited from Bataille, as it seems evident in what he writes about both Nietzsche and Bataille in the 1960s. I leave the question open as to whether it is suppressed rather than resolved in Foucault's later writings. Certainly it remains unresolved in what Bataille writes after the 1930s, as Allan Stoekl points out in terms of the whole body of his writing: 'These two sides of Bataille – "Nietzsche" and "Hegel/Marx" – do not result in a higher textual synthesis . . . In fact, they constantly risk and transgress each other, denounce the lie of the other, and devalorize each other's position. Yet at the same time each is contaminated by the other, each contains a minor residue of the other.'[27]

27. Stoeckl, 'The Death of Acéphale', p. 64.

If we ask, by way of conclusion, what the example of Bataille's essay of 1933 has to tell us about the attractions of Fascism in general, then the answer may well be that it should make us sceptical of certain concepts of myth that are still lingering in the western academic consciousness. There is still a tendency to see 'genuine' mythical experience not only as the reflection of a unified consciousness but also as intrinsically wholesome and life-affirming. Edith Wyschogrod's thought-provoking study of 1985, *Spirit in Ashes: Hegel, Heidegger and Man-Made Mass Death*, seems to incorporate such preconceptions into its characterization of the 'death-world':

> The death-world is thus the child of technological society; it is an attempt to give meaning to the alienation of that society from qualitative natural existence as well as from cultural experience. But the death-world is not the extreme expression of technological society itself, for what characterizes that society is its rationality, its divorce from mythic consciousness, its uprootedness from the life-world.[28]

True 'mythic consciousness' is thus in positive apposition to 'the life-world' and is the antithesis of the products of 'technological society', by which one can ultimately understand everything one finds negative in the modern age. In the perspective Edith Wyschogrod creates, the kind of myth-making practised by the proponents of ideologies, and especially the Fascist ideologies of this century, *has* to seem different. So it is stigmatized as shoddy, imitative, second-hand and spurious. It lacks the spontaneity of true 'mythic consciousness'; rather, it exhumes bits of the past, sews them together to make a Frankenstein-like corpus, reanimates it with a frightful electrical charge and sets it blundering about, wreaking havoc all over the 'life-world'.

Bataille's essay surely shows us how careful we must be not to accept such myths about myth. For if the strengths and weaknesses of his diagnosis of Fascism show anything, then it is surely that neither the provenance nor the ingredients of the Fascist self-representations he discusses are anywhere near as important for Bataille as is the symmetry of his own concepts. Nazi racism was a sorry patchwork of anachronistic balderdash, and Hitler's rise to power was nothing like the accession of a sacred king, but, given Bataille's proclivity in 1933 to respond to manifestations of 'force' by assigning to them the status of a myth of presence, we find his

28. Edith Wyschogrod, *Spirit in Ashes: Hegel, Heidegger and Man-Made Mass Death*, New Haven, 1985, p. 28.

critical awareness going into suspension when confronted with precisely these aspects of contemporary Fascism. When it happens to appease the hunger for 'mythical consciousness', an ideological self-representation becomes, as it were, opaque to the critical intelligence. It does not matter how it has been cobbled together or however manifest the absurdities it may contain; the opaqueness imparted to it by its reception makes it as functional a myth as any of the doings of those 'genuinely' mythical figures that Géza Róheim called 'the eternal ones of the dream'.[29]

It is a misunderstanding of the attractions of Fascism to argue that its constructs are not 'real' myths because they are the derivative fabrications of a 'demythologized' technological society or because they lack the spontaneity we readily attribute to the myths of ancient or non-literate societies. They may be quite cynical fabrications, but this does not prevent them from functioning just as effectively in a mythical framework as their more salubrious brethren – once the framework accepts them as filling a demand. It is fortunate that the conceptual antecedents of Bataille's essay are so well documented, as this enables us to see what kind of interference – from within his own thinking – Bataille's project of constructing a psychological complement to a Marxist understanding of Fascism encounters. The interference takes the explicit form of a Nietzschean predisposition towards creating myths of presence – in response to certain stimuli, such as an excess of manifest 'force'.

Ironically, the response is not much different from that which contemporary Fascist self-representation demanded from the populace at large. Given the inability of political systems such as the Weimar Republic to provide the German people with anything they could regard as an answer to their most urgent emotional demands, the success of Fascist self-representation is understandable. The masses who elected Hitler to power and the highly gifted individuals who flirted briefly with Nazism only to reject it, as did Benn and Jünger, had a common experiential base in disillusionment. Given that most European intellectuals experienced the Nihilism, which Nietzsche had so unerringly defined in the 1880s, as a personal crisis at the end of the 1920s, it is also quite understandable that in 1933 Bataille should fall back on the authority of the first and best diagnostician of the terminal illness of western culture, namely Nietzsche as he was read in those decades, and should wholeheartedly endorse his 'remedies', for all that they were likely to kill the patient if ever applied.

29. Géza Róheim, *The Eternal Ones of the Dream*, New York, 1971, passim.

PART III

Seduction of (by) the Intellectuals

–6–

Artur Dinter

A Successful Fascist Author in Pre-Fascist Germany

GÜNTER HARTUNG

In view of the present position of research into Fascism, the concept of 'the attractions of Fascism' seems to me a particularly necessary and useful one. I would like to apply it to the sphere of literature. More specifically, I want to pose the question as to what extent the actual Fascist movements and state regimes which emerged after the First World War were fostered or supported by literature. The question posed here is thus not the attractions of Fascism to writers, but rather the contribution of writers to the 'the attractions of Fascism'.

This topic suggests a broad range of issues and questions. One would need to ask, for instance, what the actual effect of d'Annunzio's and Marinetti's work was in Italy and beyond its borders both before and after the establishment of the Duce's regime; what the actual propaganda value of Ezra Pound's statements was for Italy and possibly also for pro-Fascist forces in the English-speaking world; what the books of Drieu la Rochelle, or Céline's *Bagatelles pour un Massacre* (Bagatelles for a Massacre, 1937), accomplished in France and also in Germany; and how the effect of Hamsun's work manifested itself in Scandinavia and in Germany after 1918 – to name only a few unarguably Fascistic authors.

Answers to such questions presuppose international cooperation on research into Fascism, covering comparative literature studies and empirical sociological research – a collective project which has barely begun. Nevertheless, the study of individual cases requires that one keep this problem area in mind, in order to avoid overlooking significant connections. I shall attempt to do so as I focus on the German context – or, more precisely, on the situation within Germany (that is excluding Austria, German-speaking Switzerland

This chapter has been translated by John Milfull and Joe O'Donnell.

and the German-speaking minorities in other countries).

There is, however, an underlying problem: the value of 'literary attractiveness' changes as a Fascist movement itself progresses from the struggle to gain power to its consolidation. Initially, it will generally enlist the help of avant-garde writers who sympathize with it for aesthetic reasons, but who appeal only to a small, elite audience; once established, however, its prime concern is the mass audience, and literary attractiveness is of interest only to the extent that it serves the party's political and ideological propaganda. This creates difficulties for an empirical literary-sociological approach, as its usual categories for breadth and depth of reception (the number and size of impressions, critical responses and the number and type of other reactions) lose much of their significance when these factors are regulated primarily by the state and the Fascist Party.[1]

This problem is particularly obvious in the literary events of the Third Reich. The case of Gottfried Benn provides a classic example of the fate of right-wing avant-gardism. Benn's weakness for biologistic theories of history and society led him into an alliance with the Nazis in 1933, and his name ('which had stood for the highest standards and a really fanatical purity', as Klaus Mann[2] later

1. For the literary-sociological statistics regarding distribution see Donald Ray Richards, *The German Bestseller in the 20th Century. A Complete Bibliography and Analysis 1915–40*, Berne, 1968. The reader should keep in mind possible causes of inaccuracies, particularly regarding the period after 1933. The great strength of Richards's analysis is that the author has begun with the official publishers' *Deutsches Bücher-Verzeichnis* (German Book Index) and presented its statistics in concrete terms through a detailed assessment of the practices of leading publishing houses (particularly as regards the size of editions). However, this form of analysis (in particular, the author's use of five-year time divisions) fails to account for the caesura of 1933 and the subsequent displacement to publishing houses outside the Reich. Absent, too, are those works which did not appear in *DVB*, or did so only sporadically, e.g. Theodor Fritsch's *Handbuch der Judenfrage*, which by 1939 had gone through forty-one imprints and 238,000 copies, and Hitler's *Mein Kampf*, of which by 1940 700,000 copies had been issued owing to state distribution measures. The author also fails at times to distinguish between the serious and the less serious, listing together with Mann's *Buddenbrooks* (1901; 999,000 copies) Alfred Hein's *Kurts Maler. Ein Lieblings-Roman des deutschen Volkes* (1922). This barely known book is in fact a parody of the writer Hedwig Courths-Mahler, and the number of copies (999,000) listed in Hein's book is part of the joke (only 1,000 copies were issued). The same mistake appears in the case of Hans Reimann's parody of Dinter, *Die Dinte wider das Blut. Ein Zeitroman von Artur Sünder*, where Richards again fails to perceive the parody in the information regarding editions and copies ('39th deranged and disordered edition, nos 640,000–643,000'). Reimann's parody first appeared in 1921 in an edition of 5,000, and then again in 1922 in an 'improved and expanded edition'. In that year total copies reached 20,000, and this figure probably increased in the following year.
2. *Gottfried Benn*, Ausstellungskatalog Marbach, 2nd rev. edn, 1986, p. 199.

reproached him) lent the movement considerable prestige. Yet in 1936 Benn was rejected, specifically on account of his *Selected Poems 1911–1936*, which consequently went unread.[3]

The case of Arnolt Bronnen presents a slightly different example. Bronnen described himself as a 'Fascist, but not *völkisch*'.[4] His novel *O.S.*, published in 1929, was the first 'literary attraction' of the militant nationalistic Right, and he became a protégé of Goebbels and the Strasser wing of the NSDAP (Nazi Party). However, as early as 1933 Bronnen was also rejected; in this case, on account of his expressionist past, his technical modernism and, above all, his militaristic orientation. An opposing paradigm is represented by Hans Grimm. His lengthy novel *Volk ohne Raum* (People without Room, 1926) was a minor success before 1933 since, despite its mediocre quality, it followed the tradition of the *Entwicklungsroman* (novel of personal development) beloved of the *Bildungsbürger* (educated bourgeois). It became a bestseller (seven impressions, 480,000 copies up till 1940)[5] only in the literary vacuum of the Third Reich, despite the fact that its cult of the small farmer, its sharp anti-English tendency and its advocacy of colonization stemmed from the *jungkonservativ* circle of Moeller van den Bruck rather than from National Socialism.

If one draws up a 'complete' list of Fascistic authors who, for whatever reasons, were 'attractive' to artistic or political elites or to the wider reading public – a list including, for instance, the later Stefan George, and Ernst Jünger and those around him such as Franz Schauwecker and Ernst von Salomon – it becomes even more conspicuous that there was not one 'Hitlerist' among them.

Of all Fascist movements, the NSDAP certainly had the worst relationship to literature. The strategy of 'legality' it followed after its re-formation in 1925 and its plebiscitary tactics limited its appeal to avant-garde intellectuals; on the contrary, from 1927 onward an affiliate called the Kampfbund für deutsche Kultur (League for the Protection of German Culture) was set up on the basis of opposition to modernism in the arts. The works of authors who belonged to, or were close to, the Hitler Party, such as Goebbels, Hans Zöberlein, Richard Euringer and Hans Heinz Ewers (*Horst Wessel*, late 1932) were so ideologized and so badly written that they had little impact on the public. There was indeed a relatively popular branch of NSDAP 'art', the marching songs for use by the

3. Ibid., p. 255.
4. *Arnolt Bronnen gibt zu Protokoll. Beiträge zur Geschichte des modernen Schriftstellers*, Berlin/Weimar, 1985, p. 255.
5. Richards, *The German Bestseller*, Table A.

Sturm-Abteilung (SA: Nazi storm-troops) and Hitler Youth, but here the text was of subsidiary importance; they served only an indirect propaganda function, 'a glimpse of order in a time of chaos, the impression of energy in an atmosphere of general hopelessness', as Speer wrote later in his memoirs.[6]

This incongruous relationship to literature existed already in the early phase of the NSDAP (from 1919 until the end of 1923). The movement's first poet, the Bavarian Dietrich Eckart (1868–1923), was as anti-modernist as he was anti-Communist and anti-Semitic. Although he produced for the party its first *Kampfgedicht* (poem of struggle) and its first newspaper, his poems never achieved success with the public after the seizure of power.

There was, however, one literary product of this earlier period which was unquestionably of a National Socialist character and which nevertheless achieved the status of a best-seller between 1918 and 1922, with some 200,000 copies being printed. The book was the *Zeitroman* (novel of contemporary society) *Die Sünde wider das Blut* (The Sin against the Blood) by Dr phil. nat. Artur Dinter. This chapter aims to present a closer examination of both this novel and its author. The material with which one is confronted is so repulsive that it is not surprising that until now research into Fascism has all but avoided it.[7] Yet such avoidance cannot be justified indefinitely, and to spare others this unpleasant task I shall attempt to discuss, with the necessary brevity, the whole of Dinter's *œuvre*, including his other *Zeitromane* and his political and religious writings. Their analysis is in any case essential to the investigation of National Socialism. Before proceeding to the novel itself I will present a short biography of the author by way of a reconstruction of the ideological and historical background to his work.[8]

Artur Dinter, born on 27 June 1876 in Mulhouse, Alsace and baptized a Catholic, was the son of a Prussian customs official who had emigrated after 1871. Following his secondary schooling in

6. Albert Speer, *Erinnerungen*, Ullstein-Taschenbuch, 1969, p. 34.
7. With the exception of the theological polemics of the 1930s and critical glosses from the immediate post-war years, the relevant literature mentions Dinter only in passing and without adequate knowledge of the subject. My own book, *Literatur und Ästhetik des deutschen Faschismus*, Berlin, 1983, also requires correction on p. 153 in this respect.
8. Dinter's biography has been compiled from his journal *Das Geistchristentum* (published from 1928, and quoted in the text as DG with volume and page number) and from the forewords and afterwords to his three *Zeitromane*: *Die Sünde wider das Blut*, Leipzig, 1918; *Die Sünde wider den Geist*, Leipzig, 1921; *Die Sünde wider die Liebe*, Part 1, Leipzig, 1922, and Parts 1 and 2, Leipzig, 1928 (cited in the text with the initials SwdB, SwdG, SwdL and page numbers).

Saargmünd, Dinter worked to support his studies, his aim at this point being to become a railway engineer. From about 1895 until 1900 he studied philosophy and natural sciences at Strasburg University, supported by a scholarship from the Kaiserliche Privatschatulle (Imperial Private Estate). In Dinter's own words, he was successful in 'the state examinations in chemistry, physics, botany, zoology, and in addition completed a doctorate in chemistry, physics and geology with *summa cum laude*' (SwdG, 236). Following his studies he worked as a senior secondary school teacher, as director of the Strasburg botanical school gardens, and for one year as an exchange teacher in Constantinople. He completed his military service and in 1904 took charge of the city theatre in Thann.

During these years Dinter published several scientific works, some at his own expense and some with Ludolf Beust in Strasburg, as well as an early epistolatory novel, *Jugenddrängen* (The Urges of Youth, 1897). While the book itself is insignificant, it introduces a theme recurrent in Dinter's later work and obviously based on the author's own traumatic experience: rejection by a woman who refuses to subject herself to the male's search for life and God. (Dinter's own late marriage in 1921 seems to have been preceded by two or three broken engagements.) More successful in terms of both financial return and public reception were a number of plays for the theatre written between 1904 and 1908. While this success was in the main limited to provincial productions, one piece in particular, the Alsatian 'dialect comedy' *D'Schmuggler* (The Smuggler), was produced in numerous theatres and translated into several languages, a version in High German being presented in the Berlin Schillertheater.

The theatre was obviously the means by which Dinter sought to establish himself in the Reich proper. After an appointment at the Rostock city theatre in 1906 he won a directorial position in Berlin in 1907, and in 1908 he founded, together with Heinrich Lilienfein and Max Dreyer, the Theatre Publishing House of the German Playwrights' Union, of which Dinter was also director. By this stage, the *völkisch* and anti-Semitic tendencies in his work had become clearly established. Using his own publishing house, Dinter attempted – for the most part in vain – to have accepted for performance not only his own work but also that of such writers as Eckart, Lienhard and Eberhard König.[9] He associated with writers in Thüringen such as Adolf Bartels (although scarcely, if at all, with the Weimar circle around Ernst Wachler, Peter Gast and the

9. Artur Dinter, *Weltkrieg und Schaubühne*, Munich 1916.

Nietzsche Archive), and above all with his Alsatian compatriot and senior by eleven years, Friedrich Lienhard. Although he and Lienhard quarrelled in 1920, prior to the war Dinter had often been a guest in the latter's home and in 1917 had taken over Lienhard's country house 'Waldesruhe' in Dörrberg, which he retained until 1945.

Dinter first made a real impact on the public with a 'demonstration' in June 1914. In the middle of a performance of Karl Vollmöller's comedy *Das Mirakel* (The Miracle), produced by Max Reinhardt in the Zirkus Busch, he stood up and embarked on a passionate, strongly anti-Semitic tirade against the theatrical and cultural scene in Berlin. The éclat found an echo in Karl Kraus's *Die Fackel*:

> Dr Dinter's protest is not directed against *Das Mirakel*, but against its performance in front of an audience of financiers rather than churchwardens. . . . He is concerned less with the text than with the disgrace of presenting such things as a titillation to a fashionable mob for whom 'It is finished' has been transformed into 'Let's get on with it.'[10]

But for Dinter the demonstration, which immediately cost him his directorship and later his membership in the Playwrights' Union,[11] was more than a protest: it marked his transition from an aesthetic to a religious-political existence. He took upon himself the role of reformer, which led gradually to a self-image as an anti-Semitic 'new Luther' and to the founding of a new church.

This mission found expression in his first *Tendenzroman* (directed novel), written during the war, and his post-war appearances as 'the first *völkisch* public speaker in Germany'. He was instrumental in the foundation of the Deutschvölkischer Schutz- und Trutzbund (German People's League of Self-Defence) and leapt to join the NSDAP at the first opportunity. 'When he first met Adolf Hitler in Munich in 1923 at a lecture on the Jewish Question', writes his Nazi biographer in 1928, 'he placed himself unconditionally at his disposal' (DG 1, 249). Unlike Ludendorff or Gregor Strasser, he remained faithful to Hitler during his imprisonment in Landsberg

10. *Die Fackel*, vol. 16, nos 400–3, 1914, p. 41. Also worthy of note are the lines on p. 60 which follow a long quotation from Theodor Haecker on Kierkegaard: 'Following these manly words, the attack by Dr Dinter on the *Mirakel* venture of Messrs Reinhardt and Vollmöller deserves a favourable mention, and the reaction of the professional circles which would call the man mad and then condemn him to unemployment – a contemptuous kick.'
11. Artur Dinter, *Mein Ausschluß aus dem Verbande Deutscher Bühnenschriftsteller*, Munich, 1916.

and founded a transitional organization on his behalf in Thuringia, 'the only state in Germany where, due to the representation of the National Socialists in the state parliament, the Hitler Party, under Dinter's leadership, was permitted'.[12] The re-established NSDAP was thus able to take over a stable *Gau* with 36 *Ortsgruppen*, and hold its own first Parteitag (Party Meeting) in the Weimar National Theatre in 1926. Dinter was honoured by his Führer with 'membership number 5' (DG 1, 364).

Dinter's messianic streak led in 1926, however, to the publication of '197 Theses on the Completion of the Reformation',[13] and the founding in November 1927 of his own Geistchristliche Religionsgemeinschaft (Spiritual Christian Religious Community). This was unacceptable to Hitler's *Realpolitik*, as it invited conflict with the churches, even though for Dinter it represented an expression of his loyalty. He was excluded from the party in a closed session of the next Parteitag (31 August to 2 September 1928 in Munich), in his absence and to his total consternation. (Hitler: 'The principal problem with which National Socialism must concern itself is that of state and *Volk*. Religion is least of all a National Socialist matter. Under no circumstances do founders of religions have a place in our movement' (DG 1, 273)). Dinter henceforth turned against Hitler while maintaining the fundamental convictions he had already expressed in March 1928: 'I am a National Socialist and have been one, as witnessed by my books, for a long time, even before the National Socialist Party existed, and I will remain a National Socialist until my dying breath!' (DG 1, 105). He declared Hitler first a clumsy strategist who far overestimated the power of the 'Jewish-Roman papal church' (DG 1, 214), and then a mere tactician who failed to perceive the necessity of a Christian/anti-materialist fundament. Finally, following the electoral success of the NSDAP in September 1930, he characterized the Fürer as one of the 'traitors' who had fallen in with the 'liberal-bourgeois-capitalist front' and who had abandoned 'one *völkisch* ideal after another': moral-religious renewal, anti-Semitism, socialism, the national revolution and now even 'the radical rejection of the Weimar system' (DG 3, 428ff.). At the same time Dinter sought contact with other Fascist groups and ideologues, opening the pages of his journal to groups such as Niekisch's *Widerstandskreis* (Resistance Circle), Ernst Jünger's *Kommenden* (The Vanguard) and Otto

12. Artur Dinter, *Ursprung, Ziel und Weg der deutsch-völkischen Freiheitsbewegung. Das völkisch-soziale Programm*, 1–5 tsd, Weimar, 1924.
13. Printed in DG 1, no. 7–8.

Strasser's *Revolutionäre Nationalsozialisten.* He even supported an alliance with Soviet Communism, which, as Trotsky's fate demonstrated, had become a 'Russian National Socialism' (DG 3, 440ff.).

Still shunned by the party,[14] he may well have been inwardly reconciled with his Führer after 1933, although his 'radical rejection of any kind of pogrom anti-Semitism' (DG 1, 315) may have led him to disapprove of the events following the Nuremberg Laws, if not of the laws themselves. In early 1945 he fled Thuringia before the approaching Russian army and died in Baden on 21 May 1948.

Dinter was a Nazi fundamentalist, a rigorous ideologue who envisaged an inner *völkisch* renewal and for whom 'politics, religion and race' represented 'an indissoluble unity' (DG 1, 66). The demonstration of June 1914, the first appearance of the avenging prophet in the temple, had been preceded by a 'spiritual rebirth' in 1913–14 (SwdB, 6), triggered by Houston Stewart Chamberlain's *Grundlagen des 19. Jahrhunderts* (The Roots of the Nineteenth Century) and his *Worte Christi* (Christ's Message). What emerged was an even more primitive blend of racist dogma combined with New Testament verses. 'Race is all!' reads the foreword to *Sünde wider das Blut*, and further: 'I owe my religion to my race, for only through my race is my religion possible' (SwdB, 6ff.).

For Dinter there was only one basic and decisive opposition: between Jews and Aryans. Jesus was, of course, like all his apostles but Judas (SwdB, 172), a pure Aryan, who attacked Judaism. For this he was crucified, and his message was perverted by the Jew Paul into a doctrine of sacrifice and redemption, his rejection of the Old Testament into its 'fulfilment'. As an Aryan, it was Dinter's task to cleanse both Old and New Testaments of un-Aryan additions.

The intellectual arbitrariness with which the reformer took to his task was unprecedented, surpassing by far Chamberlain's religious-historical and folk-historical speculations. Dinter rejected totally the few epistemological concepts with which his predecessor had sought to close the gap between the biologism of his racial theory

14. The Council of Evangelical Churches, which asked for some reassurance from the national leadership of the NSDAP before embarking on a polemic against Dinter, was informed by Rudolf Hess in March 1935 'that the claim that the so-called Dinter Movement is supported by the Führer and/or the party, is absolutely unfounded' (anonymous, quoted in Hans Beck, *Artur Dinters Geisteschristentum*, Berlin/Steglitz, 1935, p. 4).

and the idealism of his typology.[15] In their place Dinter, the 'all-round natural scientist', set an empiricism of the crassest kind, involving appeals to 'scientific results' and unrestricted analogies between material and intellectual processes. He repressed any fear of the Kantian critique of reason through a general attack on the neo-Kantians, 'a certain Jewish philosophical school' (SwdG, 45ff.). By way of this pseudo-scientific empiricism, Dinter sought the theological element he needed to make his mythology into a religion.

He found this element in spiritualism. 'While on convalescent leave' in winter 1914, Dinter was 'by chance present at a seance' (SwdG, 236) and was immediately convinced that 'here was *the* science of the future' (SwdG, 41). The *Geistlehre* (spiritual doctrine) he subsequently developed was based on the actual existence of pre- and extra-human spiritual entities. 'The whole cosmos is inhabited by spirits, some of which are embodied, some of which are not or are no longer embodied' (SwdG, 43). The elaboration of this doctrine produced a theology with many gnostic characteristics which attempted to amalgamate racism and Christianity.[16] It can be summarized as follows (SwdG, 103ff.).

God is spirit, self-conscious, personified spirit. In the beginning he created a world of pure and free-willed spirits, a world from which, through the Fall from Grace, emanated a number of gloomy and ever more inferior worlds. This process of degeneration culminated in the creation of the material cosmos. However, the *Urlicht* (primeval light) or *göttliche Urbewegung* (divine movement) remains inherent to matter itself and propels the progressive formation of crystal, plant, animal and human forms, thus setting in chain the resurrection of the spirits. The goal of this whole process is the return to God, the entry into the primeval light and thereby the dissolution of matter into spirit. 'This process of reversion has already begun in the present; the decay of matter observed in the radium phenomenon is nothing else but this' (SwdG, 113). Accordingly, every human life is also nothing else but a transitional stage in the resurrection of the spirits. 'The spirit of a lower sphere seeks out a particularly highly developed organism as its terrestrial

15. Günter Hartung, 'Houston Stewart Chamberlain's "Goethe"', in *Traditionssuche des deutschen Faschismus*, Wissenschaftliche Beiträge der Universität Halle 1983/30 (F 43), pp. 14ff.
16. In a review in 1928, Walter Benjamin made the far-sighted observation that 'every acute collision of the Christian world with the world of the *Völker*, the heathen, is signalled by a fierce flaring-up of gnostic speculation': *Gesammelte Schriften*, vol. III, p. 103.

abode', slips into the embryo and gives it a soul, since 'the soul is but the material garment of the spirit, which it already wore prior to its incarnation and which it retains after leaving the body and entering the purely spiritual state' (SwdG, 108). Thus results a permanent migration of souls through intermediate stages, guided and spurred on by 'higher spirits.'

In such a system, Jesus Christ clearly cannot be 'the way, the truth and the light'. He is given a position similar to that found in Origen:[17] 'Jesus is the only spirit created by God and incarnated on earth who never misused his free will to sin' (SwdG, 60). This system is then further applied to the racial question: 'In the Jews' – evidently a particularly low, animal-like 'bastard race' –

> are incarnated the evil and stubborn spirits which still rebel violently against the return to God and . . . constantly divert well-meaning human spirits on to the tortuous paths of the material world . . . It is the duty of every human being who becomes conscious of his eternal task to fight them and without mercy to renounce them and their kind with all the weapons of the spirit. Once humanity has been freed of the Jews, it will find the way back to God of itself. (SwdG, 60ff.)

The individual absurdities of Dinter's gnostic system hardly merit further mention. They are important in the present context only in so far as they indicate the nature of the system which provides a framework for the author's three *Zeitromane*, each novel dealing with a particular aspect of the system. It remains to be said that Dinter shied away from, or at least stopped short of, the Manichean and antinomian consequences suggested by his 'theology'. He neither believed – like Theodor Fritsch and the Ludendorffs – in an actually existing Antichrist,[18] nor promoted – like Lanz von Liebenfels and Hitler – the concept of a final apocalyptic battle. He also rejected the concept of eternal damnation: 'God, in his unending, all-compassionate love, has given even those of his most fallen children the possibility of the highest rapture. Their damnation, their hell, exists only in the separation from God' (SwdG, 43). These relics of Christian humanism no doubt underlay his opposition to 'pogrom anti-Semitism' and his insistence on a 'spiritual'

17. Protestant critics of Dinter often referred to this proximity to Origenes; see Beck, *Artur Dinters Geisteschristentum*, p. 9ff., or Hansgeorg Schroth, *Wider Dinters Mythus vom arischen Heiland*, Berlin, 1935, pp. 12ff.
18. The standard work of neo-Manichaean anti-Semitism, which certainly had a strong influence on Ludendorff, was Theodor Fritsch, *Der falsche Gott*, Leipzig, 1912.

and 'purely legal' solution to the 'Jewish question'.[19] Such sentiments, however, in no way lessened the fury of his *völkisch* anti-Semitic agitation up to 1933:

> To lead the spirit to victory over matter, and struggling humanity to its divine destiny: that was the goal God set himself when he created the Germans! . . . and in the Jewish race are incarnated, since time immemorial, those hellish powers which lead man away from God, and who . . . are constantly striving to block off the return of the struggling souls to their Father's house! (SwdB, 369)

With these words the hero of the novel *Die Sünde wider das Blut* ends a speech before the court, where he is on a charge of shooting a Jewish captain a few weeks before the outbreak of the war. To make the 'wider public' aware of the 'Jewish danger': this, and only this, was the motive for his deed. The defence counsel's strategy is to demonstrate that the hero's life has been 'systematically destroyed by the Jews' (SwdB, 351). This plan forms the structure of the novel; clearly, Dinter's own 'heroic act' of June 1914 serves as the vanishing point for an invented prehistory, the stations of a modern German 'Passion'.

At the beginning of the novel, the 30-year-old chemistry lecturer Dr Hermann Kämpfer (fighter, struggler) is about to discover the synthesis of protein. He lapses into memories of his father, a solid small farmer who was persuaded one Easter Sunday by the broker Levisohn to take over the repossessed estate of a neighbour and mortgage his own. His ruin and subsequent attack on Levisohn lead to gaol and suicide. Hermann's mother dies of grief, three younger brothers are scattered to the winds, sister Gretel is seduced and drowns herself, but Hermann studies chemistry with iron determination.

Awaking from his memories, Dr Kämpfer abandons his experiment (he later passes it on – forgetting to take out a patent – to his colleague Dr Siegfried Salomon, who exploits it) and heads for an 'international winter sport resort'. During carnival at the resort, the 'fair-haired student in the daring robber's costume' meets and falls in love with a 'strikingly attractive blonde' (SwdB, 70); at thirty, Hermann has never touched a girl in his life, and 'love was a stranger to him' (SwdB, 50). Elisabeth is the daughter of the Berlin businessman Burghamer (his real name is Hamburger!). After a skiing accident Hermann is driven by Burghamer ('His face,

19. Dinter, *Ursprung*, pp. 31ff. (point 6: 'The Solution to the Jewish Question').

framed by a big fur cap and the raised collar of his fur coat, had something diabolical about it' (SwdB, 65)) to his villa, where he meets Elisabeth again, and her blonde mother. ('Remarkable! All the people in this house had fair hair, except his host – even the servant.' (SwdB, 69)). Hermann solves in a trice a technical problem which has engaged Burghamer's staff for some time, and is offered a job. He takes over a factory in Berlin-Lichterfelde to be in easy reach of his beloved in Grunewald (an exclusive suburb). By dint of long lectures on Plato, Kant, Christ, New and Old Testaments, Jacob, Esau, Joseph in Egypt, the racial situation in Palestine and Galilee ('absolutely *judenrein*' (Jew free) in 150 BC; SwdB, 169), reincarnation, the spirit world and the longed-for 'new Luther' (SwdB, 179), he also wins the heart of the mother, a native of Schleswig-Holstein, and saves Elisabeth from a fancy for Baron von Werheim (alias Wertheim). Finally he marries her, despite the warnings of an inner voice, as Elisabeth hopes to find redemption through him. But 'the sensual desires of the young wife were so wild and uncontrolled that Hermann felt repelled by her' (SwdB, 225). Alas, he is unaware that her split nature, her dislike for the spiritual, 'her passionateness and sensuality, her wanton hunger for pleasure' are only the 'curse of the sin against the blood to which she owes her existence' (SwdB, 187). The moment of truth comes with the birth of their child: 'A dark-skinned object, its head covered with jet-black, tangled hair, scarcely human, screamed at him. Deep, dark eyes, with a kind of bluish shimmer, looked at him out of an ancient past from under long black eyelashes. A flat, squashed nose gave the face something of a monkey's (SwdB, 238).

The obstetrician, Hermann's encyclopaedias and the narrator explain to us that this is a case of atavism, pointing back to the animal world and the negro, as 'according to the latest research' the Jews came from Africa (SwdB, 238ff.). Hermann fails to understand this, and as Elisabeth thinks an indiscretion with Baron von Werheim may be to blame, they decide to have a second child. Before it is born, however, Burghamer dies (his boudoir full of blonde women). His papers yield appalling revelations. In order to forestall a German victory in the coming war, 'which is to make Jewish capital the dominant influence in Germany' (SwdB, 216), he and von Werheim have been systematically undermining the German race. He has founded 'blonde brothels' in all major cities, subsidized newspapers, and bribed journalists and expressionists to sing the praises of racial admixture. These revelations are too much for Elisabeth. She suffers a miscarriage; a 'pretty, dark Jew-child' emerges, only to perish with his mother soon afterwards.

Hermann now begins his campaign against Berlin and all that it stands for in earnest, devotes his inheritance of 100 million marks to the anti-Semitic cause, and founds a society for 'race research and hygiene', which admits only those who can prove that even their great-grandparents included no converts (SwdB, 296). Hermann's upbringing of his son Heinrich is disturbed by the fruit of a sin of youth: eight years before, it now appears, he had spent a night of love with Röschen Brunner, the daughter of his laboratory attendant, but had broken with her and left her letters unanswered, so that she had to bring up their son on her own till she died in poverty. The two boys now grow up together and show their opposite natures in everything. Finally, during a boat trip on the Wannsee, Heinrich, who is of course a non-swimmer, falls into the water and drags his half-brother and their tutor down into the depths with him.

But Kämpfer's last ordeal at the hands of the Jews still awaits him, before his ruin is complete. He meets a nurse, a 'well-built, blue-eyed, blonde mature woman' of thirty. '"She should be the mother of your children", was his first thought' (SwdB, 343), and he pursues it despite her revelation that years ago she had been seduced and borne a child. After nine months, alas, there appears 'a child with black curly hair, dark skin and dark eyes, a true Jew-child. Hermann roared like a fatally wounded bull when he saw it. "Whore!", he screamed at his wife.' The narrator adds a comment: 'It is an important racial law, well known from animal breeding, that a female of good stock is rendered permanently incapable of producing throroughbred offspring if she is once fertilized by a male of poor stock' (SwdB, 349). Hermann has seen the light; he searches out the seducer and kills him. On his return he finds two more corpses; his wife has taken her life and that of the child 'with morphine. The syringe was still sticking in her chest, near the heart' (SwdB, 350). The court acquits him of murder; those who hasten to congratulate him see in him the long-wished-for 'Führer' who will take up the fight against 'these traitors, poisoners of the *Volk*' (SwdB, 367ff.).

The novel is framed by a foreword, in which Dinter describes the development of his *Weltanschauung* (ideology), and an afterword, which contains a virtually complete annotated bibliography of 'scientific anti-Semitism' which Hitler was fond of consulting. The lectures and demonstrations included in the body of the novel make it clear that the author was exclusively concerned with the propagation of his doctrine and that he chose the form of the popular thriller only for 'psychological-propagandistic reasons' (DG 1, 71).

According to Dinter, he began the book in 1916 and completed it in 1917, either in military hospital (DG 1, 128) or in his Dörrberg country house (SwdB, 7). Following refusals from six publishers, including J. F. Lehmann (who rejected the novel only on grounds of form) and the *Staatsbürgerzeitung*, an unknown 'young beginner' risked a first edition of 1,000 copies for which Dinter himself bore the printing costs (DG 1, 128). A second edition of 4,000 copies, published by a certain Wolfverlag Leipzig, appeared at the end of 1918, likewise without attracting much response. This name concealed a subsidiary publishing concern established in the last year of the war which, obviously because of censorship restrictions, distributed its wares only by prepaid registered postage. However, in February 1919 the owner, Erich Fürchtegott Matthes, following the formation of a partnership with William Oskar Thost and the establishment of a branch firm in Hartenstein, changed the company's name to the more neutral Verlag Matthes und Thost, Leipzig and Hartenstein. Under this flag the novel began its rise to prominence in the latter half of 1919.[20] (There are other interesting features of the Verlag Matthes und Thost. Emerging from the youth movement, the publishing house was established in 1913 and until 1923–4 operated successfully as a *völkisch*-oriented publisher without party political allegiances. It was responsible, among other things, for collecting the successful *völkisch* literature of middle and north Germany and for the German edition of Gobineau's collected works. And yet it modestly withheld the name of its most successful author – and doubtless the source of its prosperity – from all official advertisements and prospectuses.) Between 1920 and 1921 the novel went from seven to fifteen impressions, the last one taking the total copies produced from 146,000 to 170,000; 1922 saw the culmination of the book's success and sales subsequently began to wane. In 1927, with an edition published by Dinter's old friend Ludolf Beust in Leipzig, the total number of copies climbed from 230,000 to 235,000;[21] and in 1934, with the anti-Semitic Hammer publishing house, from 251,000 to 260,000. This last edition, however, was presumably still in stock when the Leipzig publish-

20. For an account of the history of the Matthes Verlag, see the German version of this chapter in *Traditionen und Traditionssuche des deutschen Faschismus*, Sonderheft 'The Attractions of Fascism', Martin Luther University Halle/Wittenberg, Halle (Saale) 1988, pp. 79–81.

21. Not included in Richards, *The German Bestseller*. According to Dinter's report on January 1930 (DG 3, 36), a 'fully revised edition' of SwdB (taking the total copies from 246,000 to 250,000) had just appeared. However, since this edition had virtually no reception, I have not included it in the following discussion.

ing quarter was destroyed in the war.

The critical reaction, in so far as it can be reconstructed, is revealing. In the case of the assimilated Jewish *Centralvereins-Zeitung* and the communist *Volk* from Jena, it was strongly negative (DG 1, 105). So too was that of the social democratic *Dresdener Volkszeitung*, against which Dinter even brought an unsuccessful defamation suit, Thomas Mann acting as one of the paper's witnesses.[22] The racialist camp showed considerable reserve;[23] the major newspapers were silent; only a few small *völkisch* papers seem to have dared to praise the book (DG 1, 105ff.). Obviously the novel's success lay outside the literary scene: Dinter speaks in November 1922 of 'many thousands of readers' letters' which 'still reach him daily, even from Australia' (!) (SwdL 1922, 320). Typical of them, perhaps, is one from a primary teacher in Zobten, who was given the book by a friend: 'Clarity at last! . . . Now rest and peace have entered my heart' (DG 1, 43). Also revealing is the contribution of the poet, translator and racist ideologue Otto Hauser, a Hungarian-German resident in Vienna who stayed in Thuringia before the war and between 1920 and 1923, publishing with Alexander Duncker in Weimar.[24] In 1922, during a 'summer walking tour' through middle Germany, he made contact with a large number of young people, both in organized youth groups and otherwise. In the account *Ursel Unbekannt* (Ursula Unknown), published soon after, Hauser's eager adoption of Dinter's *Entrassungs-These* (thesis regarding the degradation of race) is notable, as are the still more ridiculous arguments with which he seeks to support it wherever possible (in the woman of a higher race, a chemical change takes place through coitus with a lower race, 'just as an indigo[!]-coloured solution is turned red by the addition of a drop of acid'[25]). Even more remarkable is Hauser's report of meeting many young people with a knowledge of the book and expressing tentative agreement with its thesis.[26] On reading the novel in 1920, the then 19-year-old Heinrich Himmler, a member of the right-

22. Thomas Mann, *Aufsätze. Reden. Essays*, vol. 3, Berlin/Weimar, 1986, p. 279, and notes, p. 787.
23. A good indication is provided by Dinter's series of *Xenien* (epigrams) on 'true prophets' and 'false prophets' (DG 1, 180ff.), where the theorist of racial hygiene Fritz Lenz appears together with the 'false prophets' Lienhard, Keyserling, Anni Besant, Steiner, Peter Muckermann and Spengler. (The 'true prophets' are Fritsch, A. Bartels, Chamberlain, Hitler, D. Eckart and Luther.)
24. For information on Otto Hauser see Friedrich Heer, *Der Glaube des Adolf Hitler*, Munich/Esslingen, 1968, passim.
25. Otto Hauser, *Ursel Unbekannt. Ein Wandersommer*, Weimar, 1922, p. 58.
26. Ibid., pp. 57ff.

wing Freikorps, reacted similarly and found himself 'in a blind rage of hatred for the Jews'.[27]

The novel was read and discussed mainly in the years between the Versailles Treaty (June 1919) and the great inflation, in a period when large sections of the declassed middle strata and the bourgeois youth were seeking causes and scapegoats for the German collapse. (The same period is marked by the growth of *völkisch* anti-Semitic agitation and the growth of Hitler's NSDAP.) Its audience was restricted entirely to readers of German, at home and abroad; there is no trace of reactions from speakers of other languages, and no suggestion of plans for translation. Obviously, too, the audience was not a cultured one. The literary weaknesses of the novel – the schematic plot, the didactic 'inlays', the absurd contradictions in character development, especially of the hero – were far too evident and repulsive. The briefly and brutally narrated 'surprises' with which the action is laced often border on the unintentionally comic, as Hans Reimann's parody, *Die Dinte wider das Blut. Ein Zeitroman von Artur Sünder* (1921–2; 20,000 copies) was quick to demonstrate.[28] Thomas Mann also attacked the book in the strongest

27. Josef Ackermann, *Heinrich Himmler als Ideologe*, Göttingen/ Zürich/Frankfurt, 1970, p. 26.
28. See note 1 for bibliographic details. As evidence there follow a few examples, which can easily be related to my summary of the plot. 'When Levisohn appeared again on the following Sunday, the deal was finalized. The blood-suffused pupils of the usurer Jew lit up with malicious glee. The debts grew endlessly. The new farm building burnt down two days before the fire insurance came into effect, since Father did not have the money to pay the premium. Whooping cough broke out amongst the cattle, erysipelas amongst the poultry, the horses fell down like maggots, Mother pined away, a thunderstorm devastated the barren fields, Father contracted gall-stones and, deathly sick, had to travel to Karlsbad. All this was the work of the greedy Jew' (1st edn, p. 11). 'An elderly gentleman came along in his new Mercedes and gave [Hermann] a lift. He introduced himself in return as *Kommerzienrat* [business consultant] Brodelmann. His face, framed by a big fur cap and lightly padded pigskin muffs, had something diabolical about it. Under the greenly shimmering eyebrows lurked a pair of protruding lids. From the pores of his ugly, contorted forehead grew a kind of grey undergrowth, while his unkempt moustache fluttered in long rats' tails over his protuberant negro mouth, and undulated in bleary strands over his pustular cheeks . . . An inner voice, aided by the vinegar poultices Hermann had prescribed for himself, held him back from fulfilling his promise to visit the *Kommerziernrat* at his villa.' (1st edn, pp. 16ff.) It is also worth pointing out that in the last version of Reimann's parody, in which the hero is called Dr Hermann Stänker, some information on Dinter's quite mysterious wartime activities seems to have been included: 'Hermann the Stinker volunteered as an inspector for the Helgoland tramways and wangled, like not a few others, a voluntary deportation to Sachsen as permanently fit only for garrison duty . . . When the war gave out and made way for revolution . . . he made a rapid adjustment to the new situation, false and ambiguous as it was,

possible terms: 'Poetically without any worth whatsoever, and with no aspirations in this direction, the book, through its combination of half-truth and virulent falsification, constitutes an intellectual threat. To counter the wide circulation borne by popular currents which it has achieved, I find excusable even the most severe forms of defence.' (The withering presentation of anti-Semitism in the chapter 'The Great Irritation' in *The Magic Mountain* (1924) undoubtedly refers back to this critique of Dinter. Moreover, large sections of the Joseph tetralogy can only be fully comprehended as historically located texts when one reads them in terms of Mann's 'forms of defence' against Dinter's vulgar, anti-Semitic exploitation of the Old Testament.)

The social strata reached by the novel can be roughly characterized as the lower and middle urban and rural classes, excluding the industrial proletariat on the one hand and the *haute bourgeoisie* and the nobility on the other. Dinter's term *Volksroman* is directed at this target group, but it also determines the content of the novel, which confronts a chemist who comes from a rural background with the world of financiers, *nouveaux riches*, aristocrats and officers of Jewish descent; the attempt to mobilize resentment against the 'posh', the war profiteers and the speculators is obvious. It is probably the first effective presentation of the Fascist opposition of the *Volk* against the greedy capitalists or plutocrats, and this is no doubt the reason why other anti-Semitic novels of the period of no lesser literary 'quality' were denied its success, as they were set in the *milieu* of the old aristocracy.[29]

These social impacts were consciously linked to emotional ones. Sexual repressions which the author shared with many of his bourgeois readers were expressed and addressed in the novel by offering the reader a vicarious gratification in images of the immoral life of the rich. This stops short of pornography, which

---

adopted a monocle, took to backstairs anti-Semitism, and still plagues us today with his unwelcome ranting' (Hans Reimann, *Von Karl May bis Max Pallenberg in 60 Minuten*, Munich, 1923, p. 43).

29. Freiherr Egon von Kapherr, *Im Netz der Kreuzspinne*, Weimar, 1921. This novel is set amongst the *Junkers* east of the Elbe, somewhere in East Prussia, and merits a closer reading on the grounds that – appealing to 'Master Haeckel' (p. 145) – it presents, with some system and not without artistic talent, a series of parallels between the process of natural selection and Social Darwinism. A description of the consequences of Jewish intermarriage (pp. 325ff.) contains a clear allusion to Dinter, 'The sin against the blood found its punishment here too'; and soon afterwards, referring to the November revolution, 'Juda had triumphed and the spirit of Yahweh ruled in the world.' See also *Rasse?*, a novel by Erich Kühn, Munich, 1921, which describes how a Jew makes use of the sinful pleasures of the city to destroy a Bavarian landed aristocratic family.

censorship would have forbidden, but constantly creates a 'sexual milieu', determined by Jews. Sexual activity appears as Jewish, indulged in less for erotic than for racial reasons. The really new, dangerous and destructive element in the novel is perhaps the constant interaction of social demagogy and pseudo-scientific empiricism in the sexual sphere. The anti-Semitic elements of the 'pre-history' (drawn from *deutschsozial* agitation of the 1880s and 1890s) and of the scientist subplot (fuelled by the widespread fear of competition) are conventional and relatively realistic in comparison with the 'new' elements making up the main action. Admittedly, these are opportunistic inventions or speculations of the author, from the improbable protein synthesis to 'atavism' and the crazy 'breeding theory', which even then could have been demolished by high school students with their wits about them. Their effect depends, however, on being embedded in commentaries by the narrator, which make shameless use of the suggestive diction of 'science'. It was thus not so much the theses themselves which were new and effective – the notion of *Entrassung* (racial degradation) through coitus, for example, could already be found in mythological guise in the work of the Austrian Lanz von Liebenfels – as their superficial support through the authority of the natural sciences. As Hauser observes, it was precisely this aspect which impressed the semi-educated.

A brew of this kind can preoccupy the reading public for a while, but in the long run it will only attract readers who are already inwardly convinced and need only the confirmation of an 'authority'. In this contrast between breadth and depth of reception, *Die Sünde wider das Blut* belongs to an international tradition of 'revelations', such as Leo Taxil's attack on the Freemasons (*Le diable au XIX siècle* (The Devil in the Nineteenth Century), 1893–4), or the texts that formed the basis for the production in Tsarist Russia of the *Protocols of the Elders of Zion*. Eventually, only radical ideologues and ideologized sects can believe in the truth of the material.

In Dinter's case, the Hitler circle in the leadership of the NSDAP formed such a group, as is evidenced by the words of the Nazi Julius Kaufmann in 1928: 'It [the novel] was, in the truest sense, the originator and the fanfare of today's *völkisch* movement. The literary and scientific achievements of anti-Semitic racial literature since the war are based on the model of this stirring book' (DG 1, 240).

Dinter himself rediscovered, and claimed credit for, many of his theses in Eckart's posthumous tract *Bolshevism from Moses to Lenin*, and in *Mein Kampf* (1924) (DG 1, 71). The justice of these claims can be seen in sentences of Hitler's such as: 'The black-haired Jew-boy, with a look of satanic glee, stalks the innocent girl, to violate her with his blood and rend her from her people.'[30] It is by no means an exaggeration to see Dr phil. nat. Artur Dinter as the intellectual source of the 'Aryan Clause' and the first of the Nuremberg Laws, 'For the Protection of German Blood and German Honour'.

A brief summary will suffice to deal with the other novels, in terms of both breadth and depth. The second, *Die Sünde wider den Geist* (The Sin against the Spirit), was completed in Pomerania in 1920 and was published by Matthes and Thost at the beginning of 1921 in an impression of 50,000, which sold out within a year. A larger subsequent impression (19th–20th), which took the total copies from 56,000 to 100,000, seems to have remained for the most part unsold.[31] Evidently the book appealed only to specialized circles, and disappointed the wider readership of *Sünde wider das Blut.* This is hardly surprising since, unlike the earlier work, the second book is not a *Thesenroman* (thesis novel) but rather functions simply as a makeshift vehicle for Dinter's 'spiritual' doctrine, presented in the form of a sermon given alternately by a chief engineer (!) experienced in spiritualism and by a tutelary spirit from a higher sphere – the *Segenbringer* (beneficent one). Dinter must have educated himself thoroughly in the field of occult beliefs in order to be able to convince not only his hero, a baron and fighter pilot named Armin von Hartenegg, but also readers not already biased towards such notions: '"Do you want to tell us your name now?" "Yes!" "Well then!" The table spelt out the name "Rolf". Hartenegg could hardly control himself. "Are you Rolf, my dear old Rolf?" he asked. Instead of answering, the table slowly moved towards Hartenegg [who was sitting outside the 'chain'] and nestled itself with gentle movements against him' (SwdG, 33).

Hartenegg has contemplated suicide continually since July 1919, when 'dishonourable Germans, bewildered by foreign seducers and exploiters to the point of madness, established the Republic and agreed to this ignominious and disgraceful peace' (SwdG, 10). He is awakened from his morbidity when he finds his life's task in preaching the *Geistlehre* (spiritual doctrine). Here *Sünde wider den Geist* presents the novel's female character, a young aristocrat whom Hartenegg saves from drowning and who – although then a blacksmith's daughter – had already been married to him 600 years

30. Adolf Hitler, *Mein Kampf*, Munich, 1942 (copies 727,000–731,000), p. 357.
31. Not included in Richards, *The German Bestseller.*

before. Now, as then, she fails to summon the necessary humility to subordinate herself to the male and his task, 'to take heart from him, as the weak vine climbs upwards on the stronger oak' (SwdG, 208).

The protagonist's experiences in the third novel, *Die Sünde wider die Liebe* (The Sin against Love), are equally unhappy. The hero in this case in Dr Helmut Schwertfeger, an Alsatian tutor in the house of a Pomeranian noble. Set in the revolutionary period, the novel is again overloaded with treatises. Along with his concept of German Christianity, Dinter presents his 'social ideas'. Before, during and after the storming of the castle by incited rural workers, Schwertfeger proclaims: 'This working entrepreneurial capital, which constantly creates new value, is not the enemy of the worker, but rather his friend, because it constantly provides the worker with new possibilities for income. Thus it provides him with the opportunity to save, to become independent and, if he is efficient and hard-working, to make himself into an entrepreneur.' On the other hand, 'bank and stockmarket capital creates no new, healthy value out of generated work . . . whips and subjugates the entrepreneur as well as the worker . . . and is almost exclusively in the hands of the Jews'. And, in regard to rural labour: 'The aim which, whether conscious or unconscious, is in the blood of every one of you – because you are Germans and not Jews – is only to be realized through *the collective work of the whole German Volk* . . . under the sign of Christian brotherly love' (SwdL 1922, 44ff., 48ff.).

Here the speaker presents a postulate which casts long historical shadows, reaching to the gates of Buchenwald (and which strikingly proves the critical justice of Brecht's epilogue to the *Dreigroschenroman* (Threepenny Novel), 'Das Pfund der Armen' (The Talent of the Poor):

> Christ taught that each should use the talent which the Lord God has lent him . . . taught the genuine, the true communism . . . which exists in the healthy, organic organization of human society . . . that genuine communism which our Prussian king and our Bismarck saw as the highest aim of the state and which is summarized in the words: *suum cuique* – to each his own. (SwdL 1922, 52)

Although such 'national socialist' programmes had been developed earlier and more skilfully by other Fascist ideologues, one can nevertheless understand why Hitler did not reject Dinter gladly. It was however inevitable, as the 'new Luther' endangered any working arrangement with the churches. For it was precisely the churches which Dinter attacked in *Die Sünde wider die Liebe*.

Part 1 of the novel was published in 1922 by Matthes and Thost in an edition of 25,000, which was almost unavailable by 1927, when the disputes with the Nazi leadership began. In the following year Dinter wrote the second part, which, apart from the story of a foiled marriage and Schwertfeger's decision to establish a church, contains a number of interesting arguments with Nietzsche and atheism. An enlarged edition was published by Ludolf Beust in 1928 – bringing the total number of copies to 30,000 – without provoking the slightest public response.

Dinter still had plans to develop his 'spiritual doctrine' further, and 'in a novel about Jesus, *The Hero of Nazareth* . . . to present the life of the Saviour through the shining light of this doctrine' (SwdG, 244). Fortunately, this *opus* was spared us.

–7–

Theatre and the French Right in the 1920s and 1930s

Nostalgia for 'un chef fort et autoritaire'

ALAN CHAMBERLAIN

By its nature theatre is often conservative in artistic form, but always powerfully immediate in political and social terms. The period from 1919 to 1939 in France is no exception. This was an unstable period in French history, seeing the progressive weakening of the Third Republic, the rise of the Communist Party, the wide popularity of the monarchist Action Française, and political and financial scandals. It was a period of great divisions, which culminated in the violent riots of February 1934 and a political decline which ended in the débâcle of June 1940.

Many plays which are today totally forgotten provoked strong political controversy at the time. The kings, emperors, dictators and other political leaders who strutted the Parisian stage during these years were seen in the political context of the time, sometimes with surprising results. Leaders from French history, such as Napoleon I, were contemplated with nostalgia by the Right and vilified as tyrants by the Left.[1] Other historical figures such as Machiavelli and Savonarola were actualized,[2] and fictional leaders such as Jules Romains's dictator Denis fed the political debate of the time:[3] should the security and stability of France remain in the

The detailed descriptions of events during performances, and public reactions to the plays, are taken from the collections of press reports on each play held in the Fonds Rondel, Bibliothèque de l'Arsenal, Paris.

1. Paul Raynal, *Napoléon unique*, Paris, 1937 (performed for the first time at the Théâtre de la Porte-Saint-Martin, 10 November 1936).
2. Alfred Mortier, *Machiavel*, Paris, 1931 (Théâtre des Arts, 18 September 1931); Armand Salacrou, *La Terre est ronde*, Paris, 1945 (Théâtre de l'Atelier, 7 November 1938).
3. Jules Romains, *Le Dictateur*, Paris, 1959 (Comédie des Champs-Elysées, 5 October 1926).

hands of the Third Republic, or should the nation seek 'un chef fort et autoritaire' ('a strong and authoritarian leader')[4] who would unite it and strengthen it against the rising tide of authoritarianism?

Although most of the numerous plays with kings as the main character were not overtly political, they were often given political significance by critics and the public.[5] This was largely because France was in the unique position of having a monarchist party, the Action Française, as the principal anti-parliamentary opposition. The monarchists were not amused at the continuation of the nineteenth-century tradition of demystifying monarchs on the stage, depicting them as ordinary middle-class people. These *rois bourgeois* were variously shown as weak and incompetent family heads dominated by their wives, or as naive geriatrics, invalids or lunatics, sometimes appearing in nightshirt and slippers. The peak (or rather the depths) of this demystification is reached in Saint-Georges de Bouhélier's *Roi-Soleil* (The Sun King, 1938),[6] where in one scene Louis XIV enters adjusting his dress, having just risen from his *chaise percée* (commode).

This *embourgeoisement* of the monarch was not lost on Lucien Dubech, the well-known critic of the official monarchist daily *L'Action Française*, who railed against the *bonhomie imbécile*[7] of Louis-Philippe in Louis Verneuil's enormously successful *Vive le roi!* (Long Live the King!, 1935)[8] and dismissed Paul Fort's depiction of a deranged *Ysabeau* (1924) with the comments: 'Paul Fort's play not good. Not true. All mad.'[9]

These bourgeois kings had the effect of reassuring a nervous Republic that the days of the monarchy were gone. Kings were just ordinary people, and had no more right to political power than Monsieur Dupont. Of course, the French bourgeoisie was equally nervous about Communism, and François Porché's *Tsar Lénine* (1931)[10] was an obvious attempt to depict the Bolshevik leader as

4. Sacha Guitry, *Histoires de France*, Paris, *L'Illustration*, 1929 (Théâtre Pigalle, 7 October 1929).
5. More than twenty such plays were performed in Paris during the 1920s and 1930s: Fonds Rondel, Bibliothèque de l'Arsenal.
6. Saint-Georges de Bouhélier, *Le Roi-Soleil*, Paris, *L'Illustration*, 1938 (Théâtre de l'Odéon, 13 April 1938).
7. *L'Action Française*, 7 November 1935.
8. Louis Verneuil, *Vive le roi!*, Paris, *L'Illustration*, 1936 (Théâtre de l'Odéon, 25 October 1935).
9. Paul Fort, *Ysabeau*, Paris, *L'Illustration*, 1924 (Théâtre de l'Odéon, 16 October 1924); *L'Action Française*, 26 October 1924.
10. François Porché, *Tsar Lénine*, Paris, 1932 (Théâtre de l'Atelier, 27 October 1931).

an ordinary (that is middle-class) human being as well as powerful political leader. Even the stage directions indicate that Lenin's house should be a *maison bourgeoise*. He is shown as a loving husband with a devoted and dedicated wife. In the first scene, the curtain rises on Lenin's mother-in-law knitting in the lounge room. Her son-in-law has just brought her a bouquet of lilacs!

Politically, the play attempts to be even-handed; Porché condemns the tyranny and corruption of the Tsarist regime in Act 1, and shows the 'oppression and terror' of the 'gravedigger Tsar Lenin' in the third and last act. As might be expected, reaction to the play was more political than aesthetic. According to the critic from *Le Temps*, Lenin's entry on stage was greeted with oohs and aahs of horror and enthusiasm.[11] The right-wing press wanted to know why such as 'odious' character was allowed on stage, and the socialist *Le Monde* found the first two acts 'honest' and the third act full of 'outright lies'.[12] Following an article in *L'Humanité*, Communist groups tried to interrupt several performances.

In Saint-Georges de Bouhélier's *Le Sang de Danton* (The Blood of Danton, 1931),[13] a large-scale production to which the Comédie Française devoted the greater part of its efforts for the 1930–1 season, the theme of middle-class values is again presented. This time Danton (here a good family man) and even Robespierre are depicted as political moderates who know where to stop but who are swept away and destroyed by a revolution they have begun – a revolution which is led to tyranny and destruction by the intransigent extremist Saint-Just. Writing about this play, Maurice Martin du Gard declared that the France of 1931 had only one passion – stability. France, he said, was a nation of conservatives who loved talking about revolution: 'The French public likes plays about revolution, whilst hating revolutionary plays. In revolutionary drama, it is for those who stopped on the way.'[14]

This theme of moderation versus extremism is also present in two of the most overtly political plays of the period, Jules Romains's *Le Dictateur* (The Dictator, 1926)[15] and Drieu la Rochelle's *Le Chef* (The Leader, 1934).[16] Although not without literary and dramatic qualities, both plays were relatively unsuccessful. They

11. *Le Temps*, 29 October 1931.
12. *Le Monde*, 7 November 1931.
13. Saint-Georges de Bouhélier, *Le Sang de Danton*, Paris, *L'Illustration*, 1931 (Comédie Française, 3 June 1931).
14. *Les Nouvelles Littéraires*, 13 June 1931.
15. See note 3.
16. Pierre Drieu la Rochelle, *Le Chef*, Paris, 1944 (Compagnie Pitoëff, 1934).

were in fact ahead of their time, their political *engagement* being more suited to the 1940s and 1950s. The public of the 1920s and 1930s clearly preferred the banalities of Saint-Georges de Bouhélier's bourgeois monarchs and, like the Hollywood of the 1950s, demanded romance and a happy ending even when political theses were broached.

Fascist overtones are present in both plays, most obviously in *Le Chef*. Drieu la Rochelle's leader Jean is a leader of the 'revolutionary Right' of the quasi-fictional republic of Macedonia. His party is composed largely of the disillusioned young veterans of a disastrous and bloody war. Jean describes its aims thus: 'We have to build the tower of our despair and our pride. In the sweat and blood of all classes we will build a fatherland, the like of which has never been seen before.'[17]

Jules Romains's dictator, Denis, is a more pragmatic leader. He seizes absolute power to restore order in the country, so that people will be fed, the post office will function, the streets will be lit. 'Il faut que les trains partent' says Denis, reminding us of the apologists for Mussolini and Hitler: 'At least they made the trains run on time!'

Both plays oppose conflicting political ideas through two characters: Féréol and Denis in *Le Dictateur*, and Michel and Jean in *Le Chef*. In both plays the two are close friends in a revolutionary party at the beginning and implacable enemies at the end: Féréol is arrested by Denis, and Michel is wounded trying to assassinate Jean. However, the form of the plays and their precise ideological conflict are quite different. *Le Chef* is a straight *pièce de théâtre engagé* (politically committed play), dramatically similar to works such as Sartre's *Les mains sales* (Dirty Hands, 1948) and *L'Engrenage* (The Chain of Events, 1948) although espousing a quite different ideology.

Jean's party, composed largely of veterans from the regiment he led during the war (*la Brigade des Idiots*), is 'the' party, which will 'swallow up all the others'. Its militants are 'soldiers' and 'heroes' who believe that the only salvation is in political action, no matter where it may lead: 'We don't know what we're going to do, but we're going to do something.'[18] 'We'll know who we are when we see where we've been.'[19] The overriding objective is to build a strong *patrie* (fatherland). It will be 'a block of steel, a magnet',[20]

17. *Le Chef*, p. 211.
18. Ibid., p. 205.
19. Ibid., p. 205.
20. Ibid., p. 211.

which will draw other nations to it and unite Europe, by force if necessary, and then go on to conquer the world. The sadistic Léon, leader of Jean's shock troops, puts the ideology more bluntly: 'We say "shit" to humanity.'[21] For Léon, Jean is the perfect political leader: 'You know what a leader is? A friend who kicks you in the bum!'[22]

Jean is a cynical, militaristic tyrant, the sort of leader who, according to Drieu la Rochelle's message, is not really desirable, but who inevitably rises when what he calls 'the elite' of a country is weak. This elite is defined in the play as *les chefs* (the leaders) of all the social groups in a country: the aristocrats, the army, the intellectuals, the capitalists and the workers. In other words, Drieu la Rochelle seems to be opposing two types of Fascism: a corporatist model, of which he seems to approve; and a less desirable militaristic model built around a personality cult (being the leader of Macedonia, Jean sees himself as a new Alexander the Great). Nevertheless, the militaristic model may be appropriate at certain periods in history: Michel, 'the last republican', who puts the interest of the people ahead of that of the state, 'was right yesterday, he will be right tomorrow.' But, says Jean, 'I'm right today.'[23]

Jules Romains, on the other hand, presents a complex political fresco in *Le Dictateur*, attempting to analyse all the elements in a political system which lead to dictatorship. He tries to show the relativity of moral judgements in politics. Denis is the leader of a revolutionary party in a monarchy. The King, seeing that he cannot stop Denis, makes him Prime Minister, thus separating him from his party and his friend Féréol.

Denis and Féréol represent another pair of opposing political doctrines. Féréol is the idealist for whom there can be only 'the' revolution, democratic and socialist. For him, failure and death are preferable to compromise. Denis is a pragmatist who wants 'a' revolution, one that will succeed – and one that will bring him to power. Once in power, he tries to convince his revolutionary colleagues, particularly Féréol, to join him. Féréol refuses and calls a general strike. Reluctantly, for the sake of maintaining order and for the 'good' of the nation, Denis dissolves Parliament and crushes the revolt. Féréol is arrested and the trains start running again.

At no point does *Le Dictateur* present an overtly Fascist ideology, although it was hardly the sort of play to find favour with true

21. Ibid., p. 211.
22. Ibid., p. 228.
23. Ibid., p. 264.

democrats. Indeed, *Le Dictateur* was seen as fascist by some: 'Although the author has shown himself quite openly to be a socialist, the play is obviously fascist.'[24] Of course, much of Romains's previous work did little to dispel the notion that he was at least interested in Fascist-like ideas. His well-known social theory of *unanimisme* stated that societies have a collective conscience, even a collective will, which can be represented by a single leader. This theory was best illustrated in the 1920 play *Cromedeyre-le-vieil* (Old Cromedeyre).[25] Cromedeyre is a village built out of a single piece of rock and where all the inhabitants think and act like a single person. Led by a heroic chief, Emmanuel, this *patrie de roc* (nation of stone) emerges from a period of decadence and dominates all the villages surrounding it.

Later, in 1937, Romains tried to clarify his theory, stating that there were in fact two types of *unanimisme*: a 'conscious' and 'reasoned' collective will, and another 'unconscious, blind, fanatic . . . barbaric' unanimist spirit which could be exploited by an unscrupulous political leader.[26] Still later, in 1933, Romains tried to claim prophetic qualities for his plays, stating that Emmanuel in *Cromedeyre-le-vieil* was a leader in the mould of Hitler and that Denis was a fictional precursor of Mussolini (the first version of *Le Dictateur* was written in 1912).[27]

In 1926, however, most of the Parisian critics saw in *Le Dictateur* no more than a realistic and human political drama, in spite of the fact that it presented just the set of political events which was widely feared in France. In spite of its excellent literary and dramatic qualities, and a generally favourable press, *Le Dictateur* was singularly unsuccessful. The well-known critic and producer Antoine noted this and deplored the fact that the Parisian public preferred *amusettes boulevardières* (frothy plays) to serious political theatre.[28]

Contrary to Jules Romains, Armand Salacrou denied that he had any political motivation in writing *La Terre est ronde* (The Earth is Round, 1938),[29] which describes the rise and fall of the Florentine religious leader Savonarola: 'I did not want to write a political play, or an historical play' (author's postface). On the other hand,

24. André Rouveyre, *Mercure de France*, 15 November 1926.
25. Jules Romains, *Cromedeyre-le-vieil*, Paris, 1952 (Théâtre du Vieux Colombier, 20 May 1920).
26. Jules Romains, *Pour l'esprit et la liberté*, Paris, 1937.
27. Jules Romains, *Confidences d'un auteur dramatique*, Paris, 1953.
28. *Information*, 6 October 1926.
29. See note 2.

Salacrou says in the same passage that the title of the play is meant to imply that history repeats itself: 'The earth turns. Times return'. It is thus not surprising that in 1938 the public saw Savonarola's fanatical theocracy as a parallel to contemporary Fascist regimes.

To begin with, the vocabulary of the play contains numerous echoes of contemporary political behaviour: there is a Parti Populaire which is preoccupied with 'the destiny of the fatherland'. (The main French Fascist party was Jacques Doriot's Parti Populaire Français.) Savonarola becomes 'the protector of the Republic'. His militants are 'young and pure' teenage 'soldiers'. They greet each other with slogans: 'Christ is king, comrade!' They burn 'seditious' books, spy on their families and beat up political opponents. In one particularly violent scene a Jewish citizen is hunted down and sent to his death.[30] Savonarola seizes power and mesmerizes the people of Florence with his demagogic oratory. There is no need for freedom, he says, because 'good citizens are free.'

La Terre est ronde was only moderately successful. The critics severely censured its lack of cohesion; it was supposed to be a religious drama but, because of the time (1938), the style of the production and the author's attempts to actualize certain elements, it was seen as a political drama. What is interesting is that it stirred up little political controversy in France. By 1937 a Fascist revolution was something that was not as likely to happen in France as it was in the early 1930s. But Fascist revolutions had happened elsewhere, and Salacrou's play was a frightening illustration of their consequences.

Alfred Mortier's *Machiavel* (1931)[31] is the most overt presentation of Mussolini's brand of Fascism on the Parisian stage during the period. In the author's own words, he sought to depict 'the tragedy of misunderstood talent'. In the preface to the play, he states that the character of Machiavelli was based on Pierre Laval. First a socialist, then an independent *député*, Laval was several times minister between 1925 and 1930. Mortier considered that the Third Republic would never appreciate Laval because it preferred mediocrity to talent. History was to show how tragically accurate was Mortier's judgement; Laval's talent was recognized by the Vichy government, and he was executed in 1945.

30. This scene was cut by the author in the 1945 edition of the play. Salacrou stated that it was too horrific in the light of recent events. The single copy of the original 1938 edition has also disappeared from the Bibliothèque Nationale under mysterious circumstances. Press articles confirm, however, that the scene was performed in 1938.

31. See note 2.

Mortier's Machiavelli, on a diplomatic mission for the state of Florence, meets César Borgia, an adventurer, a soldier and an ambitious, unscrupulous political leader. Borgia dreams of a unified Italy, and is prepared to go to any lengths to achieve this. Machiavelli is dazzled by Borgia's strength and vision. (He also conceives the idea of writing a book about him – a book called *The Prince.*) Borgia is equally impressed by Machiavelli's talents and invites the Florentine diplomat to join him in his struggle. Machiavelli refuses, preferring to remain loyal to the Florentine republic. However, the corrupt, weak and hypocritical republican politicians do not recognize his ability. He is wrongly accused of involvement in a state security scandal and exiled. No longer believing in any existing political doctrine, Machiavelli formulates his own: supremacy of the state to which all must be sacrificed.

There is no doubt that Mortier sought to present a Fascist-republican debate in the play. He did not hide the fact that his César Borgia was modelled on Mussolini. Several of Borgia's tirades were taken from texts by Mussolini. The play was also performed, successfully, in Milan (1937) and Rome (1938).

It is in fact Borgia rather than Machiavelli who is the political hero of the play. Machiavelli's fatal mistake is in refusing to join him and in remaining loyal to an unworthy democratic republic. For Borgia, all forms of government are simply confidence tricks. The greatest trick of all is republicanism, 'a wonderful hypocrisy, because democracy makes the flock believe it is free.'[32] 'Politically speaking, the people don't exist, because they are a group of individuals, each with only one idea – escaping from the demands of the law.'[33]

According to Mortier in his preface to the play, the above remarks are taken directly from a text by Mussolini. Similarly, the following statement by Borgia can be compared with a sentence from Mussolini's work *Fascism* (1933):

> BORGIA: God is the state, for which everything is permitted to ensure its powerful positive influence.[34]

> MUSSOLINI: For Fascism, the state is the absolute entity, compared with which individuals and groups are only relative entities.[35]

32. *Machiavel*, p. 56.
33. Ibid., p. 57.
34. Ibid., p. 153.
35. Benito Mussolini, *Le Fascisme*, Paris, 1933, p. 152.

More relevant to the political situation in France was the virulent satire of the Republic and republican politicians: shown as mediocre, hypocritical and bureaucratic, they make sententious statements about liberty and democracy, but think only about saving their own political hides. Machiavelli expresses concern at the incessant squabbling among political parties and the weakening of the Republic throughout constantly changing governments. The old Chancellor Virgilio defends this instability: 'The essential thing . . . ahem . . . if I dare to speak thus, the essential thing is that the positions do not change.'[36] This is a fairly obvious reference to the Third Republic where, as many political commentators noted, 'Ministries come and go, but the ministers remain.' Mortier's play was moderately successful and, surprisingly, caused little controversy. Three years later it may well have done so, as we shall see.

Paul Raynal's *Napoléon unique* (Incomparable Napoleon, 1936)[37] reminded the French that they once had their very own dictator. Having seen the play, the critic Gerard Bauer remarked, not without irony: 'Dictatorships may try their hardest to be like his, but they will only be a pale imitation.'[38] Although the theme of the play is sentimental rather than political (Napoleon rejects Josephine to follow his political dream), Raynal makes parallels between the French emperor and modern dictators: he came to power during a period of disorder and restored order; he exploits the notion of *patrie*, presents himself at its incarnation, and dreams of 'freeing' Europe through conquest: 'A despot, I teach liberty to all nations . . . a tamer of nations, I show them, with France as an example, what patriotism can achieve.'[39] Raynal also reminded his public that Nazism and Fascism were not simply the result of the atavistic make-up of the German and Italian peoples, as many French believed. In the play, the characters of Fouché and Talleyrand are at a loss to explain how 'the nation of Voltaire, Pascal and Rabelais' could have allowed itself to be dominated by a militaristic tyrant.

Unlike Mortier, Raynal had little success with his play in Italy. It was banned in Rome after eight performances.[40] Obviously, the scenes with Fouché and Talleyrand, which contain some violent attacks on dictatorship, would not have pleased Mussolini's govern-

36. *Machiavel*, p. 76.
37. See note 1.
38. *Echo de Paris*, 11 November 1938.
39. *Napoléon unique*, pp. 56–7.
40. *Paris-Soir*, 20 November 1937.

ment. I would suggest, half seriously, that there might have been another reason. There was already an Italian play on Napoleon's career; its French title was *Les Cent Jours* (The Hundred Days, 1932) and its author was the well-known writer Benito Mussolini.[41]

There were many French people who believed that a bit of domination by a strong, authoritarian leader would not be a bad thing for France. This may explain the success of Maurice Rostand's mawkish and mediocre *Le Général Boulanger* (1931),[42] which was performed 150 times in a theatre seating 2,000 people. Although essentially a romantic love story, Rostand's play reminded the French of the charismatic general who shook France out of the mood of pessimism brought on by its defeat in the Franco-Prussian War, and who came within an inch of seizing power in the 1880s. The journalists who saw the play could not help comparing Boulanger's period with the France of the late 1920s and early 1930s: 'Strong personalities could express themselves at that time. The nation had leaders, it had too many; today there are no more leaders, or, in a confused sort of way, we are frightened of having any. The crowd no longer loves anyone, and if it hates anyone it keeps quiet about it. No spark, no passion.'[43] In the play, Boulanger lambastes the state of politics in France with exactly the same criticisms made by the extreme Right at the time: mediocrity, venality, corruption and weakness, he says, are the order of the day.

Sacha Guitry's large-scale production of his *Histoires de France* (Tales of France, 1929)[44] was an attempt to present the same right-wing view in a more didactic form. Guitry was one of France's most successful playwright/actor/producers. He had made his reputation with light romantic comedies, and *Histoires de France* was totally unlike anything he had ever written. It was as unsuccessful as Jules Romains's *Le Dictateur*, again not so much because of its political message, but because the public was just not interested in such plays. Through a series of historical tableaux Guitry tries to show that it was the monarchy which made France great (a theme dear to the hearts of Charles Maurras and Action Française): François I, Louis XI, Henri IV, Louis XIII and Louis XIV are all shown as contributing to the unification and prosperity of the nation.

41. Benito Mussolini, *Les Cent Jours (Campo di Maggio)*, Paris, *Les Cahiers de 'Bravo'*, January 1932.
42. Maurice Rostand, *Le Général Boulanger*, Paris, *La Petite Illustration*, 1931 (Théâtre de la Porte Saint-Martin, 5 October 1931).
43. Maurice Martin du Gard, *Les Nouvelles Littéraires*, 10 October 1931.
44. See note 4.

However, it is in the long opening scene set in a *village gaulois* that Guitry presents his main political thesis. His characters represent the French people as he sees them: *le mari* (the husband), a 'Mr Everybody', well-meaning, republican, a little naive . . . and a cuckold; *la femme* (the wife), 'I'm on this earth to make love and have children. And I tell you that's enough for me!'; *le guerrier* (the warrior), convinced that 'the Iberians, the Romans and the Germans' will all invade France if given half a chance; *l'ouvrier* (the worker), who says nothing; and *le vieux tribun* (the old tribune), Guitry's mouthpiece, modelled on Georges Clemenceau.

For *le vieux tribun*, France has one overriding problem: the nation must always have *un chef*, 'a strong, intelligent, capable leader, an organizer'.[45] In spite of its contribution in the past, the monarchy is no longer a viable solution: 'Kings start off OK, but they go off after a while.'[46] This leader will suddenly appear one day, says *le vieux tribun*, and everyone will recognize him: 'He's a man who, all of a sudden, stands up, says "I'm your leader", makes everyone believe it, and is obeyed.'[47] Guitry's political ideas are, to say the least, schematic. They were not widely aired either, since the *village gaulois* scene was cut after the first performance, ostensibly because it was too long, but also possibly because it was too controversial. The play is significant, however, because Guitry was such a well-known personality, and because he spent so much time, energy and money in producing it. *Histoires de France* was the reaction of a patriotic conservative who was growing increasingly impatient with what he saw as political disorder within the nation.

Ironically, the most controversial play of the period was a version of Shakespeare's *Coriolanus*, produced at the Comédie Française during the 1933–4 season: 'Coriolanus, freely translated from the English and adapted for the French stage by René-Louis Piachaud.'[48] Piachaud was a well-known right-wing Swiss writer from Geneva. As the programme stated, his work was not a translation of Shakespeare's play but an adaptation. Some scenes were cut, others rearranged, to give more prominence to the political element in the play. Coriolanus appears as a proud and strong leader, disgusted by the venality and hypocrisy of *les tribuns*, whose language (in the adaptation) reminded the audience irresistibly of contemporary republican politicians. Not surprisingly, the 'people of Rome' appear as a Communist rabble.

45. *Histoires de France*, p. 9
46. Ibid., p. 8.
47. Ibid., p. 9.
48. Programme cover, Fonds Rondel, Bibliothèque de l'Arsenal.

The impact of Piachaud's choice of language can be judged from the following table, in which a more accurate 1911 translation of *Coriolanus* by Sonniès is compared with Piachaud's version:

Sonniès (1911)	*Piachaud (1932)*
Disorder	Anarchy
Get rid of a law	Repeal a law
The granaries	The state shops
The crowd	The masses
The 'yes' or 'no' of general ignorance	The 'yes' or 'no' of the idiotic crowd
This multiple tongue must be torn out	The representation of the people in parliament must be abolished

SONNIES First citizen: Let's kill him, and we'll have wheat at any price we want.

PIACHAUD Comrades, we only have to get rid of Caius and we'll have wheat at people's prices.

When the manuscript was first read by the Comédie Française selection committee in 1932, the director of the theatre, Émile Fabre, had strong reservations about its political content. He sought, and obtained, ministerial approval for the production before going ahead. The first performance was on 9 December 1933, right in the middle of a series of political scandals and revelations of corruption which led to serious (principally right-wing) riots in February 1934 and fears of civil war. From the first night, performances were interrupted by cheering, booing, speeches from the balcony, and fights. In spite of violent opposition from a number of government politicians, the performances continued until 3 February 1934, when Fabre was sacked and replaced by . . . the Director of National Security. On 4 February several hundred people invaded the theatre, held a meeting, then staged a demonstration on the Champs-Elysées. Performances were suspended after bloody rioting on the night of 6 February. They resumed on 11 March, and the play went on to have 152 performances in all.

The first conclusion we can draw from this brief survey is that the French public did not seem to be particularly interested in political debate in the theatre. The examples of *Coriolan* and *Le Dictateur* would not be very encouraging for either writers or producers: *Le Dictateur* left the public indifferent and *Coriolan* caused riots. The safe formula was to present the private and sentimental lives of famous leaders and to leave ideology out of it.

The second and most important point is that when political ideology was discussed, it tended to focus on the choice between bourgeois democracy and a regime with a strong, authoritarian leader. For most of the writers we have mentioned, this was not necessarily Fascism; it was a vague alternative that was never quite articulated. As Maurice Martin du Gard said, France wanted a strong leader, but was at the same time afraid of what would happen if it got one. This 'chef fort et autoritaire' never appeared for the Third Republic. In 1940, many turned to Pétain, hoping he would save France from the *décadence* of the 1930s. After liberation, it was de Gaulle's turn. Strong, imperious and charismatic, he fitted well into the image of the leader many French people thought the country needed.

–8–

Language, Modernity and Fascism

Heidegger's Doubling of Myth

KATHRYN BROWN

Martin Heidegger's official affirmation of Fascism in 1933 has evoked a wide range of reactions from critics. Since the immediate post-war period, many elements of Heidegger's philosophy have been occluded or distorted by myths concerning his activities in Fascist Germany. Complementary distortions are produced by the faction which has wilfully ignored his pronouncements as Rector of Freiburg University. The following passage by William Barrett, written in 1964, is a startling example: 'Fortunately for us, there is very little biography to get hung up on. Heidegger has been a Professor, his life has followed the usual professorial stages of development, and whatever drama clings to him has merely been what has transpired in his thought.'[1]

In attempting to determine criteria to assess Heidegger's works, readers often assume a critical bias towards the philosopher according to their extenuation or disapproval of his attitudes towards Fascism. Ernst Cassirer, Robert Minder and T. W. Adorno, for example, condemn Heidegger for distorting language and attempting to use politics to achieve philosophical aims. In opposition to these views stand interpretations by François Fédier and Walter Biemel, in which Heidegger's positive response to Fascism is described as being merely a regrettable 'mistake'.[2]

Recently, the debate on Heidegger's political activities has reopened in both France and Germany. In 1986, the Freiburg

1. William Barrett, *What is Existentialism?*, New York, 1965, p. 143.
2. Ernst Cassirer, *Der Mythus des Staats*, Frankfurt/M, 1985, pp. 382ff.; Robert Minder, *Hölderlin unter den Deutschen und andere Aufsätze*, Frankfurt/M, 1968, pp. 86ff.; T. W. Adorno, *The Jargon of Authenticity*, tr. K. Tarkowski and F. Will, London, 1973; François Fédier, 'Trois attaques contre Heidegger', *Critique*, no. 234, 1966, pp. 883ff., and 'À propos de Heidegger', *Critique*, no. 242, 1967, pp. 672ff.; Walter Biemel, *Martin Heidegger*, Reinbeck, 1973, pp. 7ff.

University journal devoted a number to the topic *Martin Heidegger: A Philosopher and Politics*; it was followed soon afterwards by Victor Farias's *Heidegger and Nazism* (1987), which led to a series of articles in German, French and English newspapers.[3] These two important studies on Heidegger are similar in that they treat the subject in a fair and moderate manner, and attempt to locate the basis of Heidegger's political views in his early philosophical writings. Furthermore, Heidegger's philosophy is analysed in a wider context, so that his susceptibility to National Socialist ideas appears as a typical phenomenon of German society in the 1930s.

I agree with those critics who view Heidegger's political engagement as based in his philosophical thought.[4] Yet the dominant structures of his thought are more interesting than the factual, biographical details of his activities in the early 1930s. This chapter will trace the major developments in Heidegger's thought which made him susceptible to the attractions of Fascism, and will relate this experience to his eventual disillusionment with the imposition of ideology on the individual.

A fundamental problem in considering Heidegger's works arises from the way in which he politicized his own philosophy. As we shall see in the course of this study, his attraction to Fascism grew directly out of claims made in his early works. The critique of modern society and the disillusionment with the development of western metaphysics, dominant in his early thought, provided the ground upon which hopes for a new Fascist age could develop. In his affirmation of Fascism, he sought to hasten the advent of a new era in which art and philosophy would provide the nucleus for human development and freedom. It is thus impossible to divorce Heidegger's philosophy from his belief in Fascism as a positive social force.

Heidegger's early disillusionment with modern society demanded a solution in both philosophical and practical terms. Initially, he saw the potential of a positive future for society in his own mythical construction of Fascism. When the practical policies of National Socialism failed to provide the desired alternative to the failure of modernity, however, Heidegger attempted to reformulate his notion of a positive future by constructing a mythicized

3. *Freiburger Universitatsblätter*, vol. 92, June 1986; Victor Farias, *Heidegger et le nazisme*, Lagrasse, 1987.
4. Cf. Pierre Boudieu, *Die politische Ontologie Martin Heideggers*, Frankfurt/M, 1976; Alexander Schwan, 'Martin Heidegger: Politik und praktische Philosophie', *Philosophisches Jahrbuch*, 1974, pp. 148ff.; Jurgen Habermas, *Der philosophische Diskurs der Moderne*, Frankfurt/M, 1985.

concept of art and the artist. In this way, his fundamental myth of salvation for society is transposed into a new area, yet still retains its original structure. A 'doubling of myth' occurs when he attempts a twofold response to these demands of his early philosophy: firstly, in a practical sense, through a mythical construction of Fascism; subsequently, by elaborating his views of poetic language and the image of an ideal leader to fill the gap left by the collapse of the initial construction.

Modernity and the Crisis of Being

To understand Heidegger's positive response to Fascism in the early 1930s, it is necessary to outline his critique of language and of the nature of Being in modern society. As his critique of western metaphysics in *Being and Time* (1927) has already been explored in detail by many authors,[5] I shall give a brief summary of only those aspects of the work that are relevant for an understanding of his susceptibility to Fascist ideology. According to Heidegger, modernity should have brought about a freeing of human consciousness from the restrictions of church rule and a feudal order, thereby providing the ground for the development of a new individual. Instead, modern society merely creates a new set of restrictions, namely the subjugation of its members to the reign of technology and the collective will. Under the tyranny of a technological society, humans are deprived of their individuality and reduced to the status of 'functionaries of technology'.[6] As automatons functioning solely for the preservation of technological society, people find themselves placed under the domination of the impersonal 'one':

> The human being [*Dasein*] stands as part of an everyday collective [*Miteinandersein*] under the sway of others. It is not itself, the others have taken being away from it. The will of the others regulates the daily possibilities of the human being's existence. These others are not particular others. On the contrary, any other can replace them . . . The who is neither this one, nor that one, not oneself, not a few and not the sum

5. Michael Allen Gillespie, *Hegel, Heidegger, and the Ground of History*, Chicago, 1984; Edith Wyschogrod, *Spirit in Ashes: Hegel, Heidegger, and Man-Made Mass Death*, New Haven/London, 1985; Robert Bernasconi, *The Question of Language in Heidegger's History of Being*, Atlantic Highlands, 1985.
6. Martin Heidegger, *Holzwege*, Frankfurt/M, 1980, p. 200. All English translations in this essay are by the author.

of all. The 'who' is the neuter, the 'one' (*das Man*).[7]

In modern society, individual human consciousness is not only placed in the service of technology, but also dominated by a generalized form of being-in-the-world. Technological society deprives people of their individuality and creates a new world in which the system of values revolves exclusively around production and further advances in technology. By accepting technology as the focal point of existence, humans alienate themselves from Being. They no longer question the nature of Being, but think exclusively in terms of *Technik* and production. This mode of human existence is described by Heidegger as the 'fallen state'. Humans 'fall' from being at one with themselves into an inauthentic mode of existence in daily life.

This 'fall' from authentic Being is understood by Heidegger in terms of neither a Rousseauistic fall from the 'state of nature', nor a Christian fall from grace. Alienation from Being is reversible if individuals are prepared to pose the question of the nature of Being more forcefully and directly. It is the task of thinkers not to understand and analyse Being, but rather to sense being as essentially incomprehensible and mysterious. Being should be sensed, not objectified, by thinkers. This is the true task of philosophy in Heidegger's terms; by posing such questions it should be possible to reverse the negative consequences of the 'fallen state'. However, largely owing to a similar 'fall' in language in the course of modernity, a reversal of human thinking has not been realized. The soteric implications of such a reversal create a basic susceptibility towards the promise of restoration, but there is nothing at this stage of Heidegger's philosophy to indicate the possibility of a political solution.

The individual 'falls' from Being into an artificially created society, yet does not recognize this condition as an inauthentic mode of existence. As a function of life in the technological world, language also undergoes a similar decline in potential. In the technological society language functions as 'information', thereby fulfilling its social role and marking a further alienation of humans from Being. Instead of unveiling being, language 'hides' it behind an institutionalized social discourse, and cannot function as a true means of communication between speakers. It rather increases the negative effects of technology and often becomes totally devoid of meaning:

7. Martin Heidegger, *Sein und Zeit*, Tübingen, 1984, p. 126.

> Because discourse has lost – or never possessed – the primary link to the addressed being, it communicates not by means of the primal frame of reference [*Zueignung*] of this being, but rather through paths of redundance and repetition. This redundance and repetition, in which the absence of ground becomes increased to complete groundlessness, characterizes the language of everyday existence [*das Gerede*].[8]

As language no longer reveals the speaker's relationship to Being or to other beings, the language of social discourse is powerless to exert any positive influence on humankind's state of being-in-the-world.

Heidegger's negative depiction of the genesis of the modern subject shows certain affinities to the philosophies of Karl Jaspers, Horkheimer and Adorno, as each of these thinkers viewed the development of individual consciousness in terms of objectification and alienation.[9] Heidegger's version distinguishes itself from these theories, however, in its emphasis on the possibility of salvation through a new consciousness of Being. The incapability of modern European society to free individual consciousness lies, for him, in the basic structures which have dominated western metaphysics. Since the division of the concept of Being in the philosophy of Plato, 'Being' and 'beings' have become confused, with the result that Being itself is left out of consideration. The history of western metaphysics is thus characterized by an alienation from Being, with the result that modern society exists in a state which has 'forgotten' being entirely (*Seinsvergessenheit*). In his inaugural lecture at the University of Freiburg on 24 July 1929, Heidegger sums up his views on this matter and the essence of his own philosophy in the following words: 'Metaphysics never answers the question concerning the truth of Being, because it never asks this question. It does not ask, because it only thinks of Being in terms of beings. It means beings in the whole sphere and speaks of Being. It says Being and means beings as beings.'[10]

In order to overcome this negative trend in the history of metaphysics, he calls for an answer to the question 'What is Being?' which aims at unquantifiable perception rather than objectification. According to Heidegger, when the nature of Being is questioned, Being automatically 'withdraws' itself from consideration by

8. Ibid., p. 168.
9. Karl Jaspers, *Die geistige Situation der Zeit*, Berlin/New York, 1979, pp. 62ff.; Max Horkheimer and T. W. Adorno, *Dialektik der Aufklärung*, Frankfurt/M, 1984, pp. 14ff.
10. Martin Heidegger, *Was ist Metaphysik?*, Frankfurt/M, 1986, p. 8.

pointing to answers which disguise its very essence. The primal error of metaphysics is to be content with such answers. Overcoming this problem implies the necessity of posing the question of Being more pointedly. There are then two options left for the questioner. It is possible either to sense Being as something essentially incomprehensible and mysterious, or to objectify it in language, thereby attempting to structure it according to human knowledge. The first possibility involves the incorporation into experience of the withdrawal of Being as a constant of perception itself. Hence perception must, again and again, renounce Being as its object. Modernity follows the second possibility, namely the objectification of Being. In the mode of inauthentic existence, primacy is given to the subject-oriented world view, in which Being, history and time become objects of language. This form of subjectification proves, however, to be a false conquering of the world by humanity. In the process of establishing dominion over the world through technology, humans themselves become objects of the technological system. Instead of positing themselves as subjects of language, speakers succumb to subjugation under the 'one'.

In order to restore the question of Being to its true significance and to displace negative 'subjectification' by an image of the new individual able to sense Being, Heidegger calls for a 'destruction of the ontological tradition' which has disguised its true essence.[11] Ultimately, this is to lead to a restoration of the pre-Socratic philosophical tradition. Throughout his work, Heidegger praises the nebulous concepts of Being he finds in the pre-Socratics and contrasts these with the negative objectification of Being prevalent in western philosophy since Plato. In his essay on Heidegger and early Greek philosophy, Hans-Georg Gadamer correctly points out that Heidegger's interpretation of the pre-Socratics is very much a distortion to suit his own philosophical aims: 'Certainly the beginning of Greek thought lies in darkness. What Heidegger recognized in Anaximander, Heraclitus and Parmenides was, in effect, himself.'[12] Heidegger's idealization of the pre-Socratics is a major aspect of his susceptibility to the image of an emotionally powerful, mythical past which played an important role in his future engagement with National Socialism. When he writes, before 1933, of a return to the philosophy of the pre-Socratics and a new sense of Being as the only possible salvation for society, his view arises not purely from

11. Heidegger, *Sein und Zeit*, p. 26.
12. Hans-Georg Gadamer, *Heideggers Wege*, Tübingen, 1983, p. 120.

philosophical questions, but also from his disappointment with the political and social climate of the Weimar Republic. He conceives of an ideal social structure in which a 'true' perception of Being is given supremacy, so that the negative subjectification of humankind will be replaced by a new form of individuality.

One may scan Heidegger's development of a social myth at this point along the axis of personalization–reification. The linked processes he terms 'subjectification' and 'objectification' of experience converge in making it not only less adequate to describe reality, but at the same time less personal. By a complementary movement, the impersonal ground of Being takes on some personal attributes: it can 'withdraw itself', elude the forms of perception, produce its own tangible absence and so on. The hubris of 'subjectification' has, paradoxically, led to the fallen state of the anonymous 'one'; redemption is for the individual alone, but – in another paradox – only for those individuals who are able to establish a new ground for the revelation of Being.

This brings us to Heidegger's concept of history. In *Being and Time*, history is discussed in terms of the temporality of human existence. Being is *Anwesenheit* (presence), and therefore humans exist only in so far as they exist in time: 'Historicity means the understanding of Being as the occurrence of the human being [*Dasein*] as such.'[13] A major step towards demolishing the ontological tradition of western thought lies in recognizing that the 'Being of beings' is presence. Divisions of history into labelled epochs are seen to be false divisions of time which objectify history. Heidegger therefore distinguishes between the historicity of Being and artificial existence in history: 'The analysis of the historicity of beings attempts to show that this being is not temporal, because it stands in a particular epoch of history, but, on the contrary, that it extends, and can only exist historically, because the basis of its Being is temporal.'[14]

Heidegger later develops the concept of *Geschichte*, the revelation of being as time; he opposes this to *Historie*, the false understanding of history which objectifies being. *Geschichte* is described as the *Schicksal* (destiny) of Being, to be revealed as time. This leads, however, to yet another paradox in Heidegger's thought: on the one hand, Being is thought of in such an abstract fashion that it must 'withdraw' from all consciousness; on the other hand, in Heidegger's mythicization it takes on the attributes of an anthropomorphic

13. Heidegger, *Sein und Zeit*, p. 20.
14. Ibid., p. 376.

entity which can fulfil a 'destiny'.

Heidegger's new *Existentialphilosophie* in *Being and Time*, based on a notion of the inauthentic nature of social existence, matched the disillusionment of Germany following the First World War. It is precisely his refusal to construct a more positive notion of the course of history and modernity that led to Ernst Cassirer's aggressive critique of *Being and Time* in 1945:

> A history of philosophy that consists of grim prophecies of the end and inevitable destruction of our civilization, and a theory of which the main feature is the projection into Being [*Geworfenheit*], have given up all hopes of an active contribution to the building and rebuilding of cultural life. Such a philosophy renounces its own principal theoretical and ethical ideals. It can, therefore, be used as a versatile instrument in the hands of political leaders.[15]

Though Cassirer's commentary may not provide a balanced view of Heidegger's first major work, it does suggest why his philosophy captured the imagination of many German intellectuals disillusioned with the traditions and conventions of the Weimar Republic.

It is on the grounds of emptiness and disillusionment, characterized by the disappearance of Being from thought, that Heidegger viewed the promises of Fascism as the dawn of a new age which offered the possibility of a true consideration of Being. In the emergence of Fascism he saw a means of restoring a system of meaning to the world. Fascism would succeed where modernity had failed. In his affirmation of the new Fascist rule, he sought to 'remythologize' society and find a way to the 'openness of Being'. His philosophies are thus inextricably bound up with the situation of the society in which they were conceived: firstly, as a reaction against the negative course of modernity, culminating in the 'forgetting' of Being; secondly, in the belief in Fascism as the means to 'overcome' the negative history of metaphysics.

Heidegger's *Rektorat*

When Heidegger was appointed Rector of the Albert-Ludwigs-University, Freiburg, in 1933, his hopes for Fascist Germany became clear. Perhaps the most revealing document on his response

15. Cassirer, *Der Mythus des Staats*, p. 384.

to Fascism is a lecture held on 27 May 1933 and published as *The Self-Assertion of the German University*. In this speech one can see how he radically distorts National Socialist policies in order to realize his own philosophical aims. The central issue of Fascism is depicted as a spiritual renewal of Germany which is to be achieved through educational reform. It is the 'destiny' of German students to bring about this spiritual revitalization of society by confirming their allegiance to the new rule. By 'following' Fascist policies, faculty members would fulfil their intellectual destiny and thereby establish themselves as society's new leaders: 'The essence of the university only attains clarity, rank and power when the leaders themselves are primarily and at all times being led – led by the relentlessness of that spiritual task which forces the destiny of the German people into the particularity of their history.'[16]

The fulfilment of 'destiny' leads to and validates existence in a new form of history. As the 'spiritual leader' of Germany, Heidegger hoped to create a system of higher education in which universities would no longer be divided into small faculties, but form a unity which would develop out of a primal ordering of existence.[17] This notion of educational reform is closely linked to the image of an idealized leader who will authorize the creation of a new system in which the reign of *das Man* will be displaced by the goal of individuality. For this reason, the leader himself must possess a model character and show resistance to the false 'subjectivity' which dominates western society:

> The decisive aspect of leadership is not merely the role of precursor, but rather the ability to walk alone, not out of egoism and love of power, but because of a deeply rooted destiny and sense of duty . . . German students are on the move . . . They seek those leaders through whom they can fulfil their own destiny in founded and knowing truth and affirm the clarity of the meaningfully effective word and work.[18]

It is the role of the leader to open a way to the truth of Being; through his ability to 'walk alone' and discover the way to the

16. Martin Heidegger, *Die Selbstbehauptung der deutschen Universität* (1933), Frankfurt/M, 1983, p. 9.
17. Ibid., pp. 13–14: 'Such questioning bursts the encapsulation of faculties into compartmentalized subjects, brings them back from the endless and useless scattering into individual fields and once again places knowledge directly in relation to the fertility and blessing of all cosmological powers of all human-historical experience: nature, history, language; the people, custom, state; poetry, thinking, belief; sickness, madness, death; law, economy, technology.'
18. Ibid., p. 15.

'meaningfully effective word', the leader has already achieved the highest stage of individual development. He can thus free the German people from the tyranny of *das Man* and effect a revolution in language, through which the empty speech of everyday communication will be replaced by the clarity of meaningful language. By finding a way out of the crisis of modernity into a future of 'authentic' existence, the idealized leader fulfils the demand for salvation in *Being and Time.* The depersonalization of the anonymous mass is replaced by a secular cult of salvation which focuses on the elite individual. This new form of individuality is to be protected from false 'subjectivity' through a mythical image of purity.

Heidegger's enthusiasm for pre-Socratic philosophy is in no way diminished during his Fascist engagement. On the contrary, his theses on the early philosophical fragments of the Greeks are transformed into an integral part of his interpretation of contemporary political ideas. In the *Rektoratsrede* (rectorship speech) he uses the ideal of a return to pre-Socratic thought as the basis of an apocalyptic vision of a new 'beginning'. In this way he manages to merge his earlier philosophical project, which focuses on the reanimation of a mythical past, with variations of Nazi propaganda:

> If science is to exist and exist for us and through us, under what conditions can it truly exist? Only when we place ourselves under the power of the beginning of our spiritual-historical existence. This is the onset of Greek philosophy . . . The beginning has fallen into our future, it stands there as the decree far above us, heralding in its own greatness. Only when we decide to accept this far decree in order to win back the greatness of the beginning, only then does knowledge become the inner necessity of existence.[19]

This concept of a new 'beginning' demonstrates the trend to apocalyptic thinking in Heidegger's philosophy at the time. His attitude to political upheaval implies that the Fascist millennium is both imminent and total. It is the collective 'destiny' of the German people to experience the wonders of this terrestrial millennium by dispensing with the traditional form of linear history and supporting an apocalyptic leap into a new form of history. This attempt to realize a new age reveals, however, a fundamental confusion between 'perception' and 'being-in-the-world'; Heidegger's desire to achieve a state in which a nebulously defined perception of Being

19. Ibid., pp. 11, 13.

takes priority over subjectification is based on the potential of a new mode of existence. His philosophy thus lies open to Fascist ideology as a means by which to change being-in-the-world and hence the forms of perception. The new beginning is seen as a means of 'overcoming' the tradition of western metaphysics; the ability to pose the question of Being in a new society is a reflection of his desire to return to pre-Socratic thought.

Heidegger clearly interprets Fascism according to his own understanding of history as an uncovering of *Geschichte* and *Schicksal/ Geschick*. In turning to Fascism in 1933, he seizes upon the current jargon and places his own meanings on Fascist terminology. Thus he is able to use Fascist ideology in an attempt to fulfil aims already present in his own philosophy. Heidegger does not, therefore, adapt his philosophy to comply with Fascist ideology, but rather constructs a preferred version of Fascism in accordance with his own theories, just as Oscar Wilde, in *The Soul of Man under Socialism* (1891), constructs a model of socialism in accordance with his own vision of a utopian society.[20] In both cases, a process of mythicization is given preference over actual social and political reality. For Heidegger, Fascism was not an end in itself, but rather a means by which to actualize his own pre-existing philosophical goals. This is clear in his interpretation of military service and propaganda about the German *Volk*.

In order to bring about a new form of educational freedom in the Fascist millennium, Heidegger sought to achieve the unity of the student body. The first step in the attainment of this unity was *Arbeitsdienst* (labour service), through which he hoped to reverse the course of technological domination of society and to achieve a new sense of closeness to the German countryside. This would increase the students' sense of community and provide them with unity through a feeling of belonging to a common ground. The second method of achieving unity was *Wehrdienst* (military service). Heidegger claimed that he did not conceive of *Wehrdienst* in terms of preparation for war. Rather it was intended to instil students with a sense of loyalty to the leader and to their own destiny: 'The second bond is to the honour and destiny of the nation.'[21] German youth would thus acquire a sense of the importance of their own destiny in the future of Germany. The third and most important unifying factor for German youth was *Wissensdienst* (the duty to acquire knowledge): 'The third bond of German students is to the

20. Oscar Wilde, *De Profundis and Other Writings*, Harmondsworth, 1980.
21. Heidegger, *Die Selbstbehauptung*, pp. 13–15.

spiritual destiny of the German people. This people fulfils its destiny by placing its history in the openness of the superiority of all cosmological powers of the new human existence and always struggles anew for its spiritual world.'[22]

Through *Arbeitsdient*, *Wehrdienst* and *Wissensdienst*, Heidegger hoped that German youth would bring about the apocalyptic leap out of history as an objectification of the past into *Geschichte*, and fulfil the destiny of the German people. He conceived of a particularly 'German' destiny, which was, however, quite different from the Nazi concept of racial superiority. For Heidegger, 'destiny' is specifically German because of the supposed deep relationship between the German language and the language of ancient Greek philosophy. His understanding of destiny was grounded in philosophical formulas that are at once different from the racial elements of Fascist ideology, yet ostensibly appropriate to the Fascist world view. If after the war he constantly stressed the significant differences between his philosophy and Fascist ideology, during his period as Rector we find a convenient interplay of terminology between Nazi jargon and many of his own claims for philosophy.

The ideal of educational reform under the Fascist rule was also seen in terms of a *Kampf*. This 'struggle' or 'battle' was to be undertaken by both students and teachers in their attempt to bring about the dawn of a new age: 'The community of teachers and students in battle will only accord the German university the place of spiritual law-giver and define the highest task of the people in the state if teaching staff and students structure their existence more rigorously, more simply and more modestly than any other members of the community.[23]

The so-called 'academic freedom' of the past was nothing more than an illusion, since education had been based on a disorganized system in which courses were carelessly thrown together, thus adding to the negative condition of the forgetting of Being. The social and political upheaval of Fascism seemed to provide the opportunity to dispense with the old system and create the new ground upon which education could lead the way into existence in the 'openness of Being'. The negative depersonalization of 'the one' would be replaced by a cult of the individual, but this cult would somehow be purified by having dispensed with the subject-oriented thought of western philosophy. A reform of the university system under Fascist rule seemed to provide the first positive step in this direction.

22. Ibid., p. 15.
23. Ibid., p. 18.

Although an esoteric view of Fascism appears intertwined with elements of propaganda in the *Rektoratsrede*, Heidegger's belief in the actual, strategic worth of the new power should not be underestimated. In a retrospective view on his actions during his time as Rector, Heidegger emphasized that there were many contrasts between his former hopes for a new Germany and National Socialist policies. Yet his argument that his *Rektoratsrede* was not understood by anyone in the audience at the time and had even aroused anger and suspicion amongst other party members is less plausible.[24] As Victor Farias has shown, these self-justifications and stylizations of his earlier comments are often suspect; Heidegger's much 'misunderstood' speech was reprinted for the third time in 1937, and 5,000 copies of it were sold.[25]

Heidegger's attraction to Fascism stems partly from his personal disillusionment with society and the wish to bring about both intellectual and cultural reform, and partly from the possibility of constructing a version of Fascism to fit the pre-existing demands of his social philosophy. Whilst he could conceive of ways in which to avert the negative course of modernity, he was faced with the necessity of bringing about concrete social change in order to realize these ideals. Fascism seemed to provide a suitable mechanism. He did not simply accept Fascist policies; he was attracted to his own construction of Fascism because he saw it as a means by which to obviate what he disliked about present society. In an interview with *Der Spiegel* in 1966, he comments:

> During the winter semester of 1932–3 we often discussed not only the political situation, but especially that of the universities and the hopeless position of the students. My judgement was as follows: as far as I can judge the situation, there remains only one possibility, namely to attempt to make the coming development one of [real] value, [working] together with the growing [political] forces, which have genuine life.[26]

Heidegger's belief in the positive potential of Fascism may thus be seen as an exercise in mythical thinking. From the supposedly 'demythologized' ground of technological society grew the necessity to provide the world with an entelechy that would, in turn, endow the German people with a positive future. The concept of 'destiny' plays an important role in both Fascist propaganda and the philosophy of Heidegger, for it is through this mythicized concept

24. Heidegger, *Das Rektorat*, Frankfurt/M, 1983, pp. 30–9.
25. Farias, *Heidegger*, p. 249.
26. *Der Spiegel*, no. 23, 1966, p. 201.

that a new system of meaning was to be imparted to society.

As Heidegger's theories on the role of art in society followed so closely upon his Fascist engagement, it may be tempting to place him in the category of those artists and writers who succumbed to the promises of Fascism in the early 1930s and adapted their work to comply with the spirit of the new era. A reading along these lines would ignore, however, his active adaptation of Fascism to accord with the structure of his earlier thought. If his theory of art shows many structural similarities to his construction of Fascism, aesthetics play a relatively minor role in his initial enthusiasm for his concept of the new regime.

Heidegger seems unaware of the paradox that his revalidation of individual experience is to proceed by means of mythical constructs that are essentially depersonalizing, and through a political transformation of the universities which must effectively impose one uniformity after another. He remained Rector of the Albert-Ludwigs-University for only one year. The details of his resignation in 1934 have been clearly documented by Hugo Ott;[27] ultimately the restrictions of Fascist ideology seemed irreconcilable with his philosophical aims. The ideological subjugation of the individual in the Nazi state was ultimately indistinguishable from the negatively judged tyranny of *das Man*.

The need to break with any form of ideological constraint is a recurrent theme in Heidegger. He rejects Marxism and 'Americanism', as both insist on the subjugation of the individual to a particular viewpoint from which the rest of existence is judged. This adds to the control by the general will of *das Man*, the alienation from Being of those trapped in a predetermined understanding of the world. The subjugation of society to an ideology also prevents the uncovering of being in history. If people view the world from a particular ideological standpoint, they must, by necessity, read history in accordance with that point of view and are forced to accept the negative form of history as *Historie*.

By allying themselves with a particular ideology, people impose an artificial system of meaning on the world, further alienating themselves from Being and increasing the tendency of western thought towards objectification. This process culminates in world views such as Marxism and 'Americanism' in which institutionalized thinking, technology and the predetermined ordering of so-

27. Hugo Ott, 'Martin Heidegger als Rektor der Universität Freiburg i.Br. 1933/34', *Zeitschrift des Breisgau-Geschichtsvereins*, 1983, pp. 121ff., and 'Martin Heidegger und die Universität Freiburg nach 1945', *Historisches Jahrbuch*, 1985, pp. 131ff.

ciety are regulated by economic and technological necessity. Fascism was itself susceptible to such an interpretation; when it became clear to Heidegger that it was not going to provide a direct escape from the crisis of modernity, he was forced to find another means by which his ideals could be achieved. Yet he did not alter the central orientation of his thinking after 1934, and his concept of a specifically German 'destiny' remained in the forefront of his philosophy. The goals of his philosophical quest were now to be achieved through a new series of mythical constructs which form the nucleus of his theories on the work of art.

Salvation and Poetic Discourse

Heidegger's most important considerations of the potential of art as an alternative solution to the problem of the absence of Being in modern society were formulated the essay 'The Origin of the Work of Art' (1935), in which his concept of a new perception of being is once again accorded supremacy. The work of art provides an area in which a revelation of being may be experienced. The revelation of being in art is equated to a process of uncovering *aletheia* (truth): 'In its own way, the work of art opens up the Being of beings. The opening occurs in the work, that is the uncovering, namely the truth of beings. In the work of art the truth of beings is effected. Art is the animation of truth.'[28]

Heidegger does not abandon his ideal of effecting a new relationship of humankind to Being. In the face of his disappointment with the practical development of National Socialism, he attempts to provide a compensation through his concept of the potential of the work of art. Central to his theories of art is the glorification of the role of the poet. While he still emphasizes that from the *aporia* of the forgetting of being a new individual must step forward to lead humankind into a new era, the political leader is displaced by the figure of the poet.

Hölderlin is for him the canonical German poet. In the Hölderlin lectures of 1935–6 he justifies this choice: 'Hölderlin has not been chosen because his work stands as one amongst many that realize the general essence of poetry, but only because Hölderlin's poetry is determined by the poetic destiny, namely to poeticize specifically the essence of poetry. In a higher sense, Hölderlin is for us the poet

28. Heidegger, *Holzwege*, p. 58.

of poets.'[29] The poet has assumed the essential characteristics of the political leader. He stands in a particular nearness to Being, so that the danger of a false subjectification is minimized. The poet, like the leader before him, is immune to the tyranny of *das Man* and thus has access to existence in the openness of Being in art. The dissolution of the everyday self in the work of art is the basis for the development of the new individual: 'the presence of the master in the work is the only true presence. The greater a master is, the more purely his personality disappears behind the work.'[30] As Max Müller argues, Heidegger creates an essentially mythicized image of Hölderlin,[31] which is largely an extension of the mythical ideal of the spiritual-political leader in his writings of 1933.

The role of the poet as leader is largely determined by his use of language. In the 'Origin of the Work of Art', Heidegger establishes a hierarchy of discourses in which poetry is recognized as the highest form of language. In his analysis of poetic discourse in the works of Hölderlin, he elaborates: 'The poet names the gods and names everything as it is . . . when the poet speaks the fundamental word, beings are named as that which they are in a primary sense. In this way they are recognized as beings. Poetry is literal creation (*Stiftung*) of Being.'[32] Poetic discourse is not the means by which humans are able to conceptualize reality. If this were the case, then the language of poetry would not differ from any other form of discourse that relies on the process of objectification. To live 'poetically' (*dichterisch wohnen*) is to use language as a means to 'call' the 'gods', a metaphor for Being, back to the world. Through poetry, individuals are able to sense the nearness of Being.

For Heidegger, Hölderlin is the 'poet of poets' because, in the age of the 'demythologized' society, he was able to 'sing on the traces of the vanished gods';[33] he was the first poet to poeticize the withdrawal of Being from consciousness in art. In his attempt to 'remythologize' society through poetic discourse, Heidegger mythicizes the potential of language. In the Hölderlin interpretations, the idea of truth as *aletheia* is expanded to encompass the possibility of bringing humans into a new closeness to Being through art. His interpretation of poetic discourse grows directly from another form of mythical thinking. Instead of trying to provide the world with

29. Martin Heidegger, *Erläuterungen zu Hölderlins Dichtung*, Frankfurt/M, 1981, p. 34.
30. Martin Heidegger, *Gelassenheit*, Pfullingen, 1986, p. 168.
31. Max Müller, in *Freiburger Universitatsblätter*, vol. 92, June 1966, p. 17.
32. Heidegger, *Erläuterungen zu Hölderlins Dichtung*, p. 41.
33. Ibid., p. 47.

an entelechy through Fascism, Heidegger now tries to import a system of meaning into society through poetry. In order to achieve this, he ignores the reality of poetry in society, closes his eyes to the everyday existence of the poet and leaves to one side poetry in which the thematic field extends beyond the theme of language itself. Heidegger's understanding of the potential of poetic discourse is based on a wildly selective reading of poetry, just as his conception of Fascism grew out of an esoteric misreading of some of Hitler's politics.

Although Heidegger's writings after 1934 place most emphasis on the salvatory potential of poetry, his idealization of Hölderlin's work and his lectures between the years 1936 and 1946 have a strongly nationalistic flavour:

> Hölderlin's word expresses the Holy and names the singular time and space of the primary decision for the existential orientation of the future history of the gods and humans. The word is, yet unheard, located in the western language of the Germans.
>
> Are not then the sons of the homeland, who are far from the soil of the homeland, offering their lives for the discovery yet to come, and offered in sacrifice, looking back at the homeland which shines towards them – are not these sons of the homeland the nearest relations of the poet? In their sacrifice is located the poetic call to the loved ones in the homeland . . . The return home is the future of the historical essence of the Germans.[34]

This aesthetic justification of nationalism – the sacrificial victims of the war are the 'nearest relations of the poet' – is by no means in conflict with the official 'line' of 1943. Once again, Heidegger contrives to fuse elements of Fascist ideology with the broader structure of his own philosophy. In the *Spiegel* interview of 1966 and other writings, however, he stylizes his emphasis on the spiritual supremacy of Germany and the notion of a specifically German 'destiny' with the help of various etymologies. His justification of his use of the word *Kampf* is a striking example. His use had nothing in common with Nazi propaganda, but was derived from its Greek equivalent (*polemos/eris*, 'argument' or 'quarrel') as expounded by Heraclitus in the fifty-third fragment: 'Quarrel . . . an argument in which the nature of those who argue puts itself at the mercy of the other, thus showing itself and coming to the fore;

34. Ibid., pp. 77, 29.

in Greek: into the open and true.'[35]

The dual nature of paradigmatic models such as 'leader/poet', 'history/destiny', and 'empty speech versus poetic discourse', indicates an essential unity in Heidegger's philosophical projects in all phases of his work. His critique of western metaphysics and his disillusionment with modernity in the period of *Being and Time* both contain elements of negative mythicization. A vacuum thus developed which could only be filled by the positive mythical image of a saviour, which in turn enabled Heidegger to construct a pattern of redemption from his vision of the potential of Fascism. His later mythicization of the image of Hölderlin repeats the model of the *Rektoratsrede*; the salvatory function of the leader is transferred to the figure of the poet. His earlier differentiation of *Historie* and *Geschichte* made possible a parallel rejection of the contemporary scene in favour of a historical construction of a mythical past in the poetry of Hölderlin.

As a philosopher, Heidegger was not content to remain outside the realm of actual social change. Even before 1933, his preference was for a social solution to the ills of the human condition rather than a retreat into aestheticism. He conceived of a 'Saviour' as first an impersonal agency, then a nebulously defined leader, and finally a depersonalized 'poet' who had very little to do with the biographical Hölderlin. In turning to Fascism, he attempted to realize his philosophical goals in the immediate social situation, yet failed to take account of the realities of the politics with which he was dealing. Subsequently, he tried to import a new system of meaning into this 'desacralized world'. The centre of his understanding of both Fascism and poetic discourse lies in the underlying structure of his philosophy, a series of paradigms in a doubled myth.

35. Heidegger, *Das Rektorat*, p. 28.

PART IV

Fascism and Sexuality

–9–

Fascism and the Hypertrophy of Male Adolescence

SILKE HESSE

This chapter takes as its point of departure an examination of ten consecutive numbers of the Berlin-based popular magazine *Am deutschen Herd. Das Blatt der Familie*, namely those published between 25 June and 27 August 1933. The magazine, which was launched just four weeks after Hitler's assumption of power, continued under the directorship of Curt Hotzel (later chief editor of the conformist satiric journal *Kladderadatsch*)[1] up to the end of 1935, when it changed its editor, publisher and title to survive till the middle of 1937.[2]

All translations from the German are by the author, unless otherwise indicated.

1. Curt Hotzel (1894–1967), who had worked as a journalist since 1921, was editor of the *Stahlhelm* radio magazine and, after 1937, of the famous satirical magazine *Kladderadatsch*, founded in 1848. Up to 1933 he had published: *Blutweihe. Gedanken über deutsche Zukunft*, 1919; *Die Stadt des guten Gewissens*, 1920; *Ernst Wachler, Ein Beitrag zur Geistesgeschichte unserer Zeit*, 1921; *Geld macht Geschichte. Das Werk politischer Bankiers*, 1933; *Ins Feld, in die Freiheit gezogen*, 1933. The anthology *Deutscher Aufstand. Die Revolution des Nachkriegs*, on the Freikorps movement, followed in 1934. His subsequent work included seven novels, two dramas and a number of stories. Ideologically, he supports the 'anti-bourgeois affect' of the post-war generation, the 'Prussian philosophy of heroism' and 'a Prussian anarchism that prefers self-annihilation to submission and that gains the strength to persevere to the end from its own doubts', and Nietzsche's philosophy of 'living dangerously'. He professes faith in 'an inherent willingness in man to suffer deprivations', rejects western democracies and their money economies, and believes in the mythical as destined to overcome the merely intellectual. See *Deutscher Aufstand*, Stuttgart, 1934, pp. 1–8 and 345–55. See also Kurt Sontheimer, *Anti-demokratisches Denken in der Weimarer Republik*, Munich, 1962, p. 56.
2. In 1936 the magazine changed publishers from the Deutscher Buchvertrieb Schmidt und Co. to the Lindenverlag H. Fischer. It was now called *Unterm Lindenbaum* and edited by Grete Fischer, continuing till May 1937. Considering that between the years 1926 and 1930 the *Deutsches Bücherverzeichnis* lists eight columns of popular magazines, between 1931 and 1935 two and a half columns, and between 1936 and 1940 only half a column, the demise of the magazine is probably attributable to economic and political austerity and Hitler's 'equalizing' policies, which led to endless repetitions.

The *Deutsches Bücherverzeichnis* describes the magazine as a 'nationale Romanzeitung' (a nationalist paper with an emphasis on fiction). There can be little doubt that, as the timing suggests, the publication was founded in support of the new era to be ushered in by the new regime.

The time segment under scrutiny is of particular interest. It is in the transitional period between the struggle for power before January 1933 and the concerted restructuring of German society that dominated the pre-war years. In mid 1933 the emphasis was on excluding the supposed enemies of the regime with the help of emergency laws. The propaganda machine had not yet begun to work effectively (the *Schriftleitergesetz* (Editors' Law) was not passed till 4 October 1933), and consequently it was still possible to define the new ideals openly and spontaneously without taking into account the pragmatism needed to dupe a nation. *Am deutschen Herd* was, so to speak, an unsolicited votive offering to the cause. By June the magazine had also had time to establish itself.[3]

Magazines specializing in popular literature are complex compilations that express both the conscious and the unconscious preoccupations of a variety of authors, as well as the expectations of

3. Among the better known contributors to *Am deutschen Herd* are the following. (1) Hanns Johst (1890–1978) was President of the Reichsschrifttumskammer and the Deutsche Akademie der Dichtung from 1935 to 1945. He began as a male nurse in Bethel, studied medicine, philosophy and art, became an actor, and was a volunteer in the First World War before he took to writing novels, stories and dramas. (2) Franz Schauwecker (1890–1964) left his studies to fight in the First World War, and wrote stories, novels, drama and poetry. He is best known for his war books. Sontheimer writes: '"The kingdom of the Germans is God's", we are told by Franz Schauwecker, and he sees this kingdom as being initially a spiritual reality that has not yet taken shape externally. "The Reich is the reality of faith. This faith is exclusively a faith of the German people." The real Germany, he continues, in which the idea of the Reich is alive and active, is, deep within its own depths, always a secret Germany, and the reality of the Reich has at most times been obscured and alienated by other forces. But this surface of reality is ruptured again and again. In this way, Schauwecker interprets his epoch as a point in time at which the Reich has once again become visible. The World War had resurrected the idea of the Reich and the power of the Reich was a mighty force in the nation today' (*Anti-demokratisches Denken*, p. 285). (3) Friedrich Hielscher (born 1902), author of the much discussed book *Das Reich*, banned by the Nazis in 1934 and, surprisingly, praised by Ernst Robert Curtius, was a right-wing mystic. Hielscher's ideas, too, revolve around a mystic Reich, envisaged by a select few, whose hour will come once western influences, epitomized by the Weimar state, have been terminated (Sontheimer, *Anti-demokratisches Denken*, pp. 290ff.). During the Nazi era, Hielscher was a right-wing activist in the resistance against Hitler. (4) Gottfried Kölwel (1889–1958) studied philosophy, then travelled widely. He was a poet, dramatist, and writer of novels and stories, with an emphasis on *Heimat* (homeland) and nature. Three volumes of his collected works were published 1962–4.

their readers. They therefore tend to reveal the mentality of a significant section of the community on which they draw, particularly if they are not in the pay of outside interests. (In this particular case only 2–3 per cent of available space was allocated to advertisements.) Consequently it seems permissible to see the results of this investigation as contributing towards an understanding of the nature and concerns of the period.

I shall briefly anticipate my conclusions. It would seem that though there is little doubt of a male bias in Fascist ideology leading to a male dominated society, the phenomenon of Fascism cannot be explained merely in terms of patriarchy, as for instance Wilhelm Reich and Kate Millett have attempted to do (see later), for it relies on significantly different social structures. This also becomes evident when one analyses *Am deutschen Herd.* Though a small sample of popular literature can hardly serve as proof of such a thesis, it may certainly suggest that the thesis is worthy of serious investigation.

Fascist Sympathies

The publication describes itself as a family magazine for hearthside reading, that is, leisure reading. It was aimed mainly at a semi-educated, lower-middle-class audience, though sections of it were clearly intended to appeal also to those with somewhat more education. Its price of 25 Pf. put it within the range of ordinary people. It was issued on newsprint and there were twenty-four pages of A4 format, including the cover.

I shall attempt briefly to outline the contents. Two pages are regularly devoted to recipes and fashion. Here the emphasis is on doing it yourself, cheaply. Fashions are depicted in small sketches, flat-breasted, ladylike, totally unprovocative, suggesting the married woman rather than the young girl. No group of women includes a man. On one occasion children are shown as a mixed group, but of separate individuals who do not interact.

The last half page of the magazine is regularly set aside for riddles, crossword puzzles and the like. Up to two pages are usually filled with fairly random snippets of conjecture or information: whether the stars are inhabited; which mammals build nests; why cities die; whether man or donkey lives longer; how fast various species of game can run; why humans have lost their fur; and so on. Just occasionally these reveal a bias, which will be more fully discussed later.

There is a non-fictional component. As to be expected, *Heimat* (homeland) is an important topic. Seven of the ten numbers have a feature on folk festivals celebrated in regional dress; all are lavishly illustrated with photographs. There are also photographs and articles on German landscape and architectural treasures (Potsdam, Nuremberg).

The wider world gets some coverage under the heading *Aus aller Welt* (from around the world). There are illustrated articles on Ireland, the struggle in Afghanistan, the Eskimos, the city of Socrates, on what is dubbed 'the market of misery in Red Russia' and on Italian Fascism (to mark the occasion of Mussolini's fiftieth birthday), and there is mention of Japanese visitors to a German sporting event.

Contemporary German politics is presented mainly in newsreel-like photographs of uniformed males of all ages. The exception is a feature on women doing rural *Arbeitsdienst* (labour service). In one number the need for air raid shelters is discussed. Aircraft technology receives a mention, as does the submarine.

There is a little history. An article on Versailles and the consequences shows the expected bias. Another on the aged Bismarck, written by the right-wing but anti-Nazi Friedrich Hielscher, argues the superiority of age and experience over youth, however inspiring the enthusiasm of the young may be. It is supplemented with five quotes from Bismarck on the preferability of peace to war. One article gives a new perspective on the famous victory of the Germanic army under Armenius over the Romans led by Varus; the theory put forward is that the long column of the Roman army was the dragon which Siegfried killed. A poem celebrates the determination of a wounded and exhausted Frederick the Great to fight on – heroism, we are told, that led to the victory of Kunersdorf. There is a photograph each of Moltke and Scharnhorst.

The magazine frequently quotes from published works. In addition to the Bismarck quotes on peace, there is a second selection that recommends a cautious approach to political and social problems. Clausewitz is heard affirming the importance of a people taking active steps to defend its dignity and freedom with every last drop of blood. We are told how the young Gneisenau is reprimanded by a military friend when he questions the concept of honour. Klopstock's poem 'Deutschland', which expresses hesitant admiration for the peaceable nature of the German people, is offset by another poem, 'Deutschland 1933', by Heinz Schauwecker, which extols a Germany which, by the grace of God, has been given the Führer in its moment of greatest need and is now aflame, united and awakened. Then, rather unexpectedly, we have Whitman on the importance of people as compared with things. A poem by a seventeenth-century German mercenary expresses confidence in armed strength and victory. A dialect poem by Gorch Fock, killed in the naval battle of Skagerrak, tells of his joy at becoming a sailor. There are aphorisms by Kurt Geucke on the lonely and misunderstood genius; Kleist, Luther, Goethe and Bismarck are mentioned. Some similarly pretentious aphorisms by a certain Schulz-Wilmersdorf present reflections on the state and the inner life.

Another passage is taken from Herrmann Reich's *Buch Michael* (The Book of Michael) and describes the Germans as a people of genius because they think only of their fatherland and are prepared to sacrifice themselves for it. A further quote comes from Willy Schlüter's *Die Mission des Mittelstandes* (The Mission of the Middle Classes). He asserts that great art was only ever born from the womb of the life of the people and was fathered by *Standesgeist* (a sense of social rank), and calls for 'sacred groves established in commemoration of the monumental deed of bringing peace to the nation. Young-Gothic dramas enacted everywhere on regional open-air stages. Young-Gothic assembl[ies], initiated for the proclamation of the cult of life in odes and hymns.' Finally, we have a quote from the notorious *Secessio Judaica* (The Jewish Secession) by Hans Blüher.

There is the occasional book review. The philosophy of Richard Benz is celebrated in an article 'Um die Bestimmung des Deutschen. Wie verhalten sich Geist und Staat' (On the Destiny of the German: The Relation between Spirit and State), which describes him as a disciple of Herder. To give an idea of the argument of Benz's book *Geist und Reich* (Spirit and Reich, 1933), the reviewer cites chapter headings: 'Nation and Idea', 'The Myth of Race', 'The Jewish Question', 'Germanness and Jewishness', 'Blood and Spirit', 'Becoming a People', 'Educated and Uneducated', 'Becoming un-German through Education', 'Technology and Capitalism', 'Film and Radio', 'Germanism and Humanism', 'Militarism as a System'. In spite of this parade of right-wing slogans the quoted conclusion of the book condemns war and recommends a united Europe composed of states that know their own worth. The youth movement is seen as the creator of the 'new German': 'Europe cannot be saved by self-mutilating power struggles, but only by a consciousness of its own worth, with the goal of a united Europe. The Youth Movement was able to achieve the creation of a new German identity.'

There are only two other reviews. The books are *Arbeit und Waffe als Grundlage der Nation* (Work and Weapon as the Basis of the Nation, 1933) by Horst von Metzsch, and *Zurück zum Agrarstaat* (Back to the Agrarian State, 1933) by Friedrich Burgdörfer. Metzsch is described as a 'tireless fighter for military-mindedness and against pacifism and defeatism'. Burgdörfer's book aims at achieving an eventual balance between urban industry and agriculture: 'Safeguarding the possessions and the future of the German nation within the territory of Germany is the ultimate goal of this direction of thought', the reviewer comments.

With the exception of the passage from Whitman (whose appeal was probably his patriotism and irrationalism), the works here drawn on all have a bearing on nationalism. But, at least to some extent, there is still an open forum for discussion, not all the ideas are extreme and, by quoting, the editor achieves a semblance of detachment. There is still quite a strong lobby for peace.

In the first of the magazines here being discussed the editors do, however, sum up the new ideals under the caption of 'Overcoming Versailles'. The slogans are: *Gefolgschaftstreue* (fealty, absolute loyalty to a leader); *Wehrwille* (willingness to bear arms); *Staatsbewußtsein* (consciousness of state and nation); *Gemeinschaftsarbeit* (communal work); *Bodenständigkeit* (sedentariness, rootedness to the soil); *Siedlung* (colonization); *Arbeitsdienst* (labour service); and *Ehrfurcht vor der Leistung* (respect for achievement). They are illustrated with appropriate photographs, subtitled as follows: 'The German Peasant Awakens'; 'The Trades Receive New Recognition'; 'Labour Service Unites the Young Nation'; and 'The Type of the German Sportswoman – a New Generation'. Though two of the seven photographs show uniformed men, they illustrate as yet *Gefolgschaftstreue* rather than *Wehrwille*. Flags are displayed, but no weapons.

The contemporary poetry published by the magazine falls into two categories. There is the poetry of sentimental and usually elegiac mood, of which 'Landschaft' (Landscape) by Hans Maria Ehringhausen is an example. Here springtime and the thunderstorms that are building up – this is already the imagery of revolution – as yet cause only a weariness comparable with that of a pale young nun yearning for love. In contrast, the poetry of Carl Ernst Wieck is dedicated to patriotic indoctrination. A prose translation of his poem to the *Volkskanzler* (people's chancellor), Hitler, reads as follows:

> Since a visible leader has arisen from the great front, the best of our youth and the warriors have thronged to him. They wanted nothing for

> themselves and everything for Germany. They sang, marched and died, laughing at bitter death. Under the ancient symbol a new people is taking shape, emerging from inherited discipline and experiences at the war front. Since the people had lost their ties with the soil, and forgotten the inheritance of their ancestors, they need stern compulsion and self-examination. But people who have been misled cannot be held to blame. Instruction and service will lead them back to the bosom of the nation, be they high or low. To him who knows nothing of the comforts that the masses lòve, who wants nothing but Germanness, to the Chancellor Hitler: *Sieg Heil*!

Finally, a revealing poem by Paul Schulz-Wilmersdorf documents the decision to move from sentimental melancholy to the sensationalist pathos of revolution.

Poems, however, are rare. More than half the space of the magazine is devoted to fiction. In the numbers examined there are two serialized novels that briefly overlap, one of eleven instalments and one of ten, and two novellas of two instalments each. In addition there are numerous stories and anecdotes. The first of the serialized novels is not quite typical of the magazine, though it seems fairly typical of the popular novel of the period.[4] The editor probably had to take what was available to him at short notice; the same applies to a novella by Gottfried Kölwel. In the case of the twenty or so other contributions, there seem to be very clear common concerns, which are of particular interest. They can be summed up as follows:

(1) Not only do all the stories have men as heroes, but in all but one case they are exclusively about men. Women and girls are never mentioned.
(2) In all but two cases, older men are also excluded from the stories.
(3) None of the men is 'attached' to women, or shows any interest in them.
(4) The children of the stories are orphans or without families; in one case, a son leaves a dying father to take part in a rally for the new state.
(5) The stories are about ordinary people. Even in the two cases where one assumes some education, the characters are shown

4. See Helga Geyer-Ryan. 'Trivialliteratur im Dritten Reich – Beobachtungen zum Groschenroman', in Ralf Schnell (ed.), *Literaturwissenschaft und Sozialwissenschaften*, vol. 10, *Kunst und Kultur im Deutschen Faschismus*, Stuttgart, 1978, pp. 217–60.

as workers among workers.

(6) The theme of all the stories is adventure, which allows the heroes to show courage.

Three of the stories are about members of the Sturm-Abteilung (SA: Nazi storm-troops) or the Hitler Youth; two describe episodes from the First World War; four have rural Germany as their setting, and one is set in England. In contrast the remaining ten stories, including the second novel, have an exotic setting. Only in the novel is the territory described a former German colony, New Guinea. None of these ten stories seems to have an obvious political bias, whereas all but one of the first group do. The exotic tales include accounts of expeditions in search of gold or zoological or archaeological treasures, of encounters with dangerous monsters such as snakes, octopuses and crocodiles, and of the training and initiation of native boys. With the exception of the novel, these contributions are all anonymous, quite possibly supplied by the editorial staff. The four stories with a clear Nazi bias were all written by one author, Carl Ernst Wieck. Only two of the non-exotic stories are anonymous. All this suggests that the exotic adventure story is compatible with an editorial policy that supports the National Socialist cause.

An all-male literature of adventure existed in the *Lanzer* stories that had followed the First World War; it was based on the activities of members of the Freikorps. This has been fascinatingly analysed by Klaus Theweleit.[5] The fact that this tradition is almost totally ignored in the magazine (even though the editor was working on an anthology in this area) suggests that in his view masculinity was of more significance for a Fascist mentality than military and nationalist subject-matter.

At this point, it needs to be emphasized again that this is supposed to be a 'magazine for the family'. It did of course supply women with recipes and fashion of a sort, and perhaps the relatively rare sentimental poems were intended to appeal to the young girl; the men could probably have been expected to show an interest in the nationalist statements quoted from various sources. What remains noteworthy is that the imaginative literature is directed entirely towards the young male and presents only his world. The family at which the paper professes to be aimed never becomes the material of fiction. For married men, for women and

5. Klaus Theweleit, *Männerphantasien*, vol. I, *Frauen, Fluten, Körper, Geschichte*, vol. 2, *Männerkörper. Zur Psychoanalyse des weissen Terrors*, Reinbek, 1980.

for girls, real identification with the heroes would not have been possible; at most there could be a nostalgic wish for a change of role, or a spectator's admiration of the young hero's deeds of derring-do. The new *Menschenbild* (image of humanity) is exclusively inspired by and oriented towards the young male.

A Male World

There is a similar bias in the photographic material. Of 150 photographs, approximately 109 depict males; twenty-nine show women and eleven show children. There is only one photograph in all ten numbers of the magazine that shows a man and a woman standing together, casually, and at some distance – beyond a small lake in a park.[6]

Of the photos of women, twelve simply display regional dress. There are two fashion photographs; the models are ladies of Potsdam society, not the class to which the magazine addresses itself. Eight are of the 'new woman', engaged in sporting or organized nationalist activities, and three are of women in foreign lands. Only one is of a young woman in her own right.

Of the male photos, eighty-eight depict politicians, men in uniform, or men taking part in mass rallies or group activities of a nationalist nature. Four depict sportsmen; four show men in regional dress; five show the 'worker'; and seven are of foreigners. Only one photo shows a grandfather, with a child on his arm, pointing out an exhibit of a bomb; even this is hardly a 'private' photo.

One or two of the stories deserve a closer look. The novella *Begegnung* (Meeting, 1933) by Hanns Johst, later the president of the Reichsschrifttumskammer (Reich Chamber of Writing) and the German Academy of Literature and a brigade leader in the SS, describes a meeting with a monk who has been transferred to another monastery. While the narrator helps him to find his way in unfamiliar alpine territory, he is told his story – the story of a young peasant lad who lives through the slaughter of the First World War and takes a vow to become a monk in gratitude for his survival and that of his comrades. The point is clear: this man has no need of women.

6. An examination of the 1934 issue of the *Völkischer Beobachter* does not show a noticeable bias towards the male sex, though photographs of couples are also missing.

> What I had never before experienced here became a reality without painful intention; free from enforced impotence, here was a man who went his way, released from the urges and oppressions of the sexes. I myself, who cannot look a woman I meet in the eye without feeling both gladdened and saddened by my desire that she might lay the grace and the courage of her arms about my neck and, face to face, give me the secret yearning of her being . . . That is, I myself, feeling thus completed by my desire for women, distrusted every man in whose life the game of love could not be perceived clearly and unequivocally. But the man beside me, whose whole being was determined by love . . . smilingly shook his head when he saw that I had asked him about the bliss of women without actually troubling him with words.

This experience arouses in the narrator the vision of a new world where a communal life of celibacy and hard unselfish labour is no longer regarded with resentment, where personal fulfilment is no longer the ideal. Woman, he realizes, is merely a distraction from true love, which, by implication, is love of the fatherland and willingness to sacrifice one's life, one way or another. It seems that we are here to be made aware of the transition from a 'normal' heterosexual view of life to a celibate, ascetic, masculine ideal, the world of National Socialism.

Carl Ernst Wieck's story 'Bastigkeit, or a Change of Substance' begins with the following paragraph:

> Malicious tongues had once claimed that the principal characteristic of Mr Bastigkeit of Widönen near Tilsit was his wife, and consequently he needed no other characteristics . . . But that was a stupid lie, though one could admit that without this splendid specimen of a wife Bastigkeit would never have become head of the district council. But how can one then explain that he was voted in again after his wife died during the birth of their eighth child? – Thus our Lord always puts the slanderers to shame, even though such damned idiots have long lost any notion of shame.

It is clearly a terrible disgrace for a man to be in any way dependent on or overshadowed by his wife, even if she is a good wife (and who could doubt it, when she has borne him seven sons?). The last child, alas, was a little girl who, as proof of her inferiority, killed her mother at birth. The oldest three sons had died defending their homeland against the Russians. Their photos, along with that of their general, are regularly adorned by their proud mother with sprigs of rosemary and the national colours, black, white and red. But as the years pass, the four men merge together for her, to become simply 'the hero on the wall'. The sons are not individuals; they are soldiers, to be sacrificed proudly.

The father, on the other hand, who, as the story points out again and again, is in control and has no need of his wife, has fastened on to the catchword 'a change of substance' and is determined to improve himself. But the times are bad, and when the old man sees his possessions diminishing, he lies down to die. The old generation cannot bring about change. It is the youngest son who storms in with news of fundamental renewal.

> 'Father, can you hear? Germany is awakening. Hindenburg has formed a national front with Hitler. There will be torch-light processions in Tilsit tonight, and in Ragnit and in Königsberg, everywhere the people are rising up, even in Berlin.
> For Hitler, Father, for freedom and bread.'
> At that the old man raised his hand: 'A change of substance – that means filling the gaps and more, because it is God's will.
> Blessed be He.'
> The lad hesitated, half out of respect and half out of pity. Then he made an about turn to march off to the torch-light procession in Tilsit, along with the other lads.

Youth does not wait for the old to die; their processions to herald the new are more important. Family bonds are of no significance when the state calls. All the same, the simple old man, part of the *Volk* as he is, knows what the nation needs: 'But the government in the Wilhelmstrasse in Berlin, the new ministers and Hindenburg knew that old Bastigkeit – who incidentally hastened to join his wife and his three oldest sons – that old Bastigkeit had been absolutely right in life and in death.' Significantly, the story is set on the outermost boundary of German territory, to demonstrate the scope of the new movement. It is in combination with stories such as these that the young male stories, in themselves innocuous, assume significance.

Martin Berger's novel *The White House on Lake Starnberg* is a rambling romance about young people and their parents from the wealthier Munich business sector. It is not characteristic for the magazine because the milieu is a little too prosperous, all sexes and ages are represented, the story is family-based, and the climax is marriage. All the same, it undeniably belongs to the period of early Nazism. The heroine has fallen in love with a young officer, subsequently crippled by war injuries. He is too noble to accept her sacrifice, as he sees marriage to a cripple, and brutally tries to be kind; but she persists, wins the hero for herself and, after the romance has been conducted with utmost chastity, we are told that within a year of marriage the young woman gives birth to a healthy son. The man may marry only when he is crippled, and then only for the purpose of procreating sons who will be heroic like their father and prepared to die for the fatherland. Though the pattern of the old popular romance still shows through, the spirit of the novel is already that of the celibate male world in which women are tolerated only as mothers of sons.

Women

Though nearly all the stories avoid mentioning women, the magazine does contain a number of short articles that define the place of woman within marriage and society. The 'Ten Commandments for the Married Woman' encourage a wife to read about politics, have an opinion and defend it, be a companion to her husband if he is intelligent and be his friend if not, but at all times to give her husband the impression that he is ultimately smarter. It ends with the admonition to respect his mother as his first love. There is no hint of a sexual relation between husband and wife; you please your man by cooking well and not humiliating him.

Another article poses the question: 'Should couples keep secrets from one another?' The answer, presented in lengthy arguments, is yes. The husband's professional secrets, the secrets the wife has been told in confidence, should not be shared. Trust is more important. It is implied that the loyalty of husband and wife to each other should always take second place, that they are to function as separate entities rather than as a pair.

Another little piece talks about thoughtfulness in marriage, and concludes that all men want women who will let them forget the burden and the struggle of their working life, who spoil them in a thousand little ways. Elsewhere, we are told that women in Hindustan have their own laws. If their husbands do not provide for them adequately they are permitted to hit back, pull hairs from their beards and stay away from home for up to ten days. The husband is the provider, to be honoured by his wife if he performs his duty well.

In a comment on the origin of the engagement ring, buying and stealing a wife are presented as the original forms of marriage. Germanic law did not require the bride to consent to the marriage, though in later times, we are told, the bride became a partner to the contract.

The only article signed by a woman in these ten numbers of the magazine is 'The Mother Educates her Children for the New State' by Elly Ostwald. Here physical fitness comes first, and next the strengthening of character. We must have masculine men and feminine women, we are told, though masculinity should not be seen as brutal egotism and femininity not as wimpishness and vanity. A sense of community is all-important – don't protect children, they must learn to defend themselves and bear pain. The meaning of life is battle. So a strong will is more important than good manners. Children must learn to be hard-working and orderly. They must learn to keep secrets. They should be introduced to politics and told what duties and hopes await the new generation. Children need ideals, leaders to follow. Only a mother who is spiritually young and has understood the goals of the new Germany, if not intellectually then with feminine intuition, and who can appreciate all the great, courageous and creative deeds of men (males), will plant the right seed in the soul of her child:

> And when a nine-year-old boy includes the Führer in his nightly prayer without being asked to do so, when a healthy ten-year-old girl declares she wants to marry one day so that she can have many children, 'for Germany must under no circumstances face extinction' – then a mother knows that she is on the right track in the way she is training her children and that she is doing her part towards the resurrection of the German *Volk*.

Here it is clearly stated that the woman exists to bear children not to her husband but to Germany, and the man exists to follow the Führer. Earlier, the point is made that only men are capable of performing great, courageous and creative deeds. The distinction between the sexes is all-important.

This is also suggested by a competition advertised in three successive numbers of the magazine. The entrant is asked to classify the photos of six young children according to sex. One suspects that clothes are intended to provide clues, so that the rate of accuracy will be high and prove that sex differences are obvious at first sight.

Finally, there is some talk of the 'new woman', represented by sportswomen who throw the javelin and by young girls willing to work as farm labourers. They are sexless ersatz men, not in competition or fellowship with 'real' men but simply their dim reflection. Increasingly, these girls were to be kept busy and out of reach of young men in the Bund Deutscher Mädel (BDM: Association of German Girls).

All this does not add up to a clear image of woman. She is the independent comrade of man, his weaker double, his intellectual inferior, his handmaiden with a duty to humour him, and the mother who bears children to the Führer rather than to her husband. But there is a common denominator: the woman is at all times a thing separate from the man, she is to keep away from him, and there should under no circumstances be a sexual bond between the two.[7]

Fascism and Patriarchy

The fear and rejection of sexuality characteristic of Fascist man has often been noted. As early as 1933, Wilhelm Reich had described Fascism in terms of the sexual repression at which the patriarchal authoritarian family aimed in order to secure and maintain the power of the patriarch.[8] Because obedience to parental authority was so deeply instilled in both women and young men, obedience to the political father figure came naturally. If we examine these magazines, however, we will find little evidence of the authoritarian family. The future is shown to be firmly in the hands of young men with no family attachments.

These tendencies are, of course, visible elsewhere as well. In an address to a youth rally in November 1934 reported in the *Völkischer Beobachter*, for example, Goebbels repeatedly makes the point that he is young enough, at least in heart, to be accepted by his audience as one of them: 'In his introduction, Reichsminister Goebbels declared that it was a particular pleasure for him to speak before young people, because he felt young enough himself to speak to people whose attitudes and status he shared.' A little later, after disparaging young people who appear to be older than their years, Goebbels reiterates: 'There are grey-heads in whose breast

7. Marianne Lehker, *Frauen im Nationalsozialismus*, Frankfurt, 1984, p. 28, comes to similar conclusions. Referring to a quoted poem she writes: 'The relationship between the sexes expressed in this poem is not based on mutual living or experience, but is evidence of a cold lack of communication between the sexes. Both live in their so-called naturally determined world; the woman remains in her house while the men "conquer" the world in their men's clubs, be they the army or the National Socialist Party. It could almost be said that male restlessness is intended to prevent closer contacts. This background, which the poem merely suggests, can be specified by any number of National Socialist texts.' See also Renate Wiggershaus, *Frauen unterm Nationalsozialismus*, Wuppertal, 1984.
8. Wilhelm Reich, *The Mass Psychology of Fascism* (1933), tr. Vincent R. Carfagno, New York, 1971.

beats a heart that is just as young as yours. They belong with you, and perceive themselves, too, as belonging with you.'[9] In a patriarchy, the father rules by virtue of his age. Goebbels also praises his mixed audience of boys and girls for the wonderful 'masculine' tent town they have erected; girls are tolerated only in so far as they work towards masculine ends.

Hitler himself, in spite of his glorification of all things masculine, was not really a patriarch. He avoided marriage, he had no children, his 'girl-friend' Eva Braun was hidden from public view. The uniform he dressed in made him look like one of the group. It is to be assumed that he figured as the leader of the pack or peer group of unmarried men rather than as their father figure.

In her classic description of sexual politics, Kate Millett writes: 'If one takes patriarchal government to be the institution whereby that half of the populace which is female is controlled by that half which is male, the principles of patriarchy appear to be twofold: male shall dominate female, elder male shall dominate younger . . . Patriarchy's chief institution is the family.'[10] The term 'patriarchy' certainly suggests fatherhood, superior age and family structures, though it is often used more loosely, as Rosalind Coward points out: 'Variously, patriarchal relations describe the oppression of all women by all men (what is often also referred to as sexism), a particular kind of kinship structure, or finally a residual ideology of male dominance. The latter is thought to have arisen from a kinship organization which has since been superseded.'[11]

In the material from our magazine – and it appears to be representative – age, paternity and family are explicitly rejected values. In the rare cases where fathers are mentioned they are weak, misguided and useless old men, who have no hope of solving the problems they and their families face. Only the young are capable of this and, as previously mentioned, most of the young heroes are orphans or without families.

Most historians today would agree that the Nazis supported the family, in the main, as a breeding ground specifically for young males. The members of a family were effectively kept apart by being locked into separate groups which left them little leisure time together, thus minimizing family influences. Children were encouraged to inform on their parents, as loyalty to the state was

9. *Völkischer Beobachter*, no. 306, 2 November 1934, p. 14.
10. Kate Millett, *Sexual Politics* (1969), New York, 1978, pp. 34, 45.
11. Rosalind Coward, *Patriarchal Precedents. Sexuality and Social Relations*, London, 1983, p. 270.

always 'higher' than loyalty to the family.[12] The education of the children was increasingly taken over by the state. The new divorce laws of 6 July 1938 further weakened the family, by making it easier for married men to become unattached entities once more.[13]

I would suggest that, rather than patriarchy, the very different structure of a gang of adolescent youths is the model of Fascist society. The political value of this model is fairly transparent. Firstly, the adolescent is the unattached person. He has outgrown the family of his childhood and has not yet acquired new commitments; he is responsible for no one but himself. This makes him more mobile than other members of society. Secondly, he is still at a formative stage in which he seeks role models to imitate. He will follow a leader and identify with him. Physically he is gaining strength, and is eager to consolidate this with exercise and exertion. In most societies, he tends to move within a pack or peer group which is both uniform and intensely competitive. His sexuality is awakened, but as yet not firmly focused; it can easily be directed towards ideals and heroes. All these characteristics tend to make him a dedicated follower of whichever hero he has chosen. This hero gains in attraction if he is also the hero of other peer group members. Because of these qualities, the male gang becomes a most efficient tool in the hands of a dictator. All armies exploit the model to some extent; in Germany it came to dominate an entire society.

It is interesting to speculate on the reasons for this development. During the First World War, Germany was still very much under the control of the fathers, who considered their sons as property to be used for their own ends and shamed them into enlisting. Perhaps it was also felt that these sons deserved to be sacrificed, as their incipient rebelliousness was beginning to become a threat. The father–son conflict, now biased in favour of the son, was a popular literary motif with younger writers. Remarque's novel *All Quiet on the Western Front* (1929) can be read as an accusation of the older generation who had betrayed their sons.

But even before the First World War, youth groups like the

12. See also Theweleit, *Männerphantasien*, vol. 2, pp. 428ff.
13. Hannelore Kessler, *'Die Deutsche Frau'. Nationalsozialistische Frauenpropaganda im 'Völkischer Beobachter'*, Cologne, 1981, p. 88, describes the central precept of the divorce laws of 6 July 1938: 'Marriage is to serve in the first place the preservation and the augmentation of the German *Volk*.' She points out that 'even a single refusal to have sex on the part of the woman offers grounds for a quick and cheap divorce to the husband. Within marriage the law delivered the woman into the power of her husband as a sex object to which he had a legitimate claim, and secondly – as a result of the ban on contraceptives and abortion – into the power of the state as a machine for bearing children.'

Wandervögel had begun to form; after it, they grew and proliferated with amazing rapidity. By the 1920s, power-mongers found it expedient to woo their support.[14] The Freikorps, made up of disgruntled young war veterans, represented a very different kind of youth group. For years after the termination of the First World War they virtually waged their own battles. And by the late 1920s, all the major parties were supported by private armies of more or (usually) less disciplined gangs of youths.

Klaus Theweleit's study *Male Fantasies* (1977) is an examination of the psyche of the Freikorps soldier as a prototype of Fascist man. He sees him as characterized by an incomplete dissociation from his maternal origin, leading to an insecure sense of self. Men of this kind perceive their nature as being amorphous and flowing, contained only by an armour of rigid habits, posturing and strict self-control. Anything that could relax their vigilance is considered a threat. The severest of these threats is sex, in which the precariously sustained identity has to encounter the 'Other'. According to Theweleit, 'not being fully born' can be caused by inadequate nurturing by the mother or by an attachment that is carried on for too long.[15] In a society like that of early twentieth-century Germany, where – in the wake of theorists like Otto Weininger[16] – motherhood was considered to be not merely a stage in a woman's life but her essential nature (if she were not a whore; the two roles were proclaimed mutually exclusive), it is not surprising that women either rejected the mother role or carried it on in perpetuity.

While youth movements were gaining momentum, the growing women's movement had for some time been provoking extraordinary outbursts of misogyny from otherwise reasonable men; Schopenhauer and Nietzsche may serve as examples.[17] Fear of an

14. See Hermann Giesecke, *Vom Wandervogel bis zur Hitlerjugend*, Munich, 1981, p. 85: 'There was a veritable cult of youth that was reciprocally confirmed: many adults projected their hopes and expectations on to the young generation, which, on the whole, defined itself as the "true" substance of the people – right through all the strata of society and party groupings. In this way "youth" was stylized as the elite of the nation or the class struggle.'
15. Theweleit, *Männerphantasien*, vol. 1, p. 212.
16. Otto Weininger, *Geschlecht und Charakter*, Vienna, 1903.
17. Cf. Arthur Schopenhauer, *Parerga und Paralipomena* (1851), anticipating NS ideas: 'Because fundamentally women exist solely for the propagation of the race and find in this their entire vocation, they are altogether more involved with the species than with individuals, and in their hearts take the affairs of the species more seriously than they do those of the individual. This gives their entire nature and all their activities a certain levity and in general a direction fundamentally different from those of the man: which is why dissension

upsurge of female values was widespread. This, too, may have fuelled a separatist and aggressive male reaction.

The Fascist gang model, as it developed in Germany, negated woman rather than subordinated her. With the beginning of the war, the men marched out of the country, often never to return. More and more women were left to fend for themselves and were obliged, in spite of the official ideology, to join the workforce and take over the running of their families. The women's groups, whose initial purpose had been firstly to segregate women from men and secondly to make them subservient to the male cause, actually gave opportunities for female solidarity. The defeat of the patriarchs by their sons necessarily weakened patriarchy. The deaths of the sons diminished male influence further. Fascism can perhaps be seen as the extreme and self-destructive final phase of *patriarchy*, and not merely of capitalism as in traditional Marxist theory.

Every society that decisively favours one sex or age group creates an imbalance that is bound to be at least to some extent problematic. As social systems, both patriarchy and matriarchy (if it ever existed) would fall into this category. However, the father and mother are each defined in terms of their relationships to their partners on the one hand and their offspring on the other, even though these may be given inferior rank; patriarchy and its mythical counterpart matriarchy consequently must retain at least some notion of a mixed human community and the interrelation of its members. By contrast the adolescent is not attached to other social groups; a male adolescent society is extreme in its one-sidedness and consequent potential for distorting and destroying human relationships. It is both unstable and unstabilizing. It is hard to say to what extent the Fascist experience has worked for or against women. Extreme conditions tend to trigger a conservative reaction, and there is no doubt that this was also the case in Germany.

In conclusion, let me quote once more from Rosalind Coward's study *Patriarchal Precedents*:

> The application of the term 'patriarchal' to all aspects of male control and dominance can obscure the differences between familial forms, differences which are vitally important if any understanding of sexual relations is to be constructed. We need ways of talking about shifts from male dominance within the patriarchal family to male dominance outside the family.

---

between married couples is so frequent and indeed almost the normal case' (in *Essays and Aphorisms*, tr. R. J. Hollingdale, Harmondsworth, 1970, p. 84).

> In addition the term 'patriarchal' describes a form of power which does not do justice to the complexity of the problem of sexual division and society. It limits what can be said in terms of the production and redefinition of sexual identities in a number of forms.[18]

I should like to argue, with Coward, that the term 'patriarchy' is of little help in studying the phenomenon of Fascism, of which German society in the 1930s and 1940s was only one example. Feminists will need to employ at least two major models, the patriarchal family and the male adolescent gang, and will need to understand the relationship of these models to each other. Otherwise, both the past and the present are likely to be misinterpreted.

Of course, Fascism cannot be exhaustively explained merely with reference to male adolescence. Yet most of the major theories of Fascism emphasize the youthful nature of the movement and, even more, its masculinity, in terms both of participation and of traditionally masculine values. These observations need to be placed in a different context.

18. Coward, *Patriarchal Precedents*, pp. 271f.

–10–

'My Sex the Revolver'

Fascism as a Theatre for the Compensation of Male Inadequacies

JOHN MILFULL

Attempts to explain the success of Fascism in Germany and Italy which restrict themselves to the economic and political spheres often end in a curious negative reinforcement of the 'leader principle'. If the masses were persuaded to charge into the abyss like the Gadarene pigs, it can only have been the result of a manipulation so clever that the manipulators acquire an aura of diabolic cunning more appropriate to myth or fairy tale than historical analysis. Finally, too, we are required either to accept that the leaders were super-Machiavellis who, like the tragic heroes of whom they are the grotesque parodies, were marked by a fatal flaw which led them to hazard their ill-gotten gains in a ridiculous gamble; or to make them true devils, who from the beginning foresaw and affirmed the self-destructive momentum of Fascism, building their own funeral pyre with Luciferian glee.

I find it far easier to assume that Hitler, Mussolini and their cliques, for all their manipulative skills, were actually convinced of the truth of their own mythologies, that these mythologies grew out of their own socialization patterns, and that the decisive element in their ability to persuade others of the attractions of the Fascist 'millennium' lay in the promise of acting out repressed phantasies and wishes shared by leaders and led. This is not to plunge into some metaphysics of 'human nature' or a dehistoricized 'mass psychology', but to affirm that socialization patterns are the 'real face' of the dominance relations in a society, that the family is not only the 'smallest cell' of society (in both senses of the word?) but its microcosm.

For many years we have been too embarrassed to confront the phenomenon of 'ethnic differences', fearing to fall into the morass of biologism or racism, but the experience of multi-culturalism, and the anthropological debate, puts the question back on the agenda in a different and vital sense. Are all cultures, and the socialization processes in which they are reflected and through which they survive, essentially 'equal'? Taken to its extreme, an 'anthropological approach' can suggest an endless stasis, in which cannibalism or clitoridectomy are cancelled out by nuclear weapons or pollution, and any concept of progress disappears without trace. Walter Benjamin tried to ensure the success of historical materialism by enlisting the services of 'the dwarf theology' to provide a direction for history which his angel, turned backwards to the past, was unable to perceive in it. It seems to me even more essential that, under the shadow of nuclear and ecological catastrophe, we summon the dwarf of humanist ethics, emaciated and battered as he or she may be from the experience of two centuries of 'enlightenment', to guide our hands in the ultimate game of chess that humanity is playing, lest it become an 'end-game' in a sense more frightening than Beckett's. If 'human nature' is not to remain merely an Ozymandias-like message etched on the ruins of history, but to become once more an object and subject of change, we must free ourselves from an 'objectivity' which contains our own death-warrant. And yet, the 'object' is extraordinarily complex. If we refuse to accept 'human nature', and the socialization processes that produce it, as immutable, we are nevertheless forced to admit that, while these processes can react rapidly to changes and fashions in the social environment, they also 'fossilize' reactions to much earlier stages of development. One has to assume, for instance, that patriarchal forms of society evolved in response to specific social and environmental conditions; yet their 'fossilization' in socialization processes survived the disappearance of these conditions, and it is by now a truism to state that equality between the sexes cannot be achieved merely by legislation or 'social engineering'. It is hard not to agree with Irmtraud Morgner that this question is directly linked to the even more basic issue of our survival. A society which transmits patterns of behaviour based on dominance and violence to its male children can scarcely be surprised if they show themselves susceptible to these viruses in later life, however 'rational' and 'humane' its explicit values may seem.

As an eruption of violence and brutality into an apparently 'civilized' society, Nazism offers itself as a horrific 'test case' for such hypotheses. If we assume, as I suggested above, that the manipulations of the German Right could not have succeeded if they had not, consciously or unconsciously, (re-)activated phantasies of dominance and violence shared by 'Führer' and *Volk*, we must also ask to what extent this propensity to violence was itself grounded in shared socialization processes. In this chapter I can do no more than offer some preliminary observations, based on a rather random selection of literary texts which reflect this problem, directly and indirectly. I cannot answer the implied question of whether specific elements in this socialization process in Germany (and Italy?), in conjunction with the economic and political determinants, 'produced' Fascism; I merely record my conviction that a comparative social psychology ought to address such issues, and not simply attempt to mediate between a set of dehistoricized Freudian 'universals' and the specific historicity of Fascism in Germany and Italy. If psychoanalysis is to be of assistance to us in an attempt to uncover the roots of destructive behaviour, it must become *dynamic* and see socialization processes not as interactions between a static 'self' and a changing environment, but as the 'precipitate' of collective and concrete reactions to this and earlier environments, changing much less rapidly than the environment itself, but changing nevertheless, and reflecting differences in environment in marked dissimilarities in attitudes. 'Socialization for peace' cannot allow itself the luxury (myth) of a value-free anthropology which sacrifices hope in the name of 'tolerance'.

It is a source of real regret to me that Klaus Theweleit was unable to attend the 1987 Sydney conference from which this volume originated, as his book *Männerphantasien* (Male Fantasies, 1977) in many ways set the agenda for the debate, while leaving its perhaps most crucial question in suspense.[1] Theweleit's analyses of attitudes to sexuality and violence in the writings of the 'first soldiers of the Third Reich' – members of the Freikorps which played a leading role in the repression of any genuine social reform after the débâcle of the First World War – construct a fascinating and entirely convincing image of the 'Fascist mentality', but ultimately beg the question as to whether Fascism is a neurosis of the patriarchal system, or whether the 'complexes' he describes are intimately linked to the social and psychological history of the Kaiserreich. I want to invert his approach by applying similar categories to a number of GDR texts which look back at the Fascist period, especially in regard to the experience of childhood, adolescence, the family and sexuality. They range from Dieter Noll's best-seller *The*

1. Klaus Theweleit, *Männerphantasien*, 2 vols, Frankfurt, 1977.

Adventures of Werner Holt,[2] which vacillates oddly between adventure novel and self-analysis, through the 'autobiographical reportage' of Erich Loest's 'A Pistol at Sixteen',[3] to Heiner Müller's 'The Iron Cross'[4] and Franz Fühmann's 'The Jews' Car',[5] both highly structured attempts to explore the basis of Fascist attitudes. For all C. G. Jung's strictures about the difficulties of a psychoanalytical approach to 'reflective' texts, I hope to demonstrate that the 'uncomplicated' narratives of Loest and Noll support and confirm the analytical insights of Fühmann and Müller.

Four male writers? In this context, I think, no apology is required. I was very struck by the title of Silke Hesse's contribution 'Fascism and the Hypertrophy of Male Adolescence' (chapter 9), and was almost tempted to change the 'and' to an 'or' and borrow it. For however unpleasant the revelations of Gisela Kaplan and Carole Adams (chapter 11) about the attractions of Fascism to women, no one would deny that in an almost absolute sense Fascism was 'male business', supported and tolerated by women, but excluding them from any important role within its scheme of things other than that of breeders and feeders. It seems, therefore, not only reasonable but necessary to focus on male responses to Fascism, and on Fascism as essentially a 'male response'.

Dieter Noll's *The Adventures of Werner Holt* (1960, 1963) has a curious history. Originally conceived as a trilogy, which was to accompany the development of the semi-autobiographical 'hero' from his adolescence in the Third Reich to final integration in GDR society, it was abandoned after the appearance of the second volume to a fairly negative critical reception, despite the fact that the first volume, published in 1960, had become one of the great popular successes of GDR literature. The reasons for this failure to complete the original plan are to be sought less in changing directions in cultural policy than in inherent contradictions in the first volume, which the author was manifestly unable to resolve in its sequel, and which both determined its success with a wide audience and made it an unusually interesting subject for our investigation.

2. Dieter Noll, *Die Abenteuer des Werner Holt* (1960, 1963), 2 vols, Berlin/Weimar, 1980, 1983.
3. Erich Loest, 'Pistole mit 16', in *Etappe Rom*, Berlin, 1975, pp. 73–120.
4. Heiner Müller, 'Das eiserne Kreuz' (1955), in Klaus Wagenbach (ed.), *Lesebuch. Deutsche Literatur zwischen 1945 und 1959*, Berlin, 1980, pp. 148–9.
5. Franz Fühmann, 'Das Judenauto' (1968), in Klaus Wagenbach (ed.), *Lesebuch. Deutsche Literatur der sechziger Jahre*, Berlin, 1980, pp. 19–25.

In retrospect, Werner Holt seems an ideal identification figure for readers who wanted to come to terms with their own past in the Third Reich. He is not a 'true' Nazi, but a confused child from a broken marriage, whose values have been disturbed by the separation of his incompatible parents. His father is a scientist with moral scruples, who refuses to cooperate in the development of bacteriological weapons; his mother is the caricature of a capitalist's daughter. As a result Werner is forced to seek his models elsewhere; his attraction to Gilbert Wolzow's Prussian militarism is carefully balanced by his weakness for Uta Barnim and her aristocratic-aesthetic rejection of Nazism, and for the daughter of a member of the resistance. Later, he is even given the chance to allow two captured Czech partisans to escape the terror of Nazi retribution. These 'alibi' elements conceal the essential questionableness of Noll's undertaking; he has transformed the experience of growing up under Nazism into an 'adventure novel', which can be read as 'entertainment' without the author or the reader admitting it to themselves.

Read in this light, Holt's 'adventures' conform to easily recognizable patterns, many of which correspond closely to the structures Theweleit identifies in Freikorps literature. The common element is the desire to prove an insecure 'masculinity' by impressing a male peer group. The result is a curious mixture: a Karl May cum Boy Scout cult of 'roughing it', escaping from the 'discreet charm' of the Fascist bourgeoisie into the 'outlaw band' (a late, perverted offspring of Schiller's *Robbers*) to show nature, and the peer group, who's boss; echoes of the experiential war novel, '*men* struggle against appalling odds'; and perhaps even more significantly, a kind of sexual *Bildungsroman* (novel of education), verging sometimes on soft-core pornography. The witch versus Virgin Mary polarity, so devastatingly analysed by Theweleit and much recent feminist criticism, is perhaps the secret centre of the novel. The problem is prefigured in the marriage of Holt's parents, in which a decent bourgeois intellectual is seduced by an immoral capitalist witch, and extended to Holt's vacillation between Frau Ziesche, the demonically named wife of an SS official and *stepmother* of the group 'nasty', who corrupts his innocence while her husband is off brutalizing Eastern Europe; the aesthetic and inaccessible Uta; and the 'little girl' Gundel, to whom he can feel paternal and protective. It is more than a coincidence that Werner's initiation into the mysteries of sexuality by Frau Ziesche is accompanied by relevations about gas chambers and concentration camps. On an unconscious level, both Dieter Noll and his protagonist clearly identify Fascist brutality and despiritualized sexuality as the Scylla and Charybdis through which the boat of true 'manhood' must be guided. Yet this concept of 'manhood' is built on too many premises shared with its Fascist inverse to allow such comforting separations. It is not female sexuality which is the ally of Fascism, but the fear of it, and the attempt to compensate this sense of male inadequacy through the construction of a male myth of power and dominance. If Fascism is the ultimate perversion of this myth, it is also its ultimate critique; in 'sharing' Frau Ziesche with her SS husband, Holt (and Noll) betray their fascination with the 'other' man they contain in themselves. Noll's failure to penetrate these contradictions revenges itself in the sequel, where Werner, robbed of the author's vicarious participation in his (s)exploits, no longer appropriate in the context of socialist reconstruction, rapidly demonstrates his inability to maintain the identification between author and reader which was the basis of the novel's original 'success'.

Erich Loest's 'A Pistol at Sixteen' (1975) offers a refreshingly frank and direct account of male adolescence under Nazism, which resolutely resists the temptation to distance the experience through fictionalization or the construction of 'mitigating factors'. Against the background of the collapse of the democratic tradition in his home town, Mittweida, Loest recounts the construction of a heroic myth of adolescence through the Nazi youth organizations and his own seduction by it. The element of compensation appears here consciously and openly: from the comedy of the opening pages, where Erich profanes the 'holiest moment' of taking the oath to join the Jungvolk by an irresistible desire to pee, which leaves him in the men's toilet pushing his little penis through the leg of his shorts, to the pistol of the title, a present from his father on his sixteenth birthday and the certificate of manhood. He had 'often watched his father clean his weapon from the First World War, and knew how to manage the complicated safety catch'. But the pistol comes too late, and his father's message, 'You're old enough now, don't do anything silly with it', seems meaningless in the aftermath of Stalingrad and his imminent call-up. The 'weak heart' that sidelines him in the training rituals of the master race, and his own increasing awareness that he is no Siegfried, are accompanied by the recognition of the objective function of the Hitler Youth, to prepare cannon fodder for a lost war. The 'theatre' of Nazism, the torch processions, the outings and the mass rallies, crumble before the reality of war and the realization of his own inadequacy; the pistol, the symbol of his manhood, and the insignia of the Hitler

Youth are disposed of, along with the role whose costume they were. And although Loest's purpose is less to analyse the evidence of his own adolescence than to break with the taboo he so trenchantly criticizes and present it 'uncorrected' by later perspectives, he leaves the reader in no doubt as to the more general relevance of his own seduction, both by its implicit extension back to the world of the fathers, the gun from the First World War and the collapse of opposition to the Nazis, and by his explicit recognition of the need to explain how 'people who had no power, and perhaps didn't even want any, were transformed when power, however petty, fell into their laps.' Loest's male narrative is unusually and disturbingly honest about the link between this latent desire for power and the rituals of male socialization under Fascism, which legitimate and make overt a goal of the process which had previously been covered by an ideological fig-leaf: the revolver-penis as the sign of manhood, ready to subdue the 'enemy' (and) the woman.

Heiner Müller's 'The Iron Cross' (1955; prose version of a scene from *Die Schlacht* (The Battle), 1951) makes such connections even more explicit. The paper manufacturer who decides in 1945 to follow his leader and shoot himself, his wife and his daughter retains the revolver he wore as officer of the reserve, as symbol of his status, and the Iron Cross that legitimated it. But the 'heroic act' seems inappropriate in the family flat; with the Iron Cross pinned to his lapel, he leads wife and daughter on the last family excursion, to the forest which seems the only appropriate backdrop for such combinations of sexuality and violence. He sends them ahead, unsure whether he fears they will run away, or if he wants to himself; but realizes that he is too frightened, and wishes *they* would. This unheroic mood communicates itself to his bladder, like little Erich's; while he relieves the pressure, he feels the coldness of the revolver through the thin material of his trouser pocket, and, as he runs after them, its slapping against his thigh. Just as he has decided to throw it away, he comes on them waiting for him, and has, after all, to play his role to the end. But after shooting daughter and wife he realizes that the 'play is over' – both the family play, whose audience is dead, and the theatre of the Third Reich. He throws away revolver and Iron Cross and heads for the West, stripped of his 'costume' and ready to don a new one.

The subtle equation between male role, revolver and penis, the reproduction of the 'theatre of the Third Reich' as 'family theatre', demonstrates Müller's intention to ground the Fascist mentality in the family itself. The need to act out a concept of masculinity based on the ideology of militarism and the dominance of the 'weak' is finally dependent on, and determined by, the 'audience' it has created, the women against and before whom this masculinity was to be proved. Behind the mask of the Fascist 'hero' is the inadequate male, trapped in the contradictions of his own socialization, unable to run away from it and transforming his insecurity into brutality. The revolver is no longer a symbol of caste, for shooting lame horses and putting 'common' soldiers out of their misery, but one of the violence that underlies, and results from, the patriarchal-militarist society. It will be replaced, in the 'new life' of Müller's protagonist, by more up-to-date symbols of dominance: the Mercedes and, perhaps, the hunting rifle. That his concern with the nexus between masculinity and violence is not restricted to Fascism is apparent from Müller's plays on the Russian Revolution, *Cement* (1973) and *Mauser* (1970) from which my title is drawn. Gleb Tschumalow's inability to overcome the male role that his service in the Red Army has only reinforced, and to redefine his relationship to his wife, echoes the revolutionary tragedy of *Mauser*, where the 'necessary violence' of the Revolution deforms its agent to the point where man and Mauser, sex and revolver become one. These parallels, however, result from no simplistic attempt to equate all forms of violence, but from the conviction that genuine emancipation will only be possible if the relics of earlier forms of socialization can be recognized and overcome.

It is perhaps appropriate that I conclude this brief and tentative investigation with a text which attempts to reconstruct the 'attractions of anti-Semitism', since it is the final displacement of Fascist brutality into the genocide of the Jews which is both its saddest historical specific and the element which most resists political-economic analysis of the type I referred to at the outset. No 'manipulative' theory can hope to explain the ease with which populations apparently no more anti-Semitic than their neighbours were brought to connive in this genocide, and it is simply offensive to treat the issue as if it were on the same level as the construction of the *Autobahn*. Again, it makes far more sense to me to assume that the 'liberation' by Fascism of repressed wishes and phantasies was the precondition for this slaughter of the 'weak', who shared, in Nazi propaganda, many of the attributes of the tabooed female, a weakness and submissiveness coupled with a demonic ability to corrupt and destroy male Aryan innocence which finds its parallel, sadly, in Noll's depiction of Frau Ziesche. It is thus peculiarly appropriate to turn to Franz Fühmann's 'The Jews' Car' (1968) as a final text, as it relates the propensity to anti-Semitism to the compensation of male inadequacy we have seen as the underlying link between the attempts of Noll, Loest and Müller to understand Fascism.

The early memories of Fühmann's narrator – the warm green of the tiled stove and its relief of a gypsy camp, the kindness of an alcoholic tramp – have been censored by a society which liquidated both. In his conversion to anti-Semitism, the demands of male socialization play an even more direct part. The story of his classmate Gudrun K. about a 'Jews' car', which cruises the hills performing the classic task of religious anti-Semitism, stealing young girls to make *matzohs* from their blood, interrupts the discussions of the boys' group about their hero Tom Shark, who kills wolfhounds with his bare hands; it offers more tangible rewards, the possibility of saving the girls from this menace and impressing them with one's heroism. In the climate of Nazi indoctrination, he has no difficulty accepting the rumour, but immediately transforms it into a day-dream in which he rescues one of the girls from his class from the evil Jews in true Wild West manner. The dream, a distillation of male theatre, has a disturbing end, the awakening of his pre-adolescent sexuality. He identifies the girl in reality and, after suffering the punishment for day-dreaming at school, carried out with familiar brutality, takes a detour home through the fields, planning to use an invented encounter with the Jews' car to explain his lateness after detention. But nature has suddenly become sexualized; the erotic contact of his dream has transferred itself to the landscape, the animals and plants. Totally confused and alienated, he mistakes a passing car for the Jews' car and runs home in terror.

This reaction, so much at odds with the bravado of his dream, demands to be heroicized at school the next day; but, as luck would have it, the story of his daring escape is interrupted by the revelation of his new love-object herself that the car belonged to her relatives, who had seen him run off in terror after asking him the way. In her mocking glances he sees all the threatening sexuality of the afternoon before; he flees from the gale of laughter to the 'black-tarred, chlorine-reeking boys' toilet', screaming and vomiting his hatred against the 'Jews' who bear the guilt.

I know of no other text, literary or theoretical, in which this connection is made so convincingly. Sartre's identification of anti-Semitism with the fear of the 'Other' in oneself points in a similar direction; Frantz Fanon 'sexualizes' this fear in his critique of Sartre's theory as applied to colonialism; and Leslie Fiedler and the novelist William Styron have uncovered similar complexes in the attitudes of American Whites to Blacks. But it is the specificity of Fühmann's narrative which gives most cause for further thought: the separation of male and female roles, the 'hypertrophy of male adolescence' (if I may again borrow from Silke Hesse) as a dominating and destructive myth, and the displacement of aggression resulting from the experience of inadequacy into brutality against the 'weak', the underlings and scapegoats of society. If it was the 'success' of German Fascism in liberating this aggression that made possible its diversion against the millions of victims of the Second World War, we will not be able to stop at an analysis of the methods it employed, but will have to investigate the construction of a socialization process which produced the aggressions thus liberated, and which predates Fascism. The curtain may have sunk on this particular episode of the Fascist play, but one is uncomfortably reminded of Fanon's provocative description of anti-Semitism as a 'family squabble' – which is perhaps not a trivialization at all, but a deeply disturbing statement.

–11–

Early Women Supporters of National Socialism

GISELA T. KAPLAN AND CAROLE E. ADAMS

Analyses of the appeal of German Fascism have long focused on men, and with good reason, for Nazi Party membership and leadership were almost entirely male, and pre-1933 electoral records indicate that more male than female voters usually chose Nazi slates.[1] This has meant, however, that women sympathetic to Nazism have until recently been ignored. We seek, as have other recent feminist scholars, to use a woman-centred analysis to explore the appeal of certain aspects of Nazi ideology to women. Why would any woman find Nazi ideology attractive prior to the seizure of power in 1933 (that is prior to a time when personal profit or propagandist manipulation might have played a role)?

This chapter will examine specific writings by National Socialist women during the *Kampfzeit* (period of struggle) before 1933. The writers selected are Guida Diehl, Paula Siber and Sophie Rogge-Börner. Both Diehl and Siber initially held posts in the Nazi Party that made them leading female figures, while Rogge-Börner provided the party with 'scholarly' credentials in anthropology. By 1936 at the latest, all three had lost any appreciable political influence or organizational role.[2]

All three women were minor writers by today's standards. The mystical tone, the sickly pathos, the lofty (and usually incongruous) metaphors were obviously more palatable in that period than today, for they compare well with similar writings by their male counterparts. Their essays were usually published in cheap and slim

The authors would like to thank Professor Richard Bosworth for his comments on the conference version of this chapter.

1. Jill Stephenson, 'National Socialism and Women before 1933', in P. D. Stachura (ed.), *The Nazi Machtergreifung*, London, 1983, pp. 35–6.
2. For biographical information see Claudia Koonz, *Mothers in the Fatherland: Women, the Family and Nazi Politics*, London, 1987.

paperback editions or as volumes of small journals. To date there are no studies of the circulation of such popular texts. However, both Paula Siber and Guida Diehl had large followings.[3] Despite the fact that these early enthusiasts were unacceptable to the party after it attained power, they belonged to the group of important image-makers, and their writings therefore contribute to our understanding of why thousands of women joined Nazi organizations before 1933.

The texts contain a surprising number of references to sexuality, within discussions of feminism and the reconstruction of the feminine role, but also with reference to eugenics debates and to attacks on the Weimar Republic, indicating that sexuality was a central concern at that time. In addition, the links posited by early Nazi women supporters between the areas of sexuality, reproduction, woman's role and woman's 'liberation' become particularly important when one recognizes that their analysis is disturbingly akin to some theories put forward by feminists of the late 1970s and the 1980s.[4]

This chapter argues that Nazi women attempted to construct a counter-image of womanhood which they hoped not only would assure women high status and self-esteem within the home, but in addition would establish women's freedom from male sexual control. Women who found Nazi ideas and policies attractive were attempting to develop a rational response to a real threat to their roles and identities within a capitalist and patriarchal society. Even if it was rational, however, their strategy was misguided, for it was based on the acceptance of a patriarchal order that could never realize their vision of a female-centred world. And the world they sought represented in any case a mythical past unobtainable in an industrialized and urban Germany, structured by class as well as gender.

The women who wrote in support of Nazism developed their arguments within a particular historical context. The chapter therefore begins with a discussion of feminism in Wilhelmine Germany and explains feminist theories of women's nature and role in society, as well as the relationship between the private and the public, particularly in sexual matters. It then examines the changing nature of feminism after the First World War, when single

3. Ibid., and Jill Stephenson, *The Nazi Organisation of Women*, London, 1981, p. 77.
4. See, for instance, Alice Rossi, 'A Biosocial Perspective on Parenting', *Daedalus*, no. 106, 1977, pp. 1–32; Judith Stacey, 'Are Feminists Afraid to Leave Home? The Challenge of Conservative Pro-Family Feminism', in J. Mitchell and A. Oakley (eds), *What is Feminism?*, Oxford, 1966, pp. 219–48.

women became more marginal, and all women seemed robbed of autonomy and influence, both in the intimate sphere of sexuality and in economic and political life. Finally, writings of Nazi women in the *Kampfzeit* will be analysed to explore both their critique of feminism and their view of female sexuality and womanhood.

The Definition of Women's Nature before the First World War

The German 'bourgeois' women's movement before the First World War, which used that label to set itself apart from socialist feminism, held a particular view of women and the impediments they faced. Bourgeois feminists argued that women should be granted full rights because both they and men were essentially the same human beings. Yet they also stated firmly that women were essentially different from – and in some ways superior to – men, and that, since the two sexes were complementary, women had to be granted rights in order for society to function successfully.[5] This claim derived from their belief in innate biological differences between the sexes, in particular a female instinct to nurture.

The belief in innate differences between men and women developed along with the Victorian cult of domesticity, which removed women from their traditional stereotypic role as lascivious tempters of men, and instead placed women on a pedestal of moral purity, with the task of providing men (now the sex driven by uncontrollable instincts and lusts) with 'spiritual uplift'. By the late nineteenth century, this view became linked to Darwinist assumptions claiming that certain instincts, values and character traits were both sex linked and biologically determined. Such scientific 'evidence' gave support to the notion that separate male and female roles were natural and immutable. (This is the position now taken by sociobiology.)[6]

5. Irene Stoehr, '"Organisierte Mütterlichkeit". Zur Politik der deutschen Frauenbewegung um 1900', in K. Hausen (ed.), *Frauen suchen ihre Geschichte*, Munich, 1983, pp. 221–49; Carole E. Adams, *Women Clerks in Wilhelmine Germany: Issues of Class and Gender*, Cambridge, 1988, pp. 39–52; Elisabeth Meyer-Renschhausen, 'Zur Geschichte der Gefühle. Das Reden von "Scham" und "Ehre" innerhalb der Frauenbewegung um die Jahrhundertwende', in C. Elfert and S. Rouette (eds), *Unter allen Umständen. Frauengeschichte(n) in Berlin*, Berlin, 1986, pp. 99–122.
6. See Stephen L. Chorover, *From Genesis to Genocide. The Meaning of Human Nature and the Power of Behavior*, Cambridge, MA, 1979; Gisela T. Kaplan and Lesley J. Rogers, 'The Definition of Male and Female: Biological Reductionism and the

Gertrud Bäumer, a leader of moderate bourgeois feminism, argued in 1905 in an important theoretical essay that because women's innate nature was different from that of men, equality could not be achieved by giving women the same life roles as men. Employed mothers, she claimed, suffered from the loss of their ties to home and children, and recognized 'that they had traded the many-sided, often changing, personally involving work in the home for monotonous, mechanical factory work that was totally split off from anything personal or inward'. What counted for Bäumer was 'the full effect of [woman's] special feminine characteristics within the cultural totality', and she claimed that women should be given more opportunities to marry and have children.

Central to Bäumer's analysis was her belief that sexual relations should change. Women's superior morality had to become the standard for both sexes, creating something 'finer and deeper', and men's domination of the arena of love and marriage had to end, for their control meant 'a painful annihilation of [women's] strongest and most inner life instincts'.[7]

Bäumer's analysis was far from unique. Indeed, the campaign against prostitution and sexual harassment and the movement to reform family law, both of which began in the late 1890s, rested on a conviction that the double sexual standard oppressed women and that women's powerlessness in the private sphere of the home was interrelated to their exclusion from the public sphere of civil and political society.[8] A description of tasks undertaken by the bourgeois women's movement is beyond the scope of this chapter. What must be emphasized, however, are the interrelationships posited by feminists within the areas of sexuality, women's roles in the home, and women's emancipation in both the private and the public spheres.

Implicit in feminist writings, speeches and actions was a belief that women's sexuality was linked to instincts of nurturance and caring, which made women essentially more moral than men.[9] This claim had a number of consequences of utmost importance for

---

Sanctions of Normality', in S. Gunew (ed.), *Feminist Knowledge as Critique and Construct*, London, in press.

7. Gertrud Bäumer, 'Was bedeutet in der deutschen Frauenbewegung "jüngere" und "ältere" Richtung?', *Frau*, vol. 12, 1904–5, pp. 321–8.
8. Stoehr, 'Organisierte Mütterlichkeit'; Adams, *Women Clerks*, pp. 114–16; Meyer-Renschhausen, 'Zur Geschichte'.
9. Bäumer, 'Was bedeutet'; Kay Goodman, 'Motherhood and Work. The Concept of the Misuse of Women's Energy, 1895–1905', in R. Joeres and M. Maynes (eds), *German Women in the Eighteenth and Nineteenth Centuries. A Social and Literary History*, Bloomington, 1966, pp. 110–17.

women's freedom of movement. First, it made women's powerlessness in the private sphere and exclusion from the public sphere unjustifiable. Second, however, and more radically, it could be used to challenge the prevalent notion that women were useless unless married. For if women's sexuality was not a rapacious drive to conquer (as was men's) but rather was more diffuse and linked to traits of altruism and nurturance most typically seen in motherhood, then single women could also act according to their natures. They could remain unmarried without being unnatural women by carrying out tasks of 'social motherhood'.[10]

Feminists asserted further that women's motherly tasks could not be limited to the private, domestic sphere. They argued that owing to modern technology there was less and less for women to do at home. In addition, many women could not marry, given their greater numbers in the population. Women therefore had to take their particular female qualities – nurturance, patience, virtue – and introduce them into the public sphere, through paid employment and new roles in welfare, service and even sociopolitical activities. Like feminists in other countries, German feminists insisted that by bringing their maternal qualities to public life, women would help the economy, create new values and contribute in a unique way to the national culture, complementing those contributions made by the other sex with its different nature. By engaging in tasks of social motherhood, by using their innate feminine talents for the good of their nation, single women could also fulfil their calling.[11]

This explicit permission given to single women to enter the public sphere was eagerly taken up by many before the First World War. It not only justified their careers, but also allowed them to postpone marriage indefinitely and to enter into close and intimate relations with other unmarried women. A number of German feminist leaders, for instance, shared holidays and homes with particular friends.[12]

10. Stoehr, 'Organisierte Mütterlichkeit'; Adams, *Women Clerks*, pp. 80–2, 163–8; Birgit Sauer, 'Den Zusammenhang zwischen der Frauenfrage und der sozialen Frage begreifen. Die "Frauen und Mädchengruppe für soziale Hilfsarbeit"', in Elfert and Rouette, *Unter allen Umständen*, pp. 80–96.
11. Bäumer, 'Was bedeutet'; Helene Lange, 'Moderne Streitfragen in der Frauenbewegung', *Frau*, vol. 13, 1905–6, pp. 70ff.; Bund Deutscher Frauenvereine (ed.), *Internationaler Frauenkongress. 1904. Officieller Originalbericht*, n.d., and *Deutscher Frauenkongress, Berlin, 27. Feb.–2. März 1912. Sämtliche Vorträge*, Leipzig, n.d.
12. Cf. Lida Gustava Heymann with A. Augsperg, *Erlebtes–Erschautes: Deutsche Frauen kämpfen für Freiheit, Recht und Frieden*, ed. M. Twellmann, Meisenheim, 1972.

The (Re-)Discovery of Female Sexuality in the Weimar Republic

Feminism changed after the First World War, however, and for a number of reasons. The creation of the Weimar Republic had led to formal political equality for women, which many naively accepted as real equality.[13] In addition, four years of war made women more visible in society, a continuation of trends begun in the empire but intensified. Women were now more likely to work outside the home, and the war marked the end of customary limits upon women's freedom in public, so that they now went about unchaperoned, smoked cigarettes in public and dressed in less constraining ways. These breaks with custom were also taken as signs of real equality. Finally, a new generation of young women was present within the German feminist movement of the 1920s, unacquainted with the struggles waged by an earlier generation of women to gain education or paid employment. This generational conflict was much discussed throughout the 1920s in feminist journals.[14]

The final cause for changed emphases within feminism lay in the impact of the movement for sexual reform. Such reform had been an area of interest before the war and had indeed often been linked to the campaigns against prostitution and for changes in family law.[15] The movement shifted focus in the Weimar period, however, when feminists interested in sexual issues joined with a group of male sexual researchers whose theories had come to predominate the sex reform movement. As a result, a new definition of female sexuality was constructed that was much more constricting than that urged by pre-war feminists.[16]

13. Susanne Rouette, '"Gleichberechtigung" ohne "Recht auf Arbeit", Demobilmachung der Frauenarbeit nach dem ersten Weltkrieg', in Elfert and Rouette, *Unter allen Umständen*, pp. 159–82.
14. Irene Stoehr, 'Neue Frau und Alte Bewegung? Zum Generationskonflikt in der Frauenbewegung der Weimarer Republik', in J. Dalhoff et al. (eds), *Frauenmacht in der Geschichte. Beiträge des Historikerinnentreffens 1985 zur Frauengeschichtsforschung*, Düsseldorf, 1986, pp. 390–402.
15. Ann Taylor Allen, 'Mothers of the New Generation: Adele Schreiber, Helene Stöcker, and the Evolution of a German Idea of Motherhood, 1900–1914', *Signs*, vol. 10, 1985, pp. 418–38.
16. See Atina Grossmann, '"Satisfaction is Domestic Happiness": Mass Working Class Sex Reform Organisations in the Weimar Republic', in M. Dobrowski and I. Wallmann (eds), *Towards the Holocaust. The Economic and Social Collapse of the Weimar Republic*, London, 1983, pp. 265–93, and '*Girlkultur* or Thoroughly Rationalised Female: A New Woman in Weimar Germany?', in J. Friedlander et al. (eds), *Women in Culture and Politics. A Century of Change*, Bloomington,

The new definition maintained the link between female sexuality and motherhood, but altered the older definition in two important ways. First, the sexologists' explanation of female sexuality emphasized the enjoyment of heterosexual intercourse rather than the earlier diffuse notions of caring, mothering, bonding; women who did not respond were abnormal, 'frigid' or even 'lesbian'. In addition, they defined female sexual response in ways supportive of male dominance. Men were encouraged to continue taking the active role in sexual matters, initiating and teaching 'their' women, who were either passive or even resistant (in which case they had to be subdued). Sexual activity centred on intercourse with penetration, which was defined in stages with the goal of orgasm. Although this now granted that women were sexual beings and indeed had a right to achieve sexual pleasure, it was on male terms.[17] In addition, this 'orgasm consciousness' led to new stress for many women in sexual relations, for those unable to reach orgasm now had either to 'confess' when they did not, and risk labels of 'frigidity' or unfemininity, or to fake it. In the case of the former, new unhappiness resulted for both partners (he was not the man he thought he was; she was unsuccessful in her most womanly role). In the latter case, a new dishonesty crept into the most intimate relationships.

The negative implications of the sex reformers' message were not always apparent at once and, of course, there were women who were not constrained by the new dictates. Many young feminists found the message of the sexologists personally appealing. The flapper could not only dress with less restriction and go out on her own, but enjoy sexual relations as well. For the young professional women sympathetic to feminism (teachers, doctors, social workers), the reformers' emphasis on contraception and abortion seemed to grant new independence to women in their relations to men, particularly for their working-class clients.[18] Furthermore, sexol-

---

1986, pp. 62–80; also Sheila Jeffries, 'Sex Reform and Anti-Feminism in the 1920s', in London Feminist History Group (ed.), *The Sexual Dynamics of History*, London, 1983, pp. 177–202.

17. Magnus Hirschfeld, *Sex in Human Relationships* (1928), tr. John Lane, London, 1935; Jeffries, 'Sex Reform'; Heide Solltau, '"Erotik und Altruismus", Emanzipationsvorstellungen der Radikalen Helene Stöcker', in Dalhoff et al., *Frauenmacht*, pp. 65–82; Beatrix Campbell, 'A Feminist Sexual Politics: Now You See It, Now You Don't', in *Feminist Review* (ed.), *Sexuality, A Reader*, London, 1986, pp. 19–39.

18. Atina Grossman, 'Berliner Ärztinnen und Volksgesundheit in der Weimarer Republik: Zwischen Sexualreform und Eugenik', in Elfert and Rouette, *Unter allen Umständen*, pp. 183–217.

ogists appeared to deal with the same issues as had pre-war feminism – both insisted on a single sexual standard and stressed the importance of motherhood, for instance – so that the sex reform movement appeared to expand on, rather than to undermine or change, pre-war feminist analysis and strategies.

In reality, however, the views of the sexologists challenged the very basis of some key feminist claims from the pre-war era. Their analysis denied single women the right to remain single and to have close emotional and/or erotic ties to other women, for 'normal' sexuality was now linked to male-centred intercourse and was confined to marriage or heterosexual 'partnerships'. This then undercut the feminist argument of social motherhood, for the only model offered by the reformers was that of the heterosexual woman planning real motherhood. Feminism shifted to emphasize a depoliticized, individualized role for women, in which the single woman no longer had a valid social role in civic or political life, while 'normal' women gave primacy to sexual relations and motherhood.

The National Socialist Construction of Womanhood

There are a number of similarities between the issues taken up by women Nazi supporters and German feminists, an observation that has led some scholars to contend that German feminism contributed to the acceptance of Nazi ideas by women.[19] Certainly, similarities existed in particular elements of their analyses, for both feminists and Nazi women shared important insights. They recognized that their society was ordered by gender (that is, that humans were divided on the basis of sex and that this division was hierarchical). Further, both groups maintained that the private sphere (the family, sexuality, personal behaviour) interacted with the public world – a connection that feminist theorists today have also emphasized. Awareness of this connection has been hindered by western male traditions of political thought and activity, both liberal and socialist, which insist that the two are separate and that political actors and citizens inhabit the public sphere alone.[20]

19. Richard Evans, *The Feminist Movement in Germany, 1894–1933*, Beverly Hills, 1976, p. 253; Claudia Koonz, 'Some Political Implications of Separatism: German Women between Democracy and Nazism, 1928–1934', in Friedlander et al., *Women in Culture and Politics*, pp. 269–85.
20. Susan Moller Okin, *Women in Western Political Thought*, Princeton, 1979; Karen Honeycutt, 'Socialism and Feminism in Imperial Germany', *Signs*, vol. 5, 1979,

But although feminists shared certain insights with pro-Nazi women, the two groups nevertheless held essentially different theories of society and politics and had very different goals. Unlike German feminists both before and after the First World War, Nazi women accepted a patriarchal order and an all-male political order. They expected men to guard their interests by doing no less than removing liberal, urban, industrial capitalism and returning German society to a harmonious pre-industrial community in which each sex had its own valued role. The home would regain central importance, and within the household sphere women expected to achieve autonomy, respect and increased status.

The link posited by Nazi women between female autonomy, motherhood and a particular definition of women's sexuality is worth exploring. The writings of all early Nazi women, including the three authors selected here, identified feminism with both a rejection of motherhood and a lustful sexuality, which led to a decline in women's status in German society and to a loss of esteem. The most notable feature of the texts is the authors' conscious attempt to imagine a new woman who was completely different from the Weimar new woman, but nevertheless strong and autonomous. They sought to elaborate a female role model that was neither 'feminist' nor 'un-German'.[21] Their reconstruction of the good German woman was bound up in their reconstruction of German history as a history of the 'Germanic race', in which the mother was the source of the race. A note of urgency entered their writing, a plea for speedy actions and programmes to prevent further contamination (biologically, sexually, morally), further decline and even the death of the German people.

Sophie Rogge-Börner's small volume *At the Sacred Well* (1928?) was no exception. Her work presented the ideals of German womanhood combined with an interpretation of the racial history of the 'Germanic' people. She offered two contrasting paradigms: the 'Nordic/Germanic' woman of early times, and the bourgeois 'Gretchen' of the industrial age. As Ehmke has noted, Germans have never been very sure of their fatherland, and have therefore felt the need to keep reinventing it.[22] The pro-Nazi women living in that unreliable fatherland, which shifted, changed and dissolved, likewise felt the need to ask where they came from and who they were.

---

pp. 30–41; Carole Pateman, *The Sexual Contract*, Stanford, 1988.

21. Contrast Dörte Winkler, *Frauenarbeit im Dritten Reich*, Hamburg, 1977, p. 33.
22. Horst Ehmke, 'Was ist des Deutschen Vaterland?', in J. Habermas (ed.), *Stichworte zur geistigen Situation der Zeit*, vol. 1, *Nation und Republik*, Frankfurt/M, 1980, p. 51.

Rogge-Börner's work therefore opened with a quote from Tacitus's *Germania*, which presented German women as companions to their husbands in work and in conflict, both tilling the fields and wielding the sword. Rogge-Börner's heroine and example of a good Germanic woman was Hedwiga, whose pagan husband Odoaker was defeated by the Byzantine Christian Theodoric in the fifth century at the battle of Ravenna. In legend, Hedwiga fought that battle and goaded her male soldiers to action. For Rogge-Börner, the defeat and death of Hedwiga and Odoaker marked the end of women's equality, legal rights and high status, and ushered in those dark ages from which women had only begun to awaken in the nineteenth century, as if from a deep slumber, from *Betäubung* (stupefaction).[23]

Rogge-Börner's statements contained major historical inaccuracies, of course, but, given her intention, that did not matter.[24] Her purpose in creating a Nordic heroine becomes clearer in the next section of the book, in which she quotes Icelandic sources to prove that Nordic women participated fully in the economic and political life of their people, running farms, distributing property to former serfs and riding alone on horseback to join the *Thing* (assembly). It is interesting to note that this pre-modern Nordic heroine had much in common with the modern emancipated woman against whom Rogge-Börner railed.

Rogge-Börner's Germanic woman offered not only a model of liberation to her contemporary sisters, but a sexual ideal as well. It might even be argued that at the centre of the entire construct of the new heroic woman was the author's concern with sexuality, for her image of Hedwiga on horseback suggests a position of power and independence for pagan women that included control over their sexuality. But Rogge-Börner went beyond this hint. Since the topic was evidently sensitive, Rogge-Börner brought sexuality into her argument by using the authority of a male Danish scholar, whom she described as both eminent and *feinfühligst* (sensitive). She quoted this person – who was thrice removed from herself, being male, from another (albeit Nordic) country, and with unassailable expertise – as stating that 'in sexual love, the "Germanic" tribes

23. Sophie P. Rogge-Börner, *Am geweihten Brunnen. Die deutsche Frauenbewegung im Lichte des Rassegedankens*, n.d. (1928?), chapter 1 (unpaginated).
24. Hedwiga belonged to a tribe found predominantly in Asia Minor and was therefore scarcely a representative of Nordic/Germanic womanhood. Further, Rogge-Börner's idealized version ignores passages in Germanic legal codes that indicate women's inferior status.

were as cold as perhaps no other people.'[25] She followed this approvingly with her own observation that as a result of this coolness, marriages of the Germanic tribes had extremely strong bonds and were characterized by a natural monogamy that produced many healthy children.

This somewhat triumphant conclusion was followed by a long disquisition on the virtues of motherhood and on the importance of that role for the future survival of the German people, as a people who had rediscovered their true heritage, an *Erbwissen* (racial knowledge) essential to successful motherhood.[26] With this, the author was carefully distinguishing between deserving and undeserving mothers, a notion that had already become commonplace in the eugenics and sex reform movements[27] and that the Nazis later realized with their forced sterilization programme.[28]

In Rogge-Börner's view, the dispersion of the Germanic tribes and their intermixing with inferior racial groups for over 2,000 years (*sic*!) had undermined their pure hearts; Christian morality had done the rest. Therefore the woman who suddenly rediscovered her racial responsibilities and the bliss of the Aryan hearth could *aufarten* (invigorate) her race. This discussion of motherhood also contained a sexual component. According to Rogge-Börner, it was common knowledge that 'only people who are not slaves to a wild, untempered sexual drive are capable of begetting high-quality children.'[29]

Woman's racial strength was thus in some way bound up with denying or controlling sexuality. The image of coldness fits with the sword (cold metal) and with struggle (the 'cold, calculating' business of survival). Sexuality became a *Triebhaftigkeit* (biological drive) that was evil, foreign, irrational and therefore dangerous. Monogamy, meaning in fact *sexual* fidelity to a single partner, along with bearing eugenically perfect children, had positive consequences for the race. But the fidelity was not perceived to be sexual, but rather became disembodied into a compatriotic quality

25. Rogge-Börner, *Am geweihten Brunnen*, chapter 2.
26. Ibid., chapter 3.
27. Atina Grossman, 'The New Woman and the Rationalisation of Sexuality in Weimar Germany', in A. Snitow et al. (eds), *Desire: The Politics of Sexuality*, London, 1983, pp. 190–218; Grossman, 'Berliner Ärztinnen'.
28. Gisela Bock, 'Racism and Sexism in Nazi Germany: Motherhood, Compulsory Sterilization, and the State', in R. Bridenthal et al. (eds), *When Biology Became Destiny. Women in Weimar and Nazi Germany*, New York, 1984, pp. 271–96; *Zwangssterilisation im Nationalsozialismus. Studien zur Rassenpolitik und Frauenpolitik*, Opladen, 1986.
29. Rogge-Börner, *Am geweihten Brunnen*, end of chapter 3.

dedicated altruistically to the race.

Rogge-Börner constrasted her powerful image of pagan womanhood to 'Gretchen' and 'Klärchen', symbols of bourgeois and capitalist Germany. She described them as pitiable and pathetic little 'hothouse' creatures, bred for centuries to *Sittsamkeit* and *Unmündigkeit* (modesty and dependency). They were artificial and even unnatural: '[She] stays a poor locked-up silly thing, remaining far behind the male in education and integrity and only existing, like a flower, to be seen and plucked, without any value of her own.'[30] The author recognized that Gretchen's dependency was unnatural for an adult woman, and that the modesty she displayed was artificial. Gretchen was housebound, passive, and basically asexual (*das* Gretchen – she had neuter gender), and would eventually be 'plucked' because one could do with her as one pleased. Rogge-Börner could so forcefully denigrate the image of Gretchen, who after all was none other than the bourgeois wife and mother at home, because she had defined Gretchen as passive and artificial. She was unworthy of motherhood, for she allowed herself to be sexually 'plucked', unlike the Germanic woman who was coolly in control of her sexuality and who therefore achieved a close marital bond and eugenically fit motherhood.

In her short book Rogge-Börner gave new meaning to discourses dating from the Second Empire that concerned definitions of female sexuality, women's roles in the public and private spheres, and the function of eugenics programmes. Where bourgeois feminists aimed to redefine politics and widen the areas open to female participation within a capitalist state, however, Rogge-Börner had another purpose. She emphasized the return to the pre-industrial Germanic past, while insisting upon women's autonomy within the family sphere. There was no need for them to leave the home in order to regain esteem and status as long as the home itself and women's role within it were redefined. Gretchen needed to take on the attributes of the woman of Germanic mythology – as if a twentieth-century woman of the petty bourgeoisie, cooking cabbage in a two-room apartment, had anything to do with a tenth-century Icelandic landowning woman riding to a political assembly!

In Rogge-Börner's eyes, if the modern woman could understand her *Erbwissen* (heritage) and begin to identify with her supposed Germanic predecessors, she would not have to succumb to her husband's every sexual whim, nor would she be bound to seek

30. Ibid., chapter 1.

pleasure or to lie about orgasms. She could be cool without being frigid. At the same time, the new Germanic woman could pride herself on her superiority to single women, for her sexuality was linked to motherhood and thus to national and racial service. It was the wholesome, self-chosen (rare but perhaps satisfying) sexual act that produced healthy children. Woman was mother, but not as the male-centred sexual reformers had defined her. Indeed, the truly feminine Germanic woman took on many traditional male attributes: she was rational, cold and strong.

Guida Diehl and Paula Siber presented similar views with a different historical perspective. Unlike Rogge-Börner, whose vision encompassed aeons of time, they only addressed the plight of their contemporaries in the Weimar Republic. In Diehl's view, the emancipatory movements of Weimar had achieved little if anything for women. In fact, women had been cheated. They had been forced on to the labour market, but paid employment, according to Diehl, had not improved women's life circumstances or increased their happiness. Working-class women in particular suffered the stress induced by poverty and the combination of work and family duties. At the same time, Diehl believed that the educated elite of women was also dissatisfied. If they followed male educative and career paths, they became bewildered when job opportunities failed to materialize. If they became home-makers, they felt frustrated because they accepted the view that work meant liberation. In addition, training lasted too long for many women, causing serious loss of reproductive strength.[31]

Siber painted an equally dismal picture of the situation of Weimar women, who not only had not benefited from their experiences in the workforce during the First World War but, on the contrary, had been simply declared *Frauenüberschuß* (redundant), suggesting that there were too many of the sex and that this was deplorable. For Siber, millions of women had had their lives destroyed after the war, becoming demoralized and degraded through meaningless work in countless offices and department stores.[32] She too believed that it was an urgent task to restore dignity to these women's lives.

With such opinions, both writers had a ready-made audience. Diehl and Siber, like an increasing number of women, felt that the women's movement had failed to address the appropriate questions

31. Guida Diehl, *Die deutsche Frau und der Nationalsozialismus*, Eisenach, 1932, pp. 57–64.

32. Paula Siber, *Die Frauenfrage und ihre Lösung durch den Nationalsozialismus*, Wolfenbüttel, 1933, pp. 6, 11.

and had let women down. They insisted that feminists' efforts to integrate women into the economic and political life of the nation had been misguided and counter-productive. But, in addition, they believed that the feminist view of the feminine had been wrong.

For Diehl, the policies of the women's movement had resulted in *Entsittlichung* and *Entmütterlichung* (a devaluation of morality and motherhood).[33] But although Diehl emphasized morality, it was rather sexuality that continually emerged as the thread within her argument. She attacked with outrage both the campaign against the abortion laws (paragraph 218) and the advocacy of contraceptives and of sexual pleasure, asserting that they were extremely harmful to women. In her view the separation of sexuality and reproduction was tearing apart women's souls and creating a perilous situation in which women failed to continue to guard the innermost values of the *Volk* soul. For her, sexual pleasure became elided into *Geschlechtslust* (sexual lust) and promiscuity.[34] She asserted that personal feelings of shame and modesty were a biological necessity for reproduction, so that lust resulted in women losing their motherly instinct. If they did bear children, they sent them to crèches rather than providing loving care at home.[35]

Her analysis also linked female sexuality with a certain fear of internationalism and capitalism. For Diehl, women were lured into sexual lust not only by the programmes of feminists and sex reformers, but also by the shameless literature spread by international, largely Jewish, capital (her examples of the 'vilest' writings included highly acclaimed periodicals and papers such as *Simplizissimus*, *Weltbühne*, *Literarische Welt* and *Vossische Zeitung*, and authors such as Zuckmayer). Racial mixing, especially with Jews, also stimulated the female sex drive and enticed women into lust.[36] Diehl's position, her crass anti-Semitism aside, was far more uncompromising than Rogge-Börner's, for she completely rejected any notion of sexual fulfilment, 'cool' or otherwise.

Common to all three writers was the vision of a previous physical and psychological strength, which individual women and the *Volk* as a whole had once possessed, but which had now been sapped and eroded. The very 'marrow' of the German people had been *angenagt* (gnawed away), wrote Siber.[37] Such loss of strength was repeatedly connected in their writings to the sexual act itself.

33. Diehl, *Die deutsche Frau*, p. 58.
34. Ibid., pp. 53, 57, 61.
35. Ibid., pp. 58, 97.
36. Ibid., pp. 60, 97.
37. Siber, *Die Frauenfrage*, p. 8.

The energy expended in achieving sexual pleasure was seen as harmful because it was presumed to diminish woman's reproductive abilities, which were for both Siber and Diehl intricately linked to the life of the *Volk*. The future of the *Volk* lay in the *Schoß* (womb) of the woman. If the womb were destroyed or endangered – which the annual decline in birthrate indicated was indeed the case – then the strength and future of the *Volk* were also in danger.[38]

The vision of the womb's destruction is itself an interesting and complex issue.[39] For both Diehl and Siber, promiscuity and licentiousness in women not only marked the individual but spoiled and even destroyed the womb for the life of the *Volk*. Siber hoped for the 'deliverance of the German *Volk* soul from the false theories of decay', by which she meant women's emancipation from sexual and feminist theories. She expected to achieve this through women's awakening to their role as mothers to individual children and to the race.[40]

Emancipation from emancipation was not only the wish of Siber and other female supporters of Nazism, but was also reinforced and thoroughly supported by male Nazi writers. Alfred Rosenberg wrote in 1930 in *The Myth of the Twentieth Century*: 'Emancipation of the woman from the women's emancipation movement is the first demand of a female generation that seeks to save *Volk* and race, the eternal unconscious, the basis of all culture, from perishing.'[41] Male Nazis also wrote on female sexuality and the link between sexuality and motherhood. In his book *Sexual Hygiene* (1939), Max von Gruber wrote that

> if sexual intercourse is practised from the start only for the purpose of pleasure, it poisons the relationship of the spouses to one another and in particular harms the morality of the woman. She will no longer view the execution of intercourse, as nature inclines her, as an act of awe and meaning and of great consequences in which the mysterious primeval forces of life are the hidden driving power, but she will gradually learn that it is nothing but a pleasure.[42]

38. Ibid., p. 10.
39. A popular work by early Nazi supporter Artur Dinter describes a German woman involved in a sexual relationship with an Aryan who gives birth to a half-human 'Jewish' child because she had had intercourse with a Jewish man years earlier; see chapter 6 by Günter Hartung in this volume.
40. Siber, *Die Frauenfrage*, pp. 14–15.
41. Alfred Rosenberg, *Der Mythus des zwanzigsten Jahrhunderts* (1930), quoted in George Mosse, *Der nationalsozialistische Alltag. So lebte man unter Hitler*, Königstein, 1979, p. 66.
42. Max von Gruber, *Hygiene des Geschlechtslebens*, rev. W. Heyn, Berlin, 1939, p. 101.

Earlier, Karl Beyer had written in *The Equality of Women in National Socialist Germany* (1933) the interesting and pathetic statement that 'all man's work must wither without the nourishing juices and strength that rise out of womanhood and motherhood . . . Without the equality of women no German people exists.'[43]

Both von Gruber and Beyer linked sexuality and reproduction; Beyer added the notion of women's equality to men, although his metaphor appears to drown women in their own juices. But note that women are valued only for their bodies (which produce 'juices' in acts of sex and motherhood); the woman becomes equal only as a baby machine. Although the *Männerwerk* (man's work: *Werk* means work, edifice, accomplishment) might 'wither' without the 'juices' of women, this sexual threat was lessened by the emphasis on woman as the mother who protected and nurtured and taught her sons to suffer and endure.

What is going on here? Certainly there are reasons why these messages would appeal to some men, for, as Theweleit has shown in relation to proto-Nazi men of the 1920s, their positive image of women was limited to those who were mothers or sisters, desexualized creatures who related to men within the constraints of kin, with no threatening erotic femininity.[44] Hedwiga fits this mould, as a loyal helpmeet, strong and nurturing in her support of her husband, and therefore not threatening to men. Indeed, the portrayal of husband and wife standing together as equals facing the world was readily taken up by Nazi mythology. In a report on a Nazi women's organization mass meeting held in Berlin in 1936, the Nordic woman was praised, while Gretchen again took a beating: 'It is not the "Gretchen" type . . . who is the ideal of today's German man, but rather a woman who is also intellectually able to stand at her husband's side, comprehending his interests and his life's struggle. This is a woman who is above all also capable of being a mother.'[45]

But this cannot explain why the image appealed to women. Research indicates that women supported Nazism in the hope of undoing the mistaken policies of the Weimar Republic. Labelled as 'double earners', blamed for the cultural as well as the economic problems of the post-war era, some women found it appealing that they should no longer be forced to compete on the labour market

43. Karl Beyer, *Die Ebenbürtigkeit der Frau im nationalsozialistischen Deutschland*, Leipzig, 1933, p. 21.
44. Klaus Theweleit, *Male Fantasies* (1977), vol. 1, *Women, Floods, Bodies, History*, tr. S. Conway et al., Minneapolis, 1987, chapter 1.
45. *Völkischer Beobachter*, 27 May 1936, quoted in Mosse, *Alltag*, p. 67.

or in the political forum, but should return to the safety of the home.[46] From the security of their own domain, and with their own special reproductive abilities, they could insist upon respect and justify a measure of independence for themselves while remaining within a stable and comforting environment.

Nor would their domain be without power. German women who watched and listened to Nazi women received a message based on distinct roles for the sexes in separate spheres. Arguing on the basis of biological determinism, National Socialist women leaders insisted that women were biologically entirely different from men and should therefore be allowed to live a different social existence, fulfilling different roles and occupying different spaces. The women's sphere therefore would provide separate training for girls, separate female organizations and institutional self-management.[47] Hedwiga's belligerence, and the cool, non-lustful, self-controlled woman portrayed by the three authors considered here, indicate their mistaken belief that the Nazi Party represented the dawn of a new and better age for women.

In addition to these economic, political and cultural concerns, however, the view of female sexuality that Nazi authors offered could also appeal to a wide range of German women. Hedwiga, the cold and daring warrior woman (complete with sword) who came from the Germanic past, when sexual relations were marked by extraordinary coolness, represented to women the possibility of some autonomy in sexual matters. In addition, the Nazi image emphasized morality and an end to the licence of the decade.

Unlike the pre-war generation of German feminists, the Nazi authors examined here were not willing to extend the concept of motherhood beyond the biological role, which meant that they excluded tasks of social motherhood. Nor did they agree with the views of younger feminists, who accepted women's right to sexual pleasure but in male-centred terms.[48] By defining female sexuality as non-lustful, even 'cold', Nazi authors sought not only to raise women's status through motherhood, but in addition to control male sexuality and provide women with some autonomy within

46. Jill Stephenson, *Women in Nazi Society*, London, 1975, chapter 1; Koonz, *Mothers*, chapters 2, 3.
47. Koonz, *Mothers*, pp. 70–2.
48. A similar analysis can be made for the support women in contemporary industrialized countries have given anti-abortion campaigns. See Janet Sayers, *Biological Politics. Feminist and Anti-Feminist Perspectives*, London, 1982; Deirdre English, 'The Fear that Feminism will Free Men First', in Snitow et al., *Desire*, pp. 97–104.

the intimate sphere. Insisting upon the 'sexual coldness' of true German women meant that women did not have to submit themselves to male sexual urges, did not have to define themselves as 'frigid' when they refused sexual intercourse, and could be both feminine and strong. Nazi women thus tried to give womankind a separate space, albeit a completely non-political one with no decision-making power.

Nazi women preferred not to enjoy themselves but instead to sacrifice themselves, to become iron women of courage rather than to speak about a sexual fulfilment that included new forms of subordination, or to question patriarchy itself. Their fear of turning into sex objects and victims of their own feelings made them accept an image of womanhood perverse in a different way – women as reproductive machines, uteruses essential to maintain and develop a eugenically improved race of sons.

PART V

The Fascist Society: Ideology and Reality

–12–

The Attractions of Fascism for the Church of Rome

JONE GAILLARD

There have been many attempts, by Catholics and others, to gloss over, or in some way justify, the Roman Catholic Church's attitude and policies towards the Italian Fascist regime, in spite of massive evidence suggesting a substantial degree of agreement and collaboration between the two powers. We find a tendency even among sincerely anti-Fascist historians such as Jemolo to underrate the responsibility of the higher clergy and of Pius XI for the church's role by 'regretfully' conceding that certain 'errors' were committed, but attributing these to an overriding concern with the 'avoidance of greater evils to the flock entrusted to [the Pope]'.[1]

Pius XI had actually stated, in 1924, that 'some ideas of dangerous interpretation are unfortunately going around. It is said, for instance, that any reason relating to the common good justifies cooperation in evil. But this is wrong; such cooperation . . . cannot be justified except when strictly necessary to avoid greater evil.'[2] However, this was not to justify his attitude towards Fascism, but to condemn the decision of the Partito Popolare Italiano (Italian People's Party; a Catholic organization) to ally itself with socialism against the Fascist Party for the imminent elections. He thus identified the 'greater evil' by no means with Fascist power, as Jemolo and others try to suggest, but with the old 'red' enemy.

In further attempts to demonstrate that the collaboration between the Holy See of Rome and Fascism was brought about by

All translations are by the author.

1. Arturo C. Jemolo, *Chiesa e Stato in Italia*, Turin, 1981, p. 215.
2. Speech to the FUCI (Italian Catholic University Federation) students, 9 September 1924, in Francesco L. Ferrari, *L'Azione Cattolica e il 'regime'*, Florence, 1958, p. 85.

circumstance, and was suffered rather than sought by the church,[3] the irreconcilable nature of the two institutions has been affirmed. Though we may agree that 'Fascism is instinctively anti-clerical',[4] the converse proposition, that is, that the church is instinctively anti-totalitarian, does not necessarily follow. Regrettably, the history of the church from the distant past to recent times supports the opposite view, as some of its advocates indicate[5] and as Pius XI himself stated unequivocally: 'if a totalitarian regime exists – totalitarian in fact and by right – it is the regime of the church'.[6]

Ever since the Middle Ages, in fact, the object of the church's policies had been the constitution of a universal, non-pluralistic, hierarchical society, under the strong leadership of the Pope and the priestly caste. Though in modern times this has seemed to become more and more impracticable, it remains the final, *ideal* goal of the Catholic Church.

This ecclesiastic totalitarianism found its 'champion' in Pius XI; after he was elected to the papal throne, he resolutely began to reverse the more democratic tendencies of his predecessor Benedict XV, slowly re-establishing a complete centralization of power. A perfect example is the Azione Cattolica (Catholic Action) as it was restructured by this Pope; it differed little in its totalitarian organization from the Fascist Party itself.[7] Pius XI's policies aimed to unite 'all Catholic forces in a single conservative, anti-democratic party'.[8] In order to achieve this purpose he did not hesitate to ally himself with 'the devil', inexorably sacrificing those of his 'children' who dared to oppose this alliance.[9]

3. See for instance Giulio Castelli, *Il Vaticano nei tentacoli del Fascismo* (The Vatican in the Tentacles of Fascism), Rome, 1946.
4. Jemolo, *Chiesa e Stato*, p. 185.
5. In his work *Studi filosofici e politici sulla società moderna*, Rome, 1863, p. 8, Bonfiglio Mura, of the Order of Mary's Servants, comments bitterly on the Westphalia Treaty (the first international treaty in which pontifical representatives had not been invited to participate) and identifies democracy with the 'heretical Protestant varieties' which fought to destroy 'Catholic unity'.
6. Quoted in Ernesto Rossi, *Il manganello e l'aspersorio*, Bari, 1968, p. 210.
7. 'In the local organizations and in the central organs of the Catholic movement, the democratic praxis to elect leaders . . . had been replaced by the designation from the highest hierarchy, revived by the doctrine and the practice of the Fascist Party. The nomination of all central leaders of the Azione Cattolica was up to the Pope, and these leaders, no longer under the control of the dependent organizations, answered only to him and to his court in regard to any action accomplished in the course of their duties.' Ferrari, *L'Azione Cattolica*, p. 167.
8. Ibid., p. 138.
9. I here refer to his opposition to and dismissal of the Partito Popolare Italiano, to which I shall return later.

We may agree with Luigi Sturzo[10] and others that Fascist theory and practice were incompatible with some of the values traditionally attributed to Christianity – at least those which Jemolo scrupulously enumerates: 'sacrifice, patience, meekness, humility . . . the man who, having been beaten, offers his other cheek'.[11] However, the historical evidence available points to the conclusion that the Fascist regime in Italy and the Vatican organization were by no means incompatible. In fact, the two institutions had much in common, as was proclaimed in a manifesto by a group of Catholics in Rome on 30 June 1923 – and not disavowed by the Holy See:

> Our consent [to the Fascist government] has now to be manifest and absolute. Such consent is determined by the fact that Fascism . . . openly acknowledges and honours those religious and social values which constitute the base of any sound political regime, and professes, against the obsolete and sectarian ideologies of democracy, principles of discipline and hierarchical order in the state. All this [is] in harmony with the religious and social doctrines always affirmed by the church.[12]

Fascism and the Catholic Church shared some common enemies. The first was liberalism, labelled *deliramentum* by Gregory XVI as early as 1832, several times condemned by Pius IX as *errore pernicioso* (pernicious error), and pointed to by his successors as the source of all evils in modern society:[13] There followed socialism and Bolshevik Communism, always considered the worst peril to be avoided and combatted;[14] Freemasonry,[15] the 'natural' ally of

10. 'The essence of the theories that Fascism borrowed from nationalism, or those that result from the political practice of the party-government, is fundamentally pagan and in antithesis to Catholicism . . . Besides, immoral actions such as murder are allowed, encouraged and applauded for the sake of the state. Instigation to violence is in direct opposition not only to the rightful state but, even worse, to love as stated by the Gospels.' Luigi Sturzo, interview with *La Stampa*, 10 February 1924, quoted in Pietro Scoppola, *La Chiesa e il Fascismo*, Bari, 1976, pp. 92–3.
11. Jemolo, *Chiesa e Stato*, p. 191.
12. *Civiltà Cattolica*, 1923, vol. III, p. 184.
13. Pius IX in *Quanta cura*, with the included *Syllabus* (1864); Leo XIII in *Inscrutabili* (1878), *Immortale Dei* (1885) and *Libertas praestantissimum* (1888); Pius XI repeatedly in speeches, letters and addresses.
14. In his first encyclical *Qui pluribus* (1846), Pius IX was the first Pope to denounce Communism, defining it as *esecrabile dottrina* (an execrable doctrine); in *Quod apostolici muneris* (1878) Leo XIII remonstrated against this 'deadly plague, this sect of men who with different and almost barbaric names, are called socialists, Communists or nihilists'. Pius XI recalled and reconfirmed the content of this encyclical in *Divini Redemptoris* (1937).
15. Freemasonry was officially condemned by Leo XIII in *Diuturnum* (1881) and in

evil forces;[16] and, last but not least, democracy itself, too often the origin of 'terrors, threats, open rebellions and other similar disorders'.[17]

Much of the Catholic social doctrine enunciated by Leo XIII in his major encyclical *Rerum novarum* in 1891 was effectively appropriated and put into practice by Mussolini in 1926. Pius XI pointed this out in *Quadragesimo anno* (1931), in which, after some timorous initial reservations due to his constant apprehension about the future of the Azione Cattolica, he officially approved and sanctioned Fascist corporativism.[18]

Convergences can also be found in other 'minor' areas of public life: in the close control of individual actions and thought, and in the demand for complete and blind obedience;[19] in the treatment of women, relegated to the role of meek, subservient and prolific 'angels of the hearth'; in anti-Semitism, whose manifestation within Fascism, however, never reached the pitch of vehemence displayed by some of the church's leaders during the long history of Catholic 'hate' for the Jews.[20] Even the dogma of papal infallibility can be equated with the well-publicized Fascist slogan 'il Duce ha sempre ragione' ('the Duce is always right').

Whatever differences did occur were therefore due not so much to alleged radical incompatibility but, somewhat ironically, to an excessively close convergence of interests. Both church and state were trying to subdue completely and *pro suo* the Italian people; both were fighting in the same field. The Fascist Party too was a

---

Humanum genus (1884) and was declared illegal by the Fascists in 1925, with loud praise from the church.

16. 'The wicked international Freemasons, Communist demagogy and Protestant Pharisaism conspired together in a less than noble and ideal marriage [against] Italy.' Father A. Gemelli, 1935, quoted in Rossi, *Il manganello*, p. 255.
17. Pius XI, *Ubi arcano Dei*, 23 December 1922.
18. After succinctly mentioning the basic points of Fascist corporativism, Pius XI concludes: 'Little is needed to see the advantages of the system, however limited the details; the peaceful cooperation between the classes, the repression of any existing or attempted socialist organization, the moderating action of a special magistrature.'
19. Compare: 'To be a Catholic, not only in name but in fact, there is but one way, and one only, indispensable and irreplaceable: to obey the church and its leader', Pius XI, quoted in Rossi, *Il manganello*, p. 207; and the oath which candidates for membership of the Fascist party had to take, 'I swear to execute without discussion the Duce's orders.'
20. It is very significant that in 1938, to support its own anti-Semitic policies, Fascism recalled a violently anti-Jewish publication by the Jesuits in *Civiltà Cattolica*, 1889, with the title 'Della questione giudaica in Europa' (On the Jewish Question in Europe).

church which, as Jemolo says, 'sidetracked its faithful from all their other interests'.[21]

It is perhaps pertinent to quote at this point a 'definition' which Noel O'Sullivan gives of the 'Fascist style in politics':

> [The Fascist] new activist style of politics [is] a style which conceives of the highest good for man as a life of endless self-sacrifice spent in total and highly militant devotion to the nation-state, the claims of which are held to embrace and override every other object of human attachment and to require unconditional allegiance to a Fascist 'leader', whose arbitrary personal decree is the sole final determinant of right and wrong in every sphere of national life.[22]

Cannot these words, *mutatis mutandis*, be applied to Catholicism as well? After all, the final purpose of both institutions was the complete submission of any other authority to their own power. Mussolini always considered religion as an *instrumentum regni*, and the church tried 'to take the opportunity of an authoritarian and personal government to eliminate all opposition in Italian public opinion nurtured on anti-Vatican prejudices and brought up to be afraid of clericalism'[23] and to re-establish a Catholic state.

Since, however, neither of them was able to subdue the other by means of a direct frontal attack, and both were aware of this, each one used the tactic of reciprocal 'taming', turning into a temporary ally the party it could ill afford to antagonize.[24] Mussolini, who as late as 1920 still used abusive language and threats against Christianity and the church, changed his style as soon as he entered Parliament and perceived the road to power before him.

Let us compare two passages, the first from an article of Mussolini's in *Popolo d'Italia* (1 January 1920), and the second from the speech that he made in Parliament on 21 June 1921:

> We have torn up all revealed truths, we have spat on all dogmas, we have rejected all paradises and sneered at all charlatans – white, red,

21. Jemolo, *Chiesa e Stato*, p. 92.
22. Noel O'Sullivan, *Fascism*, London, 1983, p. 33.
23. Luigi Sturzo, *Chiesa e Stato, studio sociologico-storico*, quoted in Scoppola, *La Chiesa e il Fascismo*, p. 228.
24. In this regard, reference could well be made to the long article in *Civiltà Cattolica*, 16 August 1924, with the title 'La parte dei cattolici nelle presenti lotte dei partiti politici in Italia' (The Role of Catholics in the Present Fights between Political Parties in Italy), in which, after 'impeccable' Jesuitical reasoning, there is the conclusion – amongst other things – that since it is impossible to remove Fascism from power 'without great damage to the common good', all good Catholics must 'obey' it.

> black – who put on sale miraculous drugs to give 'happiness' to humanity. Two religions contend today for mastering over souls and the world: the black and the red. From two Vaticans today come encyclicals: from the one in Rome and the one in Moscow. We are the heretics of both these religions. We alone are immune from the contagion.[25]

> Fascism does not preach or practise anti-clericalism . . . I here affirm that the Latin and imperial tradition of Rome is today represented by Catholicism . . . I think and affirm that the only universal idea existing today in Rome is the one radiating from the Vatican.[26]

For its part, the church soon conveniently 'forgot' the crude anti-clericalism and vulgar atheism of the man who was by now vilifying liberals, 'reds' and the *Partito Popolare*. In reality, Don Sturzo's newly formed party was 'inconvenient' to and disliked by the Holy See for its over-insistent emphasis on 'pernicious' freedom.[27] Above all it placed in jeopardy, through its declared anti-Fascism, the advantages which the church expected from the man who, one month after his 'masterfully executed revolutionary *coup d'état*',[28] had already acknowledged Catholicism as the 'dominant religion of the state'.[29]

Although the Pope did protest each time his organizations, such as the Azione Cattolica, suffered at the hands of the regime, he never formally and explicitly denounced or condemned the government, which had 'undeniable merits, especially with regard to (the Catholic) religion . . . thanks to the exceptional personality of the man who is its leader'.[30] Those who maintain in defence of the church that in those very protests total opposition to the regime is evident, who give as an example of explicit condemnation the

25. Quoted in Rossi, *Il manganello*, p. 24.
26. Quoted in Scoppola, *La Chiesa e il Fascismo*, p. 53
27. In the new party programme of 18 January 1919 'the essence of the new society' was affirmed to be 'the true sense of freedom corresponding to the civic maturity of our people and to the highest development of their energies; religious freedom, not only for individuals but also for the church, for the performance of its high spiritual mission in the world; freedom of teaching without state monopoly; freedom for the organization of social classes, without preferences or privileges; communal and local freedom in line with the glorious Italian traditions', and a few days later Luigi Sturzo specified that the new party recognized religious freedom 'for all faiths'. *Civiltà Cattolica* reacted immediately, asking in total disbelief 'how it [the PPI] is different from the liberals who recognize in their false theory the same rights to truth and to error'. Quoted in Scoppola, *La Chiesa e il Fascismo*, pp. 22, 26.
28. Cardinal Gasparri, quoted in Rossi, *Il manganello*, p. 52.
29. Ibid., p. 55.
30. *Civiltà Cattolica*, 7 August 1924, p. 299.

encyclical *Non abbiamo bisogno* (We Have No Need; 1931), forget to consider how and in what words, on which occasions and towards which other governments political parties or ideologies, the Vatican expressed its disapproval.[31] In no speech or document, not even in the above-mentioned encyclical, did the Pope officially condemn (let alone excommunicate) the Fascist Party and its doctrine, although it included the legitimization of violence and political murder. In fact, several times before and after *Non abbiamo bisogno* the church expressed its approval of the government of Mussolini, this *incomparabile ministro* (incomparable minister) as Pius XI called him in 1939, upon whom *copiosa benedizione di Dio* (God's bountiful blessing) was always invoked.[32]

Not even in his speech (never delivered – the Pope died on 6 February 1939) in commemoration of the decennary of the signing of the Lateran Treaty did Pius XI speak out openly against Fascism, as the racial laws of the previous year had led some Catholics to expect.[33]

Both parties gained substantially from their alliance. Though Mussolini never 'converted' to Roman Catholicism,[34] the majority of Catholics, including most of the high clergy and the Pope himself, were essentially pro-Fascist. There were too many aspects of Fascism which attracted the church, over and above an opportunistic support dictated by circumstances, that is the alleged 'good shepherd's duty to protect his flock'. Firstly, there was a certain (unchristian?) feeling of satisfaction on the church's part at what it saw as a redressing of ancient 'wrongs', and at the humiliation and oppression of old enemies.[35] Then there were undeniable financial

31. I refer here not only to the 'historical' condemnations preceding Fascism (such as the already mentioned fulminations against liberalism, socialism, Freemasonry), but to those made during the regime (the condemnation of the Spanish Republic in *Divini Redemptoris*, 1937) and after it (the excommunication of Communists in 1949).
32. Quoted in Rossi, *Il manganello*, p. 321.
33. The major points of this speech were made public by John XXIII on 6 February 1959, in his *Lettera all'episcopato d'Italia* (Letter to the Italian Bishops), published by the *Osservatore Romano* three days later, but although it could be said that the old Pope did not direct any praise to the regime, it is also true that he did not make any direct accusations either. See Scoppola, *La Chiesa e il Fascismo*, pp. 334–41.
34. There is much proof of this, from Mussolini's behaviour in public (see Jemolo, *Chiesa e Stato*, p. 188) to his private conversations, often quoted in Galeazzo Ciano's *Diary* (1980 edn, Milan, ed. R. de Felice), and official speeches.
35. 'A movement which presented itself as a revenge not only against the socialists, not only against the liberals, but, looking even further, against Jacobins and Girondists, against encyclopaedists and illuminists, against the values and

and political advantages accruing to the church from the Fascist state, well before those provided by the Lateran Treaty. From as early as 1922–5, for instance, the obligation to register securities was abrogated, which allowed the Vatican considerable possibilities for financial 'manoeuvres'. In addition, Gentile's school reform reintroduced the compulsory teaching of the Catholic religion; the Vatican was 'given' the Biblioteca Chigiana; and there were various substantial financial increments for the clergy.[36]

There was also a clear, unequivocal confirmation of the principle of absolute authority, constantly preached by the church and badly shaken by the free-thought movement and others. There was now a chance, on the church's part, to make up for fifty years of political isolation, self-imposed but no less hurtful for that, and to make a triumphant comeback in a position of ascendancy. Pius XI had detected all these potential advantages arising out of the formation of a Fascist state, and was therefore justified in judging Mussolini, from his own point of view, as a man 'sent to us by Providence itself'.

---

principles of the French Revolution, could hardly appear to Catholics irreconcilable with their faith.' Jemolo, *Chiesa e Stato*, p. 193.

36. Rossi, *Il manganello*, pp. 90–1; 119–20.

–13–

Italian Fascism, Legality and Author's Right

DAVID SAUNDERS

Introduction

Anyone seeking to take the *legal* relations of literature and culture seriously finds that – with the exception of censorship issues – literary and cultural studies are notable for their lack of attention to law and legislation. Where the Fascist period in Italy is concerned, this lack marks both traditional and revisionist inquiry. A bibliographical guide such as Laqueur's *Fascism: a Reader's Guide* (1979) offers no indication on any legislative work in the *ventennio* (twenty-year Fascist rule).[1] The same is true of much revisionist historiography. We search in vain the index of a cultural history such as de Grazia's *The Culture of Consent* (1981) for an entry under 'law' or 'legislation'.[2] If we try J for 'juridical' we find only James Joyce. Forgacs's *Rethinking Italian Fascism* (1986) is the same: under L is Lawrence, D. H., but neither 'law' nor 'legislation'.[3] Without reading too much into the indexing conventions of histories of Italian Fascism, such absences suggest that certain positions of argument have been pre-empted or simply neglected.

The absence of such inquiry could lead us to suppose two things: either there was no law or legislation under Fascism; or there was law and legislation but they were a sham and not to be taken seriously. The first possibility is, of course, empirically false. The second is the case argued in 1948 by Calamandrei, that the Fascist regime was 'the regime of legal illegalism: of *manipulated* illegalism

1. W. Laqueur (ed.), *Fascism: a Reader's Guide*, Harmondsworth, 1979.
2. V. de Grazia, *The Culture of Consent: Mass Organisation of Leisure in Fascist Italy*, Cambridge, 1981.
3. D. Forgacs (ed.), *Rethinking Italian Fascism: Capitalism, Populism and Culture*, London, 1986.

or, in terms that are now fashionable, of *planned* illegalism'.[4]

For a Calamandrei, Fascist law and legislation are wholly a *simulation*. If this were the case, then that law and that legislation could perhaps rightly be dismissed by historiography, on principle as it were. However, there are at least two reasons to hesitate. Firstly, for all its familiarity, opposing arbitrary and absolute despotism to the rule of law remains largely a *philosophical* gesture. In other words, it does not guarantee a description of historical reality. Indeed, in the terms of this canonical opposition, 'law' is less a matter of actual legislative and judicial procedures than a pure ethical or rational principle. However, the very fact of the persistence of a highly *technical* legislative competence might have an importance in the circumstances of Italian Fascist rule. At the very least, as in the instance considered in this chapter, the technicality of legal reasoning reminds us that the arbitrary exercise of power had its limits. This was not the message reiterated by Fascist ideology. Whether or not it is the case that silence on Fascist law and legislation is motivated by principle and by the assumption that when the idea of law is questioned legal institutions are rendered valueless, the second reason to hesitate is the following: apart from the instance of censorship, analysis of legal relations is largely missing from studies of English and American literary and cultural production too. In other words, the absence of reference to the legal in a Laqueur or a Forgacs is perhaps the sign of a current distribution of topics in cultural historiography that excludes mention of the multiple legal relations of literary and cultural production.

To propositions in the style of Calamandrei, some responses have of course been made, for example by Ungari:

> The Fascist regime was one with a dual basis, where to each of the state's legal institutions there corresponded one of the party's illegal counter-institutions (today it would be termed a counter-power) which paralysed it. There was the King and there was the Duce; the Senate and the Fascist Chamber; the Army and the Militia; the School and the Littorio Youth; and, if you will, there was private enterprise and there were the agencies of privilege, and so forth.[5]

4. P. Calamandrei, 'La funzione parlamentare sotto il fascismo', in A. Aquarone and M. Vernassa (eds), *Il regime fascista*, Bologna, 1974, p. 59.
5. P. Ungari, 'Ideologie giuridiche e strategie istituzionali del fascismo', in Aquarone and Vernassa, *Il regime fascista*, p. 56.

Ungari continues:

> when considering a period embracing a quarter of a century, it is inadequate to assert that this was the period of the 'violated Statute' or of 'legality trampled underfoot' or of the 'counterfeit Constitution'. True the Statute was violated, legality was trampled underfoot in many ways and for long periods, the Fascist Constitution was in more than one respect a counterfeit Constitution. But, above and beyond this assessment, it remains a task for the historian to complete the account of what was then happening by asking precisely what was – over and above the violated Statute – the constitution which actually regulated the country and what type of legality it was which in some sense provided the norms of existence. This task cannot be rushed with some quick formulations: it is necessary to study just how things actually were.[6]

Ungari's *prise de position* is cited less for its Rankean tones than to legitimize research that takes Fascist legislation seriously as one element in the 'normalization' that he refers to. Romano too makes a point about legitimacy and the Fascist regime that encourages such research: 'The present is almost always transformist, the past and the future are revolutionary. This contradiction, which to many Italians of that epoch seemed like evidence of national coherence, paradoxically constitutes one of the regime's sources of legitimacy.'[7]

To illustrate Fascist transformism, Romano offers another version of the 'doubling' signalled by Ungari:

> Just as in the towns, until the eighteenth century, festivals produced an ephemeral architecture superimposed on the permanent architecture and decorating the truth but not suppressing it, so Fascism traces and corrects Italian reality, revolutionizes its appearance without altering its substance. Fascism does not suppress the device of the House of Savoy, but sets it alongside the Fascist emblems; it does not suppress the Sunday observance but flanks it with the Fascist Saturday; it does not suppress religious processions but performs next to them its lay masses where its acolytes celebrate the mysteries of the new faith; it does not abolish the distinctive symbols of the pre-Fascist hierarchy but recuperates and renews them in a carnival of uniforms, flags and banners.[8]

6. Ungari, 'Ideologie', p. 56.
7. S. Romano, 'Le fascisme', in M. Duverger (ed.), *Dictatures et légitimité*, Paris, 1982, p. 239, my translation.
8. Ibid., pp. 238–9, my translation.

Ungari and Romano respond to all peremptory dismissals of Fascist law and legislation – Calamandrei in effect treats 'Fascist legality' as a total and undifferentiated oxymoron – with a call to suspend judgement and to pursue detailed historical inquiry into persisting institutions and their fascist doubles. The nature of this inquiry has been well put by Arcangelo de Castris:

> Minute 'horizontal' inquiries into Fascist cultural organization, in other words into the everyday forms in which the regime transmitted its ideas and myths and into the handling and orientation of common sense during the Fascist years, constitute beyond any doubt a significant contribution to our ever-deeper knowledge of the reactionary mass regime and the molecular reality of Italian society.[9]

What follows is a further 'horizontal and minute' inquiry into Fascist cultural organization. The specific topic is a law on author's right.

The Italian Law of 22 April 1941 (no. 633) on Author's Right exemplifies a minority theory of literary and artistic property: the theory of labour. As such, this legislation would merit mention in any theoretical and historical reconstruction of the domain of copyright and author's right. But it is important firstly to reconstruct the cultural context of this instance of Fascist legislation.

The 1941 Italian Law on Author's Right in its Fascist Context

On 13 November 1936 the Minister of Popular Culture, Dino Alfieri, established by decree a Commissione per la riforma della legislazione in materia di diritto di autore (Commission for Copyright Law Reform). Senator Eduardo Piola-Caselli, authority on literary and artistic property law, was appointed *relatore generale* of the commission.[10] The objectives were the updating and improvement of the existing legislation, the so-called Rocco Law of 1925. This, in its turn, had reformed the previous Law,[11] bringing Italian

9. A. de Castris, *Egemonia e fascismo*, Bologna, 1981, p. 11.
10. I have relied extensively on E. Piola-Caselli, *Codice del diritto di autore: Commentario della nuova legge 22 aprile 1941-XIX n. 633*, Turin, 1943. In relation to earlier legislation, Piola-Caselli had published *Trattato del diritto di autore secondo la legge italiana comparata con le leggi straniere*, Naples, 1907, and *Trattato del diritto di autore e del contratto di edizione*, Turin, 1927.
11. Prior to 1925, literary and artistic property was regulated primarily by the 25 June 1865 legislation, augmented in 1875 and 1882 but not substantially re-

legislation into line with the international norms laid down in the Berne Convention of 1886. A particular concern of the Law of 22 April 1941 was, however, to provide a more distinctively national (that is Fascist) character to the granting of author's right in Italy, albeit without departing from the broader principles of the moral right tradition that has differentiated continental civil law jurisdictions from Anglo-American law of copyright.

Over the signature of its president, Amedeo Giannini, the commission reported to Minister Alfieri on 20 July 1939. In the thirty-two months since its establishment, the commission had moved from a series of initial plenary sessions on the always complex issues of the law on literary and artistic property, to several sub-committee inquiries into the specific areas that constitute this juridical domain, such as the periodical press, the association of literary authors,[12] radio, recorded music and the film industry. On the basis of the commission's report, a bill was drafted and presented to the Camera dei Fasci e delle Corporazioni by the new Minister of Popular Culture, Alessandro Pavolini.[13] The bill was accompanied by a detailed *Relazione* in 145 parts by Piola-Caselli, covering the 206 Articles of the bill.

The legislative history of the new law on author's right is briefly as follows.[14] On 27 November 1940 it was approved by the Joint Legislative Commissions for Justice, Popular Culture, the Arts and Professions, of the Camera dei Fasci e delle Corporazioni. On 28 January 1941 it was amended by the Senate Joint Legislative Commissions for Internal Affairs and Justice and for National Education and Popular Culture. On 19 February 1941 it was further amended by the Joint Legislative Commissions of the Camera. Finally, on 4 April 1941 it was further amended and given final approval by the Joint Legislative Commissions of the Senate. The bill was passed

---

formed, despite the efforts of four commissions of reform between 1897 and 1921, none of which succeeded in gaining legislative sanction. Hence the importance of the Rocco Law in reforming the Italian jurisdiction in the light of the Berne Union of 1886, providing international norms for copyright protection.

12. Article 204 of the 1941 Law concerns a new denomination for the Società italiana degli autori ed editori (SIAE), namely Ente Italiano per il Diritto di Autore (EIDA). This organization was the object of the decree of 18 May 1942, no. 1369. In 1945 the EIDA became the SIAE again, by the decree of 20 August of that year.
13. Pavolini replaced Alfieri in October 1939. On this change, see L. Salvatorelli and G. Mira, *Storia d'Italia nel periodo fascista*, Milan, 1970, vol. 2, pp. 322–3.
14. For the full record of discussions in the Camera dei Fasci e delle Corporazioni and in the Senate, see Piola-Caselli, *Codice*, pp. 52-169.

into law on 22 April 1941, thus realizing Alfieri's 1936 initiation of a reform that would update author's right legislation in Italy in the light of technological developments and of the perceived need to correlate the law with the requirements of a corporative state structure.

In the 145 sections of his *Relazione* on the bill, Piola-Caselli enlarges on the terms in which the law accommodated these technological and political factors. Above all, it was a matter of handling authorship and literary creation within the terms of labour law. In the new legislation, as anticipated by Piola-Caselli,

> what is recognized as the fundamental principle is that the original prerogative of author's right flows from *the creation of the work*. To this has been added: 'as a particular expression of intellectual labour'. By this means a clear distinction is drawn between the author's personal and property rights.
>
> A single original source of the prerogative is admitted, that of the creative act, conceptualized as an expression of labour and thereby attached to the strongest justification which Fascist law recognizes for the right of the subject: the right that flows from labour.[15]

The *Relazione* also signals the exception proposed to the legal principle deriving from the 'carattere intimamente personale dell'atto creativo che giustifica l'acquisto del diritto di autore':[16] the proposal that the law recognize the Partito Nazionale Fascista as a subject able to hold author's right. This capacity was withheld, by contrast, from private companies.

The formal origins of the reform of author's right in Fascist Italy thus date back to 1936, with the establishment of the Alfieri commission setting in train a legislative series that was to reach its completion in 1941. Within the tranquil domain of doctrinal legal historiography, all that need be said about the 1941 Law on author's right is that it embodies a particular theory of literary and artistic property: the theory of labour. Yet it is difficult not to go further and express some surprise that a law on author's right should be promulgated in Italy in the circumstances of 1941.

Externally, Italy was then locked into the war alongside Nazi Germany. Since June 1941 Mussolini had been sending small contingents of Italian troops as a symbolic presence on the Russian

15. For Piola-Caselli's *Relazione sul progetto ministeriale* see *Codice*, pp. 12–46; here p. 14.
16. Ibid., p. 15.

front, behind the slogan 'guerrafondismo'. Yet Mussolini was at the same time confiding to Ciano his hope for an English victory over Hitler; Nazi pressure on the Fascist regime would be relieved, reducing the war economy costs of having Italian forces in action in North Africa, Yugoslavia and Greece. Internally, hopes for an end to war, and with it disengagement from the Ciano-Ribbentrop Pact of May 1939, were dissolving. Pro- and anti-German positions were forming within the PNF. This political confusion was marked by growing economic crisis: the policy of economic *autarchia* (self-sufficiency) was not working; controls were being imposed on an ever-wider range of goods, including food (in September 1941 all *pasticceria* production was forbidden), soap, clothes and paper. By the following year, the twentieth anniversary of the regime, there was daily Allied bombing of the major cities.

Yet, in the midst of this, a detailed and substantial statute on author's right was promulgated. What were the motivations behind the move to legislate, with an elaborate statute containing over 200 articles, on the regulation of author's right in 1941? Explorations lead us in at least three directions: censorship; cultural autarchy; and the generalization of labour and production.

Censorship

Copyright and censorship were once related, both on the Continent and in England. But that relation was ended in the eighteenth century. Before then censorship had been exercised, in particular against works held to be seditious or blasphemous, through the mechanism of witholding the grant of royal privilege allowing the production of copies. This mechanism could also take the form of a compulsory registration procedure, such as entry in the records of the Stationers' Company where English books were concerned.

Is it possible that some nexus between author's right and censorship is at work in the 1941 Italian legislation? It is the case that in late 1938 the Commissione per la bonifica libraria, a subsection of the Direzione generale per la stampa italiana, was established to police the field of publishing. For instance, this commission had the works of Tolstoy, Chekhov and Gogol seized on the grounds that all Russian writing had an association with Bolshevism. In addition, we would anticipate a general tightening of controls with wartime circumstances. However, we should also recall that, prior to the 1940s, the Fascist regime did not in fact pursue a thoroughgoing *dirigisme* where cultural production was concerned. Cannistraro can thus state:

> It is certainly true that the regime destroyed in principle the cultural freedom of many Italian intellectuals and artists . . . but it is also true that it did little to alter their underlying attitudes and the nature of their work. Most artists continued to paint in their own preferred style, just as teachers continued for the most part to teach according to the old ideas.[17]

The limited nature of censorship is confirmed by de Castris, who moves to specify the limits of intervention in terms of a high culture left untouched, and a mass or popular culture increasingly organized – 'Fascistized' – by the party and Mussolini:

> An organizational practice which oscillated between respectful liberality and administrative control (the Academy and the *Italian Encyclopaedia* on the one hand, but on the other the 'Fascist-ization' of existing cultural agencies, the white collar unions, the 1925 Institute) continued to characterize the regime into the 1930s, even after the oath of allegiance was made compulsory in schools and universities. On the one hand, there was an abandoning of attempts to use the major intellectuals and a substantial acceptance of the autonomy of high culture (the regime's incapacity to alter the content of the old organization of knowledge); on the other hand, there was the ever more pervasive and obsessive mass propaganda, with the establishment of an ever present organizational and policing apparatus (in the areas of sport, press and media), coordinated by the Ministry of Popular Culture and increasingly directed towards the forming of a relation of immediacy between the myth of the Duce and the consent of the masses.[18]

The weight of argument seems to confirm that high literary culture was the object of a perhaps surprising degree of official toleration. And this was not just in the aesthetic domain. Major enterprises such as the *Enciclopedia Italiana*, initiated in 1925 and completed in 1937, represent cultural undertakings open to the contributions of non-political specialist and technical expertise.[19] Indeed, as Pertile has put it:

> Despite its deep contempt for high culture, Fascism came quickly to share the intelligentsia's belief in the quality and separateness of intellectual work. In other words, it aimed to integrate high culture rather than stamp it out. While high culture was ineffective as an opposition, its

17. P. Cannistraro, *La fabbrica del consenso*, Bari, 1975, p. 54.
18. De Castris, *Egemonia*, p. 70.
19. On the *Enciclopedia Italiana* see G. Turi, 'Ideologia e cultura del fascismo nello specchio dell'*Enciclopedia Italiana*', *Studi storici*, January–March 1979.

> survival was essential to the regime's respectability and prestige. It proved that the totalitarian system was able harmoniously to integrate all human activities under the banner of work and production, while controlling and keeping them separate within their spheres of specialisation, that is, while making them innocuous.[20]

Thus a certain tolerated deployment of literary culture allegedly served as legitimation for the regime. However, whilst it would be wrong to minimize the intensity of press censorship through the Office of the Press (to 1935), the Ministry of Propaganda (1935–7), and then the Ministry of Popular Culture, other recent arguments suggest that even the general distinction between a largely immune high culture and a totally controlled mass culture must be qualified, for instance where the cinema is concerned. Here too, official interventionism was limited, not total:

> The absence of a cultural policy [on the cinema] in the Fascist period is striking: if anything the post-war Christian Democrats were more explicit in their ideological pronouncements than the Fascists had been, but then they had more of an opposition to contend with. If Fascism had an identifiable effect on the films made when it was in power, it was not through directives and acts of censorship (though censorship was quite powerful) but more as a diffuse result of the general quiescence imposed on cultural life. For the cinema to keep going it was enough for it to stay quiet and attract audiences without exciting them.[21]

The censorship conditions within the field of mass culture were thus not uniformly severe.

None the less, such exceptions as these were to the notion of a generalized and repressive censorship do not mean that, by April 1941, wartime controls were not activated. On the contrary, the whole weight of the Ministry of Popular Culture under Pavolini was marshalled, from the time of Italy's entry to the war in 1940, for the purposes of propaganda and censorship. This work, undertaken in collaboration with the military authorities, marks a constant process of concentration of cultural controls.

A process of this sort, one might think, could extend to include legislation bearing on author's right. Legal protection could be granted only to works approved. However, in the record of the

20. L. Pertile, 'Fascism and Literature', in Forgacs, *Rethinking Italian Fascism*, p. 177.
21. G. Nowell-Smith, 'The Italian Cinema under Fascism', in Forgacs, *Rethinking Italian Fascism*, pp. 159–60.

preparatory works leading to the Law of 22 April 1941, there is nothing to suggest that censorship concerns in any way penetrated the new legislative provisions on author's right.

Cultural Autarchy

There is no need to dwell on the general commitment of the Fascist regime to a policy of autarchy.[22] However, a brief reference to the bearing of the policy on cultural production is appropriate. The case of the cinema will serve. Nowell-Smith has suggested that the Fascist regime, especially in its early years, had no cinema policy because in Italy the cinema was American.[23] By contrast, the years from 1938 onwards stand out as 'a brief interlude when the majority of films publicly screened in Italy were not American'.[24]

The use of author's right legislation to protect a national film industry from foreign competition is entirely plausible. Indeed, this is precisely the object of the French Law of 3 July 1985, in which the terms of film and television production contracts are specified in such a way that the economic exploitation of the film by the producer is enhanced, albeit at the cost of various curtailments of creators' moral rights. The grounds for such legislation are precisely autarchic: the survival of the French audiovisual industries in the face of foreign competition.

The example of the 1985 French legislation invites us to consider the Italian Law in relation to protectionist moves against foreign films. Indeed, Piola-Caselli's *Commentario* on the section of the law dealing with cinematographic works is explicit on there being an economic rationale for the legislation: 'The film industry is now of international importance. A series of laws has provided for restrictions on the importing of foreign films into Italy, for the creation and supervision of an indigenous film industry whose development is supported both as an organ of publicity and as an educational instrument.'[25] The 1941 Law on author's right is therefore to be counted alongside other institutions of cultural autarchy established

22. Indicative materials from Vannutelli and Santarelli on the policy of autarchy are found in R. Sarti (ed.), *The Ax Within: Italian Fascism in Action*, New York, 1974, pp. 144–5 and 158–60, and pp. 178–80, respectively.
23. On the Americanization of popular culture in Europe in this period, see V. de Grazia, 'La sfida dello "star system": l'americanismo nella formazione della cultura di massa in Europa, 1920–1965', *Quaderni storici*, vol. 1, 1985, pp. 95–133.
24. Nowell-Smith, 'The Italian Cinema', p. 146.
25. Piola-Caselli, *Codice*, p. 384.

in the 1930s: the Direzione Generale per la Cinematografia, the Centro Sperimentale di Cinematografia and the Cinecittà Studios. Reorganization on this scale, with the involvement of state capital, generates legislative action. That in 1941 the conditions for such action existed is suggested by Nowell-Smith: 'The government's need for consent and the industry's need for markets were consonant with each other, since there was no market outside the area of consent. Only if either the economic or the political ideological situation became unstable was dissonance likely to emerge, and this indeed begins to happen during the last years of the regime.'[26] Unfortunately – but consistent with the practice of almost all cultural commentary – no reference is made by Nowell-Smith to the legal relations of Italian film production at this point.[27]

The Generalization of Labour and Production

If the first two possible motivations for legislating on author's right in 1941 can be broadly termed political and economic respectively, the third is more properly discursive. It concerns the Fascist cult of labour and production. As already noted, the 1941 Law embodies a particular theory of literary and artistic property: the theory of labour.

Pertile's statement that the regime was able to integrate high culture 'under the banner of work and production' makes absolutely no reference to the specifically *juridical* framework in which this integration was projected. Yet some reference is surely appropriate to the 1927 *Carta del lavoro* (Labour Charter), of which article 2 reads:

> Labour in all its forms – intellectual, technical, manual, organizing, and executive – is a social duty. By virtue of this fact, and this fact alone, labour falls within the purview of the state. When considered from a national point of view, production in its manifold forms constitutes a unity, its many objectives coinciding and being generally definable as the well-being of those who produce, and the development of national power.[28]

26. Nowell-Smith, 'The Italian Cinema', p. 160.
27. On the indigenous cinema under Fascism, see also C. Wagstaff, 'The Italian Cinema Industry during the Fascist Regime', *The Italianist*, vol. 4, 1984, pp. 160–74.
28. English translation in C. F. Delzell (ed.), *Mediterranean Fascisms, 1919–1945*, New York, 1970, p. 121.

The centrality of labour in the regime's symbolic self-production is evidenced by the fact that the *Carta del lavoro* was promulgated by the Fascist Grand Council on 21 April 1927, the 21 April having been celebrated since 1922 as the Festa del lavoro.

The Fascist regime is not alone in according labour a central place in its ideological discourse. The notion of the dignity of human labour has served many purposes, political and religious. But the integrating symbolic function accorded to labour by Fascism marks a particularly strong development. Or so it would seem from Mussolini's speech on 20 March 1919 to the Dalmine metal workers. The speech elaborated on the ethical concept of the inherent dignity of labour:

> In you it is labour that speaks, not stupid dogma or an intolerant church, even a red one. It is labour which in the trenches consecrated its right to be no longer fatigue, wretchedness or despair, because labour had to become joy, pride, creation, the prize of free men in a great and free fatherland, within and beyond these limits. . . . You are not the poor, the humble, the despised, as the antique rhetoric of literary socialism would say. You are the producers, and it is in your status as producers that you demand the right to treat as equals with the industrialists.[29]

Commenting on this speech, Asor Rosa notes the echoes of Sorel and Corradini. But he also shows how the speech manipulates the notion of the dignity of labour so that Mussolini can appeal to a consecration which is 'antisovversiva ma rivoluzionaria'.[30]

The appeal to the Dalmine workers centres on the Mussolinian notion of the 'creative strike', a new and productive form of industrial action:

> The intrinsic meaning of your action is clear . . . You have placed yourselves on the terrain of class, but you have not forgotten the nation. *You have spoken of the Italian people, not solely of your own category of metal workers.* For the immediate interests of your category, you could strike in the old style, the negative and destructive strike. But, conscious of the interests of the people, you have inaugurated the creative strike, which does not interrupt production.[31]

The proposition of the creative 'working strike' – this surely is an oxymoron – shows the extending and generalization of labour

29. Quoted in A. Asor Rosa, *Scrittori e popolo*, Rome, 1965, vol. 1, p. 93.
30. Ibid., p. 94.
31. Quoted in ibid., p. 94.

suggested by Article 2 of the *Carta del lavoro*. However, we should heed Asor Rosa's warning before we smile:

> We should not, however, laugh too much at these crude Mussolinian definitions, because from them will materialize things of undeniable importance, such as the corporatist theories and the corporations. The relation of class and nation, of category and people, the ethic of the producer and of production, the subordination of individual interest to the general (i.e. popular) interest: these constitute so many strongholds of that leftist Fascism which will play such a large part in the formation of the new intellectual and political cadres from 1924 to 1940, and which precisely this Mussolini and this early Fascism will bear in mind, not least in order to use them to resist the establishment of a far more explicitly conservative and bourgeois Fascism.[32]

This caution is appropriate. The labour ethic is self-evidently part and parcel of the 'ethical state' whose configuration is outlined in the Mussolini-Gentile entry under 'Fascism' in the *Enciclopedia Italiana*; however, it is by no means limited to Fascist discourse, recurring for instance in Gramsci.[33]

The extension of labour and production into non-work time and space involved not only the strike but also leisure. The Opera Nazionale Dopolavoro or OND was introduced into Italy by Mario Giani, the manager of a Westinghouse Corporation subsidiary at Vado Ligure. The bill proposing establishment of the OND was approved by the Council of Ministers on – inevitably – 21 April 1925. The rich symbolism and political competition around labour are demonstrated by the fact that Mussolini had King Victor Emmanuel sign the bill into law only on 1 May, although May Day celebrations had been banned since April 1923. The stated object of the OND was, according to the founding statute, to promote 'the healthy and profitable occupation of workers' leisure hours by means of institutions for developing their physical, intellectual and moral capacities.'[34] According to de Grazia, Mario Giani argued that the organization 'held in itself the possibility of producing a totally reformed citizen-producer'.[35] This new subject, produced in the practices of healthful leisure activities that would restore it for even greater labour, would itself enhance the national interest by improved productive effort whilst no doubt remaining impervious

32. Ibid., p. 94.
33. As shown for instance by Romano, 'Le fascisme', p. 245.
34. De Grazia, *The Culture of Consent*, p. 35.
35. Ibid., p. 35.

to such divisive or distracting interlopers as class, gender and politics.

In this generalization of labour and production we shall find the central motivation for the labour theory orientation of the 1941 Law, of which the definitional article 6 reads as follows: 'The original prerogative of the author's right is constituted by creation of the work as a particular expression of intellectual labour.' At the heart of the legal matter is the reference to creation as intellectual *labour*. This reference, the topic of my next section, will be seen to reinforce Mercer's comment on Gentile's striking formulation that 'at the root of the "I" there is a "we"': 'The project of . . . fascist ideology . . . can be seen as a sometimes pragmatic, sometimes systematic series of transactions which would attempt to write the subjective "I" with the collective "we".'[36] The 1941 Italian Law on author's right thus conceptualized individual creators within the framework of a juridical national collectivity.

The 1941 Italian Law on Author's Right and Theories of Intellectual Property

Just as literary and cultural studies proceed with only a rare mention of the *legal* relations of their object, so studies of law, particularly those that treat doctrine in terms of some timeless logic or general juridical rationality, proceed with barely a mention of the *cultural* relations of law and legislation. In my previous section, I began to redress this latter deficit where the 1941 Law on author's right is concerned. However, some attention to the doctrinal context of such legislation is also required.

The 1941 Law conceptualizes the creation of works in terms of a 'particular expression of intellectual labour' (article 6). On this ground the Fascist legislation is treated, in studies of the doctrine of author's right, as an example of the labour theory of author's right, a distinction shared with Soviet legislation.[37]

36. C. Mercer, 'Fascist Ideology', in J. Donald and S. Hall (eds), *Politics and Ideology*, Milton Keynes/Philadelphia, 1986, p. 228.
37. Whilst he would doubtless accept the parallelism of the two legislations in so far as both Fascist and Soviet legislations ground themselves on the principle of labour, Piola-Caselli none the less draws a distinction between the 1941 Italian Law and that of the Soviet Union, noting that the reform commission had examined 'the French Bill of 13 August 1936 but only in order to delimit the principles which inform it. Such a bill in fact grounds author's right on the concept of remuneration for the work, thereby aligning itself in a war far removed from the Fascist perspective with the old Soviet legislation dating

Beyond the familiar distinction between *copyright* regimes (as developed in English and American law) and *author's right* regimes (as developed in the civil law tradition of continental European states), we can note that author's right is in practice a loose nomination for two distinct sets of rights: the patrimonial and the paternal. These are distinguished as *property* rights and *moral* or *personality* rights respectively. (The latter can be thought of as rights attaching to the person of the author, extending to the protection of the work in so far as this is taken to be the 'mirror of the personality' of the author.)

The 1941 Italian Law was oriented to this author's right tradition, but with a new grounding in labour theory. What does this imply? The brief answer is as follows: the 1941 Law is grounded in a labour theory of author's right in that the 'personality' mirrored in the work is defined according to labour criteria. This is the import of Article 6, as cited above, with its criterion that recognizes creation of the work 'quale particolare espressione del lavoro intellettuale'. This phrase is critical for Piola-Caselli in defining the 1941 Law as both appropriate for author's right protection and also exemplary of Fascist values. From Piola-Caselli's monumental *Commentario* on the new statute, we can reconstruct the argument that leads him to this position. We note firstly his interpretation of Article 6; secondly his alignment of author's right with labour law

---

from the first period of the Revolution (the decree of 26 November 1918), a concept which we consider harmful and dangerous for those very authorial interests which the Italian Bill aims to safeguard' (p. 45). The point at issue is the recognition of the object of author's right as defined not in terms of expenditure of a quantity of energy ('locazione di energia umana') but of the creative act considered as 'la più nobile espressione del lavoro umano'.

On Soviet copyright legislation see M. Newcity, *Copyright Law in the Soviet Union*, New York, 1978. In relation to labour theory and the practices which might flow from it, the following observation by Newcity (p. 84) on the Soviet law can be cited: 'Soviet jurists maintain that royalties paid pursuant to these fixed schedules are equivalent to the wages paid workers in the USSR; authors are compensated in proportion to the quality and quantity of their work.' Newcity notes that the 1928 statute establishing different scales of royalties according to a judgement on the work as outstanding, good or satisfactory (from an ideological viewpoint) has been superseded by the 1960 Law. However, the rates of royalty are still fixed by government decree. Criteria determining the rate include genre, length, size and number of editions. For instance, in the literary domain, sixteen genres are recognized, whilst the length of a work is measured in units of 'author's sheets'. In prose works one author's sheet is 40,000 printed characters including spaces, whilst for poetry the base unit is 700 lines. Logically, in a labour theory regime, the author's heirs or successors in interest get less than a full rate of return on a work after the author's death, in fact 50 per cent of the authorial rate.

rather than with law about property; and finally his observations on the political relations of this legislation.

Article 6 is the point of alignment of the 1941 Law on author's right and the general codification of all forms of labour in the *Carta del lavoro*. The latter is several times invoked by Piola-Caselli as the overriding authority for the author's right provisions:

> The labour Charter stands as a constitutional statement of Italian private law and, as such, is transcribed at the head of the Fascist Civil Code.
>
> What is more, author's right is recognized and regulated in the said code in the book concerning labour.
>
> In the same way, Article 6 of the new law declares that the original prerogative of author's right is constituted by the creation of the work, as a particular expression of intellectual labour.[38]

In a subsequent reference, this alignment with the *Carta del lavoro* is recognized as marking off the new conceptualization of author's right from a property right:

> Thus it is now beyond doubt that in Fascist positive law author's right is considered a specific type of right, not assimilable to a property right because it forms part of the systematic framework of labour law, being a prerogative constituted by the creation of the work as a particular expression of intellectual labour.
>
> The norms of this juridical institution do not belong to the field of norms which govern property rights. They relate to labour law on the basis of the general provision contained in article 1, book 5 of the new Civil Code, which declares: 'Labour is protected in all its forms: organized and executive, intellectual, technical and manual, according to the principles of the Labour Charter.'[39]

There is nothing self-evidently erroneous in locating author's right within labour law. In fact Piola-Caselli claims that a labour law context is the most justifiable of the several theoretical contexts within which literary and artistic production and distribution might be regulated:

> The Fascist conception transforms and rectifies juridical positions, plac-

38. Piola-Caselli, *Codice*, p. 179.
39. Ibid., p. 193.

> ing author's right in the field of labour law and thus furnishing authors with the powerful protection afforded by corporative law. In this respect, this part of the civil law has been coordinated with the corporative system, thus consolidating and reinforcing a *de facto* state of affairs which has existed since authors became part of the fascist Confederation of Artists and Professionals.[40]

Here the claim is emerging of the *superiority* of the labour law framework for the protection of the rights of the author's personality. The assimilation of author's right to property right is, in fact, held to be positively harmful for Italian authorial interests, as well as ill-conceived, the property relation between author and work being terminated once the work is published.[41] Hence Piola-Caselli's conclusion:

> Examination of these doctrines thus confirms in full the correctness of the solution adopted by Fascist civil law, that is to say the decision to consider author's right as a specific prerogative, the content of which, within the broad framework of labour law, consists of two closely interrelated faculties destined to assure the author both remuneration for his creative work and also at the same time the protection of those personal interests which flow from the creation itself.[42]

The conclusion is that in Italy author's right is neither a conventional property right, nor a conventional right of personality, but a *sui generis* right ('di natura giuridica particolare') that belongs within a labour law framework.

There is no avoidance of the political relations of this legislative organization:

40. Ibid., pp. 193–4.
41. Whilst not of central concern to my present inquiry, Piola-Caselli's distinctive argument on the 'representative form' as the object of author's right protection merits mention. For Piola-Caselli, the notion of the work as representation is fundamental, whether of ideas, facts or feelings. From this notion it follows that the protected object of author's right is the representation of a content, not the content *per se*. However, if the ideas, facts or feelings that constitute the content can be reproduced with impunity, definition of the limits of the exclusive right will often prove contentious, the distinction of content and form being far from self-evident in every case. Novelistic plots, for instance, would tend to be unprotected in any strict limitation of representation to exclude the content represented. Indeed, in order to broaden the category, Piola-Caselli has recourse to the category of 'inner form', which he borrows from the nineteenth-century German jurist Josef Kohler (*Codice*, pp. 180–3).
42. Ibid., p. 201.

> To a superficial look, this concept might appear as one whose value is purely political. This is not so. The concept can and must direct legal thinking in the interpretation and application of all the norms of the new law. In interpreting and applying these norms, the judge will have to be guided by the idea that it is a question not of objective protection for an economic good but of protection for an intellectual labour, an activity which constitutes at one and the same time a property and a value, the one economic and objective, the other spiritual and personal.[43]

Earlier, Piola-Caselli had already asserted that, as an exclusive patrimonial right, author's right is justifiable only as a grant made by the state in recognition of an individual's intellectual labour. However small, provided it is original, the outcome of that labour is considered as a contribution to the intellectual life of the nation. And Piola-Caselli observes: 'Today, this second justification of author's right has assumed in the Fascist conception the importance of a political conception. Property can have for us today no political basis other than that of labour.'[44]

We can now ask: what is at stake when authors are protected under labour law? What is the type of relationship that labour law, with its collective entities of employee and employer, can typically recognize? The measure of what hangs on these questions can be gauged by a brief comparison between the 1941 Italian law and the 1985 French Law on the *droit d'auteur.*[45]

Section 2 of the French Law of 3 July 1985 establishes for the first time a style of author's right for performers, and delineates the conditions of its exercise (notably by the mechanism of a presumed ceding of such rights to the producer). In Article 19, performers are actually referred to as 'wage earners', that is as a collective entity, even though these same performers are newly individualized by their recognition as holders of a moral right – a right of personality – in their performance. This reference might be an inadvertently retained fragment of the *Code du travail* where the status of performing artists was formerly defined. None the less, the logic of the new law, as the French jurist Bernard Edelman has shown, marks a shift away from what he approvingly terms the 'wildly individualistic' tradition of French moral right.

43. Ibid., p. 249.
44. Ibid., p. 179.
45. In commenting on these extensions of French author's right to new subjects and objects beyond its traditional boundaries, I am indebted to B. Edelman, 'Commentaire de la loi no. 85–660 du 3 juillet 1985 relative aux droits d'auteur et aux droits voisins', *Actualité Législative Dalloz*, special issue, 1987. All translations from Edelman are mine.

One sign of this shift is the blurring of legal boundaries. Section 5 of the 1985 French Law extends protection under author's right to producers of software and their works. However, 'authors' of software are individualized as holders of moral rights only to be recollectivized, in Article 46, as employees who cannot exercise their moral right to alter, to withdraw or to refuse their employer's wish to alter their work. As Edelman observes: 'Here we reach the very *limit* where authors' rights disappear to be replaced by a hybrid right which is closely related to labour law.'[46] The 1941 Italian Law was not, of course, concerned with software protection. However, like the 1985 French Law, the earlier Italian legislation raises questions on how to conceptualize the authorship of original intellectual work.

What is at stake becomes evident in Edelman's comments on 1986 French Court of Cassation findings on cases involving the extension of author's right to software. At issue was the definition of an originality in software production that could qualify for protection under author's right criteria. This definition involved an important rupture: 'Author's right was emptied of all its aesthetic substance: creative will was displaced by "intellectual effort" and the product obtained became the result of this effort.'[47] For Edelman the rupture is profound: 'From being a creator, the author is transformed into a worker.' Furthermore, the law loses an historical capacity to distinguish between intellectual effort, and intellectual effort *that produces an original work.*

My reference to this transformation and to the fuzzy boundary emerging in contemporary French legislation has three purposes. Firstly, it shows that the turn to labour theory in the 1941 Italian Law was not an entirely peculiar and Fascist phenomenon. Secondly, it shows that the broadly defined tradition of author's right legislation has no single theoretical ground. Where the Italian Law recognized labour as its ground, French Law recognized (at least prior to 1985) individual creativity. Thirdly, the French and Italian Laws serve as a joint reminder that English copyright law does not ground its provisions in any theoretical principle whatsoever, whether creativity or labour. The formal basis of authors' rights under a copyright regime is the statute, currently the Copyright, Designs and Patents Act (1988) in the UK, not some underlying principle attaching to the act of intellectual creation.

46. Ibid., p. 6.
47. B. Edelman, 'Note', *Recueil Dalloz Sirey*, vol. 31, 1986, p. 414.

The argument is not, therefore, that the theory of labour is an improper theory to apply to literary authorship. Rather, the Italian labour theory marks a particular juridical framework for constituting individuals as legally protected authoring subjects. The detail of how different juridical frameworks constitute different authoring subjects cannot be pursued here, but Edelman's stark opposition of 'worker' and 'creator' suggests certain of the resulting options. It is important to recognize that the choice between a labour theory law and any other theory of author's right cannot be resolved by reference to some allegedly independent knowledge of what authorship really is. What we count as authorship will always be defined, at least in part, by the classificatory decisions made between the forms available within one juridical framework or another, for instance between classifying authors and works according to the labour principle, or according to the principle of individual creativity.

The 1941 Italian Law, in other words, exercises a juridical option, elements of which are quite capable of emerging in other jurisdictions and times, as shown by the labour law elements in Soviet law and in the recent French legislation on author's right.

Future consideration of the historical relations of the categories of person, property and labour would establish a set of genealogies for the slippery concept 'labour'. It would not be just a matter of showing that 'labour' designates a denial of 'creativity' (as Edelman fears). After all, it could just as easily lead to notions of workers' control (which Edelman might welcome). Rather, what is needed is an exploration of the different ways in which the concept of 'labour' has been transfused with notions of 'creativity' (whether in Marx, Morris or Mussolini). Analysis would lead to historical inquiries into how 'labour' came to provide a discursive basis for notions of property as exclusive right:

> Every man had a property in his own labour. And from the postulate that a man's labour was peculiarly, exclusively his own . . . so was that with which he had mixed his labour. This was the principle that Locke made central to the liberal concept of property. . . . Even Bentham, scorning natural rights and claiming to have them replaced by utility, rested the property right on labour . . . A man's own labour, as well as capital and land, was made so much a private exclusive property as to be alienable, that is marketable. The concept of property as nothing but an exclusive, alienable, individual right, not only in material things but even in one's own productive capacities, was thus a creation of capitalist society: it was only needed, and only brought forth, when the formal

> equality of the market superseded the formal inequality of precapitalist society.[48]

Against this background it would then be possible to explore other arguments, such as that there was no necessity for authorial labour to generate a right to property. After all, '[we] do not ordinarily create or modify property rights . . . solely on the basis of labour expended.'[49]

Conclusion

Tranfaglia observes that the analysis of Fascist legislative work remains almost entirely to be done.[50] He is concerned with public law, in particular legislation on constitutional matters, not with the specialist private law domain of author's right. Yet the objective remains to make legislative work visible. Once visible, the probability is that it will show itself not as a complete rupture with what went before Fascism and what came after. Hence Tranfaglia's comment on Alfredo Rocco, Minister for Grace and Justice: 'Despite rhetorical exaltations to the contrary on the part of the Fascists and cries of grief from anti-Fascist liberal democrats, the Fascist legislation of Alfredo Rocco and Mussolini did not constitute a profound rupture at the institutional level.'[51] In other words, because legislation of the Fascist years is in part continuous with what went before, it is not totally reducible to a Fascist episode apart. After all, the 1941 legislation on author's right is still the fundamental operative statute in republican Italy.[52]

Reconstructing the context of the Law does not mean attributing any ideally oppositional capacity to that Law. Tranfaglia refers to judicial memoir evidence for the argument that anti-Fascist judges maintained a minimum of autonomy, noting that the party's 1926 establishment of the Tribunale Speciale (not composed of professional judges) has been cited in support of this argument. Yet

48. C. B. Macpherson, 'Capitalism and the Changing Concept of Property', in E. Kamenka and R. S. Neale (eds), *Feudalism, Capitalism and Beyond*, Canberra, 1975, p. 114.
49. S. Breyer, 'The Uneasy Case for Copyright: A Study of Copyright in Books, Photocopies and Computer Programs', *Harvard Law Review*, vol. 84, 1970, p. 289.
50. N. Tranfaglia, *Dallo stato liberale al regime fascista*, Milan, 1975, p. 47.
51. Ibid., p. 136.
52. On the persistence of Fascist legislation into the present see F. Spotts and T. Wieser, *Italy, a Difficult Democracy*, Cambridge, 1986.

Tranfaglia remains sceptical, finally aligning himself with Aquarone's view that if, as a whole, the judiciary was not complicit with the will, excesses and more glaring illegalities of the regime, judges none the less did not constitute a centre of opposition.[53] The subsequent reference to Neppi Modona suggests that the Fascist executive had little need to alter the pre-existing system of relations between government and judiciary.[54] The judges' aura of non-complicity, therefore, lies less in some individual act of will than in the persistence of a specialist legal-technical competence, something similar to the technical competences that persisted in the professions or in the Vatican.

At this point, revisionist historiography can advance its claim of 'horizontal' and 'minute' description against the certainty for a Calamandrei that Fascist legality is a self-evident oxymoron. The trouble with such a certainty, as with the Crocean assertion that Fascist culture was not culture, is that, once stated, it leaves nothing more to say about the detailed mechanisms of twenty years of right-wing, authoritarian, police state, one-party rule which none the less registered a convergence between the national regime (in the broadest sense) and all categories of producers of intellectual property, scientists and historians as well as *letterati*. Of the 1250 university professors, 1237 consented to take the oath of loyalty to the regime (two took early retirement instead). This convergence, this consent, and the elaboration of detailed statutes on specialist matters such as the 22 April 1941 law on author's right are what historians such as Tranfaglia seek to penetrate and describe.

In this chapter, the question of legality has been considered at the level of a particular law. It is of course one thing to consider a particular law, and another to judge an entire legal system. Let us suppose, nevertheless, that the 1941 statute was the only surviving piece of Fascist legislation. Would we, on the basis of this one instance, doubt the legality on which such legislation stands? In so far as the 1941 law can appear in surveys of the domain of author's right alongside English and American, French and German laws, it would seem that no such doubt need follow from this one sample.[55] True, the Italian Law is unusual in its grounding on the theory of labour. But this is only to record an historical preference

53. Quoted in Tranfaglia, *Dallo stato liberale*, p. 178.
54. G. Neppi Modona, 'La magistratura e il fascismo', in G. Quazza (ed.), *Fascismo e società italiana*, Turin, 1973.
55. See, for instance, F. J. Kase, *Copyright Thought in Continental Europe*, South Hackensack, 1967.

for one doctrinal current rather than another, albeit one which blurs the boundaries between intellectual property law and labour law.

It would therefore be difficult to justify any general dismissal of Fascist law in terms of an illegalism evident in everything legislative done in the *ventennio*. I would certainly want to pre-empt any moral argument that might justify silence on the legal relations of Fascist literature and culture by invoking a general illegality of Fascist law.

–14–

'Material Incentives'

The Lust for 'Jewish' Property

KONRAD KWIET

There is still no adequate historical interpretation of the attempted extermination of European Jewry; none of the various theories of Fascism is in a position to explain this central complex of crimes committed by the National Socialist regime. The virulent *Historikerstreit* (historians' dispute) in West Germany, which began in response to Ernst Nolte's remarks and has now spread to the international scene, is symptomatic of this state of affairs; few of the participating historians have any expertise on the Holocaust. One of the major problems of research in this field is the issue of continuity and discontinuity in the National Socialist persecution of the Jews; the so-called 'intentionalists' and 'structuralists' have developed contrasting models of description and interpretation. The course of this debate has been determined by the late Martin Broszat.[1] A few years ago he presented his 'improvization thesis', claiming that the 'Final Solution' arose not only from the prevailing wish to exterminate the Jews, but also as a 'way out' of an impasse into which the National Socialists had manoeuvred themselves. Once initiated and institutionalized, the practice of liquidation set its own priorities and developed into a comprehensive 'programme'.[2]

1. For the development of research in this area see K. Kwiet, 'Zur historiographischen Behandlung der Judenverfolgung im Dritten Reich', *Militärgeschichtliche Mitteilungen*, vol. 1, 1980, pp. 149–94; O. D. Kulka, 'Major Trends and Tendencies in German Historiography on National Socialism and the "Jewish Question" (1924–1984)', *Yearbook Leo Baeck Institute*, vol. XXX, 1985, pp. 215–42; M. R. Marrus, 'The History of the Holocaust: A Survey of Recent Literature', *Journal of Modern History*, vol. 59, 1987, pp. 114–60.
2. M. Broszat, 'Hitler und die Genesis der "Endlösung"', *Vierteljahrshefte für Zeitgeschichte*, vol. 25, 1977, p. 753. See also C. Browning, 'Eine Antwort auf Martin Broszats' Thesen zur Genesis der Endlösung', *Vierteljahrshefte für Zeitgeschichte*, vol. 29, 1981, pp. 97–109, as well as *Fateful Months. Essays on the*

My chapter attempts to modify this thesis. I will restrict myself to an aspect which has so far attracted little attention[3] – the termination of German–Jewish cohabitation, the 'living together' of Germans and German Jews, which formed an integral part of the social and economic process of expulsion and thus paved the way for the 'Final Solution'.[4]

Immediately after their seizure of power in 1933, the National Socialists set about undermining the basic conditions for the continued existence and survival of the Jews in Germany, thereby fulfilling the old promise from the *Kampfzeit* (time of struggle) to force the Jews out of the economy and society and effect a 'clean break' between Jews and Germans in preparation for total *Entjudung* (de-Jewing).[5] Until the early stages of the Second World War, they hoped to solve the 'Jewish question' through segregation and expulsion. When it became clear that this strategy was no longer possible, the 'Final Solution', in the form of systematic extermination, presented itself as the 'alternative'. The realization of this alternative presupposed not only the ideological 'will' but also the perfection and unswerving execution of a process of social exclusion, which had been carried out single-mindedly, without interruption and with remarkable consistency – allowing for regional nuances – from 1933 onwards. Laws and regulations, sporadically organized outbursts of 'people's rage', boycotts and other acts of oppression were among the measures employed. Government officials and party functionaries worked hand in hand with

---

Emergence of the Final Solution, New York/London, 1985; E. Jäckel and J. Rohwer (eds), *Der Mord an den Juden im Zweiten Weltkrieg*, Stuttgart, 1985; G. Hirschfeld (ed.), *The Politics of Genocide*, London, 1986; W. Scheffler, 'Probleme der Holocaustforschung', in *Deutsche-Juden-Polen*, Sonderband der Historischen Kommission zu Berlin, Berlin, 1987.

3. See especially G. Botz, *Wohnungspolitik und Judendeportation in Wien 1938 bis 1945. Zur Funktion des Antisemitismus als Ersatz nationalsozialistischer Sozialpolitik*, Vienna/Salzburg, 1975. See also the excellent case study by M. Buchholz, *Die hannoverschen Judenhäuser. Zur Situation der Juden in der Zeit der Ghettoisierung und Verfolgung 1941 bis 1945*, Hildesheim, 1987; and recently J. Tabor, 'In Beethovens Lieblingswohnung hausten Juden. Der Bau-Raub als Form des gewalttätigen Antisemitismus in Wien 1938–1945', in *Der Novemberpogrom 1938. Die 'Reichskristallnacht' in Wien*, Historisches Museum der Stadt Wien, Vienna, 1988.
4. This chapter is based largely on my contribution 'Nach dem Pogrom: Stufen der Ausgrenzung', in W. Benz (ed.), *Die Juden in Deutschland 1933–1945. Leben unter nationalsozialister Herrschaft*, Munich, 1988, pp. 545–659.
5. See R. Rürup, 'Das Ende der Emanzipation: Die antijüdische Politik in Deutschland von der "Machtergreifung" bis zum Zweiten Weltkrieg', in A. Paucker (ed.), *Die Juden im Nationalsozialistischen Deutschland*, Tübingen, 1986, pp. 97–114.

representatives of economic organizations. They were supported by a broad public consensus: the isolation and expulsion of the Jews meant freedom from irksome competition, and promised handsome profits. Many 'Aryan businessmen' were able to amass a considerable fortune. Initially, the attitudes of foreign countries and exchange markets had still to be taken into consideration. As relieving mass unemployment and building up an effective weapons industry had top priority, a number of large Jewish enterprises were spared. The expulsion of Jews from the free professions and the 'Aryanization' or dissolution of small and medium-sized businesses could be carried out without 'disturbances' or 'disadvantages' for the German economy. At the end of 1937, against a background of considerable successes in foreign policy, of preparations for war and institutional restructuring within the National Socialist power apparatus, the last phase of the *Entjudung* of the economy began. The pogrom of November 1938 heralded its onset: the forced 'Aryanization' and closure of businesses, the final bans on professional activity and the confiscation of remaining assets led swiftly to the economic and financial ruin of the Jews.[6]

This was the context in which the National Socialists began driving the Jews out of their much coveted houses and apartments. The prelude was set in Austria. Approximately 10,000 dwellings were 'freed' immediately after the annexation in March 1938. Uncoordinated and spontaneous action rapidly developed into organized theft, sanctioned by the authorities. Up to 1942 the Viennese were offered a further 60,000 'vacant' apartments; in Berlin more than 30,000 homes were confiscated, in Munich about 3,000, in Düsseldorf 700. Hamburg boasted an additional 1,900. Every city experienced a similar expansion in real estate. The seizure of Jewish homes was motivated both by racist ideology and strong material interests. Nazi ideology dictated an end to German–Jewish cohabitation, the physical separation of Germans and Jews, a measure which was essential to the planned solution of the 'Jewish question'. But the herding together of Jewish families under one roof released accommodation to ease the housing shortage. In 1933 the National Socialists had announced the introduction of a comprehensive housing programme. As Gerhard Botz has convincingly shown, this was one of the many promises they failed to keep; anti-Semitism served as an *Ersatz* for social policy. Top

6. See the comprehensive study by A. Barkai, *Vom Boykott zur 'Entjudung'. Der wirtschaftliche Existenzkampf der Juden im Dritten Reich 1933–1945*, Frankfurt/M, 1987.

priority was given to rearmament and preparations for war, including the costly and much publicized building of the *Autobahn*. From 1936–7 onwards, in the context of preparations for war, they concentrated their efforts on the planning and construction of the massive edifices which were to symbolize the glory and splendour of the *Tausendjähriges Reich* (thousand-year Reich). Confronted with an acute housing shortage which took on catastrophic proportions with the outbreak and spread of the war, the National Socialists turned their attention to Jewish dwellings. The greater the housing shortage, the more single-mindedly they pursued the policy of *Entjudung*. There is a clear link between the need for accommodation and the final expulsion; an unbroken line leads from ghettoization to deportation and finally to mass murder. This was no improvization, but the product of careful planning.

In contrast to the practice in the occupied territories, ghettoization was to be carried out 'inconspicuously' in Germany. A few weeks after the November pogrom, Göring informed the ministers of the Reich of Hitler's decisions on Jewish housing. The decree of 28 December 1938 reads: 'Generally speaking, tenant protection will continue to apply to the Jews. Nevertheless it is desirable that, in individual cases and wherever rental conditions permit, the Jews be placed together in one building. The "Aryanization" of property ownership should thus only be carried out in individual cases where there are compelling reasons for it.'[7]

The guidelines soon became regulations. The Law Concerning the Letting of Property to Jews, passed on 30 April 1939,[8] legalized the eviction without notice of Jews from so-called 'Aryan' buildings and apartments, provided that they could be guaranteed alternative accommodation. The requirement of alternative housing ensured that the evacuated Jewish tenants would not become a burden on the 'welfare services for the homeless'. Jews were now permitted to sign leases only with other Jews. Jewish landlords were obliged to accept Jews as tenants or subtenants 'at the request of the local authorities'. The law prescribed registration, so that all utilizable living space was recorded. Freedom of movement was restricted and subject to strict controls. Every letting and every change of residence required the permission of the authorities. Later, these records were to facilitate the 'rounding-up' of the Jews for deportation, and it was far more difficult to escape from these new enclaves into illegality.

7. Anordnung no. 1/39g, 28 December 1938, Nbg. Doc. PS 069.
8. *Reichsgesetzblatt* 1939 I, 864f.

With the support of these new regulations, city and local authorities, and especially housing offices, landlords and real estate agents, set about evacuating all Jews from 'Aryan' buildings, in close cooperation with the regional Gestapo and NSDAP (Nazi Party) representatives. In many cases they even evicted the tenants without notice to meet the cost of improvements and repairs requested by the new tenant. The Jews were assigned alternative accommodation in buildings which had not yet been selected for 'Aryanization'. These included not only houses, apartments and boarding-houses owned by Jews, but community buildings such as kindergartens and schools, nursing homes and hospitals, public offices and communal halls, prayer rooms and funeral parlours, which were converted to accommodate the new homeless. This was the first step in the establishment of *Judenhäuser* (Jews' houses). Apart from this, there were efforts to urge 'Aryan' tenants to move out of Jewish-owned property of their own accord. As they still enjoyed tenant protection, the authorities appealed to their *gesundes Volksempfinden* (healthy *völkisch* feelings) or suggested an exchange of accommodation. Once new regulations had invalidated the conditions of tenancy in Jewish-owned buildings, a further eviction procedure was introduced. An official circular of the Darmstadt Gestapo (15 January 1941) reveals the motives for this measure and its consequences:

> According to our survey here, unmarried Jews, childless Jewish couples or couples with few children are very often occupying buildings which are suitable for the accommodation of families of German blood and are thus in urgent demand. In order to relieve the prevailing housing shortage at least in part and to effect a separation of people of German blood and Jews, it is proposed that the Jewish occupants of such properties be made to vacate their homes. Any dwelling which becomes superfluous through the uniting of several Jewish families under one roof may be reserved or sold in accordance with the prevailing currency regulations.[9]

The isolation of the Jews proceeded swiftly and by decree. It was taken for granted that living conditions in the *Judenhäuser* would be ignored. The process of impoverishment was executed with ruthless determination, as shown in a letter dated 18 September 1941 from the Gestapo in Düsseldorf to the local authorities in Kleve:

9. D. Rebentisch and A. Raab, *Neu-Isenburg zwischen Anpassung und Widerstand. Dokumente über Lebensbedingungen und politisches Verhalten 1933–1945*, Neu-Isenburg, 1978, pp. 278ff.

> It is most important to make even greater use of Jewish living space acquired through the uniting of several Jewish families under one roof . . . The Jews are to be assigned only the dirtiest and worst accommodation, whilst current sanitary regulations must be observed and care should be taken that not all the apartments or houses are contiguous. The Jewish living space thus vacated is to be made available to the German population, without involving the Reich or local councils in additional expense.[10]

This solution did not satisfy the fanatics. Even before the systematic deportations, they were anxious to declare their residential, administrative (and recreational) areas *judenfrei* (Jew-free). The National Socialists showed a deliberate preference for the high holidays of the Jewish calendar, combining persecution with the violation of Jewish laws. In Vienna one eviction was carried out on the night of Yom Kippur, 5 October 1938. Jewish families expelled from homes in Ottakring, Hernals, Währing and Döbling were sent to the railway stations to be dumped across the Reich border, free of charge and without any travel documents.[11] This procedure became commonplace. In February 1940 Jews from Stettin were deported to occupied Poland. At the end of October 1940 almost 7,000 Jews from Baden, Rheinpfalz and the Saarland were transported to southern France. These deportations were supplemented by local *Umsiedlungsaktionen* (resettling action); some cities and communities, afraid of missing the opportunity, adopted a model recommended by the Austrian National Socialists, the erection of barracks classified as *Arbeitslager* or *Selbsterhaltungslager* (work camps or self-maintenance camps). The Ulm city council was clearly concerned to spirit away its Jews as quickly as possible. A decrepit castle in Oberstotzingen offered the solution; the council generously declared its readiness to spend 6,000 to 10,000 Reichsmarks on necessary renovations, mindful, no doubt, of the effect of these 'vacancies' on its housing problems. The clearing of several buildings would probably be cheaper than construction of a new one; the local council of Oberstotzingen had to be offered a modest compensation, but only as long as the Jews stayed in the castle. It was a rewarding investment. The mayor reported of 19 December 1941: 'The city cannot withhold its assistance in the resettlement of the Jews. It has assured the *Gauleiter* of its cooperation in the expectation that, in allocating Jewish rooms and dwellings, state

10. H. G. Adler, *Der verwaltete Mensch*, Tübingen, 1974, p. 47.
11. Report by Dr Josef Löwenherz, in H. Rosenkranz, *Verfolgung und Selbstbehauptung. Die Juden in Osterreich 1938–1945*, Vienna/Munich, 1978, p. 157.

and party will take the demands and wishes of the city into account.'[12]

In Essen, Jews were taken to Holbeckshof, a camp erected on the site of a former coal mine. Nine barracks awaited them, 50 metres by 15 metres and divided into small rooms. Fifteen Jews shared each room. In Dresden Jews were 'resettled' in barracks at Hallersberg. More than 300 Jews were housed in one wing of the Vincentine nunnery in Berg am Laim, Munich. The Munich National Socialists referred to this detention centre as a *Heimanlage*. They praised their second *Judensiedlung* (Jewish settlement), constructed by Jewish forced labour on a 14,500 square metre site in Milbertshofen, 7 kilometres from the city centre, as a 'model . . . pointing the way'. By October 1941 eighteen wooden barracks, designed to accommodate a maximum of 1,100 inmates, were ready for occupation. This number was soon exceeded and eventually reached 1,376. From Milbertshofen and other *Transitlager* or *Sammelstellen* (transit camps or collection sites) the Jews set out on their last journey to the extermination camps in the east. Once they crossed Germany's borders, their homes – sealed and locked by the Gestapo, the keys deposited at the local police station – and all their confiscated possessions became the property of the German Reich.

The German population accepted the dissolution of German–Jewish cohabitation in silence. A few voices were raised in protest. Landlords occasionally refused to turn their Jewish tenants on to the streets. Some Aryan tenants ignored the appeals of the National Socialists and stayed in their Jewish-owned buildings. Some even tried to relieve the plight of the Jews in the *Judenhäuser* and *Judensiedlungen*. They were vastly outnumbered by those scrambling to stake their claim on Jewish property. A small-town hairdresser wrote in October 1939:

> Dear Housing Office!
>
> I should hereby like to make the polite and urgent request that the apartment above my shop at 9 Kaiserstraße no longer be let to Jews, especially as this is a prestigious street. I should like to reside here myself, next to my shop, a privilege which has been denied me for almost nine years. I would be grateful if you could inform me of the rent of the apartment and, if possible, consult me on the matter. Jews should

12. H. Keil, *Dokumentation über die Verfolgung der jüdischen Bürger von Ulm/Donau*, Ulm, 1961, p. 237.

> keep to themselves, out of sight, if possible, and certainly should not be living in a commercial district.
>
> I trust that this reasonable request will find the response it deserves.
>
> With German greetings . . .
>
> Heil Hitler.[13]

Such requests increased in number when the order for deportation was given 'from above', and massive pressure 'from below' began to speeed up the process of *Entjudung*. A report from the Lübeck NSDAP in October 1941 states under the heading 'The Jews and the Housing Shortage':

> The housing problems in the district of Lübeck are out of control. They can only be described as catastrophic. It has, for example, not escaped my attention that the local police station here has more than 200 families on record as occupying unsatisfactory living quarters, some of which are totally unsuited for human habitation. These families want to be declared homeless [to be eligible for rehousing]. On the other hand, some of the Jews here still occupy highly desirable quarters. It should be considered whether these unpleasant creatures should not be deported to the east and disappear from the towns in our area once and for all.[14]

In Munich, vacated Jewish homes were allocated to families with several children or to other worthy 'Aryans'. The best homes were presented to deserving party members and high-ranking officials, to officers and artists. The grandest of the confiscated buildings served as offices and public rooms for the National Socialists. A Party Court and the Gestapo moved into the Auspitz Palais in Vienna. The Rothschild Palais housed the Zentralstelle für Jüdische Auswanderung (Central Office for Jewish Emigration), where Adolf Eichmann organized the exploitation and expulsion of the Viennese Jews.[15] Members of the SS did not go empty-handed. In November 1940 Reinhard Heydrich and Albert Speer agreed to place a number of Jewish apartments and houses at the disposal of the Gestapo. In an effort to ease the prevailing need for housing, officials were asked to submit their applications immediately, so

13. Adler, *Der verwaltete Mensch*, p. 56.
14. *Stimmungsbericht* (informal report) of the NSDAP Kreisleitung, Lübeck, October 1941, Institut für Zeitgeschichte, MA 138.
15. Tabor, 'In Beethovens Lieblingswohnung', p. 106.

that the most suitable buildings could be made available through the Reichsvereinigung der Juden (Reich Union of Jews) and the leases drawn up. Speer had been assigned the task of administering and distributing Jewish properties in his capacity of Chief Building Inspector in Berlin, and showed understanding for the special wishes of other party and state officials. He had no qualms in laying claim to Jewish homes himself; they were 'cleared' and demolished as part of his mammoth plan to redevelop Berlin as Germania, the future capital city. Several *Großaktionen* (major campaigns) were carried out. A Jewish teacher recalls:

> Speer demanded 1,000 apartments in so-called 'Aryan' buildings, [currently] occupied by Jews, for victims of air raids, and instructed the Jewish community to evict the tenants and accommodate them in *Judenhäuser* . . . The lists we received from the authorities revealed, to our amazement, that 7–8 per cent of all private buildings in Berlin were classified as 'Jewish'; in Wilmersdorf, in Schöneberg and other areas there were about 450 each . . . As a surveyor with a measuring tape, a pencil and a certain authoritarian clout, I spent eight weeks inspecting all the Jewish apartments in Schöneberg, and settled Jewish families who had only had temporary accommodation.[16]

The work was in vain. The *Judenhäuser* disintegrated with the deportations. The plan for a *judenfreies* Berlin had already been drawn up in the Ministry for Propaganda, by experts from the NSDAP, the SS and the Housing Office, in March 1941. The minutes of the meeting record under 'Housing':

> Gutterer informed us that during a lunch conversation with the Führer, Dr Goebbels's attention had been drawn to the 60,000–70,000 Jews still resident in Berlin. In discussion it was agreed that it was intolerable that the capital of the National Socialist Empire should house such a large number of Jews. Eichmann (SS Reich Security Main Office) reported that Heydrich, who had been commissioned by the Führer to evacuate the Jews once and for all, had presented a proposal to the Führer some six to eight weeks ago. It had only not been carried out because the general government of occupied Poland was at present not in a position to accept a single Jew or a single Pole from the Altreich [old Reich]. A representative from Speer's office revealed that 20,000 apartments were currently occupied by Jews. Speer needed these apartments vacated and held in reserve in case of extensive air-raid damage and, later on, for clearing as part of the redevelopment of Berlin. He went on to say that

16. Wiener Library (no number). Photocopy in possession of the author.

there were currently 160,000 to 180,000 too few apartments in Berlin. Consequently, Eichmann was asked to submit a plan for the evacuation of the Jews from Berlin to *Gauleiter* Goebbels.[17]

When the plan was put into action in autumn 1941, representatives from the Jewish community were summoned to Gestapo headquarters and informed of the beginning of the deportations. The housing issue was once again at the forefront. Hildegard Henschel, wife of the last president of Berlin's Jewish community, reports:

> The Gestapo wanted to combine the evacuation with a large-scale plan to acquire living quarters for Nazi families. This is why the discussion took place in the presence of the head of the district housing office. The acquiring of apartments for Nazi families had gradually become a matter of major concern to the Nazi authorities. Air raids had destroyed many buildings, the construction of countless new office buildings had turned residential space to commercial use, and finally the expectations of high-ranking Nazis, who often came from quite poor families, had risen to such an extent that only the relatively attractive Jewish apartments in the better districts of Berlin could satisfy them. We were therefore informed of the Christian-owned buildings in which Jews were to be given notice; the local authorities were to request the tenant to surrender the apartment. [They] . . . were given the task of providing new accommodation for those affected, usually by placing them in apartments in Jewish buildings. We were further instructed that the synagogue in Levetzowstraße was to be turned into a *Sammellager* [collection camp] for about 1,000 people; a deadline was set for its establishment, but no date was announced for the evacuation. The housing plan was executed, every tenant given notice was allocated new accommodation; but before the moves could take place, 15 October 1941 arrived. At the onset of dusk, two Gestapo officers appeared without warning in each of the apartments of those who had been given notice and asked the families to pack the necessary things and follow them.[18]

The link between the housing shortage and deportation was also clear in Vienna. At the beginning of November 1941 Martin Bormann, as leader of the Party Chancellery, conveyed an instruction from Hitler to Baldur von Schirach, *Gauleiter* and *Reichsstatthalter* in Vienna. The following is an extract from this strictly confidential letter:

17. Institut für Zeitgeschichte, MA 423; see also Adler, *Der verwaltete Mensch*, pp. 152ff.
18. H. Henschel, 'Aus der Arbeit der Jüdischen Gemeinde Berlin während der Jahre 1941–1943', *Zeitschrift für die Geschichte der Juden*, vol. 9, 1972, pp. 34ff.

> The Führer emphasized that you should see your task not in the creation of new living quarters but rather in the cleaning up of existing conditions. Firstly, in cooperation with the Reichsführer SS, all Jews are to be pushed out as soon as possible, followed by the Czechs and other foreign races, who make it so difficult to achieve a unified political direction and opinion among the Viennese. If you reduced the total population . . . from 1.5 to 1.4 million, you would easily and quickly resolve the housing shortage.[19]

According to an ordinance of the *Reichstatthalter* in Hamburg, vacated apartments were to be given in the first instance to those who had suffered war injury and those with large families. The authorities expected access to about 1,000 vacant apartments through the *Wegschaffung* (removal) of 5,000 Jews by Christmas 1941. Welcome as this acquisition of additional living space was, it could in no way compensate the losses incurred in the Allied air raids. By November 1941 more than 1,200 buildings were already in ruins; between 2,200 and 2,300 buildings were classified as extensively damaged and 1,400 as slightly damaged. In August 1942 the authorities in Hamburg drew a provisional balance. In a document classified 'top secret' the Department of Social Services reported on the *Entjudung*:

> The Jewish apartments were a great help; there was a total of 1,900, of which 570 were one- or two-room apartments (old people's homes); of the remaining 1,330, about 130 were used to house the Jews still resident here (privileged and non-privileged mixed marriages), so that only 1,200 Jewish apartments could be made directly or indirectly available to the victims of bomb attacks. In 1933, the number of Jews in Hamburg was 34,000. By September 1939, 21,500 had emigrated. Of the remaining 12,700, a further 2,000 emigrated and 5,150 were deported. In addition, 4,100 died between 1933 and 1942. There are now 1,540 still resident: 1,200 are living in mixed marriages, 200 are ill, and 50 are employed as nursing and administrative staff. As more move into the Jewish old people's homes, approximately 400 further apartments will become vacant. This will, however, completely exhaust our supply.[20]

Faced with their own annihilation, representatives of German Jewry attempted to safeguard their diminishing living and survival space. They attempted to follow the instructions of the National

19. Botz, *Wohnungspolitik*, p. 199.
20. A. Ebbinghaus et al., *Heilen und Vernichten im Mustergau Hamburg*, Hamburg, 1984, doc. 22, 68.

Socialists and assumed responsibilities. This strategy of survival soon backfired. Jewish officials were forced to act as intermediaries between the authorities and the Jewish community; they relayed orders and performed administrative tasks which assisted the National Socialists in their collection and isolation of the Jews. As in the forced labour programmes, they were urged to assist in rehousing or resettlement measures. They helped keep records of the housing situation, drawing up lists and locating new accommodation. As Dr Martha Mosse, the head of the Housing Department of the Jewish community in Berlin, writes:

> The implementation of the rehousing measures was primarily the responsibility of the Chief Inspector and the Central Planning Office in Berlin. At the wish of these authorities and the Gestapo, the Jewish community participated in the carrying out of these measures. The board was prepared to cooperate on the justifiable assumption that they could thereby ease the severity of the procedures. The Jewish community set up a Housing Advisory Board, which it was my job to run and which was there to help Jewish tenants who had been forced to give up their apartments, and to find suitable living quarters for them. The Jewish community was always informed of the apartments to be vacated and the appointed date. Through the land register, the Housing Advisory Board was able to trace both Jewish property owners and the Jewish tenants living in these buildings, where tenants forced to give up their apartments had to be re-accommodated as subtenants. This was done with all possible sensitivity. The professions of the parties concerned, their family status, the residents' state of health and the sanitary condition of the building were all taken into consideration. Given the relatively large Jewish ownership of property in Berlin, the procedures went quite smoothly . . . If the parties could not agree on a subletting fee, the Housing Advisory Board stepped in. Such differences of opinion were rare, however. The parties involved settled down to a peaceful coexistence. A very different state of affairs prevailed in Vienna . . . where the Jews were herded together in a very small number of apartments . . . widespread misery, illness and infestation resulted.[21]

Community members were repeatedly warned to follow official instructions. Precise records of the various rents and subletting fees had to be maintained. Inspection of 'vacant areas' could only be undertaken with official authorization. House keys were to be kept in an agreed location, to allow inspectors access at any time. Furthermore, they were constantly exhorted to support the resettlement measures.

21. Adler, *Der verwaltete Mensch*, pp. 46ff.

The surrender of their homes affected many Jews deeply. They were forced to uproot themselves from places they had lived in for years, often for generations. In the first phases of the regime they had at least been able to escape public defamation and discrimination by withdrawing into the relative security of their home environment. This refuge was no longer available. Familiar pieces of furniture and household items, books and pictures, domestic animals – all had to be abandoned, along with the memories of childhood and schooldays, of profession and family. Some made pilgrimages back to their old address, to gaze at their old apartments and houses from outside. Such feelings of sorrow and anguish were echoed, years later, by Jews returning from emigration to the scenes of their childhood. They, too, had had to bid a painful farewell to their families. The wave of emigration loosened many close family ties; evictions hastened the sorry process. The old and feeble disappeared into old people's homes, other family members moved into Jewish boarding-houses, *Judenhäuser*, or barracks. Those who retained the privilege of temporary residence in their own apartments frequently took in relatives and friends. They were soon joined by strangers: unmarried, married couples, or families with children. They had to adjust to these heterogeneous new communities and survive under wretched physical and psychological conditions, until the Final Solution put an end to this existence as well.

The Liebmanns, an elderly artist couple, found refuge in a room in a Jewish boarding-house on Munich's Akademiestraße. One visitor recalls:

> The living area . . . was quite uncomfortable. Not that it was dirty or even untidy, that it was certainly not. But the innumerable cases, cardboard boxes and small chests, wardrobes and cupboards piled on top of each other, took up every inch of space and stood in the way. The furniture they hadn't known what to do with after being driven out of their previous home had been stored with a removal firm, there was no place for it in the furnished room in the *Pension*. Everything that they had previously kept in drawers and cupboards – clothes, underwear, shoes, books, and all their painting and drawing materials – was packed away in this pile of parcels and boxes. Alexander Liebmann referred to his new residence ironically as the 'night refuge'. One day, with tears in his eyes, he showed me his German war decorations, and asked me the question: 'And suddenly I'm not supposed to be a German any more?'[22]

22. K. Weininger, *In München erlebte Geschichte*, Munich, 1985, p. 64.

Joel König visited his parents in Berlin at the beginning of 1940. They had sublet the apartment of a former Jewish businessman, close to the Hansaplatz:

> The one and a half rooms of the apartment were so crammed that one literally had to worm one's way between the furniture. Titian's Lavinia gazed at us from the corner of the room where mother cooked lunch on a primus stove. There was not enough coal to keep the rooms warm. My father had a flannel blanket draped about his shoulders, and tried to stay close to the lukewarm stove. Despite the cramped conditions and the cold, my parents were happy to have this apartment.[23]

Others complained about the cramped conditions: 'My mother and I lived in a five and a half room apartment with eleven other people, who all had to share a single kitchen, bathroom and toilet. The order to vacate a building usually came from one day to the next, and many Jews began to sell off their furniture, to be prepared.'[24]

Theodor Tuch left us this description of the situation in Hamburg:

> All Jews must now live in buildings which belong to a Jew, mostly in the Grindel area. Whole districts of the city are *judenfrei*. Usually, people live two to a room; Dora, for example, moved in with Paul's mother-in-law. The room is about 3 by 4 metres. You can work out for yourselves how much freedom of movement they have. Sleeping, eating, washing. Pick up the bed cushions, but where can they be stored? In the three-room apartment there are five or six people; in the kitchen, the washing is drying. Four wardrobes stand in the narrow hall, holding the remains of those possessions which the people were allowed to keep. Everything else had to be auctioned off.[25]

Until they were called up for deportation, the Jews were contained within the walls of an invisible ghetto. The waiting, the uncertainty, and the fear of transportation contributed to this slow torture, as did the fear of attacks by fanatical anti-Semites. *Judenhäuser* were preferred targets for members of the NSDAP and the Gestapo bent on showing their hatred of Jews in acts of brutality. Inspections provided the perfect excuse for molestation, plundering and ill-treatment.

23. J. König, *Den Netzen entronnen*, Göttingen, 1967, p. 164.
24. Wiener Library PIId, no. 192.
25. U. Randt, 'Theodor Tuch: An meine Tochter. Aufzeichnungen eines Hamburger Juden 1941/42', *Bulletin Leo Baeck Institute*, no. 70, 1985, pp. 20ff.

Before their deportation, German Jews were subjected to a period of 'ghettoization', in which they already experienced ostracism and banishment – a total expulsion from society. Thus prepared, they were to embark on their last journey. In autumn 1941, three years after the November pogrom and on the eve of the deportation, there were still 164,000 Jews living in Germany, one-third of the Jewish population in 1933. Most of them still intended to leave Germany. The National Socialists, however, no longer permitted this escape from the German-Jewish existence; by October 1941, emigration was forbidden. The 'Final Solution' was to be executed. Decimated and ageing, separated from their families and cut off from the outside world, stripped of all rights and impoverished, pressed into forced labour and undernourished, restricted in their freedom of movement, herded together in *Judenhäuser* and finally branded with a yellow star, the remaining Jews had become a *minorité fatale*, a burden to society which the Nazis were allowed to dispose of in secrecy. When, finally, 134,000 German Jews were dragged from their last refuges and loaded on to the trains, the public silence was undisturbed. Only 8,000 returned.

–15–

Politics and Canonicity
Constructing 'Literature in the Third Reich'

MARTIN TRAVERS

How does one speak of the unspeakable? Clearly, with difficulty. The subject of German literature in the Third Reich has remained a *thema non grata* for the great majority of scholars and critics working within the area of twentieth-century German literature in the post-war period. Until very recently, questions concerning literary life during the years 1933 to 1945 had not only been left unanswered and unexplored but even, in many circles, positively repressed, displaced from an historical agenda that moved out of the expressionism of the early years of this century, through such 'classics' as Thomas Mann, Kafka and Brecht, to re-emerge into the post-war sobriety of Böll and the post-modernist enthusiasm of Grass. One looked in vain through many of the standard literary histories for any mention of literature under National Socialism; even when the talk was of 'tradition' or 'exorcism', the coverage of this period conspicuously hovered around an absence.[1]

The reasons for this neglect of a whole era in German literature are complex, and deserve their own full-length enquiry. We would need to look at a constellation of factors, from moral distaste and aesthetic rejection through to political expediency and the traditional German abhorrence of *Nestbeschmutzung* (fouling the nest); these are all factors which impinged upon the process of *Vergangenheitsbewältigung* (coming to terms with the past) during the post-war period.[2]

1. This, at least, is the case in such standard studies as Hans Friedmann and Otto Mann, *Deutsche Literatur im 20. Jahrhundert*, 2 vols, Heidelberg, 1961; and Fritz Martini, *Deutsche Literaturgeschichte*, Stuttgart, 1952. The specific references are to Ronald Gray, *The German Tradition in Literature, 1871–1945*, Cambridge, 1967; and Michael Hamburger, *From Prophecy to Exorcism: The Premisses of Modern German Literature*, London, 1965.
2. The secondary material that attempts to deal with the national trauma of

I said above that the area had been 'largely' neglected, but not 'entirely'. For, existing alongside this institutional neglect, there appeared, rather like the trace of a conscience pressing for recognition, a small number of works which did indeed try to confront the writing of the Nazi period, and make it cohere into an object of literary enquiry. The authors of this body of scholarship posed, albeit often implicitly, a number of questions that confront any scholar facing a period or a movement without any agreed canonical status, questions such as: 'Which authors were central and which were marginal?', 'Which texts were viewed as classic, which were seen as peripheral?', 'Is it possible to speak of schools or movements within this period of literature?', and 'How can this period be related to the broader tradition of German literature?'[3]

In answering these questions, critics have realized that there are problems about applying in this field the standard categories of literary classification and assessment; that questions about authorial development and originality, stylistic innovation and literary value cannot be unproblematically posed about the literature produced in the Third Reich. Critics have responded to this methodological impasse in a number of ways. Some have dispensed entirely with conventional literary-critical categories, choosing instead, in a *polemisch-didaktisch* spirit, the more politicized priorities of ideological analysis. Others, focusing upon certain components of the literary representation of National Socialist ideology, have drawn upon the metalanguage of intellectual history.[4]

What these critics and others have in common is, above all, a tendency to set up their problematics within a methodological framework established by those political historians who first came to grips with the subject in the immediate post-war period. In

---

Vergangenheitsbewältigung is vast. For an excellent early discussion of the problem see Harry Pross, *Vor und nach Hitler: Zur deutschen Sozialpathologie*, Olten, 1962, particularly pp. 154–62. Pross's argument that we should not treat the Third Reich 'as a methodologically separate area' but should see it as something that is 'connected by a thousand threads with what went before and what came after' (p. 144) is a suggestion that I have tried to follow in this chapter.

3. Uwe-K. Ketelsen, in what is probably the most systematic attempt to establish the literary-historical parameters of the subject to date, addresses himself to such questions in his excellent *Völksch-nationale und nationalsozialistische Literatur in Deutschland, 1890–1945*, Stuttgart, 1976. See also his more recent essay, 'Die Literatur des 3. Reichs als Gegenstand germanistischer Forschung', in J. Kolbenbrock et al. (eds), *Wege der Literaturwissenschaft*, Bonn, 1985, pp. 284–302.
4. The studies alluded to here are Franz Schonauer, *Deutsche Literatur im Dritten Reich: Eine Darstellung in polemisch-didaktischer Absicht*, Olten, 1961; and Rolf Geissler, *Dekadenz und Heroismus: Zeitroman und völkisch-nationalsozialistische Literaturkritik*, Stuttgart, 1964, particularly pp. 76–103.

particular they have taken over a key assumption, or set of assumptions, inherent in much of the historical and historiographical writing about National Socialism, namely the totalitarian thesis or totalitarian model, a systematic approach first developed in the work of Hannah Arendt and Carl Friedrich.[5]

The central argument of this thesis is well known. Totalitarian political systems, which are meant to include not only those of Nazi Germany and Fascist Italy, but also that of the Soviet Union, are distinguished from the political systems found in liberal democracies by a number of key structural features: they possess an all-pervasive official ideology; they are governed by a single mass-based party led by a charismatic leader; a total control of the nation is exercised both through the terroristic intervention of a police force and through propagandistic media; and there is a central control of the economy. In short, totalitarian societies stand rigidly 'closed' to the pluralistic values of 'open' societies. The totalitarian model has, it is true, been modified in recent times by its more sophisticated exponents such as Karl Dietrich Bracher, but the essential assumption of total control of state over civil society has been largely retained.[6]

It is precisely this thesis that has been taken on board, sometimes unconsciously, by previous critics trying to construct a canon of literature in the Third Reich, and has been permitted to become the guiding light for their approaches. Scholars working within this area will be familiar with the major titles.[7] There is much good scholarship here, and on the whole I have no disagreement with the ideological analyses undertaken in these studies, or with the political sympathies that underwrite such approaches.[8] It is certainly

5. Here the seminal texts are Hannah Arendt, *The Origins of Totalitarianism*, New York, 1951; and Carl Friedrich and Zbigniew Brzezinski, *Totalitarian Dictatorship and Autocracy*, Cambridge, MA, 1956. Putting the totalitarian thesis on a firm political-historical foundation, and incidentally adding two key terms to its rhetoric, was the achievement of Karl Popper; see his *The Open Society and its Enemies*, 2 vols, London, 1945.

6. For an excellent résumé of the arguments involved, expounded with a clear eye to their German relevance, see Ian Kershaw, *The Nazi Dictatorship: Problems and Perspectives of Interpretation*, London, 1985, pp. 11–12, 20–3.

7. In chronological order: Walter Muschg, *Die Zerstörung der deutschen Literatur*, Munich, 1958; Schonauer, *Deutsche Literatur im Dritten Reich*, Olten, 1961; Josef Wulf, *Literatur und Dichtung im Dritten Reich*, Hamburg, 1963; Hildegaard Brenner, *Die Kunstpolitik des Nationalsozialismus*, Hamburg, 1963; Dietrich Strothmann, *Nationalsozialistische Literaturpolitik: Ein Beitrag zur Publizistik im Dritten Reich*, Bonn, 1968; Ernst Loewy, *Literatur unterm Hakenkreuz*, Frankfurt/M, 1969; J. M. Ritchie, *German Literature under National Socialism*, London, 1983; Günter Hartung, *Literatur und Ästhetik des deutschen Faschismus*, East Berlin, 1983.

8. It is, however, highly significant that most of these studies, such as those by

undeniable that the conditions under which literature was produced in the Third Reich were exceptional, and involved a series of widespread injustices that need to be both politically and morally confronted. But the moral distaste evident in some of these early works, such as the Wulf volume, can easily lead to a misrepresentation of the scope and extent of Nazi control of literature.

Even in the most recent studies of literature in the Third Reich, assumptions about the total control of the state over the production of literature have come to harden into an orthodoxy. Ralf Schnell, for example, introduces a collection of essays on the topic with the following observation about the nature of the Nazi system of total control: 'The unity of Fascist rule . . . was . . . an indicator of the systemic coherence of all its cultural expressions . . . an entire social order was determined by the influence of politically imposed *Gleichschaltung* [policy of bringing all areas of social life into line].'[9] Likewise Ronald Taylor, in an English study of this period, seems to adopt uncritically the major premises of the totalitarian thesis: 'State control was absolute and ruthless, and *Gleichschaltung* both demanded and received conformity of public utterance to the principles of the regime.'[10]

It is the central argument of this chapter that this assumption –

Brenner and Strothmann, are concerned more with the institutional framework in which the literature was produced than with the literature itself, almost as if the former focus must necessarily exclude the latter. This problem has been partly redressed in two more recent compilations of essays: Horst Denkler and Karl Prümm (eds), *Die deutsche Literatur im Dritten Reich: Themen, Traditionen, Wirkungen*, Stuttgart, 1976; Klaus Bohnen and Conny Bauer (eds), *Nationalsozialismus und Literatur*, Copenhagen, 1980.

9. See the foreword to Ralf Schnell (ed.), *Kunst und Kultur im deutschen Faschismus*, Stuttgart, 1978.
10. See Ronald Taylor, *Literature and Society in Germany, 1918–1945*, Brighton, 1980, p. 236. The lure of the totalitarian thesis is so strong that many authors retain its methodological priorities even in the face of conflicting evidence presented in their own works. Christa Kamenetsky, for example, in her *Children's Literature in Hitler's Germany: The Cultural Policy of National Socialism*, Ohio, 1984, concludes her study by revising her previous assumptions about the total control exercised by the state over literature (p. 311): 'Some of the shortcomings of the censorship system became particularly evident in regard to the popular Karl May novels and old fashioned girls' books. These works and others that were widely read did not meet the Nazis' *völkisch* criteria, and yet, the publishers supported them and the authorities tolerated them, at least for the time being. The real implications of the Nazis' censorship as a whole, however, should not be estimated in view of what was actually accomplished during the Twelve-Year Reich, but from the perspective of what the Nazis still hoped to accomplish in the future, for only from that angle is it possible to perceive the direction into which the totalitarian regime was moving.'

that the state was able to exert total control over individual writers – hinders rather than promotes a recognition of the true relationship between literary production and state control in Nazi Germany. Further, by recognizing that this relationship was far more complex and far less monocausal than has previously been assumed, we will be forced not only to redefine our view of 'Nazi' literature and hence to allow a different canon of writing to emerge, but also to rethink the whole concept of political or politicized literature.

More specifically, I want to argue that those previous approaches which have, by and large, accepted and worked within the assumptions of the totalitarian model have neglected three important dimensions of literary activity in the Third Reich. Firstly, they have disregarded the contradictions, tensions and dysfunctions within the apparatus of Nazi cultural control. Secondly, they have given insufficent attention to the lapses in the control and surveillance exercised over individual writers and certain literary institutions and journals. Thirdly, they have underplayed the overlaps and continuities that exist between the literature produced under the aegis of the Third Reich and literature produced in literary communities generally typified as 'liberal' or 'democratic'.

These areas have begun to be opened up by recent historians working in this area, and I have, to a certain extent, taken my cue from the work of Tim Mason (on workers' resistance to Hitler), Jill Stephenson (on the role of women in the Third Reich) and Ian Kershaw (on the knotty issue of Hitler's popularity).[11] To be sure, there are important differences of methodology and political priority between these historians. But where they do converge is in their attempt to revise the totalitarian thesis, and to move the debate's emphasis away from control and manipulation towards an analysis of the mechanics of resistance and opposition. They would all concur with the sentiments expressed in the conclusion to Kershaw's 1983 work: 'The material we have reviewed reveals . . . beneath the surface unity of the propaganda image, a remarkably disunited society. Under the propaganda varnish of the 'National

11. Recent work by Mason would include 'Intention and Explanation: A Current Controversy about the Interpretation of National Socialism', in Gerhard Hirschfeld and Lothar Kettenacker (eds), *Der Führerstaat; Mythos und Realität*, Stuttgart, 1981, pp. 23–40; and 'Open Questions on Nazism', in Raphael Samuel (ed.), *People's History and Socialist Theory*, London, 1981, pp. 205–10. For Jill Stephenson see *Women in Nazi Society*, London, 1975 and *The Nazi Organization of Women*, London, 1981; and for Ian Kershaw see *Popular Opinion and Political Dissent in the Third Reich: Bavaria, 1933–1945*, Oxford, 1983.

Community', old antagonisms continued unabated, heightened even by Nazi social and economic policy, and new ones were added to them.'[12] Literary historians have, as I indicated above, lagged in their analyses behind the attempts of these historians and others to revise our image of the Third Reich, although there is some evidence that things are beginning to change.[13]

This chapter, then, is an attempt to apply to the subject of German literature in the Third Reich the insights won by those political and cultural historians who have sought to revise the totalitarian thesis. The central question it addresses is: 'What would be a view of literature in the Third Reich which is constructed beyond the methodological parameters and political priorities of the totalitarian thesis?' Owing to exigencies of space, the attempt to answer this question made here must necessarily be schematic – the basis for a more extended analysis carried out elsewhere.[14] I shall address those three areas neglected by previous studies, beginning with the debate about the operation and constitution of the Nazi literary establishment. It is in this area that the first revision of the totalitarian thesis must be made. The received opinion is that the Nazi regime was a monolithic structure united in aims and policies, possessing a 'unified ideology'.[15] This view needs to be modified in two ways: firstly, by foregrounding the struggles within and between the various policy-making organizations; and secondly, by highlighting the changing, arbitrary and often conflicting nature of the cultural policies themselves.

The former area is perhaps the most difficult to analyse, since it seems in the logic of all bureaucratic organizations to disguise internal divisions and to try to produce the effect of unity and consensus of opinion. This logic was particularly prevalent in the organizational life of the Third Reich, where a high premium was set on persuading the public of the values of national harmony and collective purpose. It is probably an exaggeration to claim, as one historian has done, that 'the Third Reich was a bedlam of rival hierarchies, competing centres of power, and ambiguous chains of

12. Kershaw, *Popular Opinion*, p. 373.
13. I am thinking of the approaches adopted by Jan Berg, Walter Fähnders and Peter Zimmermann in their *Sozialgeschichte der deutschen Literatur von 1918 bis zur Gegenwart*, Frankfurt/M, 1981. Above all there is the seminal contribution of Hans Dieter Schäfer to a comprehensive cultural history of the Third Reich: see his *Das gespaltene Bewußtsein: Deutsche Kultur und Lebenswirklichkeit, 1933–1945*, Frankfurt/M, 1981.
14. See the forthcoming *German Literature in the Third Reich: A Study in Text and Context*, by the author.
15. See George Mosse, *Nazi Culture*, New York, 1966, p. xxii.

demand',[16] but recent historians are surely justified in modifying the assumption adhered to by the practitioners of the totalitarian thesis, that the cultural apparatus of the Third Reich was a tightly knit, monolithic structure, the embodiment of a single will and purpose. On the contrary, recent research has shown that, like any newly formed organizational structure, it was rent with a series of conflicting and competing claims for power and influence.

Of particular importance here were the tensions between Goebbels, as Head of the Ministry of Propaganda, and Alfred Rosenberg, who, in his capacity as the Führer's Delegate for the Entire Intellectual and Philosophical Education and Instruction of the National Socialist Party (to give him his full ungainly title), was in control of those publications concerned with articulating party ideology. The ensuing struggle between the two to gain responsibility for censoring literary production in the Third Reich has been well documented.[17] It was only the direct intervention of Hitler himself that made possible a negotiated agreement, and helped demarcate the sphere of influence of the two *apparatchiks*. But similar tensions within the system continued, involving in-fighting between Goebbels and Göring (relating to responsibilities for the state's radio network), and between Otto Dietrich, the Nazi press chief, and Max Amann, head of the state's publishing house (relating to control over the accreditation of journalists).[18]

It was inevitable that tensions and conflicts played out at the institutional level should be reflected at the level of policy. Indeed, it is arguable that debates about policy direction were often simply the means of continuing and resolving power struggles initiated at the institutional level. This certainly seems to have been the case with perhaps the most controversial and divisive cultural debate conducted during the early years of Third Reich, which centred on whether expressionist art forms could be accepted into the new canons of Nazi art. The debate that was conducted throughout 1934 – between Goebbels, the tentative defender of certain aspects of the expressionist style, and Rosenberg, a full-blown reactionary in the arts, who proposed a return to the classic styles favoured by

16. D. G. Williamson, *The Third Reich*, London, 1982, p. 20.
17. For a fuller discusssion of the tensions between Goebbels and Rosenberg see Reinhard Bollmus, *Das Amt Rosenberg und seine Gegner: Studien zum Machtkampf im nationalsozialistischen Herrschaftssystem*, Stuttgart, 1970, particularly pp. 61–103.
18. See the relevant documentation in J. Noakes and G. Pridham, *Nazism, 1919–1945: A Documentary Reader*, 2 vols, University of Exeter, 1984, vol. 2, pp. 382–97.

mainstream academy art of the nineteenth century – took over two years to resolve and spilled over into the literary arena, putting an end *en passant* to the career of Gottfried Benn, who had nailed his colours to the expressionist mast. This time it was Rosenberg who emerged the victor, but only after yet another timely intervention by Hitler, who felt his own Biedermeier tastes were more in keeping with the conservative image that the new national government wished to cultivate.[19]

The point that needs above all to be registered is that, in the final analysis, policy decisions and the implementation of cultural criteria were not the culmination of a rationally formulated and coherent aesthetic, but the consequences of overt and covert power struggles within the cultural bureaucracy of the Nazi regime. In the end, the continuing nature of these power struggles and the shifting centres and deployment of power often left official cultural policy in an indecisive and vacillating state.[20]

The second set of assumptions that needs to be challenged concern the exercise of control. Here the received opinion in many circles is that the state was entirely successful in manipulating the literary behaviour of the public sphere. This set of assumptions needs to be modified in three ways: firstly, we need to distinguish between National Socialist policy and legislation on the one hand, and its effect or realization on the other; secondly, we need to distinguish between the different targets (social groups, individuals and institutions) of that legislation; and finally, we need to be clear that the Nazis had only limited success in eradicating the private means of literary education and self-cultivation. The central assumption challenged by all three points is the idea that the state was successful in its penetration of all aspects of civil society. In other words, this set of modifications to the totalitarian thesis does not so much concern the controlled production of literature in the Third Reich, but rather its reception and dissemination. There were numerous instances of the reception of literature taking place beyond and contrary to the dictates and stipulations of official policy. Werner Bergengruen was just one of a number of authors who felt, as a writer and a reader, relatively untouched by the

19. There is no full-length study of this aesthetic conflict, but for a brief résumé of events and positions see Berthold Hinz, *Art in the Third Reich*, London, 1979, pp. 34–6, 55–8.
20. Thus Hans Hinkel, the general secretary of the Reich Chamber of Culture, felt able in 1945 to reverse the previously supportive party policy on *Blut und Boden* (blood and soil) literature; see Noakes and Pridham, *Nazism*, pp. 409–10, which should be compared with Goebbels's earlier directive, pp. 408–9.

interventionist tactics of the Nazi state. In his account of the genesis of his novel *Der Großtyran und das Gericht* (The Great Tyrant and the Court), which was published in 1935, Bergengruen argues that the control exercised by the various cultural surveillance bodies in the Third Reich was both fragmentary and inefficient, and that the whole system of cultural surveillance soon found itself out of touch ('in einer sonderbaren Isolierung') with developments in the cultural sphere.[21] Bergengruen's account acts as a useful antidote to those historians, both political and literary, who wish to convince us of the 'unified' and all-pervasive nature of Nazi control.

Bergengruen is often typified as a writer of the 'inner emigration', a not unproblematic term coined to describe those writers who felt they could resist, in both senses of the word, the pervasive influence of the state's policies; who tried, in other words, not only to remain impervious to such policies, but also to inscribe into their fiction, through allusion, allegory and symbol, values that stood, at least implicitly, in direct opposition to those of the regime. In the final analysis, it might be necessary to query the success of this inscribed or covert opposition; encoded messages could only be deciphered by readers in possession of the relevant codes. For other readers, not trained to problematize the 'surface' of the text, the implicit moment of political opposition would have gone unregistered.[22]

The existence of the work of the literary emigrants does, however, serve to emphasize one important but frequently overlooked point, namely that any adequate analysis of the success or failure of Nazi intervention in the literary sphere must take into consideration previously installed techniques of reading, which vary across social groups and age differences. There is increasing evidence to show that Nazi literary policy had its greatest successes amongst

21. See the pamphlet 'Rückblick auf einen Roman', Wiesbaden, 1961. To prove convincingly that Bergengruen was not a rare exception would require greater documentation than can be provided here. However, the case of Ernst Wiechert is yet a further example of a writer who felt that the regime, at least in its early days, was sufficiently disorganized in cultural matters to permit the expression of critical views; see his essay 'Der Dichter und die Jugend', given as a speech at Munich University in 1936.

22. This is a point not sufficiently discussed by Ralf Schnell in his otherwise excellent *Literarische Innere Emigration, 1933–1945*, Stuttgart, 1976. One author who does subject the concept of inner emigration to a more detailed theoretical analysis, paying attention to the problem of literary hermeneutics involved, is Gisela Berglund; see her *Der Kampf um den Leser im Dritten Reich*, Worms, 1980, pp. 213–44.

the youth and the very young, groups they specifically targeted.[23]

The difficulty the Nazis encountered in eradicating deeply installed reading assumptions and practices is nowhere better exemplified than in the cases of those individuals and institutions who were able to preserve their own private libraries or, at least, had frequent access to them. Information is understandably scarce concerning this area, and much of it is of an anecdotal nature. The philospher Wolfgang Harich, for example, who was ten years old when the Nazis took power in 1933, tells of his formative years in the Third Reich and of the decisive influence of the writings of Thomas Mann, to which Harich had access through the continuing existence of his father's library in spite of the ban put on Mann's writings in 1936.[24] Harich's account of his autodidactic contact with forbidden or *unerwünscht* (undesirable) literature is not without retrospective embellishment, or a tendency to idealize Mann; but his point is an important one, namely that reading literature in the Third Reich did not, as is sometimes assumed, commit one to the passive acceptance of the products of the Nazi literary establishment.[25] Harich's reading experience of Thomas Mann could be applied to the reception of a number of other established writers. The young poet and critic Felix Hartlaub, for example, tells in his diary of the importance to him of the works of Kafka and Proust during the war.[26]

The third area in which we must revise the totalitarian thesis relates precisely to the intrinsic nature of the literature published and disseminated during the Third Reich. Here, in response to those critics who insist upon the *sui generis* nature of 'Nazi' literature, a number of points need to be made: firstly, much of the writing valorized and canonized in the Third Reich was published well before 1933; secondly, many of the most popular authors of this period continued to publish in Germany after 1945; and

23. See Peter Aley, *Jugendliteratur im Dritten Reich*, Gütersloh, 1967; and Kamenetsky, *Children's Literature*.
24. See Harich's account in Marcel Reich-Ranicki, *Was halten Sie von Thomas Mann? Achtzehn Autoren antworten*, Frankfurt/M, 1986, pp. 29–35.
25. That the Nazis themselves were also aware of this fact is borne out by the pronouncements of Will Vesper who, as editor of the Nazi-oriented journal *Die Neue Literatur*, played a major role in directing literary taste in the Third Reich. Vesper was highly indignant that the work of Thomas Mann, Franz Werfel and Jakob Wassermann could be readily bought well after the *Machtergreifung* (seizure of power). See Berglund, *Der Kampf*, p. 14.
26. Hartlaub is mentioned, and further examples are given, in H.-D. Schäfer, 'Die nichtfaschistische Literatur der "jungen Generation" im nationalsozialistischen Deutschland', in Denkler and Prümm, *Literatur im Dritten Reich*, pp. 459–503.

thirdly, the Nazis tolerated and in some cases cultivated a good deal of literature which had no affinity with their ideology or policies.

These three points, all controversial to varying degress, would require detailed documentation and careful argumentation to substantiate in a convincing way. But for the purposes of this chapter, a number of more general observations must suffice. We should start by conceding that the advent of the Third Reich did allow the emergence of types of literature which, peculiar to that period, conformed to and openly celebrated the policies and general ideology of the Nazi Party. Examples of this *Parteidichtung* include both the work of poets such as Heinrich Anacker, Herybert Menzel, Gerhard Schumann and the leader of the Hitlerjugend (Hitler Youth), Baldur von Schirach, and that of the playwrights of the so-called *Thingspiel*. The latter was a dramatic form prevalent in the early years of the Third Reich, in which plays, frequently of a ritualistic or pseudo-cultic nature, were performed in purpose-built amphitheatres, often in front of audiences of up to ten or fifteen thousand people.[27]

Both these subgenres were products of a group that soon became designated as the Junge Mannschaft (Young Crew). This was not a tightly knit school or movement, but rather an *ad hoc* grouping of writers of similar age and background, idealists in the cause of National Socialism, who had been marginal, not to say unknown, figures in the world of Weimar *belles-lettres*. They had been party members prior to 1933, and had come to the fore in the early days of Hitler's chancellorship in order 'to mobilize' the population in the direction of the 'national revolution'.[28] Their work, in both poetry and drama, is interventionist; it interpellates the reader or audience directly. The poetry is meant to be sung, chanted or recited, around camp fires or during political rallies; the drama is intended to draw the spectator into the spectacle, either literally as a choric respondent, or more metaphorically through emotional or psychic absorption in the ceremony of the drama. It is a literature that hovers between magic and manipulation, and thus represents, as Walter Benjamin would have noted, a fateful blurring of the discursive distinctions between politics and aesthetics.[29]

27. See Henning Eichberg et al., *Massenspiele, NS-Thingspiel, Arbeiter-Weihespiel und Olympisches Zeremoniell*, Stuttgart, 1977.
28. The rhetoric stems from a speech given by Goebbels on 15 March 1933. It is reprinted in Noakes and Pridham, *Nazism*, pp. 380–1.
29. I am thinking here of the final words to Benjamin's famous essay 'Das Kunstwerk im Zeitalter seiner technischen Reproduzierbarkeit' (1935), in *Illuminationem*, Frankfurt/M, 1961, pp. 148–84. For a more sustained analysis of

The work of the Junge Mannschaft can justifiably be seen as *sui generis*; its producers, its ideological content and its *modus operandi* fully conform to the interventionist goals spelt out by the propaganda minister, Goebbels, in his directives to writers and artists in the early years of the regime.[30] Though it had a high profile within the academy of Nazi literature, this literature nevertheless represents quantitatively but a small portion of the literature actually written and published in the Third Reich. Indeed, evidence suggests that it reached its heyday as early as 1935, after which it declined in popularity until it was revived during the war years.[31] The reasons for this lie, paradoxically, in its very success. The work of the Junge Mannschaft was functional; it was aimed at specific groups of the population, such as youth and the party faithful, into which it sought to instil the militant values of the 'national revolution' on specific occasions during the year (such as national holidays or party rallies). Its task therefore was a limited one, and this it seems to have carried out with conspicuous success. It was part and parcel of the national revolution; once this was officially recognized as having been achieved (in the months following the Röhm *Putsch* in July 1934), the *raison d'être* for such a militant type of literature ceased to exist.[32]

What the Nazi cultural apparatus required after that date was a literature that could promote the image of the regime as a stable and respectable government of the conservative centre, bent on restoring law and order and political continuity to the public and private institutions of an impoverished and strife-torn Germany. What the Nazis proffered in their policies and election programmes was a reactivation of the traditional German values threatened and partially obliterated by the march of liberal democracy and the 'foreign' spirit of republican politics. It was for this reason that the greatest official encouragement was given not to the writers of the Junge Mannschaft (although their 'idealism' and selfless commitment to the cause continued to demand respect) but to the elder statesmen of the conservative Right, the support of whose middle-

---

attempts to aestheticize politics in the Third Reich see Klaus Vondung, *Magie und Manipulation: Ideologischer Kult und politische Religion des Nationalsozialismus*, Göttingen, 1971.

30. The goals were spelt out by Goebbels, but formulated and reformulated by critics such as Helmut Langenbucher; see his *Dichtung der jungen Mannschaft: Betrachtungen zur deutschen Dichtung der Gegenwart*, Hamburg, 1935.
31. See Egon Menz, 'Sprechchor und Aufmarsch: Zur Entstehung des Thingspiels', in Denkler and Prümm, *Literatur im Dritten Reich*, pp. 330–46.
32. Ibid., p. 341.

class readership was regarded as essential for the political continuity of the new national government.[33]

The majority of these writers, who had made their reputations long before 1933, were from a generation formed in the apolitical traditions of German culture, and hence did not always openly evince any commitment to the policies or ideology of the Nazi Party, preferring instead to celebrate what they saw as the eternal verities of German *Volk* and nationhood. Because such a celebration often contained an implicit critique of the modernist ethos supposedly inscribed into the Weimar Republic, they were often brought under the rubric of the 'conservative revolution'. This term was coined in the later years of the Weimar Republic to describe those writers, philosophers and politicians who hoped to achieve the overthrow of the democratic system of government and to replace it, not with a socialist state, but with one founded on the pre-republican values of patriotism, conservatism and even, for some, monarchism.[34] Amongst the literary representatives of this reactionary grouping we should include Hans Friedrich Blunck, Emil Strauss, Hans Grimm, E. G. Kolbenheyer, Ina Seidel and Hermann Stehr. Prior to 1933 this was a diverse group of writers, the producers of a subcurrent of literature running under the mainstream modernist writing of authors such as Thomas Mann, Alfred Döblin, Robert Musil, Hermann Hesse and others. They were the authors of *Heimatromane* and *Dorfromane* (homeland and village novels), historical sagas, nature and religious poetry, war novels and other work that, although marginalized by the progressive publishing houses and journals, nevertheless found a wide reading public in more traditional middle-class circles. It was this social group who felt most threatened by the rapid progress of modernization, which not only put at risk the financial welfare of large sectors of the white collar and small farming sectors, but also undermined their sense of status and even personal worth in the Weimar Republic. The growing support of this social group for the

33. This was not always admitted by a regime that claimed to be in the throes of constructing a classless *Volksgemeinschaft* (community of the people). A fuller analysis of Hitler's social policies and how they squared with the professional and economic realities of the Third Reich can be found in David Schoenbaum, *Hitler's Social Revolution: Class and Status in Nazi Germany*, London, 1966.
34. Standard studies of the policies and philosophy of the conservative revolution include Klemens von Klemperer, *Germany's New Conservatism: Its History and Dilemma in the 20th Century*, Princeton, 1968; and Kurt Sontheimer, *Antidemokratisches Denken in Deutschland: Die politischen Ideen des deutschen Nationalismus zwischen 1918–1933*, Göttingen, 1962.

policies of the Nazis has been well charted.[35] What the writers of the conservative revolution offered to this group – in works such as Hermann Stehr's *Das Geschlecht der Maechler: Romantrilogie einer deutschen Familie* (The Maechler Clan: Trilogy of a German Family, 3 vols, 1929–44), Karl Heinz Waggerl's *Brot* (Bread, 1930), Friedrich Griese's *Der ewige Acker* (The Eternal Soil, 1930) and Emil Strauss's *Das Riesenspielzeug* (The Giant Toy, 1934) – was a fictional world in which the threat of modernization was met and largely overcome by the reinstatement of the *Gemeinschaft* (community) values of an idealized rural existence. A similar compensation was offered in the war fiction of Werner Beumelburg, E. E. Dwinger and Josef Magnus Wehner. But in the case of the latter group of writers, it was not the 'softer' values of rural integration and domestic harmony that were on offer, but the 'harder' values of martial prowess, front-line comradeship, and a general idealization of the ethos of military *Einsatz* (service).[36]

These authors continued publishing in the Third Reich, and it is their writings, rather than those of the Junge Mannschaft, that came to form the canon of Nazi literature. The important point to stress is that even where new titles appeared, the content and style of this literature after 1933 differed in only minor ways from the literature published by the same group prior to 1933. Indeed, for many of these writers of the conservative revolution, new publications were hardly necessary; as was the case with Hans Grimm, the author of the best-selling and politically influential *Volk ohne Raum* (People without Space, 1926), the majority of these conservative writers were able to sustain both reputation and income through new editions of earlier published works.[37] For such writers, 1933 represented not so much a radical break as a renewed opportunity to occupy more central positions within the literary life of the nation – to become, in short, lionized and canonized figures within the literary establishment. Few, in fact, joined the Nazi Party; indeed like Gottfried Benn, who found himself, as a member of the Prussian Academy of the Arts, an unlikely associate of this group, few seem to have even bothered to familiarize themselves

35. For a recent view see Lothar Kettenacker, 'Hitler's Impact on the Lower Middle Class', in Peter Stachura (ed.), *Nazi Propaganda: The Power and the Limitations*, London, 1983, pp. 10–28.
36. For an extended treatment of the political role of war fiction in the Weimar Republic see Martin Travers, *German Novels on the First World War and their Ideological Implications, 1918–1933*, Stuttgart, 1982.
37. This is according to the account given by Benn in his autobiography, *Doppelleben: Zwei Selbstdarstellungen*, Wiesbaden, 1950.

with the contents of the Nazi political platform.[38] They were fellow-travellers of the radical Right, and the perpetrators of a massive *trahison des clercs*; but they can only be typified as 'Nazi' from the point of view of their willing occupancy of high office, which helped lend the Nazi state a certain legitimacy, and not from the point of view of their literary production.

The second set of overlaps and continuities between Nazi and non-Nazi areas of literary production concerns the continuing publishing record of canonized Nazi authors in the post-war period. This is a vexed and controversial subject; the essential issues became obscured by the political rhetoric brought forth in the subsequent Cold War between East and West. Once again, it is important not to overstate the matter and claim that nothing changed for these authors of the radical Right after 1945; on the contrary, all went from positions of power and prestige to positions of marginalization. But remain they did. Many, such as E. E. Dwinger, Werner Beumelburg and Paul Alverdes, continued to write and publish new fiction; others, such as Hans Grimm, were content simply to oversee the republication of earlier work, which in many cases reappeared in the form of a collected edition.[39] To be sure, these writers were more circumspect in voicing their previous political views; positions were modified, anti-liberal sentiments mollified, and explicit conservative rhetoric largely abandoned. Some, such as Ernst Jünger, even undertook a complete revision of all earlier fiction, expurgating the more trenchant expositions of previously nationalist credos.[40]

On the other hand, little was taken back; one looks in vain for any expression of remorse or admission of complicity. And even when this takes place, as in the case of Hans Friedrich Blunck or the nationalist critic Paul Fechter, the *mea culpa* is often hedged by references to the pitfalls of political inexperience and a regrettable surrender to the tide of the times. The same values of the small-town *Untertan* (underling) are defended and allowed to inform a continuing rejection of the politics of a pluralist society. It was only

38. See E. E. Dwinger, *General Wlassow: Eine Tragödie unserer Zeit*, Frankfurt/M, 1951; Werner Beumelburg, *Hundert Jahre sind wie ein Tag: Roman einer Familie*, Oldenburg, 1950; Paul Alverdes, *Grimbarts Haus*, Konstanz, 1949.

39. This is the case with the most recent Klett edition of his *Werke*. For a highly enlightening account of this process of self-expurgation see Ulrich Böhme, *Fassungen bei Ernst Jünger*, Meisenheim am Glan, 1972.

40. See Hans Friedrich Blunck, *Unwegsame Zeiten: Lebensbericht*, 2 vols, Mannheim, 1952; and Paul Fechter, *An der Wende der Zeit: Menschen und Begegnungen*, Gütersloh, 1949.

the noted *apparatchiks* of the Nazi state like Hanns Johst who remained subject to *Schreibverbot* (literary prohibition) in the post-war period.[41]

This brings us to the third point that needs to be made about the nature of literary production in the Third Reich. It is often assumed by literary historians and scholars working within the assumptions of the totalitarian thesis that the radically changed political conditions brought about by the *Machtergreifung* (seizure of power) were necessarily reproduced in the cultural and literary sphere: 'new state, new literature' seems to be the catchphrase here. It is an interpretation which is not only erroneous but, unhappily, close to the National Socialists' own view of things.[42] As I have tried to show above, even if we focus on those literary groupings that were granted canonical status in the Third Reich, the case for claiming them as purely 'Nazi' is not a strong one. But if we turn our attention to the general picture of literary production at this time, and examine the political proclivities of the great bulk of literature in circulation between 1933 and 1945, we shall have to conclude that the advent of the Nazi regime changed far less than is generally assumed in the reading habits of the nation.

This is not to deny that the Nazi intervention into the institutional terrain of cultural and literary production was not a radical one; it is undeniable that the construction of regulative bodies such as the Reichskulturkammer (Reich Chamber of Culture) and the Amt Rosenberg (Rosenberg Office), which sought to control both production and dissemination in the Third Reich, had a decisive impact on the literary life of the nation. The result of these checks and controls was the elimination of whole schools, styles and even genres of writing. Literature with a clear liberal or left-wing bias, or with stylistic affinities with any of the various modernisms, could no longer be published or openly discussed. For this reason it is understandable that most literary historians – who tend to equate the movement of literature in the twentieth century with the progress of experimental, avant-garde or, to adopt a phrase from the world of film criticism, 'art-house' literature – should seek to stress the totalizing effect of the Nazi intervention into the cultural

41. Perhaps the classic study of the continuing presence of National Socialist sympathies in the post-war period is Heinz Bräudigam, *Der Schoß ist fruchtbar noch . . . : Neonazistische, militaristische, nationalistische Literatur und Publizistik in der Bundesrepublik*, Frankfurt/M, 1965.

42. This proximity of views is brought about, it must be quickly added, not by any political sympathy but as the consequence of the application of a certain methodology.

sphere. Here the line is that all great writers left in a mass exodus in 1933, whilst those that decided to stay either went into inner emigration or were condemned to silence. It is a picture familiar to anyone conversant with the secondary material on the subject.[43]

Such a view neglects, however, an important 'middle' stratum of literature lying between 'Nazi' literature proper (however that is interpreted) and the writings of the inner emigrants. This stratum consists of the great mass of 'everyday' literature: novels, plays, poetry and short stories which exhibit no evident concern for political policies but understand themselves as having a diverting, entertaining or amusing function – in short, the 'bread-and-butter' offerings of all but the most minority-based avant-garde publishing houses prior to, during and since the Third Reich. The range of this material was enormous: domestic fiction, adventure stories, biographies, humour, travelogues, nature poetry and even detective fiction.[44]

Certain authors within this popular mode were, indeed, ideologues of the new state. For example, the journalist and cultural commentator Friedrich Sieburg published a number of travelogues throughout the 1930s in which criteria drawn from the foreign policies of the National Socialists are clearly implemented.[45] Countries such as Portugal and Japan, with their new and 'vital' systems of government, are valorized over countries like England, whose days as a world power are held to be numbered. But Sieburg is a rare case within this literature. On the whole, the writings of Hans Fallada, Erich Kästner, Heinrich Spoerl and Erwin Petzold (to name the better-known writers) carefully avoid the explicitly political; the goals, different in each case, are diversion, compensation and consolation. It is a body of work that has generally been overlooked in previous studies of writing in the Third Reich,

43. This is how Gerhard Schoenberner describes the effect of the Nazi *Machtergreifung* of 1933: 'The emigrants included thousands of scientists, including many Nobel prize winners, actors and producers, a large part of the elite of the German theatre, writers and journalists, including almost all authors of world fame. The representatives of literary and intellectual Germany turned their backs on the new regime. Many fled because they saw their life, freedom or existence threatened, but not a few left the country because they were not prepared to sell their conscience and convictions.' *Artists against Hitler: Persecution, Exile, Resistance*, Bonn, 1984, p. 6.
44. Recent work on the German cinema has come to recognize the existence of this broad area of 'popular' or 'everyday' culture. See Arthur Rabenalt, *Film im Zwielicht: über den unpolitischen Film des Dritten Reiches und die Begrenzung des totalitären Anspruchs*, Hildesheim, 1978.
45. See, for example, his *Neues Portugal: Bildnis eines alten Landes*, Frankfurt/M, 1937.

because it is a literature that does not unambigously fall into either the pro-Nazi or the anti-Nazi camp, and hence cannot be recognized by those critics working within the totalitarian thesis.[46]

A comprehensive account of the work produced by the writers of this 'middle ground' of literature has not been attempted to date, and cannot be attempted here. But such an account is essential if we are to understand the attractions of Fascism, and, more specifically, if we are to explain why the National Socialists met with such little resistance to their seizure of power in 1933. We have been informed in great detail about the control exercised by the Nazis over writers in the Third Reich, about the successes of the propaganda machine, about the processes of *Gleichschaltung*, and about the systematic persecution of individuals; in short, about the imposition of Fascism from above. This has tended to produce a picture of a nation kept in a state of political and psychological bondage, the despairing victims of a highly instrumentalized irrationality.[47] We have heard less about the emergence of Fascism from below, of Nazism as something if not actively desired then at least deeply tolerated because, far from representing the breakthrough of demonic forces, it actually brings into play and consolidates values and desiderata that are part of shared subjectivities which exist in non-Fascist societies as well. In short, the existence of this 'middle ground' of literature in the Third Reich testifies to the perpetual possibility of Fascism.

It is for this reason that we need to look again at the apparently 'apolitical' nature of much of this 'middle-ground' or 'popular' literature. We might begin by asking questions about the implications of the compensatory function of such literature, particularly in a state bereft of many of what we would now call civil rights. In works such as Erich Kästner's *Drei Männer im Schnee* (Three Men in the Snow, 1934) and Edlef Köppen's *Vier Mauern und ein Dach* (Four Walls and a Roof, 1934), the reader is offered a world where political impotence in the real world is sublimated into a *Märchen* (fairy tale) social world in which the private tasks of self-cultivation and material advancement are extolled. In such works, the pervasive feeling is of *res non mihi agitur*, of the main course of public

46. This corpus of literature is simply not on the agenda for Wulf, Schonauer and Loewy, but it is disappointing to discover that it does not warrant even a minor coverage in Denkler and Prümm, *Literatur im Dritten Reich*, and Bohnen and Bauer, *Nationalsozialismus*.

47. This is the thesis represented by Vondung, amongst others, in his *Magie und Manipulation*.

affairs developing beyond not only personal control but also personal relevance.

More seriously, much of this 'middle-ground' literature is predicated upon a series of assumptions about the 'normal' basis of social behaviour which, if not co-terminous with the ideology of Nazism, are at least conducive to it. This area is both politically controversial and theoretically obscure, but it is worth arguing that in their descriptions of domestic hierarchies and the role of women, in their valorization of financial and property values and in their emphasis upon charismatic individualism, such works as Hans Fallada's *Wir hatten mal ein Kind* (And We Had a Child, 1934), Ernst Penzoldt's *Kleiner Erdenwurm* (Little Earthworm, 1934) and Conrad Muschler's *Sucher und Versucher* (Seeker and Tempter, 1935) interpellate the reader, in their different ways, as an at least willing accomplice in the politics of Fascism proper.[48]

Earlier in this chapter I asked the question: 'What would be a view of literature in the Third Reich which is constructed beyond the methodology of the totalitarian thesis?' I have tried to answer this question in a schematic way, which has often run the risk of an overly polemical painting in black and white. I should perhaps stress in conclusion that it has been my intention not totally to undermine or replace the assumptions of the totalitarian thesis, but rather to revise and supplement them. I have accordingly placed the emphasis upon the weaknesses of the totalitarian thesis, what it neglects or represses, rather than upon its strengths, which are well known and have been worked up into a historiographical orthodoxy in the secondary literature on the topic. It is perhaps best to think of the two competing models as Weberian ideal types which, when applied to a series of empirical phenomena, allow different objects to emerge and different sets of questions to be answered.[49]

Unless, however, the findings of the set of questions aired in this chapter are admitted into standard accounts of the Third Reich, the attractions of Fascist politics must remain inherently irrational and impervious to systematic reconstruction, their sources the barely fathomable workings of parapsychology. Were we to accept this as

48. It is no easy matter to reconstruct these values from within the text, but the concepts of the *Erwartungshorizont* and the implied reader, developed in the reception theories of Jauss and Iser, provide at least a starting point. For a systematic analysis of their approaches see Rainer Warning (ed.), *Rezeptionsästhetik: Theorie und Praxis*, Munich, 1979.

49. For a modest amount of theory see Max Weber, 'The Ideal Type', in Kenneth Thompson and Jeremy Tunstall (eds), *Sociological Perspectives*, Harmondsworth, 1971, pp. 63–7.

being the case we would, unhappily, be close to compensating Fascism for its political and military defeats by granting it, retrospectively, a methodological victory within the academy of historiographical explanation.

–16–

The Ritual and Stage Management of National Socialism

Techniques of Domination and the Public Sphere

WOLFGANG BENZ

The rule of National Socialism was founded on the ecstasy of the ruled. The conquest, exercise and consolidation of power involved, to an extent unrealized by any other regime, the devising of institutions and mechanisms whose purpose was to transport the populace into a form of permanent intoxication and to generate and maintain a climate of mass hysteria – a climate in which a constant, unreflected acclamation of the regime thrived.

The ideology of National Socialism was meagre in the extreme, in essence confining itself to several stereotypes of the enemy, the most well known being the Jew and the Bolshevik; to the propagation of Social Darwinism and abstruse racial and hereditary theories; and to the postulates of an aggressive all-German nationalism, namely the acquisition of colonial territories in Eastern Europe and aspirations to the status of a world power. Added to this, as a substitute for the building blocks of a unified political, economic and social programme, was the glorification of rural life, the cult of militarism, the propagation of the master race doctrine, and the mystification of the German past, Fatherland, native soil, folklore, custom and tradition – however these might be understood. These ideological set pieces, which could be arranged arbitrarily, were constantly deployed in daily political life in the form of slogans: *Blut und Boden* (blood and soil), *Volk ohne Raum* (a people without space), *Fronterlebnis* (front experience), *Blutzeuge* (martyr), *alter Kämpfer* (old warrior), *Volksgemeinschaft* (community of the people).

The most important element of National Socialist ideology was the identification of Hitler, the Nazi movement and the German

This chapter has been translated by Joe O'Donnell.

people as a type of mystical unity which was continually invoked through ritualistic and consecratory acts, demonstrations and acclamations. The most important aim of the techniques of National Socialist rule was the establishing and stabilizing of the Führer cult. As long as the masses believed in their idol, the regime was stable; failures, excesses and crises did not constitute a threat to the continuation of rule and the consent of the ruled. Of course, the systematic use of terror and violence against critics of the regime, political opponents and minorities declared hostile also played a considerable role in Hitler's state. Nevertheless, what needs to be emphasized are the methods through which the positive commitment of the majority of the population to the National Socialist state was achieved.

The five major elements of National Socialist rule, through which the fascination of the German people for the regime was achieved, were:

(1) Propaganda.
(2) The orchestration of public life.
(3) The self-representation of the regime in the form of its own aesthetic.
(4) Ritualistic acts as a substitute for religion.
(5) Stylization of the people as a cultic fraternity.

Propaganda

The implementation of the National Socialist propaganda programme was the responsibility of a state bureaucracy created specifically for this task. The Reichsministerium für Volksaufklärung und Propaganda (Reich Ministry for the People's Enlightenment and Propaganda) was a unique innovation, and the regime regarded it with pride as the only ministry of its kind in the world. With a master of demagogy at its head, the task of the propaganda programme was the cultivation of uniform opinion and consent and the suppression of unwanted information. In this sense, Hitler's state did not differ from other dictatorships; its distinctive aspect lay perhaps in the rigour and virtuosity with which Goebbels, in the role of Minister for Propaganda, directed the apparatus, steering press, radio, film, theatre, music and all other spheres of culture on to a uniform course.

Within the ideological framework of the Nazis, propaganda was defined as an 'element of the constitution', and its function was described as that of a binding link between 'the political will, as embodied in the party, and the people'. The Nazi state, seen as a whole system, was described as a new and higher form of democracy, a concept which included the postulate of a unity between Führer and people with the party as a selective elite of the people mediating this unity. 'Without the personal relationship between Führer and people which is achieved through propaganda, the authoritarian democratic principle of the new Germany is unthinkable. Propaganda is therefore an integral element of the unwritten constitution of the Third Reich', declared an article written for the occasion of Goebbels's thirty-ninth birthday, which represents one of the few attempts to grasp theoretically the specificity of National Socialist propaganda.[1]

While certainly no theoretician, Goebbels himself formulated this concept of propaganda more clearly during his speech 'Essence, Methods and Aims of Propaganda', given at the Reichsparteitag (National Party Day) in September 1935 in Nuremberg before the assembled propaganda directors of the party. Propaganda, he declared, was above all else an instrument for the preservation of power; the propagandist needed to be an 'artist of the popular psychology' and himself a 'part of the people's soul' in order that he be able to make clear to the people the necessity of unpleasant measures. During the same speech, Goebbels also attempted to clarify the distinction between propaganda and *Volksaufklärung* (enlightenment of the people):

> Of a different character to propaganda is *Volksaufklärung*, which can also claim its rightful place in the political programme of the state. One cannot *always* beat the drum, because if one does so, the public gradually becomes accustomed to the sound and no longer hears it. The drum must be kept in reserve . . . If we always want to shout and make a noise, then the public will gradually become used to this din.[2]

Goebbels employed in this context the term *Volksbehandlung* (handling of the people), a term which expressed exactly the nature of the process involved. To this concept also belonged the policy of granting the people a rest period between large organized political events. Accordingly, with a few important exceptions, there were

1. Wilhelm Haegert, 'Propaganda als Verfassungselement. Zum 29. Oktober', in *Der Angriff*, Sonderbeilage zur Zehnjahresfeier des Gaues Berlin, 30 October 1936.
2. 'Rede am 16.9.1935 bei der Sondertagung der Gau- und Kreispropagandaleiter anläßlich des 7. Reichsparteitags', in *Goebbels-Reden*, ed. H. Heiber, Düsseldorf, 1971, vol. 1 (1932–9), p. 238.

no political radio broadcasts – one of the most important means of propaganda – for several weeks following the party meeting; the broadcasting time was used instead for musical performances.

Entertainment in general played an extremely important role in the National Socialist propaganda apparatus and flourished accordingly. Operetta and popular song – particularly since they were hardly politicized – were the most favoured genres. These, along with the series of innocuous feature films produced, can be understood as part of the regime's social policy. The aim was to maintain the mood of the *Volksgemeinschaft* with the melodies of Nico Dostal, Paul Linke and Franz Lehar; with popular songs trilled and bellowed by Zarah Leander, Evelyn Künneke, Marika Rökk and Hans Albers; and with the people's favourites, Heinz Ruhmann, Johannes Heesters, Luise Ullrich, Victor de Kowa, Willy Birgil, Brigitte Horney and many others. The state radio and state-controlled film industry were highly popular means of mass entertainment. The 'request concerts' broadcast by the Großdeutscher Rundfunk (Greater Germany Radio) were as enthusiastically received at the front following the outbreak of the war as they were at home. With the production of comic and sentimental films, the vision of an unproblematic world was preserved on the cinema screen. Films such as *Quax der Bruchpilot* (1941), *Wiener Blut* (1942), *So ein Früchten* (1942), *Münchhausen* (1943) and *Feuerzangenbowle* (1944) were in every case more popular than technically well-made propaganda pieces of the type *SA-Mann Brand* (1935), Leni Riefenstahl's film of the national party meeting, *Triumph des Willens* (1935), and the war films *Pour le Mérite* (1938), *Legion Condor* (1939), *Über Alles in der Welt*, *Stukas*, and *Kadetten* (all 1941). Some success was eventually achieved with agitational and *Durchhaltefilme* (endurance films) such as Veit Harlans *Jud Süss* (1940), the anti-British film *Ohm Krüger* with Emil Jannings (1941), *Der Große König* (Harlan, 1942), the euthanasia film *Ich klage an* (Liebmeiner, 1941) and *Kohlberg* (1945). More popular was the newsreel *Deutsche Wochenschau*, a report on political and later especially war events, which was shown before the feature programme in cinemas and which entertained rather than informed an audience of 20 million every week.

The Orchestration of Public Life

Following the establishment of National Socialist rule in 1933, the implementation and elaboration of the methods developed during the struggle for power resulted in the thoroughgoing organization of public life. This orchestration of the public sphere was the most important and effective political instrument employed by the Nazi leadership and in no other area was so much effort expended. The catalogue of forms employed ranged from the social evening in the home to the local meeting of party members, the village communal evening and the collective reception of Hitler's speeches over the radio; and from local rallies and celebrations on state holidays to parades, marches and the great key commemorative events of the party, culminating in the annual Reichsparteitag in Nuremberg.

The aim of every National Socialist meeting, irrespective of the scale of the event, was the mesmerizing of the individual participant. This was achieved through the organization of events around a uniform model, one designed to avoid argumentation and to captivate the senses. Events were so organized that participation constituted an experience in itself. The incorporation and dissolution of the individual in the *Volksgemeinschaft* was calculated and the means employed were chosen purely to this end: speeches, official ceremonies, the mass declaration of allegiance, rituals of worship, parades and roll-calls, and so on.

The mass spectacle represented, so to speak, the climax of the National Socialist dramaturgy. The Day of Potsdam on 21 March 1933 was designed to legitimate the new masters who had appropriated the Prussian tradition and claimed the identity of their position and that of the old Reichspräsident Hindenburg. The official opening of the newly elected Parliament, staged as the aligning of the German bourgeois establishment and the National Socialist parvenus, took place in the Potsdam garrison church. The main programme of events was located in Berlin and included various field services in the Lustgarten and before the Stadtschloss (city palace), a march-past by the police force, SS, SA and Stahlhelm reviewed by the police commander, parades, gun salutes and an evening torchlight procession which lasted several hours.[3] On 10 April 1933 Hitler held what the *Völkischer Beobachter* called the longest roll-call the world had ever seen; 600,000 SA and SS men, experienced in the hall and street fighting of NSDAP (Nazi Party) rabble-rousing bands, were assembled from throughout the nation in order to hear a speech by their supreme commander in the Berliner Sportpalast. This huge event was directed by Goebbels,

3. See 'Der Tag von Potsdam. Zum 21 März 1933', commemorative edition of *Die Woche*, Archive of the Institut für Zeitgeschichte. Schutzstaffel (SS), Nazi elite corps; Sturm-Abteilung (SA), Nazi storm-troops; Stahlhelm (Steel Helmet), veterans' organization.

who employed the radio as a megaphone for directing the masses. Realizing that the quasi-transcendental character of the radio medium made it an excellent means for representing the omnipresence of the Führer, the Nazi propaganda machine took over German radio and employed it until the fall of the regime. It was clearly not by chance that Goebbels attributed great potential to experiments at the time with television.[4]

In 1936 Hitler's state presented its best face to the public, the most important arena being Berlin. The opportunity for this presentation of National Socialist splendour, German efficiency and perfect organization was provided by the XIth Olympic Summer Games. Berlin was covered in a sea of banners and the anti-Semitic slogans were temporarily removed. The desired effect soon became apparent, and it was not only the foreigners who were astonished; following the successful hosting of the Olympiad, the prestige of the Nazi regime also increased considerably within Germany itself.

One of the high points of the regime's self-presentation was the Sommerfest der Reichsregierung (Summer Festival of the Reich Government), held on the Pfaueninsel in the river Havel, to which Goebbels invited the guests of honour of the Olympiad. The correspondent for the *Völkischer Beobachter* wrote with rapture of the display of splendour:

> The spell which radiated from the unusual setting was skilfully enhanced with artistic embellishments. Little wonder that the participants, particularly those from other lands who, during their visit to Berlin, had experienced many an example of the most generous German hospitality, were very quickly drawn into the mood of festive relaxation, one which brings even the most unlikely people together.[5]

The offerings were many-sided. A ship's bridge was erected upon which the guests were received by sappers with presented oars. Pageboys clad in white then conducted the visitors to the festival grounds on the island. Amidst Chinese lanterns and fireworks, Goebbels presented himself as the kindly host of this 'Italian night'. Artistic entertainment was offered by the opera ballet and the cream of society dined and danced until morning.

The year 1937 saw what was probably the most powerful political-military review that the Third Reich produced. The event was organized in honour of Mussolini and was presented in Sep-

4. 'Adolf Hitler spricht zu 600 000 Mann S.A. und S.S.', *Völkischer Beobachter*, 10 April 1933.
5. *Völkischer Beobachter*, 17 August 1936.

tember in Berlin. Almost 1.5 million marks – a staggering sum for the time – was squandered on decorations, forests of banners, light domes and other baubles. The highpoint was a mass rally at which Goebbels, continually interrupted by cries of 'Heil', greeted the Duce and Hitler. 'I report: on the Maifeld in Berlin, in the Olympic Stadium and in the forecourts of the National Sports Ground, one million people; in addition, on the drives from Wilhelmstraße to the National Sports Ground, two million people; in total, three million people assembled for this historic mass rally of the National Socialist movement!'[6]

On such occasions the people were used as a backdrop, as a false façade for the mock metropolis that Berlin in some respects was at this time. In reality there were obstacles to the remodelling of the Prussian metropolis into the megalopolis of Hitler's grandiose visions of power – obstacles which for the time being were overcome by the illusory world of the mass spectacle. It was not by chance, then, that the sound of marching feet and the mass spectacle expressed most clearly the peculiarity and self-perception of National Socialism, and its leader and his generals competed in martial splendour. Goebbels, ill-favoured by nature, faced considerable difficulty in this area, certainly more so than the popular and seemingly jovial Hermann Göring, who occupied the second position in the state hierarchy. However, sometimes the state elite could also demonstrate warmth and emotion, at least during Christmas, which the 'new pagans' of National Socialism preferred to call Julfest (Yuletide). The rulers of the Nazi state gathered needy children around themselves, giving out Christmas gifts, exploiting the propaganda potential of the event. At Christmas 1935, Göring invited 500 children. Music was provided by the music corps of Göring's regiment, a children's choir sang and the children's ballet of the Prussian state opera danced. A record of the event was provided by the *Völkischer Beobachter*:

> Frau Göring, leading two children by the hand, goes from table to table guiding the parents and children to their places where gifts lie piled up. General Göring, followed by Santa Claus and two elves, moves through the rows of tables, here pulling out a toy, showing a tot the mechanism of an aeroplane, a model tank, there pressing silently the hand of a mother who approaches him moved and speechless, here taking a little girl on his arm, giving her a doll taken from the package-bedecked coat

6. 'Begrüßung auf der Großkundgebung anläßlich des Besuches Mussolinis in Berlin, 28.9.1937', in *Goebbels-Reden*, vol. 1, p. 287.

> of Santa Claus, there beginning to speak with a father and here again asking a mother about her home, her children.[7]

The orchestration of public life in the Nazi state did not exhaust itself in the organization of unique events. A canon of forms was consistently utilized throughout the year, transforming the everyday into a series of National Socialist events which functioned to construct and maintain the national community. The National Socialist calendar began on 30 January with a speech by Goebbels to the nation's school children and a speech by Hitler before the Reichstag. In the evening a torchlight procession commemorated the *Machtergreifung* (seizure of power). The Heldengedenktag (Day of Commemoration of Heroes) in March, celebrated with army parades in Berlin, replaced the Volkstrauertag (People's Day of Mourning) established during the Weimar Republic. On the last Sunday in March, those who had reached the age of fourteen were formally inducted into the Hitler Youth, and on the evening prior to Hitler's birthday the roll for ten-year-olds was called for the Jungvolk. The Führer's birthday on 20 April was celebrated with the greatest pomp, including military parades in all garrison cities and a party celebration usually held in the Parteiforum on the Königsplatz in Munich. May Day (1 May) was celebrated as the Tag der nationalen Arbeit (Day of National Labour) with traditional and folk dance groups, and was created to take the place of the original Day of International Worker Solidarity. This was followed on the second Sunday in May by Mother's Day – also not a Nazi discovery – which carried an official stamp from 1939 onwards following the first conferral of the Mutterkreuz (Mothers' Cross) on three million women. (The order was established in 1938 and incorporated three categories: gold after eight children, silver after six or seven, and bronze after four or five.)

The summer solstice (21–2 June), celebrated since 1933 in numerous places throughout the nation, was officially observed in the form of a mass event in the Berlin Olympic Stadium from 1937 until 1939. The official calendar reached its zenith each year in September with the spectacle of the Reichsparteitag in Nuremberg. This was followed in October by the Harvest Thanksgiving which drew hundreds of thousands to the Bückeberg near Hameln. In the evening of 8 November the *alte Kämpfer* (Nazi veterans) met in the Bürgerbräukeller in Munich to commemorate the Hitler putsch of 1923. On 9 November the *Blutzeugen der Bewegung* (martyrs of the

7. *Völkischer Beobachter*, 25–6 December 1935.

movement) were honoured in a macabre ceremony, and on the same day the older members of the Hitler Youth were inducted into the NSDAP. Finally, in the evening, a new generation of SS members participated in nocturnal pledges of loyalty.

The two final events on the Nazi calendar, namely the winter solstice celebrations introduced in 1935 and the Germanification of Christmas as Julfest, found less resonance among the public. However, the catalogue of festivals and rituals extended far beyond these major events, with provincial party days, song and gymnastic festivals, the monthly frugal Sunday in support of the Eastern Front soldiers (Eintopfsonntag des WHW) and almost every other possible occasion for celebration, at which the uniformed marched, the party prominence spoke and celebrations were prescribed. On 1 June the SS assembled in Quedlinburg in order to pay homage to Heinrich Himmler's idol, Heinrich I, the 'creator of the First Reich'. In addition there was a whole series of celebrations within the framework of the Betriebsgemeinschaft (Community of Management and Workers) and events involving the subdivisions and associations of the party, for which the coordinators of the national Nazi propaganda programme provided a detailed set of 'Recommendations for National Socialist Celebrations'.

The Self-Representation of the Regime

The attempts of the Nazi regime to develop a specifically National Socialist aesthetic were based on the maintenance of political power; the efficacy of these efforts was consequently measured in terms of their success in creating a community and in intimidating, suppressing and dominating it. Integration and exclusion were represented simultaneously through parades and collective singing in formation (*die Reihen fest geschlossen*). One of the few genuine National Socialist art forms, the *Thingspiel*, while drawing on a range of older dramatic forms ranging from Greek tragedy to the mystery and passion plays of the Middle Ages, in essence represented a wider development of the parade and the political rally. As exemplified on 1 October 1933, when 60,000 spectators assembled to watch 17,000 uniformed players in the Berlin Stadium, the guiding principle of the *Thingspiel* was the interaction of audience and actors, both mobilized on a massive scale.[8]

8. See Egon Menz, 'Sprechchor und Aufmarsch. Zur Entstehung des Thingspiels', in H. Denkler and K. Prümm (eds), *Die deutsche Literatur im Dritten Reich.*

However, *Thingspiele* and their arenas, the *Thingstätten*, remained marginal and episodic phenomena. The most important expression of the National Socialist creative urge was architecture. Until well into the war the Third Reich had the character of a giant building site: housing estates in the *Heimatschutzstil* (conservation style), youth hostels and communal buildings, barracks and *Ordensburgen* (pseudo-medieval castles), stadiums, squares and, above all, large-scale projects bespeaking omnipotence and the claim to power. This function was also served by the *Autobahn* for which, in terms of the degree of motorized traffic at the time, there was technically very little need. Accordingly the propaganda for these *Straßen des Führers* emphasized their recreational value, their stylization as art works and their symbolic value as connecting lines to the German population outside the national borders. (The military significance of the 3,000 kilometre *Autobahn* network completed in December 1938 was and is for the most part over-emphasized; the transportation of troops and materials remained predominantly the task of the railways.)

The National Socialist claim to power manifested itself in an architecture of subjection. Consciously designed for effect, the representational architecture of party and state proliferated in the form of a brutalized neo-classicism of grossly heightened dimensions which, with its monotonous, monumental character, its endless rows of simplistic elements and forms, produced a series of colossal, intimidating structures. The leading figures in establishing this style were Paul Ludwig Troost, who designed the Haus der Deutschen Kunst (Hall of German Art) in Munich (1933), and his disciple Albert Speer, who conceived of the Reichsparteitaggelände in Nuremberg – the central location for the national roll-call – in terms of an architecture of cultic ritual and domination, as the stone backdrop of the uniformed multitude. 'In order to achieve their full effect', as one description put it at the time, the structures in Nuremberg required 'the tens of thousands of German men, marching in strict columns and moved by one will'. Although the whole complex was not completed, the National Party Day celebrations took place there until 1938 (they ceased following the outbreak of the war). The event took the form of a march-past lasting several hours by the different party organizations and associations, including the army after 1934; nocturnal rallies were held under the Lichtdom (light dome), created by using anti-aircraft

---

Themen-Traditionen-Wirkungen, Stuttgart, 1976, pp. 330–46; Hildegard Brenner, *Die Kunstpolitik des Nationalsozialismus*, Reinbek, 1963, pp. 95ff.

searchlights, the illumination of which could be seen from as far as 200 kilometres away, thus providing a showpiece for National Socialist power. The supernumeraries assembled for Hitler's speech were numbered in the hundred thousands, and a fresh cast took the place of the old one several times during the events, which lasted four to eight days. All given this opportunity regarded their participation as a privilege.

Nazi architecture was an architecture of subjection in several senses. The despotism of the omnipotent leadership was not only expressed in the anachronism of the forms utilized, the materials and the huge dimensions. It could not have manifested itself without the appropriation of resources regardless of economic benefit or cost, nor without the methods of ancient barbarism: the regime's architecture was realized through the extensive enforcement of slave labour in the concentration camps. The monumental structures also served directly as instruments of political pressure, as in the case of the Neue Reichskanzlei (New Reich Chancellery), built in the record time of less than a year, in which Hitler committed suicide in the spring of 1945. At the end of January 1938 Hitler sent for his personal architect Speer, who reports in his memoirs: '"I have a most important task for you", he said solemnly, standing in the middle of the room. "In the coming time I must hold some most important discussions. For this purpose I require great halls and rooms with which I can impress lesser rulers."'[9]

The new buildings were ceremonially opened on 9 January 1939 and were declared to express in outstanding fashion the culture and creative will of National Socialism. In one of the rooms, on the night of 14 March 1939, the Czechoslovakian state president Hacha was coerced into delivering up the rest of his nation to Hitler's Germany. The architecture of the Reichskanzlei, with its 145 metre gallery through which Hacha had to walk in order to reach Hitler, formed part of this orchestrated event. The cabinet chamber, which never actually housed a sitting of the national government, measured 600 square metres, whereas the corresponding room in the old Reichskanzlei had been barely one-tenth this size. *Gebauter Nationalsozialismus* (constructed National Socialism) was the name given to the results of this new *Bauwille* (will to build); *Gemeinschaftsbauten* (community buildings), another official term current at the time for this architecture of the cult of power, they certainly were not.

The motivations of the National Socialist building style included aspirations to permanence and the aim to establish everlasting relics

9. Albert Speer, *Erinnerungen*, Frankfurt/Berlin, 1969, p. 116.

– again, elements reminiscent of ancient oriental despots. Such visions of Hitler's have been handed down by Speer:

> It is scarcely comprehensible what power is conferred on a small spirit over those around him when he can appear amidst such great proportions. Such chambers with a great historical past elevate even a small successor to the ranks of history. You see, that is why we must build this within my lifetime: so that I will have lived there and imbued this building with my spirit. It will suffice if I only live in it for a few years.[10]

The final climax in the dramatization of National Socialist power was planned to be the remodelling of Berlin into the world capital, into the megalopolis 'Germania'. Hitler outlined the programme in November 1937 in the following words:

> It is therefore my unalterable will and resolve to provide Berlin with those streets, buildings and public places which will render it well suited and worthy in all times to be the capital of the German Reich. The dimensions of these structures and works should not be measured according to the necessities of the year 1937, 1938, 1939 or 1940. Rather, they should be measured in accordance with the knowledge that it is our task to build for a thousand-year people with a thousand-year historical and cultural past an equally matched thousand-year metropolis for the boundless future which lies before this people.[11]

The dictator contributed his own ideas to this project, ideas which he had already outlined long before. He saw himself as a gifted architect, while Speer and his colleagues accepted him as a congenial dilettante. The subject of Hitler's blueprint was a domed hall of dimensions never before realized. Ten times as high as the Brandenburg Gate, it was matched by a triumphal arch of just as stunning dimensions. Planned on an axis, these edifices were envisaged as forming the nucleus of a future world capital with monumentally pompous administration and government buildings.

Ritualistic Acts as a Substitute for Religion

National Socialist rule was based on an irrational devotion; *Gefolg-*

10. Ibid., p. 172.
11. 'Rede bei der Grundsteinlegung der Wehrtechnischen Fakultät Berlin, 27.11.1937', in *Hitler. Reden und Proklamationen 1932–1945*, ed. M. Domarus, Würzburg, 1962, vol. 1, p. 765.

schaft (allegiance) and *Treue* (fealty) were among its most significant slogans. In fact, these terms referred to unconditional faith and blind obedience. Submission to the omnipotence of the National Socialist leadership was also realized with the help of pseudo-religious rituals which promoted the mythology of the Nazi movement and its Führer. In some scenarios the structural models developed in the ceremonies of the Catholic Church were still recognizable, while other details represented adaptations of Italian Fascism. These roots were most clearly manifested in the rituals surrounding the cult of the dead and the honouring of heroes, rituals which were performed annually on 9 November in commemoration of the events on that day in 1923. The idea of revering relics, combined with the specific blood mysticism of Nazi ideology, was acted out in the cult of the *Blutfahne* (blood banner) and the *Blutzeugen* (martyrs), with macabre ceremonies. Also of religious origin was the partly realistic, partly symbolic re-enactment of the events of 1923 which had been given the status of legend. These ceremonies, presented in the same ritual form since 1935, had the character of a secularized procession in which martyrs and high priests were united, as well as that of an extreme emotionalizing – and thereby heightening – of National Socialism as a kind of religion of eternal validity.[12]

A separate department, the Amt für den 8./9. November, was responsible for the rituals, which followed the same scheme every year. An army of banner-bearing supernumeraries re-enacted the march from the Bürgerbräukeller to the Feldherrnhalle, passing pylons crowned with blazing sacrificial bowls and bearing the names of the *Gefallene der Bewegung* (the fallen of the movement), the martyrs of the National Socialist cult. There was also a special costumery with wind jackets and ski caps *à la* 1923. The 'Horst-Wessel-Lied' was played synchronously and continuously from loudspeakers, interrupted only when the front of the procession reached one of the 'altars' where the name of the dead man was solemnly read out. The high point of this emotive ritual was reached when Hitler arrived at the Feldherrnhalle and sixteen artillery salvos announced the honouring of the heroes. This part of the ceremony, endowed with a form of sacrificial tradition, was followed by the movement of the procession to the Königsplatz, where from 1935 onwards the Letzter Appell (last roll-call) took

12. See Ernst Niekisch, *Das Reich der niederen Dämonen*, Hamburg, 1953, pp. 102ff. Niekisch interprets the Third Reich as a secularized church, as a synthesis of Rome and Potsdam.

place. Here the sixteen who had died in the Hitler putsch of 1923 were buried in temples of honour (which were completely destroyed in 1945). The ceremony of the Letzter Appell combined in typical fashion necromantic, spiritual and religious elements. As each of the names of the sixteen dead was intoned by the head of the Munich Nazi administration, the voices of those present responded with 'here.' On the following day a guard of honour was formed by the Hitler Youth, and the swearing in of SS men on the Königsplatz ended the ceremonies. After 1936 the flags were no longer flown at half-mast. The event was thus reconstituted as a feast of the resurrection of the dead soldiers with the intention of demonstrating the unity of party and fatherland. The religious days of commemoration falling in the month of November, All Saint's Day and Totensonntag (the Sunday prior to Advent), were reduced to insignificance, as were the Langemarck ceremonies (see chapter 4 in this book), in the face of the 9 November events. That 9 November was also the anniversary of the reputedly ignominious end of the First World War was also not lost on the directors of this dramaturgy of resurrection and redemption.[13]

That the *Hitler-Mythos* took on clearly religious dimensions is hardly surprising, given that a saviour figure with a charismatic and absolute claim to authority stood at the head of the Nazi movement, ready, as it were, for religious interpretation. As Baldur von Schirach wrote: 'We heard often the sound of your voice, listened mutely and clasped our hands.'[14] Göring too styled the leader of the NSDAP a saviour (and himself the high priest) when he declared in September 1935, at the National Party Day ceremonies: 'A whole people, a whole nation feels itself joyful and strong today, because in you is not only the leader of the people, because in you the saviour of the people is also come into being.'[15] The words of Robert Ley two years later already had the character of a creed: 'Adolf Hitler! We are bound to you alone! In this hour we want to renew the vow: on this earth we believe in Adolf Hitler alone. We believe that National Socialism alone is the faith that makes our people blessed.'[16] And on 13 September 1937 Goebbels dictated his impressions following the National Party Day to his diary in the form of the following apotheosis: 'An almost religious celebration

13. Karlheinz Schmeer, *Die Regie des öffentlichen Lebens im Dritten Reich*, Munich, 1956, pp. 101ff.
14. Quoted by Hans-Jochen Gamm, *Der braune Kult. Das Dritte Reich und seine Ersatzreligion. Ein Beitrag zur politischen Bildung*, Hamburg, 1962, p. 24.
15. Ibid., p. 38.
16. Ibid., pp. 38ff. ('Der Schulungsbrief der NSDAP, Nr. 4/1937').

of fixed unchanging tradition. The Führer speaks deep into the hearts of the people. The consecration of the new standards is clothed in a boundless mystical magic. As the Führer speaks, the sun breaks out for several minutes.'[17]

All the elements of this surrogate religion were thus combined: tradition, ritual, mystical emotional captivation of the ritual participants, and a godlike being at whose very speech the sky broke open.

The People as Cultic Fraternity

It was not only its Byzantine features and enforced allegiance which won for National Socialism its success with the masses. The figure of the saviour presupposed the yearning to be saved, and this predisposition was evoked and maintained with all possible means of mass suggestion. The function of the Führer myth was ultimately that of offering an object to the need for religious devotion. Mass ceremonies and rituals, the cults of blood and banner, the concept of the order and the 'sworn community' all served this purpose. So too did the permeation of the religious domain and the adaptation of religious features, as seen in the construction of a specific chronology, the building of church-like community halls where ritual acts took place, the organization of processions and the creation of a mystical darkness in place of rational reflection. The result of these efforts to create a propagandistic dramaturgy of self-representation was the short-lived realization of the idea of the people as a *Schicksalsgemeinschaft* (community bound by destiny).

Naturally there were outsiders and critics who did not adapt, and coercion was used in dealing with such individuals. However, the degree of conformity and silent toleration for the regime was, as is well known, extraordinarily widespread. The archetypical enemies of National Socialism – Jews, Communists, 'subversive intellectuals' – were also the enemies of those who were not supporters of Hitler. In this sense, even those opponents of the regime who had the possibility of active resistance shared the sense of belonging to a 'community bound by destiny'.

To a great extent, National Socialist propaganda and orchestrative skill succeeded in manufacturing the *Volksgemeinschaft* as the realization of one of its most popular slogans. The power of this fascination remained considerable even following the military

17. Goebbels's diary, 13 September 1937, Archive of the Institut für Zeitgeschichte.

catastrophes of the war. The amalgamation of National Socialism and nation, of the Hitler movement and patriotism, had succeeded, and proved astoundingly resilient. At the summer solstice celebrations in June 1933, Goebbels hailed the attendance of so many party comrades despite the bad weather as 'proof of our invincibility', as 'proof of blind faith and willingness'.[18] And indeed the preparedness for sacrifice among the people was to prove itself under far more terrifying circumstances, even when the Hitler myth itself had already paled.[19]

It goes without saying that the dictator himself understood his people as a *Kultgemeinschaft* (cultic community) and claimed them as such. A promise implying the future *Heilserwartung* (the expectation of salvation) thus formed an appropriate close to his political testament: 'Out of the sacrifice of our soldiers and out of my own solidarity with them to the point of death, the seed will inevitably grow once again in German history which will lead to the glorious rebirth of the National Socialist movement, and thereby the realization of the true national community.'[20]

The final report by the Supreme Command of the German Army, announcing the unconditional capitulation of the German nation on 9 May 1945, stated as follows: 'Even the enemy will not refuse respect for the achievements and sacrifices of the German soldiers. Every soldier can, therefore, remaining upright and proud, lay down his weapon, and in these most trying hours of our history, courageously and confidently go to work for the eternal life of our people.'[21]

18. *Goebbels-Reden*, vol. 1, p. 127.
19. See Ian Kershaw, *Der Hitler-Mythos. Volksmeinung und Propaganda im Dritten Reich*, Stuttgart, 1980, pp. 131ff.
20. 'Politisches Testament, 29.4.1945', in *Hitler. Reden und Proklamationen 1932–1945*, Würzburg, 1963, vol. 2, pp. 2236ff.
21. *Kriegstagebuch des Oberkommandos der Wehrmacht*, with introduction and notes by P. E. Schramm, Frankfurt/M, 1961, vol. IV/2, p. 1282.

PART VI

The 'Export' of Fascism

–17–

An Old-Style Imperialist as National Socialist

Consul-General Dr Rudolf Asmis (1879–1945?)

JOHN PERKINS

A Diplomatic Career

By the time of his arrival in Sydney in June 1932 to succeed Dr Büsing as Consul-General of the Republic of Germany, the senior commercial and diplomatic posting of that country in Australia, Dr Rudolf Albert August Wilhelm Asmis already had a long, varied and interesting career behind him. Born at Mesekenhagen in the Pomeranian county of Grimmen in 1879, the son of a Prussian official whose forebears had been predominantly pastors, minor landholders and teachers, he was in many ways a typical product of his class and its milieu in the burgeoning Second Empire.[1] After completing a doctorate on a legal topic at the University of Greifswald, and his military service in 1900–1 with the Colberg Grenadier Regiment, he followed in his father's footsteps into the public service. While serving as a judicial official in Germany he was awarded a second doctorate, in 1906, for a thesis on 'British East Africa in the Planned Imperial Customs Union'. Thereafter, he joined the (German) Imperial Colonial Administration and was invited to Togo by the Governor, Julius Count von Zech, to take up the position of Director of Education.

From 1907 to 1910 Asmis was mainly employed in Togo investigating customary tribal law and Bezirksleiterrecht, the mixture of

The author wishes to acknowledge the permission of the Royal Australian Historical Society to reprint material from his article 'Dr Asmis and the "Rescue of *Deutschtum*" in Australia in the 1930s', *Journal of the Royal Australian Historical Society*, vol. LXXIII, 1988, pp. 296–312.

1. 'Ahnentafel Asmis', in *Deutsche Ahnentafeln*, Leipzig, 1936, vol. II.

the German criminal code and local tribal law that was practised by individual district officers. The result was a draft for a uniform legal code for the colony which Asmis presented in 1910.[2] The governor, however, was unable to institute it, and the only lasting result of Asmis's efforts was a series of published studies on tribal law and customs.[3] While working on the legal code, Asmis also acted as the chairman of a land commission engaged in investigating treaties for the alienation of land concluded between German companies and native rulers. The outcome of this activity was a publication on the land tenure of one district of Togo and judgements against the Deutsche Togo-Gesellschaft (German Togo Company) in respect of most of its treaties. This created some controversy in Germany and placed the German Colonial Office, established in 1907, in a position of some embarrassment.[4] In 1912 he joined the Foreign Office and was appointed Consul for the Belgian Congo and French Equatorial Africa.

Asmis spent the First World War as an official in the German civilian administration of Belgium, where he was initially concerned with matters relating to the Congo. In 1916 he moved to the Political Department and by the end of the war headed the Flemish Policy Section. After the Armistice and a relatively brief period with the Foreign Office in Germany, he transferred to the Ministry of the Interior and remained there for approximately fifteen months. He returned to the Foreign Office in March 1921 to head the Economics Department. In 1923 he was promoted to the rank of embassy counsellor and, after a few months as Germany's representative in Outer Mongolia, was sent to the Moscow embassy for 'special duties'. The latter included extended tours of Soviet Central Asia and the Caucasus, on which he reported to the German government and gathered material for a later book.[5]

2. *Das Deutsche Führerlexikon, 1934/35*, Berlin, n.d., p. 37; Australian Archives (hereafter AA) ACT, A377/10A, Nazi Activities/Fascist/Communism; A. J. Knoll, *Togo under Imperial Germany 1884–1914*, Stanford, 1978, pp. 62–3; D. E. K. Amenumey, 'German Administration in Southern Togo', *Journal of African History*, vol. X, no. 4, 1969, pp. 627–8.
3. R. Asmis, 'Die Stammesrechte des Bezirks Atakpame', *Zeitschrift für vergleichende Rechtswissenschaft*, vol. XXV, 1911; 'Die Stammesrechte der Bezirken Misahöhe, Anecho und Lomeland', vol. XXVI, 1911; 'Die Stammesrechte des Bezirks Sansame Mangú', vol. XXVII, 1912; 'Landschaft und Grundeigentum im östlichen Teil des Misahöhegebiets', *Blätter für vergleichende Rechtswissenschaft*, Berlin, 1910.
4. Knoll, *Togo*, p. 134
5. *Das Deutsche Führerlexikon*, p. 37; W. A. Mommsen, *Die Nachlässe in den Deutschen Archiven*, Boppard am Rhein, 1983, p. 54; R. Asmis, *Als Wirtschaftspionier in Russisch-Asien*, Berlin, 1924.

During his time in the Soviet Union he also met and married, in Moscow, the daughter of a former Tsarist official of Baltic German descent who had been raised to the Russian hereditary nobility in 1913.[6]

In April 1925, after a brief period at the Peking embassy, Asmis was promoted to the rank of ambassador second-class and sent to represent Germany in Thailand. After seven years of service there, he was appointed a consul-general first-class and came to occupy the post in Australia, where he was to serve until the Second World War. The outbreak of hostilities actually found him on home leave for consultations. He subsequently joined the Colonial Policy Office of the Nazi Party, under General Ritter von Epp. There he was engaged for the duration of the war on the planning for a future German colonial empire and became the state-secretary designate for a proposed ministry of colonies, under von Epp, which was never to be realized.[7] He was arrested by the Soviet NKVD (the precursor of the KGB) on 17 June 1945, at his home in the village of Klein-Machnow near the western border of West Berlin. Subsequently, in November 1945, the Soviet authorities confiscated all his and his wife's possessions – 'on the grounds', she was informed, 'that her husband was a Nazi war criminal'.[8] He was later reported by the Soviet authorities to have died in the same month at a camp in Vortuka in Siberia.[9] Asmis has been described, by a French authority, as 'one of the most outstanding personalities in German colonial thought'.[10]

The Rescue of *Deutschtum* in Australia

At the time of his arrival in Australia in mid 1932, Asmis was far from sympathetic to the Nazi cause. At heart he was a monarchist, a man who desired nothing more than the restoration of the Hohenzollern dynasty and the entire sociopolitical order of the Second Empire. From his perception at the time, Hitler was an

6. See 'Ahnentafel Asmis'.
7. See W. W. Schmokel, *Dream of Empire: German Colonialism, 1919–1945*, New Haven, 1964, pp. 148–54. Asmis was the head of section II of the Colonial Policy Office, which was responsible for 'Organization for the Reacquisition of the Colonies'.
8. AA ACT, A1533, 53/77, Australian Military Mission Berlin to Secretary for External Affairs, 19 May 1947.
9. AA Sydney, SP1714/1, N4319.
10. R. Cornevin, *Histoire du Togo*, 3rd edn, Paris, 1969, p. 442.

upstart and his followers an unruly mob. By late 1932, he came to see Hitler's 'great historical contribution to have been the formulation of a unified national movement to express the demands of the masses for an end to the swamp of party politics and to the mass unemployment produced by the Great Depression'. However, he believed that Hitler's refusal to join the von Papen cabinet, and his negotiations with other parties, would cost him votes in the future.

It was unwarranted, in Asmis's opinion, to call Papen's a *Junker* government. It was, he believed, 'more an accident that the leading personalities belong to the nobility. They are actually nothing more than the best representatives of the old Prussian-German bureaucracy, serving without personal interests and in their decisions influenced only by the real interests of the state.' Also, in his opinion, the economic programme of the NSDAP (Nazi Party) required 'substantial reworking before it could be implemented'.[11] It must have been about this time that he informed a local Nazi Party member that 'his class . . . could never join up with Hitler'.[12] His gardener-chauffeur later recalled the consul-general's response to the *Machtergreifung* (seizure of power) of 30 January 1933: 'I remember the day that the news came through that Hitler had taken the throne [*sic*]. I remember Asmis coming down the steps into the garden, and saying, "Well, what do you know? Hitler is the boss of Germany now." That was in a quite disgusted way. He was not a Nazi then.'[13]

In his initial readiness to serve the Hitler government, Asmis was doubtless influenced by the traditional code of behaviour of the Prussian bureaucrat, of obedience to the 'state', and by the fact that Hitler headed a coalition cabinet in which the major positions concerned with the economy and foreign affairs were occupied by men of the conservative Right rather than members of the NSDAP. Officials (of non-Jewish origin) suffered no conflict of loyalty with the cabinet appointed by President Hindenburg on 30 January 1933 such as they had felt with left-of-centre Weimar governments.

Although originally far from being a Nazi himself, the consul-general rapidly developed into an ardent supporter of the regime. He first applied to join the party in 1933, on the day that news

11. Politisches Archiv des Auswärtigen Amtes (hereafter PAdAA) Nachlaß Asmis, Paket 50, Asmis to Dr E. Hirschfeld, 22 November 1932.
12. Ibid.; AA Sydney, C414 [3] Nazi Activities, B. von Bülow to Gauleiter Bohle, 20 August 1934.
13. AA ACT, A367, C66427, Wolf, A. M. Boll, who was positively apolitical, considered Asmis 'a good boss' who treated him 'as a gentleman' (ibid.).

arrived in Australia of a decree permitting officials to join.[14] This effort was thwarted by Dr Johannes Becker, a medical practitioner at Tanunda in the Barossa Valley of South Australia, who was the *Landesvertrauensmann* (official representative of the NSDAP) from about 1930 and the first *Landeskreisleiter* (local leader of the party) in Australia, from 1933 to 1937.[15] Asmis finally withdrew his application in October 1935 and did not reapply until 1938, this time successfully, when a large number of Foreign Ministry officials joined after the career diplomat von Neurath was replaced as Foreign Minister by the Nazi von Ribbentrop.[16]

Becker, an *Altkämpfer* (old fighter) who had joined the Hitler movement in the mid 1920s while a medical student at the University of Marburg, was almost ideal-typical of the pre-1933 Nazi. He had served in the trenches through the Great War, where he was wounded at Ypres and Verdun, was awarded the Iron Cross and ended the war a corporal. His war and other experiences had left him with a pronounced antipathy towards the Prussian *Junkers* or nobility, whom he considered to have been 'tyrants as officers and landlords', and by association towards Prusso-German bureaucrats like Asmis.[17] In becoming a medical practitioner, he joined a profession that was significantly over-represented amongst the membership of the NSDAP in proportion to the number who were eligible.[18]

Amongst the factors impelling 'Aryan' German doctors towards the NSDAP were the influence of biological theory inherited from the nineteenth century and the assumed excessive numbers of Jewish students in medical faculties in the 1920s.[19] It was later to be claimed of Becker that in 1936 he had observed of Hitler: 'In his endeavour to keep his country racially clean he is making a mistake by his treatment of the Jews.'[20] However, the medical practitioner's library, which was confiscated on his internment at the outbreak of war, contained an extremely large number of anti-Semitic works, including *The Protocols of the Elders of Zion.*[21] He believed that

14. AA Sydney, SP1714/1, N39039, Walter Ladendorff, Asmis to Admiral Menche, 4 August 1938.
15. AA Adelaide, AP308/1, SA20419(1), Nazi Party in South Australia.
16. AA Sydney, SP1714/1, N39039.
17. AA Adelaide, AP308/1, SA20419(1).
18. M. H. Kater, *The Nazi Party: A Social Profile of Members and Leaders 1919–1945*, Oxford, 1983, pp. 73, 112–13.
19. Ibid.
20. Letter from E. Kock, School of Pianoforte, Tanunda, *Adelaide Advertiser*, 3 December 1947.
21. AA Adelaide, AP308/1, SA15163.

'Jewish interests' effectively ruled Australia and would 'move against him sooner or later'; and he is on record as referring to the German clubs of Australia's capital cities as 'Jew infested'.[22]

Anti-Semitic remarks were also expressed by Asmis. They were, however, very occasional indeed. He was certainly made aware of the persecution of the Jews in Hitler's Germany, by the Australian press and the stories of Jewish refugees. These sources he chose to ignore or disbelieve. In early July 1938, for example, when reporting to Admiral Menche of the Foreign Organization of the Party on the growing anti-Nazi tone in the Australian press, he remarked: 'The Jews who are streaming into Australia in growing numbers help with their interviews and fairytales of terror of their experiences in Austria.'[23]

The quite senior position that Asmis came to occupy in the party bureaucracy on his return to Germany shortly before the outbreak of war may have provided him with a knowledge of the Final Solution that was denied the German public in general. Overall, however, Asmis's anti-Semitism was on a par with that of his middle- and upper-class peers in the rest of Europe – and in Australia. (Somewhat ironically, in the late 1930s the forceful opposition of the South Australian branch of the British Medical Association to Becker's registration was motivated almost entirely by the fear that it could become a precedent in the face of an influx of refugee Jewish doctors from Central Europe.) Asmis was more indifferent to the fate of the Jews than an active participant or proponent of Nazi policy on this issue.

The consul-general's rapid drift towards embracing the Nazi cause as his own appears to have been motivated by a number of considerations. On one occasion, Asmis urged his gardener-chauffeur Johnnie Boll to join the party. His reasoning, that membership might be of advantage should Boll decide to return to Germany, may have reflected one of his own motives for applying to join.[24] There were, however, more important reasons. In the first place, Hitler promised and soon embarked upon the restoration of Germany's former position as a major European and world power. Secondly, Asmis shared the Nazis' anti-Bolshevik views, from a combination of his background, his experience of the Soviet Union and the fortunes of his wife's family after the October Revolution. Thirdly, National Socialism, more than the national-

22. AA Adelaide, AP308/1, SA20419(1).
23. AA Sydney, SP1714/1, N39039, Asmis to Menche, 2 July 1938.
24. AA ACT, A367, C66427, Wolf, A. M.

ism of the German National People's Party (DNVP) or the notion of the restoration of the pre-1914 order, offered the prospect of eliminating the class conflict that seemed to weaken Germany internally and therefore also externally. Finally, and not least, the Nazi regime provided an opportunity for the realization of Asmis's primary objective in Australia: namely, the 'rescue of *Deutschtum*'. His initial purpose was to halt the ongoing process of Anglicization by reviving and intensifying a sense of a German identity amongst those of German descent residing in Australia and to translate that into a feeling of identification with Germany and its fate. Concurrently, the sense of a German identity was to be equated with, indeed subsumed in, a National Socialist one, as Nazism developed in Germany to represent exclusively a German racial ideal in the process of being transformed into reality.

The task Asmis set himself in Australia was a daunting one. No clear agreement existed on the number of 'German-Australians' residing in the country; estimates varied from 50,000 to 200,000.[25] This arose from the differing and mostly subjective criteria of definition, which included language usage and acknowledgement of a German heritage. On the other hand, where the seemingly objective criterion of antecedence was applied, it ignored personal perceptions of ethnic identity. In Asmis's view, if a *Volksdeutscher* were to be defined as a person with a German parent or having at least two German grandparents, then the commonly suggested figure of 100,000 for the size of the German-Australian community was too low. If, on the other hand, 'one counts as *Volksdeutsche* only those who feel they have a cultural tie with Germany and have at least a certain knowledge of the German language, then the number is scarcely more than 60,000'.[26]

Political events as refracted through the attitudes of the majority and hegemonic Anglo-Saxon population had a negative effect upon the survival of a German identity in Australia. Although hostility towards Germany and Germans commenced before the First World War, it was only then that it approached an hysteria that was translated into legislative enactments designed to eradicate an

25. See *inter alia* W. Geisler, 'Die Deutschen und ihre Siedlungen in Australien', *Jahrbuch der geographischen Gesellschaft zu Hannover*, 1930, pp. 125–8; *Das Echo*, vol. LIII, 1934, p. 110; C. Petersen and O. Scheel (eds), *Handwörterbuch des Grenz- und Auslandsdeutschtums*, 2 vols, Breslau, 1933, vol. I, p. 178; H. Kloss, *Statistisches Handbuch der Volksdeutschen im Übersee*, Vertrauliches Schriftenreihe Übersee der Publikationsstelle Stuttgart-Hamburg, Stuttgart, 1943, no. 1, pp. 16, 25.
26. PAdAA, Nachlaß Asmis, Asmis to Foreign Office, 22 July 1935.

ethnic identity amongst German-Australians. During the war, Lutheran schools were closed in some states, as in South Australia, or German was prohibited as a medium of instruction in them, as in Victoria.[27] German clubs and societies were compelled to disband and German-language newspapers had to cease publication. Church services could no longer be conducted in German. It was even made an offence to conduct a telephone conversation in any language other than English.[28] German citizens and a number of naturalized British (that is, Australian) citizens of German origin experienced internment. The property of German nationals was confiscated, eventually to contribute towards satisfying the absurdly high reparations demanded by Prime Minister Hughes at Versailles. After the war 696 German citizens were deported and 4,620 German-Australians volunteered for repatriation. The entry of German goods into Australia was prohibited until August 1922 and the entry of German nationals until the end of 1925.[29]

All in all, the wartime anti-German hysteria and its legislative consequences devastated a once thriving German-Australian community, and the effects of that experience were to linger on into the 1930s. Asmis himself commented in 1932 on 'the psychosis against Germany, which was stronger here than in other enemy countries, and persisted longer on account of the isolation of the country and the widespread disinterest in political enlightenment and in the developments of the post-war years'.[30] When the consul-general toured southern Queensland in 1936, a Lutheran pastor at Toowoomba (where a number of Germans had settled from the 1860s onwards) requested him to address the students at the Lutheran School in German as well as in English because: 'It would be of great importance that just the boys who no longer understand German in spite that they are of German blood and who are wholly scared of anything that is German owing to the war propaganda of that time, should have a purification bath so that they no longer would be ashamed of their German blood.'[31] On the positive side,

27. A. Lodewyckx, 'Deutsche Sprache, deutsche Schulen und Deutschunterricht in Australien', in *Deutsche Kultur im Leben der Völker*, 1934, pp. 172–3.
28. J. Lyng, *Non-Britishers in Australia*, Melbourne, 1927, p. 40.
29. K. Burggraf, *Die Deutschen in den Hauptstädten von Australien*, Sydney, 1934, p. 47. See also John Perkins, 'Germans in Australia during the First World War', in J. Jupp (ed.), *The Australian People*, Sydney, 1988, pp. 488–9.
30. German Democratic Republic, Zentrales Staatarchiv Potsdam, Auswärtiges Amt (hereafter ZSP, AA), Akten betreffend Handelsbeziehungen Australiens zu Deutschland, vol. II, 1926 onwards; *Die Deutsche Einfuhr nach Australien*, 1932.
31. AA Sydney, SP1714/1, N43197: Dr Asmis 1941–53. The syntax of this and some other quotations used in this essay is unusual; the translations from the

for Dr Asmis's purposes, the shared experience of the effects of anti-Germanism had done much to diminish the significance of class and political differences as a divisive force amongst Australians of German origins.

The basis of Asmis's initial approach to the rescue of *Deutschtum* was institutional: to create umbrella organizations for existing bodies catering for the German-Australian community, which were to be integrated within 'coordinated' quasi-governmental institutions of the Third Reich and to act as channels for permeation by Nazi ideology. Thus he worked to transform the already existing German-Australian Chamber of Commerce into an adjunct of the East Asia Association, a 'coordinated' Hamburg organization that was a branch of the Deutsche Industrie- und Handelstag (German Industry and Trade Parliament), the supreme representative body of German industry and commerce.[32] At the same time, he was active in promoting a Bund des Deutschtums in Australien und Neuseeland (Alliance of Germandom in Australia and New Zealand), which officially came into being on 30 May 1933 on the occasion of the 50th anniversary of the founding of the Concordia (German) Club in Sydney.[33]

The Bund began as an association of existing German clubs and societies, as this was a more readily achievable objective in Australia than the creation of an entirely new grassroots organization like the Bund of the United States of America. As the consul-general informed the head of the Foreign Organization of the NSDAP, *Gauleiter* Bohle, in May 1934: 'To create a cell organization over the whole continent is practically impossible or only under great cost and loss of time; therefore, I decided to unite the relatively get-atable unions and clubs in the coastal towns.'[34] Moreover, given Germany's critical foreign exchange situation in the 1930s, clubs like the coordinated German-Australian Chamber of Commerce were a prospective source of 'financial support for building up the Bund' and for propaganda and other activities amongst the

---

German were made by members of the security services and the original documents have been destroyed.

32. See ZSP, AA, Akten betreffend Deutsche Handelskammer in Australien, Asmis to Foreign Office, 1 August 1933.
33. University of Melbourne Archives, Augustin Lodewyckx Deposit, Section D, Germans in Australia, K. Burggraf to A. Lodewyckx, 9 August 1934.
34. AA Sydney, SP1714/1, N43197, Asmis to E. W. Bohle, 2 May 1934. See also Bundesarchiv Koblenz (hereafter BA), Auswärtiges Amt, Akten betreffend das Deutschtum im Ausland, Australien, vol. I, Asmis to E. W. Bohle, 22 June 1933.

German-Australian community.[35] Eventually, it was hoped to expand the direct individual membership of the Bund.

In his efforts to establish the Bund, Asmis initially faced considerable opposition from certain quarters. *Landeskreisleiter* Dr Becker, in particular, desired to take a more direct approach to the subsumation of German-Australian identity within a National Socialist one, and in 1933 he was active in the formation of groups of 'friends of the Hitler movement' amongst Australians of German extraction in the Barossa Valley and elsewhere.[36] He considered the German clubs in the capital cities, especially the one in Adelaide, with its traditional social-democratic leanings, to be 'Jew infested' and hotbeds of Communist, socialist and democratic ideas. It was in these terms that he issued a public statement in 1933 in the German-language *Queensland Herald*, warning visiting German seamen against frequenting these social venues. As for the Bund itself, Becker believed that the 'idea and goal' were 'healthy and desirable'. However, in his opinion, 'the proposals, to judge from the prospectus, are out of date and originate from before the war – from the sterile time of *Junker* rule – and do not meet the needs of today's new, budding, growing and reflowering Germany, and therefore not those of the *Deutschtum* of today.'[37]

A constant source of concern to Dr Asmis was the possibility of the Commonwealth government acting to ban Nazi Party organizations. This step was taken by a few governments during the 1930s, including those of Switzerland and South Africa.[38] Asmis feared such a measure not only for its effect on resident German citizens, who were exclusively eligible for membership of the NSDAP, but for the likely reaction from German-Australians. As the consul-general observed: 'The great majority of German-Australians . . . would straight away creep back into their mouseholes' and 'the Anglicizing would then go ahead.'[39]

Although there was a constantly perceived threat, there appear to

35. AA Sydney, SP1714/1, N43197, Asmis to Bohle, 2 May 1934.
36. Deutsche Börse zu Marburg, Nachlaß J. W. Mannhardt (hereafter DBM), private archive in the possession of Ms R. Eisinger of Marburg, Asmis to *Gauleiter* Bohle, 2 May 1934; AA Adelaide, AP308/1, SA19447, Auslands Organization of the NSDAP, Loveday Camp Interview, 9 May 1944.
37. AA Adelaide, AP308/1, SA20419(1); AA Adelaide, SA18121, German Club, Becker to the President of the SA Allgemeiner Deutscher Verein, 20 September 1933.
38. South Africa banned the NSDAP in late 1934 and Switzerland did so in February 1936.
39. AA Sydney, SP1714/1, N39039, Walter Ladendorff. On 11 March 1936 the Minister for External Affairs did go so far as to warn the consulate-general that

have been only two brief periods when the Australian government seriously considered proceeding to ban Nazi Party organizations. One was in late 1934, after the party was outlawed in South Africa. The other occurred during the first half of 1936, when Hitler revived the issue of the restitution of Germany's former colonies and when, during the absence of Dr Asmis in Germany, a more than usually intensive Nazi propaganda effort was undertaken amongst German-Australians by *Landeskreisleiter* Becker and others.[40]

During 1935 the consul-general was active in endeavouring to obtain from Germany an organizer and secretary for the Bund. In the interests of not arousing the suspicions of the Commonwealth government and perhaps a refusal to issue an entry permit, it was decided to utilize the desire of the Professor of German at the University of Sydney for a lecturer from Germany as a cover for the appointment. Initially a Dr Hildebrandt was considered ideal for the dual post, being a German language teacher and an active Party member. The proposal came to nothing, however, because Hildebrandt declined to move from a secure position at the National Political School at Oranienstein to an uncertain future as a temporary lecturer at the University of Sydney. Eventually a replacement was found who was to serve until the outbreak of war and his internment.[41]

Towards the end of 1933, having effectively established the Bund and integrated it, together with the revived German-Australian Chamber of Commerce, within institutions representing the Third Reich, the consul-general took the necessary steps to bring into being a periodical to act as the mouthpiece of both, and as a medium of propaganda amongst the German-Australian community. In November 1933 a prospectus was issued by the newly-formed German-Australian Publications Proprietary Ltd, which invited subscriptions for 7,500 £1 shares towards a capital of £10,000; the remainder consisted of 100 'special' £25 shares placed with persons trusted by the consul-general. It was presumed that this form of distribution of the share issue would be adequate for

---

'the intensive propaganda of the National Socialist organization in Australia within the German colony, and amongst those of German descent, would have to cease': BA, Reichskanzlei, R4311/1411, Consul Hellenthal to the Foreign Office, 12 March 1936.

40. AA Sydney, SP1714/1, N39039, Asmis to Admiral Menche, 3 May 1936; BA, Reichskanzlei, R43 II, Hellenthal to Foreign Office, 12 March 1936.
41. DBM, J. W. Mannhardt to Asmis, 28 January and 2 March 1936.

the retention of control of the company in the right hands.[42]

The bilingual weekly *Die Brücke* (The Bridge) was launched in February 1934, and continued to be published up to the outbreak of war in September 1939. The journal, as Asmis reported to *Gauleiter* Bohle in early May 1934, 'gives its readers the wealth of thought of the National Socialistic movement, teaches, and drives up to that borderline where the Australian reader, who also would like to grasp it all, would simply throw it unread into the waste-paper basket as a "Nazi propaganda pamphlet"'.[43] In practice, *Die Brücke* endeavoured to present National Socialism as a reasonable, harmless and 'common-sense' bourgeois ideology that only 'Communists' and 'misguided elements' could find objection to. After all, for example, with the establishment of the Nazi *Deutsche Arbeitsfront* (German Labour Front) under Dr Robert Ley, after the trade unions had been disbanded, 'the number of organized workers has increased nearly threefold since the new government took over and reorganized and rationalized all old trade unions and allocations of employees.'[44] The remarks of the wife of a Melbourne University academic, given at a talk after her return from an extended stay in Nazi Germany, were quoted with approval; she stated 'that the new ideology of Germany was clean-thinking, clean-living, service to the fellow man, and the eradication of self-aggrandizement'. In particular, she thought that 'the Nazi regime protected the worker, prevented the exploitation of the peasant and put an end to intellectual snobbishness'.[45] Some of her reasons for admiring Hitler's Germany may have had a lot to do with her experience of Melbourne University life. An academic at the University of Adelaide was reported in *Die Brücke* as stating in a radio broadcast that 'Nazi Germany stands for the same ideal of political liberty as England.'[46]

Asmis was one of a number who encouraged participation and spectator interest in such 'German' sports as gymnastics and rowing amongst German-Australians, as a means of combating the assimilatory consequences of a commitment to 'Australian' sports. Philately, one of the consul-general's hobbies, was promoted as a means of disseminating Nazi propaganda amongst Australians of German descent.[47]

The consul-general's efforts were considerably aided by assist-

42. Mitchell Library (Sydney), *Die Brücke*, prospectus.
43. AA Sydney, SP1714/1, N43197, Asmis to Bohle, 2 May 1914.
44. *Die Brücke*, 24 February 1934.
45. *Die Brücke*, 21 April 1934.
46. *Die Brücke*, 3 November 1934.
47. *Die Brücke*, 13 April 1935, 30 March 1935.

ance provided by Nazi Germany. From 1935 onwards, short-wave broadcasts from Germany were directed at an audience principally consisting of German-Australians. The visits of the cruisers *Karlsruhe* (in 1934) and *Köln* (in 1936) had a considerable impact.[48] So too did the tour by Count von Luckner in 1938. Von Luckner was the former captain of a German surface raider of the First World War, the *Seeadler*, which was responsible for sinking a considerable tonnage of Allied shipping in various waters, including the Pacific. His exploits had received considerable publicity in the Anglo-Saxon world through the popular account written by the American Lowell Thomas. He was also something of a popular hero in Germany.[49]

In the late 1930s, in view of the developing 'appeasement policy' of the British government, which was pursued up to and beyond the Munich Agreement of November 1938, many German-Australians began to feel that an identification with the 'New Germany' was not incompatible with being a patriotic Australian. By this time, thanks in no small part to the efforts of Dr Asmis, it could be said that 'The danger of Anglicization (*Verengländerung*) is . . . not as acute as it was a few years ago.'[50] In November 1939 the *Kristallnacht* aroused the Left in Australia to even more emphatic opposition to Nazism, and Asmis was savagely attacked in the *Labour Daily* until he was able to move Prime Minister Lyons to intercede on his behalf.[51] It must however be conceded that, through generations of teaching, anti-Semitism was fairly pronounced amongst Lutherans of German descent, perhaps even more so than amongst the Australian middle class. It was really only after Hitler's annexation of the rump of Czechoslovakia in March, and Chamberlain's response of a guarantee of Poland's frontiers, that public opinion in Australia began to change dramatically. By the time war was declared in September, attitudes to Germany and Germans were beginning to approach those of 1914–18 in intensity.

48. Apparently, 'mementoes of the visit of the "Koeln" were found in most of the homes of German-Australians that were searched by members of the Security Service after the outbreak of war': AA Adelaide, AP308/1, SA20418, part 6, Some Aspects of the NSDAP in Australia (SA).
49. AA Sydney, St1233/1, N40752, Count von Luckner 1938–46; L. Thomas, *The Sea Devil*, London, 1928.
50. A. von Skerst, 'Das Deutschtum in Australien', in *Wir Deutschen in der Welt*, Stuttgart, 1938, p. 170.
51. BA, Nachlaß 44 Luther, Australien 1937–8, Asmis to Dr Hans Luther, 3 December 1938.

Asmis and National Socialism

Was Asmis really a Nazi? To answer this question objectively is extremely difficult. On the one hand, it depends upon the specification of what National Socialism was. On the other hand, a lot of the evidence on Asmis's views is biased by its sources in extant documents of an official nature and the recorded statements of others. Obviously, if card-carrying members of the party are to be viewed as Nazis, then Asmis was one of them. However, such a definition is too loose, given the enormous increase in membership from 1933 onwards, which included persons with widely differing political viewpoints (or none at all).

Whether out of a sense of duty as a civil servant or from conviction, Asmis was prepared on occasions to go to quite extraordinary lengths to serve the Hitler regime. In 1935 he travelled to Darwin, then being developed as the adjunct to a British Empire defence system based upon Singapore and Hong Kong, to prepare a report for the German government on the military installations there.[52] It is not known whether or not this report was passed on to the Japanese authorities, with whom Germany was developing ever-closer relations which resulted in the Anti-Comintern Pact in the following year.

Asmis, who held an attitude of superiority towards Australians in general, considered Darwin 'the dirtiest European settlement in the tropics I have hitherto seen'. His report contained information on the location and complement of the local army garrison, in which he emphasized the increased size as compared with the publicly available figure for 1933. He noted that the Australian navy presence on shore amounted to an officer and an NCO. However, he was able to convey the information 'that in the near future it will receive a substantially increased staff'. Unable to locate more than a few defence installations around the town of Darwin, he assumed they had to be concentrated around the harbour entrance. He recorded the position of oil tanks and of a gun emplacement in their proximity. Of the airport, he reported that 'it appears to be adequately equipped with lights for night flying.' Finally, unable to locate any German citizens in Darwin, he recommended a retired Australian Post Office official of German descent, who was engaged in the Northern Territory in collecting plants for the botanical gardens at Berlin-Dahlem, as someone who

52. ZSP, AA, Akten betreffend Reiseberichte, Asmis to Foreign Office, 6 June 1935.

was prepared to furnish ongoing information on military developments.[53] He also arranged for reports to be sent to Berlin by a station owner on the Gulf of Carpentaria.[54]

If the anti-Semitism that produced the Holocaust is to be seen as the core of the ideology of National Socialism, as it is in certain quarters, then Asmis hardly ranks as a Nazi at all. From his years of contact with non-European races Asmis acquired a respect for their persons and culture which was totally at odds with the views of Hitler and the race theories of National Socialism. Admittedly, he viewed the indigenous peoples of the South Pacific as 'certainly far behind Europeans'. However, he went on to say:

> In my opinion the European is not on that account justified in denying these people the possibility of development and designating them as ripe for extermination, as was once the case . . . The expression of an American philosopher that 'civilization is impossible where the banana grows' is definitely untrue. That is demonstrated by India, Siam, Peru; and it is shown by the South Sea Islanders in their particular areas.

Where Asmis came closest to Nazi racial ideology was in his abhorrence of miscegenation. This stemmed, however, from his admiration of the cultures of indigenous peoples, his awareness of the destructive impact that contact with Europeans had upon them, and his compassion for the fate of most of those of mixed race.[55]

What particularly stands out about Asmis was his rejection of Eurocentric values. He sought to understand and came genuinely to appreciate the achievements of non-European peoples in adapting to their environment. The boomerang of the Australian Aborigine, to take but one example of his beliefs in this respect, was 'certainly evidence of considerable ingenuity'. For Asmis, 'between Papuan headhunting and European executions there is in the final analysis no difference'.[56]

Asmis cannot be described as an ideological Nazi. He retained throughout his life the conservative outlook and attitudes he acquired during the formative pre-1914 years. That is not to say that he became an opportunist from 1933 onwards. His response to the *Machtergreifung* certainly did not parallel that of Friedrich Wilhelm von Prittwitz und Gaffron, the ambassador to the United States,

53. Ibid.
54. Ibid., Asmis to Foreign Office, 6 July 1935.
55. R. Asmis, *Das Ende eines Paradieses*, Berlin, 1942, pp. 28, 35–6.
56. Ibid., pp. 30–1.

whose moral principles compelled him to resign rather than serve under Hitler. To only a limited extent, and during the early years of the Third Reich, was there an element in his response of remaining in office 'to prevent the worst', as was the case with ambassadors Hoesch (London) and Köster (Paris) and the London embassy counsellor Count Bernstorff (who was hung in April 1945).[57] Asmis's active support of the Nazi regime, however, stemmed more from a belief that it could provide a means to realize his ideals than from the desire to further his diplomatic career.

Just as Becker was the ideal-typical Nazi of the years of struggle before the achievement of power in 1933, Asmis was almost the ideal-typical Nazi of the Third Reich. Like so many of his class who rode the tiger, he believed he could use and even manipulate National Socialism to achieve ends that were his own. As the divergence in their careers after 1933 demonstrates, Asmis was far more successful than Becker. It was the Asmis approach that received the backing of the authorities in Berlin, and he eventually succeeded, in 1937, in having Becker replaced as leader of the NSDAP in Australia.[58]

Asmis's enthusiasm for the National Socialist cause became especially pronounced from 1936 onwards. In that year he took home leave and was visibly impressed by the changes that had occurred in Germany since his last leave in 1932, at the height of the Great Depression. He was similarly impressed by Hitler, who granted him an audience. The anti-Bolshevik attitude of the regime was becoming more and more overt, and the Anti-Comintern Pact was signed with Japan and Italy. Perhaps most importantly for Asmis, colonial revisionism – the demand for the return of Germany's former colonies – was adopted by Hitler as official policy from the spring of 1936. Given his background, Asmis readily responded to this direction taken by the Nazi regime. The closing years of his life were to be spent drafting an administrative apparatus ready for the day when the 'dream of empire' became a reality.

57. See W. Bussmann, 'Das Auswärtige Amt unter der nationalsozialistischen Diktatur', in M. Funke et al. (eds), *Demokratie und Diktatur*, Düsseldorf, 1987, pp. 252–65.
58. See D. Orlow, *The History of the Nazi Party 1933-1945*, Pittsburgh, 1973, pp. 10–11. Orlow stresses the continuing importance of *Altkämpfer* in Hitler's inner circle and their rapid promotion with the *Machtergreifung* of 1933.

-18-

Italian Fascism in Australia 1922–45

GIANFRANCO CRESCIANI

Filippo Tommaso Marinetti, futurist poet and, with d'Annunzio, one of the most bewildering intellectual fathers of Fascism, flamboyantly stated in his version of the Fascist Catechism that Italy's Brenner Pass was not a point of arrival, but a point of departure. Thus already in the early 1920s the ecumenical aspect of Fascist ideology was summarily announced by the man who in January 1926 would see fit to create an association called the Guard on the Brenner to counter the increasing German nationalism in the Alto Adige region. Secretary of the association was Franco Battistessa, a journalist and a *squadrista* who would emigrate to Australia in 1928.

This was by no means the only Australian connection with the prophets of an Italian Fascist 'civilizing mission'. The archives of the Ministry of Popular Culture abundantly document the Fascist expansionist aims and thrust in South East Asia and Australia during the 1930s – aims that were not necessarily proportionate to Italy's political and economic interests (understandably modest) in this region. The importance of *universalfascismo* was stressed again by Galeazzo Ciano in 1935, when he became Under-Secretary of Press and Propaganda. At a meeting with the advocates of a Fascist International, he declared: 'We will speak to the whole world. We will tell all other countries about Italy and her great men. We will use radio, theatre and the movies. And, naturally, we will use the press. But above all we will use men.'[1]

This Fascist global policy of ideological imperialism not only aimed to mobilize and regiment foreign sympathizers, fellow-travellers and fervid admirers of 'Italian civilization', that is of classicism. It also postulated the exploitation of the millions of Italians who had emigrated to foreign countries and who were now seen by Rome as the ideal vehicle for Fascist penetration of those

1. Ciano, quoted in M. A. Ledeen, *Universal Fascism*, New York, 1972, pp. 106–7.

societies. The fact that many of these emigrants had opted to acquire the nationality of their chosen country did not deter the Fascist authorities from manipulating them to their advantage; on the contrary, the migrants' new citizenship status was considered as an enhancement of their credibility, and ultimately of their effectiveness.

Moreover, the Fascist Penal Code clearly indicated Italy's refusal to acknowledge a change of nationality by any of her subjects. Its preamble stated:

> The loss of citizenship does not free the ex-citizen from the bond of fidelity to his country of origin; still less can it free him from responsibility when he loses citizenship through political misdemeanours. Otherwise, the very loss would give him immunity and encourage him to commit more and perhaps worse outrages against his country of origin or his former co-citizens.[2]

Italian communities all over the world thus became, to varying degrees, overt and covert instruments of Fascist propaganda, of Fascist influence, of Fascist power abroad. The Italian community in Australia was no exception.

The extent of Fascist penetration in foreign countries, and specifically in Australia, was dependent upon several interrelated factors, the importance of which varied according to the unfolding of political events, both nationally and internationally, during the age of Fascism. Of particular relevance among these factors were:

(1) The size of the immigrant community and the historical span of its settlement.
(2) The geographic concentration, or dispersion, of the emigrants in the new country.
(3) The social, regional, economic, political, class and gender composition of the community.
(4) The level of integration and interaction of Italians with the local environment.
(5) The presence (or absence) of, and the role played by, an immigrant cultural elite and/or an economic elite.
(6) The level and frequency of economic, information and travel exchanges with Italy.
(7) The activities and the effectiveness of Fascist officials *in loco*.

2. Quoted in Australian Archives, AP 538/1, Attorney General's Department, Commonwealth Police Force, file 3074, 'Fascism in Australia'.

(8) The nationalization of the emigrant masses.
(9) The relationship between immigrant Fascism and autochthonous Fascist movements and supporters.
(10) The dialectic relationship between Fascism and Italian anti-Fascist forces abroad.
(11) The influence of the international fortunes of Italian Fascism on local affairs and on local public opinion.

In my book *Fascism, Anti-Fascism and Italians in Australia, 1922–1945* (1980) I have dealt extensively with the activities of the supporters of the regime in Australia.[3] This chapter will instead attempt to outline some specific aspects of the popularity enjoyed by Fascism among Australians and Italian migrants. As in other Anglo-Saxon countries, Mussolini and Fascism also undoubtedly enjoyed wide and unmitigated support in Australia, at least until 1935. The press, the Catholic Church, and the conservative establishment all came out publicly in praise of the Italian Duce and of his ideology. Like Winston Churchill, Stanley Bruce and Joseph Lyons also extolled *ad nauseam* the virtues of trains running on time, of cities being cleaned up and of Communists being mopped up.

Admittedly, their laudatory outbursts fell on fertile ground. Sydney was controlled in 1922 by the 14,000 strong secret Digger Army, led by Major Jack Scott and Major-General Sir Charles Rosenthal, whose covert activities, under the umbrella of the King and Empire League, formed the historical basis for D. H. Lawrence's *Kangaroo* (1923). Melbourne was under the spell in 1923 of the paramilitary White Guard, the 5,000 special constables raised and organized by Sir John Monash under the direction of the Victorian government, to prevent looting during the police strike. Australia was visited in November 1925 by Captain James O. Hatcher, who formed branches of the British Union of Fascists in Sydney, Hobart and Melbourne.[4]

In May 1927 Brigadier-General Charles Rudkin, who had been in command of the British artillery on the Italian front in 1917, came to Australia on a lecture tour entitled 'Mussolini, Fascism and its Influence on World Politics'. In Sydney he spoke at King's Hall and at the local chapter of the Dante Alighieri Society, hosted by president and long-time friend Antonio Baccarini, who had been

3. G. Cresciani, *Fascism, Anti-Fascism and Italians in Australia, 1922–1945*, Canberra, 1980.
4. *Argus*, 3–4 November 1925; *Italo-Australian*, 7 November 1925.

Rudkin's liaison officer with the Italian command during the First World War and had been decorated by him with the British Military Cross.[5] It was the same Baccarini, the 'cultured Italian gentleman', who in the early 1930s lent 'quite a lot of literature of the propaganda type' on Fascism to the leader of the New Guard Movement, Lieutenant-Colonel Eric Campbell, who understandably declared that 'even after discounting the bias of the enthusiastic protagonist authors I liked what I read.'[6]

It must nevertheless be stated that contacts between Australian and Italian sympathizers and supporters of Fascism were few, far between and fruitless, given the social, linguistic and cultural abyss which kept Italian migrants apart from mainstream Australian society. Liaison was maintained in the main by businessmen, diplomats, travellers and the clergy. There were values common to the ideologies of both Fascism and the war veterans, namely discipline, anti-intellectualism, anti-Communism, anti-labour, the spirit of camaraderie and of 'mates', the primeval myth of the goodness of life on the land and of nature in contrast to the evil of city life, the emerging middle-class values and the thwarted aspirations. However, these values were overshadowed by the dominating and divisive influence of the myth of the God-given supremacy of the British Empire and race, whereby Italians, even when Fascist, were ultimately considered to be inferior or, at best, peculiar and uncontrollable.

This disturbing peculiarity of judgement penetrated the attitudes of even the staunchest Australian supporters of Fascism. One of them was undoubtedly Herbert M. Moran, a Sydney doctor who frequently visited Italy and was received by Mussolini several times. Moran interpreted Fascism and judged Italians in strict medical terms. Fascism, for instance, was 'the normal reaction of the national organism to the invasion of a corrupt communism, but only the comparatively healthy body is capable of properly reacting, for there comes a stage when an undermined constitution is overwhelmed by the infection',[7] an infection spread by the intellectuals, 'those mischief-makers of every country whose fertility in ideas rivals their pathetic sterility in practical statesmanship'.[8] To Moran, Italians (even the Fascist ones, we may assume) were a 'nation whose people have not assimilated the modern technique of

5. *Italo-Australian*, 9 May 1927. On Baccarini see *Australian Dictionary of Biography*, vol. 7, 1891–1939, Melbourne 1979.
6. Eric Campbell, *The Rallying Point*, Melbourne, 1965, p. 131.
7. Herbert M. Moran, *Letters from Rome*, Sydney, 1935.
8. Ibid., p. 52.

birth control . . . they had failed to practise that control which in the end means the subjugation of the white race.'[9] They were uncontrollable not only sexually, but temperamentally as well: 'It is necessary to point out,' stressed Moran, 'that in the Italian dictionary there is no word for "bluff", it has to be borrowed from the English, and the reason is this: an Italian may bluster, but he does not bluff.'[10] In the face of these opinions, one cannot help wondering about the terminal nature of Moran's sycophancy.

Another staunch supporter of Italian Fascism in Australia was Thomas Herbert Kelly, who in March 1935 became President of the Dante Alighieri Society in Sydney, following Antonio Baccarini's resignation. It was, as the *Italian Bulletin of Commerce* reported, a 'change of the guard which took place in perfect Fascist style'.[11] Vice-president of the Dante at that time was Herbert M. Moran. Kelly, a director of Tooth's Brewery, the Colonial Sugar Refining Company and the Bank of New South Wales, served as an officer in military intelligence during the First World War. When Prime Minister Bruce sought to break the seamen's strike in 1925, Kelly helped Eric Campbell to organize the deployment of 500 ex-AIF (Australian Imperial Forces) special constables to intervene if necessary. Under his leadership, the Dante Alighieri Society became even more politicized, and Kelly's connections with Italian and Japanese Fascist circles (he was also an active member of the Japan–Australia Society) grew even closer.[12]

Perhaps the most coherent and cogent theoretical attempt to 'adapt' Fascism to local conditions was made by Eric Campbell in his 1934 publication *The New Road*. In it he charted the way towards a Fascist Australia and ventured to prophesy that 'a serious and sane application of Fascist doctrines is the only hope if Australia is to preserve its freedom and to take material advantage of exploiting this veritable land of Canaan. The fact that we are in the land of Canaan constitutes one of the greatest difficulties of reform.'[13] Fortunately for Australia, the dictum *nemo propheta in patria* again proved correct in the case of Eric Campbell and his followers. The land of Canaan was too comfortable for the new Israelites to follow a black-shirted antipodean Moses through the brimstone of a Fascist *Götterdämmerung*.

Kelly, Campbell and Moran were only the tip of the iceberg. The

9. Ibid., pp. 5, 34.
10. Ibid., p. 31.
11. *Italian Bulletin of Australia* (Sydney), March 1935, p. 10.
12. Drew Cottle, letter to author, 10 March 1986.
13. Eric Campbell, *The New Road*, Sydney, 1934, p. 57.

Australia of the 1920s and 1930s looked at Italian Fascism with mixed feelings of racial superiority and increasing interest and sympathy – feelings which were not exclusively restricted to the Anglo-Irish Catholics, to Archbishop Mannix and Bishop Duhig, to the Catholic intelligentsia militating on the editorial board of the *Catholic Press*, the *Catholic Worker* and the *Catholic Freeman's Journal*. Even flamboyant and aggressively nationalist Australian intellectuals like P. R. Stephensen, although outwardly spiteful towards Fascism, embarked in reality upon a road which ultimately led them, hand in hand, a long way along the path of the apologists of that ideology. Conversely, it is indeed indicative that people like R. A. Shaw, of the Department of Italian of the University of Sydney, who in 1943 would become one of the leaders of the Italian anti-Fascist organization Italia Libera, was still lecturing at the Dante Alighieri Society in 1939 on theses such as 'Patria diva, santa genitrice' (Divine Fatherland, Holy Progenitor) and was signalled by the Commonwealth Investigation Branch as one of the lecturers who were 'fanatical Fascists'.[14] In *The Foundations of Culture in Australia*, Stephensen stated in 1936 that 'the tradition of the AIF will almost certainly, I believe, defend us against the extremes of Fascism should the nasty little plotters ever screw up their courage to the point of putting matters to the test.'[15] Yet when the ultimate test came, Stephensen, like not a few others, did not pass it. In July 1939, as the clouds of war were fast approaching, he went on flirting with the idea of the *homo novus*, with the firebrand aspects of totalitarianism. 'We need here,' he wrote in *The Publicist*, 'a Mahomet, a Hideyoshi, a Cromwell – or a Hitler – a man of harsh vitality, a born leader, a man of action, not one sicklied o'er with the pale cast of thought. Fanatics are needed, crude, harsh men, not swept and decorous men, to arouse us from the lethargy of decadence, softness and lies which threatens death to White Australia.'[16] As a result of his crypto-Fascist outpourings and association with the Australia First Movement, Stephensen was arrested by police officers on 10 March 1942 and interned.

Undoubtedly, the main channel of penetration of Italian Fascist ideology in Australia was the Italian community. In a report written in 1944 to Italian Prime Minister Ivanoe Bononi by Mel-

14. Australian Archives, series 13.P242, item Q30565, Report of Commonwealth Investigation Officer, 'Italian Organisations'. Also Australian Archives, AP 538/1, item SA 3074, ONB Sydney, Circular Letter, 28 September 1939.
15. P. R. Stephensen, *The Foundations of Culture in Australia*, Gordon, 1936, p. 132.
16. Stephensen, quoted in Bruce Muirden, *The Puzzled Patriots*, Melbourne, 1968, p. 40.

bourne businessman Gualtiero Vaccari – a report remarkable for its sins of omission and remission, and for the author's suspect protestations that he was *au-dessus de la mêlée* of the ideological dogfight – it was claimed that in Australia

> There were, occasionally, manifestations of Italian enthusiasm which arose not out of Fascism but out of attachment for far-away Italy. Also among Australians there were pro-Fascist voices and some press articles, but these carried no significance in a country where everyone enjoys full freedom of expression . . . Any semblance of Fascism amongst the Italians in Australia is dead and buried since Italy's entry into the war and . . . the large mass of the Italians in this country has never had and does not want to have the pretension to meddle with, let alone dictate, the politics to be followed in Italy.[17]

The playing down by Vaccari of Fascism's influence among Italians in Australia is reminiscent of the very same attitude adopted by scores of Italians in Italy after 1945 whereby, if one believes them, it would be difficult to explain the rise of Fascism and its staying in power for twenty-three years, let alone the famous Defelician *consensus*. Yet Vaccari, like other members of the Italian business establishment both in Australia and in Rome, had good reasons to claim the quasi-absence of Fascism and to champion the wish, on the part of Italians, 'to be left in peace'.[18] They had a vital interest in successfully riding the momentarily turbulent political waves of the immediate post-war period and re-establishing their self-appointed role as moderate, sensible and reliable leaders of the Italian community, despite their dubious political past.[19] It is hard to believe that the Fascist authorities would have allowed Vaccari, and other Italian entrepreneurs, to maintain their positions of privilege, had their feelings towards the regime been less than enthusiastic.

Despite the fact that, as Vaccari correctly points out, Fascism did not galvanize Italians in Australia to white heat, it nevertheless was present and operating to a much larger extent than admitted by the Melbourne philanthropist. A comprehensive report drafted by the Commonwealth Investigation Branch (CIB) in 1939 on Italian organizations in Australia portrays an intricate and intriguing web of clubs, organizations and interests which constitute indisputable evidence of the capillary nature of the work carried out by Fascist

17. Australian Archives, CRS A989, item 455/7/2, Vaccari to Bonomi, 7 August 1944.
18. Ibid.
19. Cresciani, *Fascism*, pp. 212–13.

officials in this country.[20] The Fascio headquarters were housed in the Consulate-General in Sydney, and one of its clerks, Felice Rando, was Inspector-General of the Fascist branches of Sydney, Melbourne, Brisbane, Adelaide, Port Pirie, Perth, Cairns, Babinda, Innisfail and Edie Creek, New Guinea. The Consulate-General also housed the Italian Chamber of Commerce and the Dante Alighieri Society, while the headquarters of the Dopolavoro were established in the nearby Club Italia. Practically all Fascist activity was confined to the two premises.

The Sydney Fascio, named after the *squadrista* Luigi Platania, had over 300 members in 1939, and was firmly in control of a female branch, a youth group 104 strong, and an Italian school which had 59 pupils enrolled in 1938. The Opera Nazionale Dopolavoro (OND) was responsible for coordinating the leisure time of Italian migrants. Its principal officers were all prominent in the Fascio and controlled the sporting and cultural activities of its 127 members. At orchestral and dramatic functions about 300 people attended, and on occasions the functions were repeated a second night to another crowded audience. The investigating officer commented that 'it would appear that the Dopolavoro is the main lure to bring Italians under Fascist influence, but all members of the Dopolavoro are not members of the Fascio; some Italians join the Dopolavoro to gratify their love of Italian music and ignore the political side entirely.'[21]

The Italian Chamber of Commerce in Australia was definitely controlled by the Fascio, and was also a main vehicle for Fascist propaganda through its monthly publication the *Italian Bulletin of Australia*. Its secretary for a time was Felice Rando, the Inspector-General of the Fasci in Australia. One of the objectives of the chamber was to place before the Australian people 'the Italian view in thought, culture, industrial development and national and world position. This', commented the CIB officer, 'is rather a comprehensive programme and with the exception of industrial development is not the function of a commercial organization such as the Chamber of Commerce.'[22]

Other organizations falling under the umbrella control of the Fascist Party were the social clubs, the veterans' associations, the cultural groups and the Italian press. Commercial support included

20. Australian Archives, series 13.P242, item Q30565, Report of Commonwealth Investigation Officer, 'Italian Organisations'.
21. Ibid.
22. Ibid.

the Australia-Italia Shipping Company, whose managing director Icilio Fanelli was also secretary of the Sydney Fascio in 1939, and whose passenger manager Luigi Gartiglio was president of the Italian Chamber of Commerce and a prominent Fascio member. Small Italian trading firms in Sydney were predictably sympathetic to or conveniently supportive of Fascism. The terrazzo and marble firms of the Melocco Brothers and A. Aguggia were controlled by Fascio members; the wine merchants and importers of Italian foodstuffs Fiorelli, Cinzano (Australia) Ltd and B. Callose and Sons subscribed to Fascist organizations. Even restaurants such as Florentino, Arminini's, Dungowan Café, Romano's, Luigi's Spaghetti Bar, and boarding houses like Lorenzi's, were kept under surveillance by the Australian authorities because their owners were members of the Fascio or were close friends of executive officers of Fascist organizations. At Arminini's, for instance, a special table was reserved by the committee of the Fascio Luigi Platania which held its weekly meetings there, while the restaurateur Orlando Romano, a faithful advocate of Mussolini, was a close friend of Thomas Herbert Kelly and his wife.

Despite the high profile adopted by the apologists of Fascism in Australia, especially during the 1930s, there is no evidence that, apart from a lot of propaganda and some espionage activities, Italian Fascists carried out carefully planned, efficient and damaging subversive activities in Australia among either the Anglo-Australian or the Italo-Australian communities. The bursts of initiative had an *ad hoc* character and were motivated by specific international or local events like the murder of Matteotti, the Concordat, the war in Ethiopia, the Spanish Civil War, the Depression, the 1935 cane-cutters' strike in Queensland, and the appearance or disappearance of Italian anti-Fascist organizations or newspapers in Australia. Between these manifestations of vitality there were the troughs of work, alienation, isolation, homesickness, poverty and ignorance of what was really happening in the world. The march, the film, the rally, the picnic, the visit to the Italian ship in port, the evening at the club, the commemoration of Fascist anniversaries, the distribution of pamphlets were in effect the only, prosaic, proselytizing acts of the immigrant apostles of Fascism. In Australia, *strafascismo* (ultra-Fascism) was redimensioned and reduced to *stra* little Italy!

When war broke out, the dreaded fear of an Italian fifth column did not materialize, despite the apprehension of the Australian military authorities. As one anonymous military intelligence officer pointed out, 'the first consideration of practically all Italians in New

South Wales is their business. Many own their business and is [*sic*], in most cases, the fulfilment of a hard struggle.'[23] Although the officer feared that some Italians might be led to commit acts of sabotage because, as he put it, 'in the hearts of this impulsive race a national characteristic – revenge – [may] take control of their reason,' no acts of sabotage were recorded.[24] Italian peasants, farmers, fruit-growers, miners, market gardeners, fishmongers, stonemasons, plasterers, shopkeepers *and* Fascist diehards were sheepishly rounded up and quickly put behind bars, in concentration camps. To most of them, Fascism embodied the evanescent chimera of faraway Italy, the voice of the fatherland which had persistently and enticingly promised grandeur, glory and a 'place in the sun' while they were besieged by a world that did not want to know, understand or even accept them.[25] They could hardly fathom the logic of a situation whereby they had been interned for alleged or proven apology of Fascism while Australian politicians were still indulging in hyperbolic and traitorous praises of Fascism. For example, Senator Darley stated in March 1942 that 'Mussolini introduced many great reforms and, if he had not become obsessed with the idea that he was a modern Julius Caesar bent on forming a new Roman Empire, Italy would have been better governed under Fascism than under any so-called democratic system.'[26]

To the core of Fascist ideological irreconcilables, who would remain behind barbed wire for the duration of the war, the long years of internment gave the opportunity to ponder about their failed efforts to 'nationalize' the immigrant masses. In reality there were no masses but scattered settlements of 'Italians' coming from vastly different geographic areas, cultures and social backgrounds, with often diverse economic interests and viewpoints concerning Australian society. To those who had embraced Fascism for convenience, to the Italian establishment and the businessmen who had supported it in the belief that their lucrative import licences would thus be secure, the war represented a temporary setback that interrupted their orderly and steadfast accumulation of profit. To the poorest immigrants, the years spent in internment were yet

23. Australian Archives, series 13.P242, item Q30565, Military Intelligence, Army Headquarters, Melbourne, 26 July 1939.
24. See G. Cresciani, 'Lo spettro della quinta colonna italiana in Australia, 1939–42,' *Affari Sociali Internazionali*, no. 4, 1985, pp. 45–61.
25. On the superficial impact of Fascism on Italians in Australia, see G. Cresciani, 'Peasant Immigration in Australia, 1920–1940', *Spunti e Ricerche*, vol. 2, 1986.
26. *New Times*, 28 March 1942. Also quoted in Ralph Gibson, *Stop this Fascist Propaganda*, pamphlet, 1942.

another calamitous, unexpected episode in their secular struggle against the insensitivity, brutality and oppression of the ruling classes, be they Italian or Australian.

All in all, the world conflict brought to a sudden end an era in which Italians in Australia had registered a marked lack of success in their efforts to integrate into Australian society. By and large, it was not their fault. The differences between the two cultures, the two ethical systems, the two societies, were too wide to allow for even a few points of contact. Besides, the myopic view of the world held by many Australians precluded them from tolerating anybody or any idea which was not a carbon copy of themselves and their deep-seated prejudices. Yet this cleavage was widened even further by the emotionally understandable, albeit historically aberrant, endorsement by the Italian immigrants of the principles of Fascism. The slogan 'Fascism is Italy. All Italians are Fascists', convincingly peddled by the apologists of this creed, ultimately proved, for those Italians in Australia who vouched for the truth of it, the speediest and most reliable passe-partout to the internment camp.

Like Rip van Winkle, some torpidly woke from their twenty-year sleep, only to find their ideological and material world in tatters and the future uncertain and threatening. Others, during the long, hard years of the conflict and afterwards, persevered in their unshaken belief in the ultimate truth of Fascism. These were the inescapable victims of Fascism, who bring to one's mind the arresting verses of the poem 'Who being dead . . .', written twenty years earlier by the Australian poet Vance Palmer on the occasion of another tragic and obscene slaughter, about other people, other fanatic disciples of the destruction of reason:

> But those who watched the evil tempest pass
> And saw not evil; drowning with trivial hum
> The small voice speaking in the thunder's quake,
> Who watched their kindred flesh consumed like grass
> And being deaf and blind remained not dumb –
> Those are the dead no trump shall ever wake.[27]

27. Vance Palmer, *The Camp*, Melbourne, 1920, p. 17.

Select Bibliography

Aquarone, A. and M. Vernassa (eds.), *Il regime fascista*, Bologna, 1974

Behrens, Manfred (ed.), *Faschismus und Ideologie*, 2 vols, Berlin, 1980

Benz, Wolfgang (ed.), *Die Juden in Deutschland 1933–1945*, Munich, 1988

Bettelheim, Bruno, *The Informed Heart*, Glencoe, 1960

Bracher, Karl D. et al., *Nationalsozialistische Diktatur 1933–1945. Eine Bilanz*, Düsseldorf, 1983

Bridenthal, Renate et al. (eds.), *When Biology Became Destiny. Women in Weimar and Nazi Germany*, New York, 1984

Cresciani, Gianfranco, *Fascism, Anti-Fascism and Italians in Australia 1922–1945*, Canberra, 1980

Diner, Dan (ed.), *Ist der Nationalsozialismus Geschichte?*, Frankfurt/M, 1987

Ferretti, Gian Carlo, *Letteratura e ideologia: Bassani, Cassola, Pasolini*, Rome, 1965

Forgacs, D. (ed.), *Rethinking Italian Fascism: Capitalism, Populism and Culture*, London, 1986

Giesecke, Hermann, *Vom Wandervogel zur Hitlerjugend*, Munich, 1981

Hartung, Günter, *Literatur und Ästhetik des deutschen Faschismus*, Berlin (GDR), 1984

Heller, Agnes, *The Power of Shame*, London, 1985

Jemolo, Arturo C., *Chiesa e Stato in Italia*, Turin, 1981

Koonz, Claudia, *Mothers in the Fatherland: Women, the Family and Nazi Politics*, London, 1987

Mosse, George L., *The Crisis of the German Ideology. Intellectual Origins of the Third Reich*, New York, 1964

Reich, Wilhelm, *The Mass Psychology of Fascism*, tr. V. R. Carfagno, New York, 1971

Schäfer, Hans Dieter, *Das gespaltene Bewußtsein: Deutsche Kultur und Lebenswirklichkeit 1933–1945*, Frankfurt/M, 1981

Schmakel, W. W., *Dream of Empire: German Colonialism 1919–1945*, New Haven, 1964

Smith, W. D., *The Ideological Origins of Nazi Imperialism*, New York, 1986

Stachura, Peter (ed.), *Nazi Propaganda: The Power and the Limitations*, London, 1983

Stephenson, Jill, *Women in Nazi Society*, London, 1975

Stern, J. P., *Hitler: The Führer and the People*, London, 1986

Theweleit, Klaus, *Männerphantasien*, 2 vols, Frankfurt/M, 1977

Vondung, Klaus, *Magie und Manipulation: Ideologischer Kult und politische Religion des Nationalsozialismus*, Göttingen, 1971

Vyschgorod, Edith, *Spirit in Ashes: Hegel, Heidegger and Man-Made Mass Death*, New Haven, 1985

Notes on Contributors

Carole Adams, Lecturer in History, University of Sydney. Publications: *Women Clerks in Wilhelmine Germany: Issues of Class and Gender*, Cambridge, 1988; numerous articles on aspects of modern German social history, especially on the situation of women. Research interests: social history of modern Germany, German women's organizations.

Wolfgang Benz, Institut für Zeitgeschichte, Munich. Publications: *Süddeutschland in der Weimarer Republik*, Berlin, 1970; *Bewegt von der Hoffnung aller Deutschen*, Munich, 1979; *Von der Besatzungsherrschaft zur Bundesrepublik*, Frankfurt/M, 1984; (ed.), *Die Juden in Deutschland 1933–1945*, Munich, 1988; numerous articles. Research interests: contemporary German history since the Weimar Republic, anti-Semitism and the Holocaust.

Kathryn Brown is currently working on a D.Phil. at Balliol College, Oxford, after being awarded a Rhodes scholarship on the basis of her studies at the University of Adelaide. Publications: articles on Mandelstam, Goethe and Heidegger. Research interests: modern German philosophy, comparative literature.

Alan Chamberlain, Senior Lecturer in French, University of New South Wales. Publications in the fields of applied linguistics and methodology of foreign language teaching. Research interests: applied linguistics, French culture and civilization.

Gianfranco Cresciani, Ministry for the Arts, Government of New South Wales. Publications: *Fascism, Anti-Fascism and Italians in Australia 1922–1945*, Canberra, 1980; *The Italians*, Sydney, 1985; *Migrants or Mates*, Sydney, 1988; numerous articles. Research interests: history of Italian migration to Australia, multiculturalism, Italo-Australian relations.

Mira Crouch, Senior Lecturer in Sociology, University of New South Wales. Publications: *The Course of Community Health in New South Wales, 1958–1982* (with C. Colton), Sydney, 1983; various articles. Research interests: the psycho/sociological dynamics in everyday life and their reflections in cultural forms, philosophy and sociology of medicine.

Jone Gaillard, Senior Tutor in Italian Studies, La Trobe University, Melbourne. Publications: articles on Italian popular literature, Pavese and Fenoglio, D'Annunzio. Research interests: literature and melodrama after Verdi, church and state, literature of the Second World War and Resistance.

Günter Hartung, Professor of German Literature, Universities of Halle/Wittenberg and Prague. Publications: *Literatur und Ästhetik des deutschen Faschismus*, Berlin, 1984; numerous articles on German literature and music from the Reformation to the present. Research interests: the Enlightenment, German classicism and romanticism, Brecht, Heinrich and Thomas Mann, Bobrowski, the literature of Fascism.

Silke Hesse, Senior Lecturer in German Studies, Monash University, Melbourne. Publications: articles on German literature from the baroque to Kafka. Research interests: modern German literature and society, German women's writing.

Bernd Hüppauf, Associate Professor of German Studies, University of New South Wales. Publications on the German novel in the early twentieth century, theory and methodology of literary criticism, literature and philosophy. Research interests: a history of mentalities in relation to the First World War, science migration.

Gisela Kaplan is currently completing a book on *Contemporary Western European Feminism* after gaining a Ph.D. in German Studies from Monash University, Melbourne; she is joint editor of the *Australian and New Zealand Journal of Sociology*. Publications: articles on Hannah Arendt, feminist theory, women's movements, sociology of welfare. Research interests: political sociology, sociology of culture, women's and ethnic issues.

Suzanne Kiernan, Lecturer in Italian Studies, University of Melbourne. Publications: articles on biography and historiography, Lyotard and Vico, Christina Stead. Research interests: early eighteenth-century ideas and letters, contemporary fiction.

Konrad Kwiet, Associate Professor of German Studies, University of New South Wales. Publications: *Reichskommissariat Niederlande*, Stuttgart, 1968; *Van Jodenhoed tot Gele Ster*, Bussum, 1973; *Selbstbehauptung und Widerstand* (with H. Eschwege), Hamburg, 2nd edn, 1986; 'Nach dem Pogrom: Stufen der Ausgrenzung', in W. Benz (ed.), *Die Juden in Deutschland 1933–1945*, Munich, 1988; numerous articles. Research interests: Fascism and anti-fascism, German-Jewish history, anti-Semitism and the Holocaust.

John Milfull, Professor of German Studies, Dean, Faculty of Arts, University of New South Wales. Publications: *From Baal to Keuner. The Second Optimism of Bertolt Brecht*, Frankfurt/M, 1974; 'Die Literatur der DDR', in V. Zmegacs (ed.), *Geschichte der deutschen Literatur*, vol. III, Königstein, 1984; numerous articles. Research interests: literature and society in the GDR, the German-Jewish experience, the constitution of male and female role-models in/through literature.

John Perkins, Senior Lecturer in Economic History, University of New South Wales. Publications: numerous articles on German and British agrarian history and, more recently, on German settlement in Australia. Other research interests include the history of German penetration of Melanesia.

David Saunders, Senior Lecturer in Humanities, Griffith University, Brisbane. Publications: articles on copyright law. Research interests: the historical relations of law and culture.

Anthony Stephens, Professor of German, University of Adelaide. Publications: *Rilkes Malte Laurids Brigge. Strukturanalyse des erzählerischen Bewußtseins*, Frankfurt/M, 1974; *Nacht, Mensch und Engel. Rilkes Gedichte an die Nacht*, Frankfurt/M, 1978; numerous articles. Research interests: Heinrich von Kleist, European thought from the Enlightenment to the present.

Silvio Trambaiolo, Senior Lecturer, Department of Italian, University of Sydney. Publications: *Altro Polo* (ed.), Sydney, 1978 and 1988; various articles. Research interests: early Italian narrative, the modern novel, politics and society in contemporary Italy.

Martin Travers, Lecturer in Comparative Literature and History, Griffith University, Brisbane. Publications: *German Novels of the First World War*, Stuttgart, 1982; *Thomas Mann*, London, 1990; various articles. Research interests: Thomas Mann, Gottfried Benn, the literature of the Third Reich, the German literary intelligentsia, the historical novel.

Index